Intersectional Decoloniality

This book assesses diverse ways to think about "others" while also emphasizing the advantages of decolonial intersectionality.

The author analyzes a number of struggles that emerge among Andean indigenous intellectuals, governmental projects, and International Relations scholars from the Global North. From different perspectives, actors propose and promote diverse ways to deal with "others". By focusing on the epistemic assumptions and the marginalizing effects that emerge from these constructions, the author separates four ways to think about difference, and analyzes their implications. The genealogical journey linking the chapters in this book not only examines the specificities of Bolivian discussions, but also connects this geo-historical focal point with the rest of the world, other positions concerning the problem of difference, and the broader implications of thinking about respect, action, and coexistence. To achieve this goal, the author emphasizes the potential implications of intersectional decoloniality, highlighting its relationship with discussions that engage post-colonial, decolonial, feminist, and interpretivist scholars. He demonstrates the ways in which intersectional decoloniality moves beyond some of the limitations found in other discourses, proposing a reflexive, bottom-up, intersectional, and decolonial possibility of action and ally-ship.

This book is aimed primarily at students, scholars, and educated practitioners of IR, but its engagement with diverse literature, discussions of epistemic politics, and normative implications crosses boundaries of Political Science, Sociology, Gender Studies, Latin American Studies, and Anthropology.

Marcos S. Scauso is an Assistant Professor of Political Science in the Department of Philosophy and Political Science at Quinnipiac University, USA. Previously, he was a research fellow at the Kroc Institute for International Peace Studies at the University of Notre Dame, USA. His research lies at the intersection of International Relations and identity politics, with a concentration on indigenous voices in post-colonial Latin America and issues of intersectionality. He holds a PhD in Political Science, with a primary focus on International Relations and secondary interests in Political Theory, from the University of California, Irvine, USA. He has directed two research documentaries about indigenous activisms in Argentina and Bolivia, which inspired his current book project.

Worlding Beyond the West

Series Editors:
Arlene B. Tickner, *Universidad del Rosario, Colombia,* **David Blaney,** *Macalester College, USA* and **Inanna Hamati-Ataya,** *Cambridge University, UK*

Historically, the International Relations (IR) discipline has established its boundaries, issues, and theories based upon Western experience and traditions of thought. This series explores the role of geocultural factors, institutions, and academic practices in creating the concepts, epistemologies, and methodologies through which IR knowledge is produced. This entails identifying alternatives for thinking about the "international" that are more in tune with local concerns and traditions outside the West. But it also implies provincializing Western IR and empirically studying the practice of producing IR knowledge at multiple sites within the so-called 'West'.

NGOs, Knowledge Production and Global Humanist Advocacy
The Limits of Expertise
Alistair Markland

Theory as Ideology in International Relations
The Politics of Knowledge
Edited by Benjamin Martill and Sebastian Schindler

International Relations from the Global South
Worlds of Difference
Edited by Arlene B. Tickner and Karen Smith

Making Global Knowledge in Local Contexts
The Politics of International Relations and Policy Advice in Russia
Katarzyna Kaczmarska

Decolonization, Development and Knowledge in Africa
Turning Over a New Leaf
Sabelo J. Ndlovu-Gatsheni

Intersectional Decoloniality
Reimagining International Relations and the Problem of Difference
Marcos S. Scauso

For more information about this series, please visit:
www.routledge.com/Worlding-Beyond-the-West/book-series/WBW

Intersectional Decoloniality

Reimagining International Relations and the Problem of Difference

Marcos S. Scauso

Routledge
Taylor & Francis Group
LONDON AND NEW YORK

First published 2021
by Routledge
2 Park Square, Milton Park, Abingdon, Oxon OX14 4RN

and by Routledge
605 Third Avenue, New York, NY 10017

First issued in paperback 2022

Routledge is an imprint of the Taylor & Francis Group, an informa business

Publisher's Note
The publisher has gone to great lengths to ensure the quality of this reprint but points out that some imperfections in the original copies may be apparent.

British Library Cataloguing-in-Publication Data
A catalogue record for this book is available from the British Library

Library of Congress Cataloging-in-Publication Data
Names: Scauso, Marcos S., author.
Title: Intersectional decoloniality : reimagining international relations and the problem of difference / Marcos S. Scauso.
Description: Abingdon, Oxon ; New York, NY : Routledge, 2020. |
Series: Worlding beyond the West | Includes bibliographical references and index.
Identifiers: LCCN 2020013428 (print) | LCCN 2020013429 (ebook) |
ISBN 9780367369552 (hardback) | ISBN 9780429352058 (ebook)
Subjects: LCSH: Citizenship--Bolivia. | Minorities--Bolivia. |
Decolonization--Bolivia. | Bolivia--Politics and government. |
International relations.
Classification: LCC JL2283 .S33 2020 (print) |
LCC JL2283 (ebook) | DDC 327.84--dc23
LC record available at https://lccn.loc.gov/2020013428
LC ebook record available at https://lccn.loc.gov/2020013429

ISBN 13: 978-0-367-53733-3 (pbk)
ISBN 13: 978-0-367-36955-2 (hbk)
ISBN 13: 978-0-429-35205-8 (ebk)

DOI: 10.4324/9780429352058

Typeset in Times New Roman
by Taylor & Francis Books

To the multiple voices of denunciation and solidary that constantly re-emerge from the corners of worlds.

Contents

Acknowledgements

The list of people and organizations that helped me throughout my career and much of the path that led to the conclusion of this book is undoubtedly endless, but I would like to emphasize some of them in a chronological narrative that might also explain much of my own positionality.

Growing up in Argentina during the "lost decade" of 1980 and the neoliberal years of the 1990s, my mother Diana and father Sergio always gave everything they had to provide me with the opportunities to have education. Even when the family went out of business and lost its only source of income, my parents tried to send me to high school and eventually encouraged me to apply for a scholarship that would allow me to become an exchange student in Hungary. Once I returned home, I met my life partner, Caroline, who was born in the United States and was an exchange student in Argentina. In 2002, I decided to enter the free National University of Argentina in Villa María, my hometown. The international context of 9/11 and the war in Iraq, together with the crisis of neoliberalism in Argentina and a vibrant environment of student political action taught me lessons that I will never forget. At the time, class-based forms of inequality seemed to explain everything to me, but my work with documentaries and public debates took me to Bolivia, where my Eurocentric understandings of the world were often confronted by different leaders and their projects of political transformation.

During my college years, Caroline and I traveled in our opposite summers to see each other. I was able to afford these trips thanks to the help of Mary and Daniel Wilson (Caroline's parents), who often paid for my tickets and patiently waited for me to pay them back with the money that I received while doing agricultural work in California. Their help kept us together and made our current life possible. In California, I encountered very different kinds of struggles. The experience of immigrants in the United States, including my own, seemed to have its own logic of identity, legal, and economic issues, which modified yet again some of my notions of class, ethnicity, hybridity, and ways of being more in general. Once we both graduated from college, Caroline and I decided to move from Argentina to California in 2009, but the financial crisis in the United States prevented me from getting any jobs connected to my sociological and political interests. Thus, I decided to apply to graduate programs, but very few institutions in the United States recognized or valued my Argentine education. In disbelief, I turned to the Argentine Ministry of Education for a letter that could prove the actual existence of my home university. After much paperwork, many translations, several letters, and a relatively big monetary investment, the Master's in International Relations at San Francisco State University accepted my application. Despite the hegemony of realist and liberal approaches in International Relations, which contradicted much of my own experience in the "Third World," Professor Sanjoy Banerjee and Professor Amy Skonieczny opened my understanding of international politics towards the world of constructivism and the diversity of approaches that are often classified within the umbrella of this perspective.

Thanks to their continuing help, support, mentorship, and guidance, I received the Master of Arts degree from San Francisco State University, but not before seeing the birth of my son, Timothy. His arrival, together with the wonderfully feminist teachings of my partner, challenged everything that I thought I knew about life, temporality, sleeping arrangements, gendered relations, divisions of labor, concerns for the future, ontological security, and so on. Nothing has humbled me more than the daily life that I shared with him and Caroline, constantly teaching me about the limitations of my own certainties and assumptions.

In 2012, I brought all the daily and academic questions that kept confronting my foundations into the beginning of my PhD at the University of California, Irvine, where I had the honor of meeting my mentors, Dr. Cecelia Lynch and Dr. Nicholas Onuf, who did not work at the University of California, but agreed to advise me nonetheless. Throughout my years in this institution, Cecelia and Nick patiently listened to my concerns and provided every tool available for me to continue my studies. Their friendship, mentorship, and guidance frequently helped me to unveil the biases of my own assumptions, moving my work beyond certainties that were implicitly sustaining colonial legacies. Dr. Daniel Brunstetter and Dr. Kevin Olson also helped me in much of my academic and professional development. As members of my dissertation committee, all four professors guided my work in different and interesting ways, but they also often went far beyond the role of academic advisors, providing the friendly solidarity that graduate students often seek. The University of California also allowed me to create new spaces of debate such as the International Relations Working Group. Within the regular meetings of this group, and also beyond, friends such as Shauna Gillooly, John Emery, Mary Anne Mendoza, Alexandra Raleigh, Misbah Hyder, Pernilla Johansson, and many others often helped in ways that continuously pushed my work beyond barriers and obstacles.

Throughout my studies at the University of California, I was also able to travel to Bolivia in order to collect documents and to learn from intellectuals that had been discussing colonialisms and notions of transformation long before I even engaged in these discussions. During my trips, Carlos Makusaya and Dr. Esteban Alejo Ticona often helped me to find important documents and also organized discussions that taught me some of the ideas that are being discussed for example at the Universidad Mayor San Andrés, La Paz. During one of my trips, I also had the opportunity to meet Silvia Rivera Cusicanqui, who promptly pointed out the problematic and colonial assumptions that I was making while talking about "harmony" and "balance" in Pachamama. While working with her hands in a beautiful piece of art, the author told me that decoloniality could not rest assured within a particular idea of justice and "harmony." To the contrary, my assumptions included masculine understandings of identity that prevented me from moving beyond coloniality. That day, I left the Cultural Center of the Tambo Colectivx with many of her books and even more questions.

Once I graduated, I was offered the opportunity to become a visiting research fellow at The Kroc Institute for International Peace Studies, University of Notre Dame. This year-long position allowed me to expand my research, beginning with the manuscript that has turned into this book. Additionally, the fruitful environment of discussion at the Kroc Institute helped me to understand some of my own ideas more clearly and explicitly. During this year, I first met my friends and colleagues Dr. Elena Stavrevska and Dr. Kate Paarlberg-Kvan, who often read my work, providing feedback and helping me to understand feminist theories. Their friendship and teachings made much of this book possible. Then, Garret Fitzgerald and Dr. Atalia Omer created the Decoloniality Reading Group, which constructed a wonderful site of discussion, exchange, and debate. After the first semester, I was also able to meet Dr. Bahar Baser and Dr. Ahmet Erdi Öztürk, both of whom became part of my group of friends at Notre Dame even after reading some of my papers and discussing the colonial legacies of International Relations. During 2019, at the Annual Convention of the International Studies Association, I also met Dr. Tamara Trownsell, Dr. Arlene Tickner, Dr. Amaya Querejazu, Dr. Isaac A. Kamola, and many others who are members of the Doing IR Differently collective. This friendly space for discussion, cooperation, and debate has not only taught me more about relationality, but also provided a refreshing possibility for finding scholars who seek to move beyond colonial legacies in International Relations.

Thanks to the teachings, confrontations, support, mentorship, guidance, and friendship of every single of one of the people and institutions included in this story, I was able to accept a position as Assistant Professor at Quinnipiac University, which has become my new home in Connecticut. As I write this acknowledgement, I continue to meet new scholars in an institution that allows me to research, teach, and practice decoloniality. Hence, the book that you are now engaging with is the result of all these relationships and more; it is an academic, political, and personal discussion of a way of knowing, being, and enacting.

Introduction

The encounter of "other" ways of knowing, being, and enacting has historically created struggles that aim to know, organize, and control these differences (Said 1978; Agathangelou and Ling 2009; Mignolo 2011). As Tzvetan Todorov asserts, the encounter of difference and "others" often leads to the organizational principle of hierarchy, which establishes conditions of possibility for different forms of colonialism and for the civilizing models that unfold henceforth (Todorov 1982). This organizational principle entails bounded notions of equality for some, but not "others;" it constructs particular ways of knowing, being, and enacting that are regarded as superior, while all "others" are organized in downward echelons. Despite the historically continuous institutionalization of colonial discourses, Todorov also examines the ways in which particular missionaries thought about the possibility of coexistence between "diverse universes" (190). The author shows how some intellectuals actively sought to understand decolonial possibilities of equality that would not lead towards excluding, exterminating, and/or assimilating "others." Of course, European missionaries are not the only ones who have thought about other ways to deal with the problem of difference. In the Americas, many indigenous uprisings, rebellions, political actions, and intellectual productions have resisted colonial orders. Many indigenous leaders and intellectuals have sought to achieve this goal in order to establish more respectful forms of coexistence.[1] As Mignolo and Walsh discuss, many movements currently continue to construct decolonial possibilities of doing "otherwise" (Mignolo and Walsh 2018). To Todorov, this struggle to define ways to deal with difference exploded in 1492, but has only become more prominent in current times (Todorov 1982, 249).

As globalization decreases some distances, increases inequalities, and reinforces a number of colonial processes of homogenization, the problem of difference continues to gain saliency in domestic, international, and global politics (Mignolo 2000; Quijano 2000; Richards 2014). On one side, colonial projects of civilization still assimilate, erase, and/or kill differences. On the other side, people, movements, intellectuals, activists, and leaders still seek possibilities of respecting differences without falling into paralyzing relativisms that ignore the denunciation of injustices. This search for decolonial alternatives entails a tension between respecting more differences and being able to oppose injustices. How is it possible to deal with different ways of knowing, being, and enacting while also enabling a possibility of decolonial praxis? How is it possible to respect differences while also opposing the differences that are "colonial"? In this book, I answer these questions by analyzing a genealogy of struggles and debates between indigenous movements, governmental projects of civilization for Bolivia, intellectuals of "International Relations" from different parts of the world, intellectuals from the Andes, and my explicit intervention.[2] As this genealogical journey unfolds throughout the book, I examine different epistemic positions that struggle to define distinct ways to deal with "others." Then, I analyze and interpret the benefits of the approach developed by Silvia Rivera Cusicanqui.

By focusing on the analysis of epistemic assumptions and the marginalizing effects that often emerge from them, I separate four sets of discourses that deal with the problem of difference in distinct ways. Each one of these approaches to the problem of difference represents a position; a discursive locus of enunciation that is found in a struggle to define a dominant possibility to deal with "others." Colonial, anti-colonial, post-structuralist, and intersectionally decolonial positions thus dispute the meaning of difference and deal with "others" in particular ways. By studying the epistemic approaches used in this struggle for the possibility to define relationships with "others" and by relating these discourses to discussions of International Relations, I thus analyze four positions in a process of epistemic politics. Then, I highlight the ways in which intersectional decoloniality moves beyond some of the limitations found in the other three sets of discourses.

The problem of difference in International Relations

Since the 1980s, the study of the problem of difference has gained saliency in International Relations through the work of several authors who deploy diverse approaches. For example, post-structuralism entered International Relations as a way to unveil dominant limitations erected by discourses such as realism and liberalism against difference (e.g., Ashley 1981; George and Campbell 1990; Ashley and Walker 1990; Walker 1993, 2010). Much of the post-structuralist literature has discussed the ways in which theories of International Relations and discourses of international politics construct binary boundaries between a "superior" inside and a "barbaric," "uncivilized," "dangerous," "mad," "irrational," or "inferior" outside (Campbell 2013). As several authors have pointed out, these classifications of "others" are often related to epistemic assumptions of different sorts (Walker 1993, 2010; Mills 1997; Seth 2010).

Feminist scholars have denounced the dominance of patriarchal ways of knowing, being, and enacting, which silence "other" voices and oppress "other" identities in international politics and International Relations. J. Ann Tickner points out that International Relations often reinforces a masculine reading of politics, which silences the voices of women, hiding consequences of state-centric and realist definitions of security and missing the opportunity to learn about new insights emerging from feminism (Tickner 1992). Other feminist scholars show how these kinds of masculine biases justify wars to "protect" women and children, but end up causing disproportionate violence against those same groups (e.g., Enloe 1993; Moon 1997; Sjoberg 2006; Shepherd 2008). Post-structuralist feminists examine the ways in which many of these biases emerge from relationships between knowledges and power, which often construct epistemological ideas that categorize "men" as authorized knowers (Tickner and Sjoberg 2013, 211). Post-colonial, intersectional, and black feminists also emphasize the specific characteristics of different experiences of oppression and they highlight the agency of "other" voices (e.g., Mohanty 1988; Crenshaw 1991; Agathangelou and Ling 2009; Mann 2013; Cho, Crenshaw, and McCall 2013; Collins 2015; Treva 2015). Many of these discussions of the problem of difference also include the study of political and epistemic alternatives. For example, intersectional feminists often discuss the problem of difference and its relationship with axes of power in order to deconstruct systems of domination and to construct innovative possibilities of equality (e.g., Fraser and Honnet 2003; Collins and Bilge 2016).

The study of the problem of difference in International Relations owes much to post-colonial literature as well (e.g., Fanon 1952, 1968; Said 1978; Spivak 2010). The renowned author of *Orientalism*, Edward Said, uncovers how power and knowledge are related to each other in the construction of notions of superiority that justify the control, domination, and occupation of "other" countries such as Egypt (Said 1978, 32). In the construction of the "Orient,":

> to have such a knowledge of such a thing is to dominate it, to have authority over it. And authority here means for "us" to deny autonomy to "it" – the Oriental country – since we know it and it exists, in a sense, *as* we know it.
>
> Said 1978, 32

Orientalism is thus a form of knowledge that constructs the "other" as a racialized, sexualized, and inferior object, which can be objectively known and controlled. Then, the "West" regards these systems of truth as epistemologically objective, which elevates these discourses above the epistemic possibility of intellectual dispute (Said 1978, 205). Post-colonial books such as *Creating Boundaries* (Manzo 1996) and *Transforming World Politics* (Agathangelou and Ling 2009) have used these insights to critique specific colonial legacies and to seek alternatives that move beyond them. Authors have also focused on the study of classifications and boundaries that silence "others" and often construct the conditions of possibility for violence (e.g., Grovogui 1996; Doty 1996; Assad 2007; Pasha 2012). These boundaries entail epistemic assumptions that validate specific kinds of knowledge, authorize particular knowers, and legitimize single projects of civilization. For example, since "secularity" is often regarded as the public realm of "knowledge" and "politics," "religion" often appears as the inferior opposite, which is "…emotional, irrational, unpredictable, and behind the march of progress" (Hurd 2008, 169). As Elizabeth Hurd asserts, "secularity" is the "…secured place for the good, rational, and universal in Western moral order, which is then opposed to series of nonrational or irrational particularism, aberrations, or variations" (169).

Together with these theoretical discussions of the problem of difference, and other theories as well, interpretivism re-emerged in the 1980s as a methodological opportunity to expand the scope of International Relations, emphasizing the complexity of meanings that are practiced in international and global politics. Although still operating from a marginalized position in International Relations, interpretivism is often involved in a mutually enabling relationship with the theories mentioned above and with other post-positivist approaches. Interpretivism aids in the construction of a more pluralistic space of knowledge production, which aims to encompass multiple theories and epistemic discussions (Schwartz-Shea and Yanow 2012, 139). To achieve this goal, interpretive scholars often question the tendencies of positivist epistemic assumptions such as the notions of truth correspondence and objectivity, which validate single ways of knowing. This methodological orientation can limit International Relations and it tends to generalize particular empirical trends. In the continuous struggle of many scholars and students to sustain a more open space of knowledge production, the enabling relationship between methodological discussions and theories has created an "existential crisis" in the old boundaries of the discipline and a fruitful proliferation of ways of knowing (George and Campbell 1990; Milliken 1999; Smith 2013; Pachirat 2014; Lynch 2014; Gofas, Hamati-Ataya, and Onuf 2018). This proliferation encompasses the theories mentioned above, but it also includes queer theory (e.g., Butler 1990; Moraga 1993; Stoler 1995; Agathangelou 2013; Weber 2016), green theory (e.g., Laferrière and Stoett 1999; Wolfe 2010; Eckersley 2013; Cudworth and Hobden 2013; Dalby 2013), and many other voices and combinations that defy the boundaries often erected among approaches, isms, and disciplines. The proliferation of approaches and perspectives in International Relations thus encourages interdisciplinarity and even transdisciplinarity; it enables conversations about a wide variety of topics, while also elevating the problem of difference as a discussion of the discipline itself. In this sense, interpretivism explicitly introduces International Relations into struggles to define the problem of difference.

In 2004, Naeem Inayatullah and David Blaney called these methodological, theoretical, and political possibilities of unveiling colonial legacies and engaging with alternatives the "problem of difference" (Inayatullah and Blaney 2004). While following much of their work to contribute to these discussions and to continue trespassing institutionalized boundaries of International Relations, I also use a decolonial perspective. Despite the saliency of decolonial approaches in other disciplines such as Latin America

Studies, Comparative Literature, and Anthropology (e.g., Quijano and Wallerstein 1992; Quijano 2000; Mignolo 2000, 2009, 2011; Lugones 2007; Escobar 2010, 2017; Mignolo and Walsh 2018), this perspective has been largely ignored in International Relations. Some scholars have discussed the advantages of bringing decoloniality into International Relations (Taylor 2012; Blaney and Tickner 2017), analyzed the possibility of decolonizing Globalization Studies (Richards 2014), and introduced fruitful dialogues between feminist notions of intersectionality and decolonial insights (Méndez 2018), but the conversation has only begun.

Decolonial scholars seek to avoid the construction of yet another singularity; they try to renounce the possibility of universalizing a single definition of decoloniality and difference, which would aim to liberate all peoples, but would inevitably create other forms of irreflexive violence (Mignolo and Walsh 2018, 1). Instead, decolonial scholars often aim to listen to multiple local histories, which might relate to each other in different ways and might confront the universalizing effects of colonial discourses in contextualized manners. In this sense, decoloniality acts as an approach that locates itself in the middle of the tension between opposing colonialisms and respecting differences. I further discuss several aspects of this approach in Chapter Seven, but one of the main advantages of this perspective is its explicit concentration on both sides of the problem of difference and their relationships. Decolonial authors simultaneously analyze colonial limitations of difference, possibilities of alternatives, and diverse epistemic relationships that emerge between these two sides (e.g., Wynter 1995; Mignolo 2000; Rivera 2015). As a result of this area of study, decolonial scholars construct a particularly fruitful locus of interpretation, which enables the discussion of a variety of positions in the struggle to define relationships with "others." Additionally, authors often examine the epistemic conditions of possibility that are necessary to construct these ways of studying and practicing decoloniality. Walter Mignolo thus asserts that decolonial studies move beyond the limits of "Western" social sciences to create a possibility of "border thinking" from the multiple localities of the "other" (Mignolo 2000, 203).

Throughout the book, I follow this decolonial concern for the multiple localities of "others" to study a genealogy of the problem of difference that is centered in Bolivia, but encourages a dialogue with International Relations and highlights the advantages of intersectional decoloniality. Similarly to other decolonial scholars who understand that "so long as we do not unsettle our inherited colonial frameworks of assessing truth, we will continue to erase ways of being and knowing that might hold a promise for a more just future" (Méndez 2018, 22), I analyze how colonial legacies continue to limit differences while some Andean intellectuals such as Fausto Reinaga and Silvia Rivera Cusicanqui construct epistemic possibilities of decoloniality. Many decolonial scholars have developed this topic, but the genealogical struggle between Andean intellectuals, the government of Bolivia, indigenous movements from the Andes, and other scholars of International Relations contributes to this discussion in several ways. First, I examine the epistemic characteristics of specific colonial discourses and I highlight their similarities with some liberal and Marxist theories of International Relations. The proximity between these understandings of difference unveils the biases and violent consequences that unfold from the universalizations of particular ways of knowing, being, and enacting. Second, I connect decolonial perspectives to discussions from different territorial and disciplinary boundaries, highlighting the advantages of trespassing siloed discussions, listening to the implications of an approach that expands the discussions of decoloniality, and contributing to the work of scholars that discuss the problem of difference in International Relations. Third, I show how the work by Rivera is related to the construction of a dynamic epistemic condition of possibility for the coexistence of multiple ways of being, knowing, and enacting. In addition to the importance that is granted to dynamic multiplicity and difference in this perspective, the author also practices a reflexive form of decolonial praxis; she creates a self-problematized and yet politically committed possibility of thinking about various ways of knowing, being, and enacting. In order to sustain a possibility of decolonial and political praxis, this approach demands the de-universalization of colonial discourses and it emphasizes the struggles, voices, and projects of those who are often othered. Fourth, I examine how Rivera's approach highlights a reflexive understanding of the epistemic boundaries that even decolonial intersectionality includes in order to sustain a possibility of transformative action against colonialisms. This reflexivity demands the problematization and analysis of all othering tendencies, but it also shows why a precarious epistemic decision is necessary if decoloniality aims to listen to the multiple struggles with oppression that "others" face. Fifth, I follow the implications of this approach to argue that decoloniality ought to begin from intersectional conditions of possibility, which avoid prioritizing specific experiences of race, ethnicity, or geo-historical locations over other struggles, identities, and projects. This perspective emphasizes the importance of understanding the ways in which multiple struggles overlap and sometimes confront each other. Hence, I study one way of thinking about the epistemic requirements that are necessary to establish a reflexive and dynamic possibility of decolonial intersectionality. Then, I examine the implications that unfold from this platform, contributing to debates that are prominent in feminist, post-structuralist, postcolonial, decolonial, and other interpretive approaches. Sixth, I follow the argument of María José Méndez about the need to think intersectionally while also moving beyond its limitations, constructing an ethics of incommensurability (Méndez 2018). Here, intersectional decoloniality enables a possibility of praxis and political action, but the goal of listening to multiple "others" also leads towards the demand of trusting ways of knowing, being, and enacting beyond "our" levels of intelligibility, understanding, and familiarity. Finally, I aim to create a possibility of dialogue and ally-ship between multiple ways of knowing, being, and enacting the problem of difference. Despite the divergences that I highlight throughout the book between intersectional decoloniality and other perspectives, I also emphasize that the possibility of differentiating discourses emerges from a moment of epistemic faith, which allows us to classify "colonialisms" and to construct praxes of transformation in a variety of ways. This epistemic notion localizes our own criteria of classification and praxis, humbling our own approaches to the problem of difference and creating a much more egalitarian possibility of inter-epistemic dialogue. My hope is to encourage post-/de-/anti-/settler-colonial approaches, as well as many others who also find themselves resisting disciplinary, territorial, political, and social domination, to contribute in discussions of the problem of difference from their own locality, teaching us to limit our voices in order to walk the here/now together and in respect at the same time.

Methodology: Archaeology, genealogy, and involvement

In order to achieve these goals, I begin the genealogical journey of this book from an approach that renounces foundations, bedrocks, and structures. "We must renounce all those themes whose function is to ensure the infinite continuity of discourse and its secret presence to itself in the interplay of a constantly recurring absence" (Foucault 1972, 129). As I discuss in Chapter Five, the possibility of abandoning ideas that attach meanings to an unquestionable, independent, universal, and intelligible "reality" allows me to study how different discourses construct their own epistemic assumptions. Hence, I begin from a dynamic, complex, and "untamed" notion of practices (Doty 1997). These sudden irruptions (i.e., practices) are the data of interpretation; they are momentary settlements of meanings, which can be interpreted in order to follow the regularities and patterns that make up discursive formations (Foucault 1972). By following Michel Foucault's archaeological approach, I analyze how each discourse endogenously includes a set of epistemic assumptions and conditions of "reality," which separate the formation from other discourses. To analyze different ways of knowing, being, and enacting the problem of difference, I thus focus on how each discourse entails ideas of what is "real" (i.e., ontology), how "reality" is knowable and who knows it (i.e., epistemology), and how "reality" can be enacted (i.e., temporality). Additionally, the construction of epistemic platforms often determines the boundaries of classification that exclude and/or hierarchically organize "other" ways of knowing, being, and enacting. They determine what is not "real," how "others" do not know "reality," who these "others" are, and how the "unreal" can be avoided, transformed, or killed. By following this epistemic focus, each chapter of the book entails an archaeological examination of a discourse, which deploys its endogenous epistemic assumptions to elevate itself above "others," determining how difference is defined and limited.

Notwithstanding this archaeological separation of distinct approaches to the problem of difference, I combine archaeology with genealogy, which is a more dynamic way to reconnect and analyze these discourses. Here, genealogy is understood as a way to interpret discourses that are included in diachronic processes of meaning contestation and definition (Klotz and Lynch 2007, 31). Genealogy enables a possibility of arranging distinct discourses as dynamic positions that confront each other to know, be, and enact the problem of difference in particular ways. Hence, the struggle between the ways in which each discourse is practiced throughout history in Bolivia and in International Relations is the thread connecting the chapters of this book.[3]

Since I specifically focus on how Indianismo – an indigenous movement from the Andes – and other Andean intellectuals confront dominant discourses, I use genealogy as a:

> … way of playing local, discontinuous, disqualified, or nonlegitimized knowledges off against the unitary theoretical instance that claims to be able to filter them, organize them into a hierarchy, organize them in the name of a true body of knowledge, in the name of the rights of a science that is in the hands of the few.
>
> Foucault 1997, 9

Of course, Andean intellectuals such as Silvia Rivera Cusicanqui, Esteban Alejo Ticona, and Fausto Reinaga have already achieved this goal, successfully confronting notions through discussions that have repercussions far beyond the territorial borders of Bolivia. However, the walls of International Relations continue to marginalize much of their work. Hence, I seek to listen in order to learn and to decolonize some of the boundaries that are more familiar in my own positionality. In this sense, genealogy does not seek to "translate" or "empower" already agentic voices. Instead, genealogy becomes a possibility of learning in order to become yet another locus of confrontation, which is now related to a different context and positionality. Here, genealogy becomes a process that explicitly includes my own contribution and set of questions as an active locus of enunciation in the dispute to define the problem of difference.[4]

In order to examine some of my own assumptions and locus of enunciation, it is necessary to highlight that the narration of a genealogical thread always entails epistemic decisions, which enable the possibility of classifying some discourses as "dominant" and others as "decolonial," "disqualified," "non-legitimized," "dominated," "subjugated," etc. This moment of classification of discourses does not consistently unfold from an approach that renounces all epistemic foundations; instead, it requires a moment of epistemic decision and settlement. Said differently, the consistent and generalized abandonment of all foundations and bedrocks leads towards an understanding that judges all discourses as equal constructions of foundations. This approach allows us to study multiple epistemic assumptions, but it also undoes the possibility of classifying "coloniality" or "domination." Insofar as I regard all meanings as equal discourses, how could I elevate a criterion above them? How could I create a discourse to analyze discourses? How could I discern what is "colonial," "dominant," "decolonial," "resistance," "alternative," etc.? How could I demand a transformation or change from whatever is "oppressive," "colonial," "unjust," and so on? Moreover, how could I commit to the prioritization of multiple subaltern ways of knowing, being, and enacting? How could I create a moment of decolonial praxis?

These methodological questions explicitly introduce my own intervention and contribution as an active locus of interpretation that is directly involved in the dispute for the problem of difference.

As the first four chapters of the book illustrate, these questions are particularly problematic for the differentiation of discourses that equally universalize and elevate their own notions above "others." Are the different branches of Indianismo equally "dominant" or "dominating" as colonial notions of liberalism or Marxism? Of course not, but what exactly distinguishes them in the struggle to define the problem of difference? The possibility of answering this question risks creating another foundation, bedrock, or set of epistemic assumptions; it leads towards the predefinition of "power" as something that lies beyond discourse and then it forecloses the problem of difference again, creating yet another set of othering tendencies.

This explains why some feminist, queer, and interpretivist scholars highlight the importance of dynamic understandings of meaning (McCall 2005; Cho, Crenshaw, and McCall 2013; Lynch 2014; Weber 2016; Wibben and Rutazibwa 2019), but this dilemma of classification introduces all possibilities of research and interpretation into the problem of difference and its tension. On one side, renouncing foundations enables the possibility of untaming meaning, which allows me to study multiple kinds of epistemic assumptions and discourses; it enables me to cope with more difference. Despite this possibility, completely untaming meaning prevents me from constructing criteria to differentiate discourses and their "colonial" tendencies. On the other side, the construction of boundaries of classification and the utilization of an extra-discursive notion of power can enable me to create decolonial praxis, but it also leads to othering tendencies that foreclose the possibility of thinking about the problem of difference. These questions turn my own genealogical narration into an explicit intervention, which includes its own way of classifying discourses and opposing "colonialities" into the struggle to define the problem of difference. This tension between the respect of epistemic differences and the possibility of creating decolonial praxis unapologetically includes me in a dispute of the problem of difference; it is the core of the plot that organizes all the chapters of the book and my own contribution in this struggle.

Genealogy and book plan

In order to collaborate in this genealogical struggle for the problem of difference, Chapter One discusses how intellectuals and governmental policies construct what most scholars regard as *colonialism* in and for Bolivia. Since much of the literature in International Relations focuses on examining colonialisms, this chapter briefly analyzes the epistemic commonalities found between the discourses that created the projects of civilization in Bolivia between 1825, which is when the country gained independence from Spain, and the end of the Nationalist Revolution in 1964. First, I analyze the constructions of an oligarchic form of liberalism, which defined the dominant shape of the state of Bolivia between 1825 and 1952. As a colonial project, liberalism encompasses a set of epistemic assumptions that fix boundaries of citizenship and individual rights within particular territories. These boundaries construct a marginalizing and assimilationist understanding of "others" for Bolivia, but some of the epistemic assumptions and othering effects of liberalism can also be found in International Relations. Second, I analyze the structuralist form of Marxism that became institutionalized in 1952, when the Nationalist Revolution gained control of the government in Bolivia and sought to move beyond the inequalities created by liberal ideas of citizenship. Despite their goal of emancipation, the Revolution imposed Eurocentric notions of class-based equality, which still hierarchicalized indigenous peoples as inferior "others." In this section, I not only examine the governmental construction of Marxism in Bolivia, but also discuss how other intellectuals continue to reproduce a similar epistemic stance in much of the literature of International Relations that focuses on "peasant" movements. Finally, the analysis of these two sets of discourses leads towards a conceptualization of the epistemic dimensions of colonial discourses. This chapter shows how the utilization of "colonial" epistemics often leads to particular definitions of power and equality, which universalize single forms of classification and create othering tendencies.

In Chapter Two, I interpret the Revolutionary branch of Indianismo, which officially emerged in 1962, when the Indianista party was created in Bolivia.[5] As an *anti-colonial* approach, Revolutionary Indianismo seeks to construct a discourse to oppose the notions and effects of oligarchic liberalism and structuralist Marxism. To achieve this goal, intellectuals create a different platform, which validates a particular kind of knowledge, promotes a specific form of ethnic and/or racial equality, authorizes a distinct kind of agent, and enacts a single type of temporality. As a result, liberal and Marxist colonialisms are regarded as the invalidated, de-authorized, and illegitimate enemy, which has to disappear through revolution and, if necessary, war. Despite the important possibility of listening to the struggle and voice of an "other," Revolutionary Indianismo universalizes a particular experience of oppression, generalizing its own notion of equality, authorizing a single kind of agent, and legitimizing a single kind of liberation. Hence, this branch of the movement views "other" struggles, voices, and projects as potential obstacles against the "true" revolution. The epistemic assumptions of Revolutionary Indianismo lead towards the universalization and romanticization of a single "other." In this sense, this Indianista possibility of establishing a bedrock of judgment to separate "colonialism" from anti-colonialism leads to the exclusion of "other" struggles, voices, and projects; it creates other "others." As Audre Lorde states, the "master's tools will never dismantle the master's house" (Lorde 2018). Here, the problem of difference re-emerges because other "others" seek to expand the possibility of encompassing more difference, while also classifying and defining the "colonialisms" that need to be resisted and transformed. Additionally, the study of these Revolutionary epistemic tendencies poses another question: how is Revolutionary Indianismo different to colonial discourses that also universalize their own singularities? Undoing all possibilities of classification and respecting all formations could lead towards ignoring the differences between Indianismo and colonial discourses such as liberalism and Marxism. Hence, I explicitly follow the demand to listen to other "others" while also avoiding the dismissal of Indianista resistance, but how is this possible? This question is related to my own examination of classifications and my intervention in the struggle to define the problem of difference, which reminds us about the difficulty of respecting differences while also creating a possibility of praxis.

In Chapter Three, I focus on how Fausto Reinaga – the father of Indianismo – seeks to move beyond Revolutionary limitations, while also constructing another *anti-colonial* discourse that opposes the projects of oligarchic liberalism, Marxism, and neoliberalism. Since it uses an anthropocentric set of epistemic assumptions to critique colonialism, Revolutionary Indianismo excludes or hierarchicalizes ecological aspects of indigenous cosmologies. Hence, Fausto Reinaga follows this critique, moving towards the construction of Indianismo Amáutico after 1974. This newer kind of anti-colonial Indianismo seeks to include inter-human and ecological equality simultaneously. In order to achieve this goal, Reinaga synthetizes a particular reading of Andean cosmology, which helps him to think about the problem of difference while including epistemic critiques of colonial discourses. Despite his concern for the problem of difference, Reinaga's construction still sustains essentialist assumptions and it creates an epistemological form of authorization that only allows for the "Indio" to know the single and universal "truth" of cosmic order. Indianismo Amáutico thus ends up imposing a single experience of ethnic and ecological equality as a form of universal liberation that everyone else has to follow. Similar to Revolutionary Indianismo, the problem of difference re-emerges in relation to Indianismo Amáutico because other intellectuals seek to expand the possibility of encompassing more multiplicity while also classifying the "colonialism" that needs to be resisted and transformed. Other "others" denounce Amáutico boundaries as well. Furthermore, the discourse does not answer the question of how Indianismo is different to colonial discourses. Fausto Reinaga sought to investigate colonial notions of epistemic foundations and universalization, but he ended up sustaining some of their tendencies by universalizing yet another singularity. With that said, how is it possible to listen to the call emerging from other "others" while also separating Indianismo Amáutico from colonial discourses?

In Chapter Four, I examine the governmental project of Evo Morales Ayma, president of Bolivia between 2006 and 2019, and Álvaro García Linera, former vice-president of the Republic. As opposition to neoliberalism in Bolivia began to unite Marxist and Indianista movements, some intellectuals sought to expand Indianista ideas to include other ways of knowing, being, and enacting in the early 2000s. By constructing epistemic notions that seek to validate multiple identities, Evo Morales and García Linera created another *anti-colonial* project, which denounces "Western" domination, but also respects aspects of "Western" identities. In order to resist neoliberal colonialism – the current expression of "Western" domination – Evo Morales and García Linera established a plurinationalist project of ethnic equality in Bolivia and they promoted their ideas of "Buen Vivir" (live well) internationally. This discourse has been used to reconstruct the state and to approve, in 2009, a new constitution, which respects "liberal" and "indigenous" identities simultaneously. This project also assimilates notions of sustainable development and gender equality. Despite the expansion of equality for ethnic identities and the important inclusion of other forms of equality, the discourse epistemologically authorizes a particular voice, institution, and leader to define who is a "true" "indigenous" person in Bolivia. Hence, the plurinational notions of citizenship, structures of the government, and characterization of representatives tend to simplify the diversity of ways of being that are practiced in the country. In this manner, plurinationality still silences voices of other indigenous peoples, feminist movements, ecological organizations, etc. Additionally, the ontological notion of "reality" that is used within the discourse validates and elevates a particular idea of equality, which hierarchicalizes other notions of struggle and justice. Environmentalism and feminism are thus assimilated within a logic of ethnic equality, which reframes these struggles through the lens of particular criteria and hierarchicalizes them as secondary issues. Despite the expansion of boundaries of validation, authorization, and legitimation, then, plurinationalism also utilizes colonial epistemics that lead to the construction of other "others." Unlike other forms of Indianismo, however, this discourse has been successfully institutionalized in the government of the country. This process of normalization and partial sedimentation emphasizes the importance and complexity of the question that I pose in previous chapters: how are anti-colonial discourses different to colonial projects? How is plurinationality different to neoliberalism? How are anti-colonial discourses different to colonial discourses that also universalize and institutionalize their own singularities?

In order to answer this question and to continue analyzing the problem of difference, the following chapters turn away from epistemic foundationalisms and strong bedrocks of judgement. The possibility of encompassing more difference turns against foundations, bedrocks, and universalizing notions of "reality," which often sediment the boundaries of a particular discourse. Despite this move, the chapters continue the search for classification in order to sustain the conditions of possibility for political action, also avoiding the idea that anti-colonial and colonial discourses are the same. How is it possible to re-think the problem of difference beyond the othering tendencies that emerge from foundations while also sustaining criteria of judgment that are necessary to differentiate "coloniality" from those who resist or seek to transform these legacies?

In Chapter Five, I discuss the approach that is proposed by Foucault. The relevance of this approach in the genealogy that I am narrating emerges from the ways in which Andean scholars, as well as intellectuals that study Andean cosmologies, deploy and critique some of the discussions that Foucault advances (e.g., Estermann 2006; Escobar 2010; Viaña, Claros, and Sarzuri-Lima 2010; Alcoreza 2014; Rivera 2015). Additionally, the work of Foucault has been used within International Relations to think about difference (e.g., George and Campbell 1990; Milliken 1999; Campbell 2013; Weber 2016). Finally, I used this approach to begin the study of the problem of difference from an archaeological and genealogical understanding of discourse. Since I explicitly introduce my own intervention into this dispute of the problem of difference, the possibility of questioning the limitation of this approach becomes important as well.

To create a possibility of encompassing more difference, Foucault constructs a starting point that validates multiple discourses and highlights their epistemic deficit simultaneously. He deals with the problem of difference by thinking about an epistemic possibility of multiplicity. Since post-structuralism validates multiple knowledges, the approach also authorizes diverse knowers and it legitimizes various temporalities. Despite this respect of epistemic differences, Foucault locates the interpreter above foundationalism and he generalizes a tendency towards deconstructing epistemic assumptions of reality, identity, and history. Hence, the approach tends to regard all foundationalist discourses as equally dominant and it undermines the possibility of committing to the subaltern. Here, different kinds of Indianismo, plurinationalism, liberalism, and Marxism appear as similarly dominant. Of course some post-structuralist authors have moved away from this tendency and have sought other ways of respecting differences while also stopping the generalization of deconstruction (e.g., George and Campbell 1990; Stoler 1995; Milliken 1999; Campbell 2013; Weber 2016), but the question that remains understudied is, how can we stop deconstruction while also staying reflexive of the boundaries that we erect? How much deconstruction is necessary in particular contexts? How can we create a criterion to think about this limitation of deconstruction? In sum, how is it possible to enable epistemic levels of multiplicity while also creating decolonial possibilities? In this sense, the question that emerges from the tension between multiplicity and decolonial praxis is still standing.

In Chapter Six, I examine the work of Rivera to propose a way to answer this question. Rivera takes into account Indianista insights and she moves beyond the limitation of post-structuralism, while also critiquing colonial projects. In her construction of a "Ch'ixi" approach ("grey" or "mestizo" in Aymara), Rivera begins from an Aymara cosmology that respects all differences and commonalities from a relational perspective, but, instead of falling into the generalization of deconstruction, Rivera creates a "profession of faith;" she constructs an epistemic moment of definition in order to prioritize the multiple forms of knowing, being, and enacting that demand the deconstruction of the universalizing discourses hierarchicalizing them. This epistemic possibility explicitly locates Rivera's locus of enunciation as a distinct position within the struggle to think about difference. Here, the "profession of faith" prioritizes the voices of "others" that confront the epistemic privilege of universalization and the oppression that unfolds from it, but this boundary does not assume the "reality," epistemic superiority, or philosophical perfection of other understandings of the problem of difference. Instead, Rivera sustains a cosmological abyss that demands constant reflexivity and problematization. Hence, the form of decolonial praxis that Rivera constructs includes a different kind of boundary and epistemic stance. Additionally, Rivera uses this strategy to emphasize multiple moments of confrontation against different kinds of colonial wounds. This creates a dynamic, circular, and intersectional form of praxis, which views different ways of knowing, being, and enacting as the moments that denounce suffering and create more agency at the same time.

In Chapter Seven, I unpack the advantages of Rivera's approach for a number of discussions in International Relations, undoing some of the disciplinary boundaries of this field of knowledge and expanding the possibility of debating about the problem of difference. This chapter shines light on two particularly important benefits that emerge from within the approach created by Rivera. First, the decoloniality that emerges from her idea of a profession of faith prioritizes voices that confront different kinds of privilege and oppression, creating a boundary of praxis that has to constantly listen to different ways of knowing, being, and enacting. That is, the boundary that Rivera constructs includes multiplicity in an intersectional and dynamic sense. Second, the author begins from a cosmology that sustains epistemic equivalence, which prevents the possibility of elevating any kind of reality, knower, and project above "others." Instead of generalizing a paralyzing form of relativism and the epistemic abys that could be philosophically created from this idea, however, Rivera makes a profession of faith, which sustains the abys while also building a momentary and reflexive possibility of walking in a here/now. The author sustains an epistemic precarity, which demands the constant reflexivity that foundationalist or generalizing discourses cannot reach.

In the Concluding Thoughts, I first discuss how this understanding of a profession of faith allows us to create a much more democratic dialogue between different approaches that are concerned with the problem of difference and international politics, constructing a more egalitarian and reflexive possibility of debate and ally-ship. This encourages important questions for approaches of International Relations and for the discussion of the relationships between them. In this sense, the concluding chapter contributes to the analysis of the boundaries of International Relationships and a possibility of constructing a different kind of locus of interpretation and praxis.

Finally, the discussion of the implications that surge from my interpretation of Rivera's work also leads towards the examination of my own methodological and ethical dilemmas. My main concern is the tension that emerges between, on one side, listening to others, answering their invitation to action, and learning from them, and, on the other side, translating their ideas, expropriating their work, and committing yet another form of colonial violence. Of course perfect translation and synthetization is impossible due to the polysemic characteristics of meaning, but abandoning the possibility of communication also entails renouncing decolonial praxis, ignoring the call to action that often emerges from the voices that we might be interpreting never without some degree of violence. In this sense, I do not aim to explain to "them," what it is that they are "really" saying. Instead, I seek to accept a call to imagine a different kind of "planetarity" and decolonial praxis (Rivera 2018, 57). This invitation includes the possibility of sharing some aspects of struggle, agency, and enactment, especially when we think and act in relationship to international politics. Additionally, interpretation and praxis can also include a localization of our struggles and positionalities in order to confront the specificities of oppressions that might affect us, as well as the privileges that we might sustain. In this sense, my goal in this book is to walk in a particular here/now, risking contributions that move beyond the safety of inaction and also undoing colonial boundaries that still constrain International Relations.

Notes

1 In 1536, for example, Manco Inca sieged the city of Lima in order to fight against racial segregation and slavery. In 1727, Juan Bautista Aruma gathered an army of 14,000 warriors to fight in the region of Tarija, which is in the south of current Bolivia. Later on, during 1780 and 1781, one of the most famous indigenous risings took place. Around the city of La Paz, Túpac Katari and Bartolina Sisa created a three-month long siege. Together with 40,000 Aymara warriors, these leaders sought to destroy the colonial order and to create an indigenous Bolivia that could respect the differences between peoples. As Waskar Ari asserts, Pablo Zárate Willka later led a strong and historic rising against the Bolivian liberal state during the 1870s. This leader sought to create an Aymara republic, separated from the colonial form of order and including the possibility of coexisting with the decedents of European colonizers. This idea of two republics, one seeking the respect of differences and the other promoting colonial homogeneity, has survived through time and it has inspired other leaders. During the 1920s, the Alcaldes Mayores Particulares also began struggling for land and decolonization (Ari 2014). Their project took into account the notion of two republics in order to create the possibility of a multi-ethnic space for all peoples. As Sinclair Thomson points out, indigenous revolts in Latin America such as the one that took place in 1780–81 often sought to redefine the relationships of power and self-determination within states or regions (Thomson 2002).

2 I use quotation marks to talk about "International Relations" as a discipline whose boundaries are constructed, sustained, and disputed by different practices of scholars throughout history. The same can be said about other disciplines and academic communities. Despite the transdisciplinary and interdisciplinary discussions of methodological and empirical issues, these boundaries of "International Relations" continue to create authorizing and silencing effects. In this sense, I use the name of "International Relations" to highlight its current boundaries and to explore the possibility of trespassing them. In the rest of the book, I seldom use quotation marks again, but I continue to regard the discipline in this manner nonetheless.

3 Despite the rhetorical separation that I use throughout the book between "Bolivia" and "International Relations," I realize that such boundaries sustain colonial notions of who is the authorized knower of the "international." These separations remain powerful, but I do not aim to reinforce them. To the contrary, the entire book aims to undo colonial boundaries of disciplinary and territorial separations, which entail hierarchical notions of knowledge production and often silence voices. Hence, my role in this book includes the possibility of contributing to the possibility of trespassing boundaries and pushing these discussions further.

4 I further discuss my own positionality, methodological tension, and ethical dilemmas in the Concluding Thoughts.

5 Bolivia has a long and complex history of indigenous movements and uprisings. While I acknowledge the antecedents of Indianismo, I focus primarily on the officialization of the movement because it has particularly fruitful and influential discussions of the problem of difference. Additionally, Indianismo recognizes other indigenous struggles as antecedents of a history of anti-colonial resistance. These connections highlight the importance and agency of indigenous voices in the region.

References

Agathangelou, Anna M. 2013. "Neoliberal Geopolitical Order and Value: Queerness as a Speculative Economy and Anti-Blackness as Terror." *International Feminist Journal of Politics* 15 (4): 453–476.

Agathangelou, Anna M., and L. H. M. Ling. 2009. *Transforming World Politics: From Empire to Multiple Worlds.* New York: Routledge.

Alcoreza, Raúl Prada. 2014. "Epistemología Pluralista." In *Pluralismo Epistemológico*, edited by Amílcar B. Zambrana, 13–55. Cochabamba: FUNPROEIB Andes. https://es.scribd.com/doc/296610165/Pluralismo-Epistemologico.

Ari, Waskar. 2014. *Earth Politics. Religion, Decolonization, and Bolivia's Indigenous Intellectuals.* Durham, NC: Duke University Press.

Ashley, Richard. 1981. "Political Realism and Human Interests." *International Studies Quarterly* 25 (4): 204–236.

Ashley, Richard, and R. B. J. Walker. 1990. "Speaking the Language of Exile: Dissent Thought in International Studies." *International Studies Quarterly* 34 (3): 259–268.

Assad, Talal. 2007. *On Suicide Bombing.* New York: Columbia University Press.

Blaney, David L., and Arlene B. Tickner. 2017. "Worlding, Ontological Politics and the Possibility of a Decolonial IR." *Millennium: Journal of International Studies* 45 (3): 293–311.

Butler, Judith. 1990. *Gender Trouble: Feminism and the Subversion of Identity.* New York: Routledge.

Campbell, David. 2013. "Post-Structuralism." In *International Relations Theories: Discipline and Diversity*, edited by Tim Dunne, Milja Kurki, and Steve Smith, 223–247. Oxford: Oxford University Press.

Cho, Sumi, Kimberlé W. Crenshaw, and Leslie McCall. 2013. "Toward a Field of Intersectionality Studies, Applications, and Praxis." *Signs* 38 (4): 785–810.

Collins, Patricia Hill. 2015. "Intersectionality's Definitional Dilemmas." *Annual Review of Sociology* 41 (1): 1–20.

Collins, Patricia Hill, and Sirma Bilge. 2016. *Intersectionality.* Cambridge: Polity Press.

Crenshaw, Kimberlé W. 1991. "Mapping the Margins: Intersectionality, Identity Politics, and Violence Against Women of Color." *Stanford Law Review* 43 (6): 1241–1299.

Cudworth, Erika, and Stephen Hobden. 2013. "Of Parts and Wholes: International Relations Beyond the Human." *Millennium: Journal of International Studies* 41 (3): 430–450.

Dalby, Simon. 2013. "What Happens If We Don't Take Nature for Granted?" In *Global Politics: A New Introduction*, edited by Jenny Edkins and Maja Zehfuss, 39–61. New York: Routledge.

Doty, Roxanne Lynn. 1996. *Imperial Encounters: The Politics of Representation in North-South Relations.* Minneapolis: University of Minnesota Press.

Doty, Roxanne Lynn. 1997. "Aporia: A Critical Exploration of the Agent-Structure Problematique in International Relations Theory." *European Journal of International Relations* 3 (3): 365–392.

Eckersley, Robyn. 2013. "Green Theory." In *International Relations Theories: Discipline and Diversity*, edited by Tim Dunne, Milja Kurki, and Steve Smith. Oxford: Oxford University Press.

Enloe, Cynthia. 1993. *The Morning After: Sexual Politics at the End of the Cold War.* Berkeley: University of California Press.

Escobar, Arturo. 2010. "Latin America at a Crossroads: Alternative Modernizations, Post-Liberalism, or Post-Development?" *Cultural Studies* 24 (1): 1–65. doi:10.1080/09502380903424208.

Escobar, Arturo. 2017. *Designs for the Pluriverse: Radical Interdependence, Autonomy, and the Making of Worlds.* Durham, NC: Duke University Press.

Estermann, Josef. 2006. *Filosofía Andina: Sabiduría Indígena Para Un Mundo Nuevo.* 2nd ed. La Paz: Instituto Superior Ecuménico Andino de Teología.

Fanon, Frantz. 1952. *Black Skin, White Masks.* New York: Grove Press.

Fanon, Frantz. 1968. *Les Damnés de La Terre.* Petite Collection Maspero 20. Paris: Maspero.

Foucault, Michel. 1972. *The Archaeology of Knowledge, and The Discourse on Language.* New York: Vintage Books.

Foucault, Michel. 1997. *Society Must Be Defended: Lectures at the Collége de France, 1975–1976*. New York: Picador.

Fraser, Nancy, and Axel Honnet. 2003. *Redistribution or Recognition? A Political-Philosophical Exchange.* London, New York: Verso.

George, Jim, and David Campbell. 1990. "Patterns of Dissent and the Celebration of Difference: Critical Social Theory and International Relations." *International Studies Quarterly* 34 (3): 269–293.

Gofas, Andreas, Inanna Hamati-Ataya, and Nicholas Onuf, eds. 2018. *The SAGE Handbook of the History, Philosophy and Sociology of International Relations.* Los Angeles: SAGE.

Grovogui, Siba N'Zatioula. 1996. *Sovereigns, Quasi Sovereigns, and Africans.* Minneapolis: University of Minnesota Press.

Hurd, Elizabeth Shakman. 2008. *The Politics of Secularism in International Relations.* Princeton, NJ: Princeton University Press.

Inayatullah, Naeem, and David L. Blaney. 2004. *International Relations and the Problem of Difference.* New York: Routledge.

Klotz, Audie, and Cecelia Lynch. 2007. *Strategies for Research in Constructivist International Relations.* New York: M. E. Sharpe.

Laferrière, Eric, and Peter J. Stoett. 1999. *International Relations and Ecological Thought: Towards a Synthesis.* New York: Routledge.

Lorde, Audre. 2018. *The Master's Tools Will Never Dismantle the Master's House.* London: Penguin.

Lugones, María. 2007. "Heterosexualism and the Colonial/Modern Gender System." *Hypatia* 22 (1): 186–219. doi:10.1111/j.1527-2001.2007.tb01156.x.

Lynch, Cecelia. 2014. *Interpreting International Politics.* New York: Routledge.

Mann, Susan Archer. 2013. "Third Wave Feminism's Unhappy Marriage of Poststructuralism and Intersectionality Theory." *Journal of Feminist Scholarship* 4 (4): 54–73.

Manzo, Kathryn. 1996. *Creating Boundaries, The Politics of Race and Nation.* London: Lynne Rienner Publishers.

McCall, Leslie. 2005. "The Complexity of Intersectionality." *Signs* 30 (3): 1771–1800.

Méndez, María José. 2018. "'The River Told Me': Rethinking Intersectionality from the World of Berta Cáceres." *Capitalism Nature Socialism* 29 (1): 7–24.

Mignolo, Walter. 2000. *Local Histories/Global Designs: Coloniality, Subaltern Knowledges, and Border Thinking.* Princeton Studies in Culture/Power/History. Princeton, NJ: Princeton University Press.

Mignolo, Walter. 2009. "Epistemic Disobedience, Independent Thought and Decolonial Freedom." *Theory, Culture & Society* 26 (7–8): 159–181. doi:10.1177/0263276409349275.

Mignolo, Walter. 2011. "Border Thinking, Decolonial Cosmopolitanism and Dialogues Among Civilizations." In *The Ashgate Research Companion to Cosmopolitanism*, edited by Maria Rovisco and Magdalena Nowicka, 329–348. Farnham: Ashgate.

Mignolo, Walter, and Catherine E. Walsh. 2018. *On Decoloniality: Concepts, Analytics, and Praxis.* Durham NC: Duke University Press.

Milliken, Jennifer. 1999. "The Study of Discourse in International Relations: A Critique of Research and Methods." *European Journal of International Relations* 5 (2): 225–254.

Mills, Charles W. 1997. *The Racial Contract.* Ithaca: Cornell University Press.

Mohanty, Chandra Talpade. 1988. "Under Western Eyes: Feminist Scholarship and Colonial Discourses." *Feminist Review* 30 (1): 61–88.

Moon, Katharine H. S. 1997. *Sex Among Allies: Military Prostitution in U.S.-Korea Relations.* New York: Columbia University Press.

Moraga, Cherrie. 1993. *The Last Generation: Prose and Poetry.* Boston, MA: South End Press.

Pachirat, Timothy. 2014. "We Call It a Grain of Sand." In *Interpretation and Method: Empirical Research Methods and the Interpretive Turn*, edited by Dvora Yanow and Peregrine Schwartz-Shea, 426–433. New York: Routledge.

Pasha, Mustapha Kamal. 2012. "The 'Secular' Subject of Critical International Relations Theory." In *Critical Theory in International Relations and Security Studies*, edited by Shannon Brincat, Laura Lima, and Joâo Nunes. New York: Routledge.

Quijano, Aníbal. 2000. "Coloniality of Power, Eurocentrism, and Latin America." Translated by Michael Ennis. *Nepantla: Views from South* 1 (3): 533–580.

Quijano, Aníbal, and Immanuel Wallerstein. 1992. "Americanity as a Concept, or the Americas in the Modern World-System." *International Journal of Social Sciences* 134: 583–591.

Richards, Patricia. 2014. "Decolonizing Globalization Studies." *The Global South* 8 (2): 139–154.

Rivera Cusicanqui, Silvia. 2015. *Sociología de la Imagen. Miradas Ch'ixi Desde La Historia Andina.* Buenos Aires: Tinta Limón.

Rivera Cusicanqui, Silvia. 2018. *El Mundo Ch'ixi Es Posible: Ensayos Desde Un Presente En Crisis.* Buenos Aires: Tinta Limón.

Said, Edward W. 1978. *Orientalism.* New York: Vintage Books.

Schwartz-Shea, Peregrine, and Dvora Yanow. 2012. *Interpretive Research Design: Concepts and Processes.* New York: Routledge.

Seth, Vanita. 2010. *Europe's Indians: Producing Racial Difference, 1500–1900.* Durham, NC: Duke University Press.

Shepherd, Laura. 2008. *Gender, Violence, and Security: Discourses as Practice.* London: Zed Books.

Sjoberg, Laura. 2006. *Gender, Justice and Wars in Iraq.* New York: Lexington Books.

Smith, Steve. 2013. "Introduction: Diversity and Disciplinarity in International Relations Theory." In *International Relations Theories: Discipline and Diversity*, edited by Tim Dunne, Milja Kurki, and Steve Smith, 1–12. Oxford: Oxford University Press.

Spivak, Gayatri Chakravorti. 2010. "Can The Subaltern Speak." In *Can The Subaltern Speak? Reflections on the History of an Idea*, edited by Rosalind Morris, 21–78. New York: Columbia University Press.

Stoler, Ann Laura. 1995. *Race and Education of Desire: Foucault's History of Sexuality and the Colonial Order of Things.* Durham, NC: Duke University Press.

Taylor, Lucy. 2012. "Decolonizing International Relations: Perspectives from Latin America." *International Studies Review* 14 (3): 386–400.

Thomson, Sinclair. 2002. *We Alone Will Rule: Native Andean Politics in the Age of Insurgency* (Living in Latin America). Madison: University of Wisconsin Press.

Tickner, J. Ann. 1992. *Gender in International Relations: Feminist Perspectives on Achieving Global Security.* New York: Columbia University Press.

Tickner, J. Ann, and Laura Sjoberg. 2013. "Feminism." In *International Relations Theories: Discipline and Diversity*, edited by Tim Dunne, Milja Kurki, and Steve Smith, 185–202. Oxford: Oxford University Press.

Todorov, Tzvetan. 1982. *The Conquest of America: The Question of the Other.* Norman: University of Oklahoma Press.

Treva, B. Lindsey. 2015. "Post-Ferguson: A 'Herstorical' Approach to Black Violability." *Feminist Studies* 41 (1): 232–237.

Viaña, Jorge, Luis Claros, and Marcelo Sarzuri-Lima. 2010. "La Condición Colonial y Los Laberintos de La Descolonización." *Revista Integra Educativa* 3 (1): 13–36.

Walker, R. B. J. 1993. *Inside/Outside: International Relations as Political Theory.* Cambridge: Cambridge University Press.

Walker, R. B. J. 2010. *After the Globe, Before the World.* New York: Routledge.

Weber, Cynthia. 2016. *Queer International Relations: Sovereignty, Sexuality and the Will to Knowledge.* Oxford: Oxford University Press.

Wibben, Annick T. R., and Olivia U. Rutazibwa. 2019. "Who Do We Think We Are?" In *Global Politics: A New Introduction*, by Jenny Edkins and Maja Zehfuss, 3rd ed., 79–101. New York: Routledge.

Wolfe, Cary. 2010. *What Is Posthumanism?* Minneapolis: University of Minnesota Press.

Wynter, Sylvia. 1995. "The Pope Must Have Been Drunk, The King of Castile a Madman: Culture as Actuality, and the Caribbean Rethinking Modernity." In *Reordering of Culture: Latin America, the Caribbean and Canada in the Hood*, by Alvina Ruprecht, 17–42. Ottawa: Carleton University Press.

1 Colonialisms in/for Bolivia and IR

Several scholars have examined how specific forms of colonialism have dealt with the problem of difference (e.g., Said 1978; Todorov 1982; Quijano and Wallerstein 1992; Rivera and Morón 1993; Manzo 1996; Canessa 2000, 2005; Mignolo 2000, 2011; Inayatullah and Blaney 2004; Seth 2010; Reinaga 2014). In his renowned account of "Orientalism," Edward Said affirms that colonial discourses create a hierarchical separation between a superior "West" and an inferior "Orient" (Said 1978). Through an essentialist epistemic understanding of "others" as discrete, eternal, fixed, observable, and controllable "objects," colonial knowledges organize "Oriental" peoples, cultures, and geographical locations within their own hierarchicalizations (Said 1978, 32). Said's contributions in discussions of colonialisms and the problem of difference are numerous, but I would like to emphasize one in particular: Said understands the hierarchical relationships between the "West" and the "Orient" as *constructions* (Said 1978, 2). By following some aspects of Michel Foucault's definition of discourse, the author avoids essentialist understandings of colonialism.[1] He studies this kind of relationship without assuming that it emerges from some kind of hidden cause, such as the deep nature of a people, the "true" characteristics of a culture, or the "real" essence of a nation or a continent. To him, the colonial problem lies in the construction of hierarchical relationships between stereotyped, coherent, and generalized identities, knowledges, cultures, geographies, etc.

Since Said aims to abandon this kind of essentialist assumption, he is able to study many of the ontological, epistemological, and temporal assumptions that are deployed within colonial discourses. He analyzes the ways in which constructions include these assumptions in order to validate, authorize, and legitimize "Western" colonialism. Additionally, Said's emphasis on the constructed aspect of colonialism shines light on the heterogenous and dynamic complexity of the geographic and historical contexts that are so often homogenized and fixed within these constructions. Here, power is understood not as a single structure that homogenously determines meanings and singularly causes all practices of domination and resistance; instead, power is much more unstable. This methodological stance can thus highlight the innovative voices that resist colonial formations inside and outside the so called "West."

Additionally, it shows the changes that take place in the construction of colonialism; it emphasizes the "palimpsest of different races and cultures" sharing various places (Said 1978, 347), avoiding the very myth that colonial discourses aim to impose when knowledges appear as corresponding to objects; when peoples, cultures, places, bodies, etc. become the very knowledge that claims to know them.

Consistent with the notion of constructed and hierarchicalized characterizations, then, I study colonialisms as discourses that imply superiority for a handful of values and ideas (Said 1978, 347), which are attached to peoples and entail privileges. Since much of the literature examines colonial discourses, and since my goal is to emphasize alternative ways of thinking, being, and enacting difference, I aim to analyze specific formations that briefly illustrate colonialisms. Throughout this chapter, I analyze how particular constructions of liberalism and Marxism seek to solve the problem of difference in Bolivia by organizing echelons of knowledges, peoples, and civilizations. Then, I examine the proximity and consistency between some of the epistemic characteristics of these colonial discourses and a number of theories of International Relations. In the conclusion, I conceptualize the epistemic characteristics of the colonial discourses that I interpret. This process of definition and abstraction aims to pose questions for other approaches. Finally, I recall the problem of difference to confront the classification of "coloniality," showing that the study of epistemic politics has enormous advantages, while also posing problems and important questions.

Reason, liberalism, and citizenship: Civilizing models of equality

As Michael Walzer affirms, liberalism is the language of individual rights such as voluntary association, pluralism, toleration, privacy, free speech, private property, and careers open to talent (Walzer 1990, 14). According to the author, this tradition emerges from the idea of an isolated individual, who has the possibility of pursuing happiness because she/he is rational (12). However, liberalism also includes a commonality or communitarian element, which avoids the complete fragmentation of society and connects its individual atoms (9). Hence, the language of liberalism unites *rational* individuals in the language of rights. Specific ideas of rights, voluntary association, freedom of speech, and liberal selves creates a community that is "a selective reinforcement of those same values" (15). Then, states preside over this union and they "foster only those (unions) that really do express communities of feelings and belief and do not violate liberal principles of association" (19). In other words, liberalism creates a bounded notion of equality and freedom for those individuals and groups that are "rational." As Walzer notices, this tradition is often confronted and critiqued because "there is no imaginable community that would not be alien to the eternally transgressive self" (15).

Walzer uses an essentialist epistemic understanding of individual human beings as the atoms of society, but he also notices that differences constantly confront liberal projects, forcing each construction to rethink its definition of commonality (i.e., "rationality"). Liberalism thus tends to settle boundaries within each definition of a "rational" individual, but "communitarian critiques" also call liberalism to "reinvent itself." Endogenously, liberalism seeks "to fix and stabilize the doctrine," which creates "voluntary associations" (Walzer 1990, 15). As other authors have asserted, these kinds of "social contracts" entail specific types of epistemic assumptions, which grant equality to those who fit within the commonality of each "rationality," sediment doctrines guarded by states, and exclude "others" who are less "rational" (e.g., Ashley 1989; Mills 1997). In turn, this form of statecraft delineates who can access rights and who is an "other" that needs to be normalized, disciplined, assimilated, or killed (Weber 2016). To illustrate specific constructions of liberalism, particular epistemic ways to stabilize the doctrine, and various consequences related to the construction of "others," I examine different ways in which ideas of "reason" have been deployed to construct colonial discourses in and for Bolivia, but also in and for International Relations. Throughout the chapter, I also highlight how each kind of liberalism tends to fix its own doctrine, only expanding its boundaries when exogenous confrontations reintroduce the problem of difference.

Reason from God and nature: Theories and governments

Thomas Hobbes and John Locke used notions of "reason" to think about politics and moral philosophy. In the *Leviathan*, for example, Hobbes constructed "reason" as a God-given and natural characteristic of "humanity" (Hobbes 1994). Since it was rooted in a "human nature" that was granted by God, "reason" itself had to be regarded as "real" and "true." However, since "humans" shared this capacity of "reasoning," they could investigate its characteristics without the authority of a religious organization. This epistemological connection between "reality" and those who "reason" authorized the state and those who govern because they represented the "true" nature of a "man" that could be known and had to be protected. Locke also used this epistemic notion when he asserted that "reason" corresponded to the law of nature, which was related to the design of God. For example, Locke stated:

> The state of nature has a law of nature to govern it, which obliges everyone: and reason, which is that law, teaches all mankind, who will but consult it, that being all equal and independent, no one ought to harm another in his life, health, liberty, or possessions: for men being all the workmanship of one omnipotent and infinitely wise maker.
>
> Locke 1980, 9

Unlike Hobbes, however, Locke described "reason" as including the ability to think about the longer term, decreasing the collective fear of each other and creating a possibility to cooperate even in the state of nature. This was understood as the basis from which the social contract could cease to need an absolute monarch who was a Leviathan or a "mortal god."

Despite their differences, Hobbes and Locke used a God-given, essentialized, and universalized characteristic of "humanity" as a condition of possibility to validate a knowledge, authorize a voice, and legitimate the enactment of states. "Reason" was the God-given reality of nature, which could be "consulted," and had to be protected by the state that resulted from the social contract. From this epistemic construction, "reason," those who knew it, and the social contract became the characteristics of a bounded basis of commonality, which classified "all" individuals as equal insofar as they were "rational." Whatever did not fit "reason" and whoever did not participate in "reason" thus appeared as "uncivilized," "irrational," or less "human." As Bhikhu Parekh notices, Locke wrote about universal equality while also excluding an array of peoples that did not quite fulfill the characteristics of "humanity" (Parekh 1995). Charles Mills asserts that this tendency can also be found in the work of Hobbes (Mills 1997). These "others" were ways of knowing, being, and enacting that were not granted the possibility of entering the social contract and thus did not access the equality and rights of the commonwealth. For example, Locke asserted that "reason" was the basis from which any "human being" could access the law of nature, which defined all "men" as equal and as primarily oriented towards the protection of their own individual self. However, in order to participate in this "reason," one had to reach a certain level of "maturity" (Locke 1980, 33).

> But if, through defects that may happen out of the ordinary course of nature, any one comes not to such a degree of reason, wherein he might be supposed capable of knowing the law, and so living within the rule of it, he is never capable of being a free man.
>
> Locke 1980, 34

Many of these epistemic notions and tendencies can be found in the specific ways in which Bolivian governments deployed liberalism between the end of the Independence War in 1825 and the War of the Pacific against Chile in 1879. Within this context, similar epistemic patterns validated a knowledge, authorized a citizen, and legitimized a project in and for Bolivia.

In 1825, Simón Bolivar wrote the first constitution of Bolivia. The intellectual stated that it was a "true liberal constitution" because it had some of the "strictest" limitations on the executive power and because the judicial power was tasked with the protection of individual rights such as liberty, equality, and security (Bolivar 2007, 128, author's translation). To Bolivar, this was the "most liberal constitution in the world, worthy of the most complete civilization" (272). This document was approved in 1826 by Antonio José de Sucre Alcalá, who became the president of Bolivia after the war of independence. Similar to the ideas of Hobbes and Locke, the 1826 constitution combined God and the faculty of the "people" to validate the document and to establish an epistemic basis for sovereignty, which then authorized the three branches of the government and the people who occupied those positions.[2] The constitution gained its validity "in the name of God" and "from the people" simultaneously (Bolivia Constitution 1826, art. VII, VIII, and IX, author's translation). Truth, sovereignty, and rule were intertwined to validate law and to authorize governing roles within a delineated territory. In the Bolivia of the nineteenth century, "reason" was a Catholic way of knowing, but a particular understanding of the doctrine was attached to the individual faculty of the "people." Despite the coupling of "reason" and Catholicism, Bolivar and the constitutions approved between 1825 and 1880 separated the state and the Catholic church. In this sense, Bolivar stated that only God had the right to found Bolivia; the creation of this nation could only obtain the blessing of the heavens through the sovereignty that emerged from the "people," the only legitimate authority of the nation (Bolivar 2007, 133). In this regard, Bolivar thought that "reason" and "God" destined men towards liberty and free will, which had to be guaranteed by the state and the government (130).

The validation of this way of knowing excluded and invalidated "other" possibilities. At first, this platform was explicitly used by Bolivar to invalidate monarchic forms of rule and to justify the war of independence against Spanish colonialism. In 1814, for example, Bolivar critiqued the "ignorance" of the monarchic system and the inquisition, "daughter of the most zealous superstition, hidden under the disgrace of human lineage." Under this kind of "ignorance," Bolivar continued, "there could be no enlightened reason, political virtue, or morality to break the scepter of oppression and substitute it with laws" (Bolivar 2007, 54, author's translation). Here, Bolivar's idea of a God-given reason and sovereignty consistently opposed the monopoly of truth that the Catholic Church and the Kings of Spain often claimed for themselves. Beyond the Church, monarchy, and Spanish colonialism, however, the Bolivian state also used this epistemic platform to exclude all other ways of knowing. For example, all 11 of the constitutions or constitutional reforms ratified between 1825 and 1880 forbid "other cults."

Together with this classification of ways of knowing, the liberal discourse of nineteenth-century Bolivia constructed an epistemological authorization of a particular knower, which appeared to participate in this kind of "reason." According to Silvia Rivera Cusicanqui, Bolivia instated this kind of liberal reforms after its independence and it created a limited form of *citizenship*, which only granted privileges to colonial elites (Rivera 2010a, 57). This form of inequality was created through a separation of two jurisdictions in Bolivia (Rivera 1990, 30). Every one of the 11 constitutions that were ratified or passed between 1825 and 1880 contained a segregation between "all the Bolivianos" in the territory and the "active citizens" of the country. The constitution thus only granted the authorization to vote and to acquire governmental positions to the men of age that "reasoned," spoke Spanish, knew how to read and write in this language, and avoided "vice" such as drinking or gambling ("Bolivia Constitution" 1826, author's translation). This authorization of a particular knower included racialized and gendered constraints. It explicitly excluded enormous parts of the population due to "their" differences.

For example, the 1826 constitution stated that Bolivianos were all the persons born in the territory, those who had Bolivian parents, those who became Bolivianos, and those who fought in wars for the country ("Bolivia Constitution" 1826, art. XI). All these "Bolivianos" had basic rights such as the guarantee of freedom (i.e., slavery was forbidden in Bolivia), individual security, private property, freedom of speech, intellectual rights, etc. This legal category of personhood also included duties such as the payment of taxes, obedience of the law, obedience to authorities, serving and protecting the country, etc. On the other legal side of segregation, "active citizens" were the men who were married or of age, knew how to read and write in Spanish, were not domestic servants, had "jobs" or property, were not "criminals," and were not "drunks." In turn, only these "active citizens" could vote in elections or become functionaries of the government; only they were authorized to pass new laws or occupy the executive, legislative, and judicial branches of the government. These legal documents thus designated "active citizens" as subjects that were authorized to define, segregate, rule, and appease "others." Moreover, these constitutions granted "active citizens" the legal capacity to suspend the basic rights of all "Bolivianos" in cases of international conflict and domestic disorder, crisis, or "commotion" ("Bolivia Constitution" 1826, art. XX). Between 1826 and 1880, then, the "other" sector of "Bolivianos," which were not "active citizens," were completely excluded from any kind of political action within or without the state.

Reason from reason: Theories and governments

During the 1870s and 1880s, Bolivians experienced a series of crises and fought the War of the Pacific (1879–1884). After Bolivia tried to nationalize Chilean mining companies due to taxation issues, Chile's armed forces invaded the port of Antofagasta. Despite its alliance with Peru, Bolivia lost its access to the Pacific Ocean and withdrew from the war in 1880. Once Narciso Campero Leyes became president of Bolivia in 1880, he faced widespread discontent and the government of the country was re-constructed by following a more Kantian idea of liberalism, which became governmentally institutionalized until the 1952 Nationalist Revolution. Discontent led to several reforms that seemingly expanded rights, but also included the expropriation of lands from indigenous peoples. On one side, the government had to rebuild the legitimacy of the defeated state. On the other side, some of these liberal reforms reactivated mining in Bolivia (Rivera 1990, 102). In turn, this form of extractivist economy allowed for Bolivian elites and the state to gain another source of taxation, which did not depend on indigenous lands to collect revenues. These policies led to the abolition of the ayllu, which entailed a communitarian form of land tenure, and it allowed for a widespread process of expropriation. Between the 1880s and 1952, this liberal project of civilization changed some of the previous epistemic notions and it reformed the state, while also sustaining a number of continuities.

As Pierre Bourdieu asserts, Immanuel Kant delineated and universalized a different definition of "reason," which also acted as a basis of judgment and hierarchicalization for "other" forms of thought (Bourdieu 1997, 44). Kant problematized the possibility of using the ontological idea of a material or empirical foundation that determined "reason." Instead of utilizing the idea of "reason" as directly emerging from a God-given "human nature," Kant began from "reason" itself. He located "reason" and its logic first, but he also claimed that "reason" was objective and universal because it was the key that opened our cognitive door towards "natural law." In this sense, Kant asserted:

> Human reason, in one sphere of cognition, is called upon us to consider questions, which it cannot decline, as they are presented by its own nature, but which it cannot answer, as they transcend every faculty of the mind. … In recent times, the hope dawned upon us of seeing those disputes settled, and the legitimacy of her claims established by a kind of physiology of the human understanding – that celebrated Locke. But it was found that … as this genealogy was incorrect, she persisted in her advancement of her claims to sovereignty.
>
> Kant 1952, 42:2

The connection between a knowledge and an ontological positivity created "certitude" and it objectivized Kant's construction, but it also gave "reason" its own "sovereignty." Then, Kant created an epistemological connection between "humanity" and "reason," which authorized particular knowers above "others." As Mills asserts, this Kantian epistemology of "reason" not only entailed the definition of a cognitive capacity, but also included racialized characteristics that excluded most non-European "others" (Mills 1997, 71). From the "certitude" of a particular kind of "reason," Kant thus validated a "true" knowledge and he authorized a single kind of knower. Here, "man" participated in that which was "real" (i.e., "reason") because he shared its characteristics (i.e., he "reasoned"). In turn, this validation and authorization led to a hierarchical classification between "civilization" and "barbarism," which then organized societies in a progressive and linear temporality. "Irrational" ways of knowing, being, and enacting belonged to the "barbaric" past that "civilized" peoples had left behind and sought to transform. The enactment of the "future" thus entailed the construction of "reason" and the banishment of the "past."

In Bolivia, this epistemic platform was introduced in the liberal idea of "active citizenship" that emerged in the 1870s. Additionally, the post-war constitution of 1880 sedimented this model of civilization and sustained it in the government at least until the end of the Chaco War between Paraguay and Bolivia in 1935 and the new constitution of 1938. Between the 1870s and 1930s, then, "reason" became more detached from "human nature" and from Catholic ways of knowing. As a result, the constitution allowed for Bolivianos to practice different cults, while also recognizing and sustaining the Catholic religion ("Bolivia Constitution" 1880, art. II). Additionally, the constitution used a particular definition of education as a pedagogical tool that could bring "Bolivianos" closer to the "reasoning" citizen. Since notions of "human nature" were less dominant in the laws of the period, the pedagogical transformation of "Bolivianos" into "citizens" became a more "real" possibility. After 1871, the constitution thus included free and mandatory primary education for all Bolivianos ("Bolivia Constitution" 1871, art. IV). Then, the category of "citizenship" required this kind of education in Spanish, together with writing and reading skills. It also demanded property, age, and inscription in a civic registry (art. XXXIII). The classification between "citizens" and "Bolivianos" thus remained very similar to all the previous constitutions, as did the notions of guarantees, duties, and exceptions, but people could supposedly become "reasoning" "citizens" because their nature did not necessarily prevent them from learning to be "civilized." The "future" of "reason" could be enacted in the present through the homogenization of the population into the model citizen. Hence, the role of education was emphasized in the constitutions of 1871, 1878, and 1880. Since it had a clear civilizing function, education had to remain under the "surveillance" of the state ("Bolivia Constitution" 1871, art. IV).

This Bolivian legal system of classification continued to exclude or assimilate "others" in the same manner until the end of the Chaco War in 1935. After the War ended, the pressure emerging from the soldiers who were not "active citizens" and from other sectors of Bolivia led to the beginning of a slow and painful process of "citizenship" expansion. The government's idea of a Kantian classification of citizens resisted transformations, but the struggle of several sectors and the turmoil in the country led to important modifications. In the post-war constitution of 1938, for example, Bolivia stopped requiring property or a minimum salary to become a citizen, "Bolivianos" gained the right to associate or form groups as long as they did not aim to act against the state ("Bolivia Constitution" 1838, art. VI, author's translation), and the constitution created a time limit to the capacity of the executive power to declare curfew (art. XXXIV). The constitution also recognized "indigenous communities" (art. CLXV). Despite these gains, the notion of "active citizenship" effectively continued to exclude the same groups of peoples or it demanded the price of their identity. As Fausto Reinaga notices, the Kantian construction of "reason" regarded indigenous peoples as "barbaric" or "savage" groups that did not "reason" (Reinaga 2014, 5:421, author's translation). Hence, "indigenous communities" still had to become assimilated through the education system in order to gain electoral rights. The state promoted the education of "peasants" through the "centers for indigenous education" ("Bolivia Constitution" 1838, art. CLXVII). Furthermore, the definition of the official "cultural regime" declared that education was organized in a centralized system (art. CLIV), which was subjected to a unique set of "official authorities, plans, programs, and rules" (art. CLV).

Due to its continuous exclusion of the majority of "Bolivianos," the constitutional reform was not enough to appease indigenous and women's movements that were becoming more salient and powerful in post-Chaco-War Bolivia. After staging a coup d'état in 1943, Gualberto Villarroel López won the elections and assumed the presidency in 1944 with the support of some left parties and unions. In May 1945, Villarroel supported the biggest Indigenous Congress that Bolivia had ever seen, with more than 1,200 leaders participating in important debates about the exclusion and exploitation of peoples. In the Congress, Villarroel reinforced old understandings of "reason" and "citizenship" by pronouncing a paternalistic speech that promoted the "integration" of indigenous peoples under the tutelage of the state and its system of education. As Elizabeth Shesko points out, the Congress ended up serving a disciplinary function that sought to bring indigenous peoples into "civilization" (Shesko 2010). Notwithstanding this continuation, the government passed in 1945 several executive orders that were designed to create indigenous rights. Later that year, Villarroel also approved a new constitution. Together, these laws protected indigenous peoples against many kinds of forced and unpaid labor, and they created specific regulations against the systems of "pongueage" and "mit'anage," which had been continuous problems in Bolivia even though "slavery" had been formally forbidden since 1826. Additionally, the 1945 constitution granted voting rights to women. Now, men and women could vote and participate in the government as long as they knew how to read and write in Spanish ("Bolivia Constitution" 1945, art. XLVI). Rights of health care, hygiene, housing, and participation in unions were also added. It was not until the Revolution of 1952, however, that voting rights and governmental participation would become legally "universal" for all "Bolivianos."

Despite important discussions of Kant's epistemic assumptions and civilizing tendencies (e.g., Foucault 1970; Bourdieu 1997; Mills 1997; Walker 2006; Reinaga 2014; Mignolo and Walsh 2018), many authors of International Relations continue to use approaches such Kantian democratic peace theories (e.g., Chan 1997; Oneal, Russett, and Berbaum 2003; Russett 2013) or Kantian peacebuilding perspectives (Paris 2004). As Campbell, Chandler, and Sabaratnam assert, many scholars still use this approach without questioning its limitations (Campbell, Chandler and Sabaratnam 2011, 1). Given the warnings of these authors, the othering tendencies of Kantian notions of citizenship and participation, and the continuation of Kantian assumptions in International Relations, several questions about the shared *characteristics* of Kantian approaches gain relevance. In much of International Relations, Kantian "reason" is related to the possibility of learning and promoting free trade, democratic states, and international organizations. In order to achieve this goal, "citizens" ought to develop their faculty of "reason" and they have to become "free," while the state has to ensure this learning process by creating the conditions that allow it. As a result of these three factors and their articulation, the relationships between states becomes more "peaceful." For Kant:

> the ultimate purpose of social life is to permit individuals to develop all of their "natural capacities," which is possible only if human beings are permitted the exercise of their "freedom of will based upon reason." But Kant also warned of the dangers of unrestricted liberty, or "wild freedom." In the absence of the rule of law enforced by a central authority, he argued, peaceful coexistence among completely free individuals would be impossible, and would collapse into a "lawless state of savagery." Peace therefore requires a powerful sovereign – a "supreme authority."
>
> Paris 2004, 49

Since this approach assumes an isolated and self-reinforcing order of cause and effect between "rational" learning, a particular kind of order, and "peace," Kantian theory often overlooks important questions. The theory isolates the study of "peace" within its discursive boundaries (i.e., between reason, order, and peace), and it understudies previous and posterior elements. In order to create "peace," Kantian notions often assume that all international and domestic "others" ought to learn, change, or disappear. As Robert Walker asserts, these epistemic assumptions of modernity validate temporalities of a "there" that is above other kinds of "here" (Walker 1993, 7). This "there" is a goal of "progress," represented by the present of those who "reason" and have already become "peaceful." Instead, "others" ought to abandon their "here" and they have to become "reason." Then, empirical studies examine the isolated and epistemically pre-defined relationship between the indicators of "reason" and "peace." The results show that increasing "reason" (i.e., democracy, free trade, international laws, and international institution) decreases war and death. But how does this isolation of "variables" hide the conditions of possibility for violence that are created by homogenization itself? How is colonial violence against "others" necessary for "rationality" and then "peace"? Is colonial violence a condition of possibility for Kantian "peace"? As Foucault famously asserts in "Nietzsche, Genealogy, History," the distant roar of battle can be heard hidden behind the blood that has dried on the codes of laws (Foucault 1986). Accordingly, how are Kantian notions of reality, reason, and peace related to pasts of colonial violence, and how do they also sustain current conditions of possibility for more violence? Moreover, wars and deaths might be decreasing over time, but who paid the price of this particular kind of "peace"?

Reason from language: Theories and International Relations

In order to continue the analysis of colonial legacies that are related to epistemic notions of "reason" in International Relations, I momentarily abandon the Bolivian genealogy in an excursus that concentrates on another epistemic transformation of liberalism. According to a number of authors, some of these liberal transformations also affected important discussions of indigeneity in the Bolivian context of the 2000s (Canessa 2005; Albró 2010), but I emphasize in this chapter the silences that they continue to create in International Relations.

According to Foucault, the human sciences continued separating "reason" from ontological objects such as "human nature" or "natural law" after the work of Kant (Foucault 1970, 326), but this field of inquiry still claimed objectivity and it still continued to validate single ways of knowing, being, and enacting. In the nineteenth century, the human sciences used the empirico-transcendental existence of "facts" as ontological foundations that could grant "reality" and "truth" to particular fields of knowledge. The fact that "man" spoke and understood meanings guaranteed the existence of signification, together with the possibility of studying this field of inquiry. Here, "reason" sustained its own logic and "sovereignty," which was now found in the empirical trends of language. "Natural law" or "human nature" no longer guaranteed "reason," but the possibility of experiencing signification still granted certitude to language. Then, insofar as "humans" could define the general characteristics (i.e., patterns or regularities) of this fact of language, they could create yet another form of "reason."

While following much of Foucault's argument, Vanita Seth asserts that this form of "reason" made "man" a full sovereign subject (Seth 2010, 188). Through these assumptions, "reason" could be studied in each context-dependent set of trends of signification, but the results of empirical research could also be generalized as *the* characteristics of "reason" because they were epistemically guaranteed by the fact that "humans" spoke. Then, the connection between the "fact of signification" and these specific empirical patterns epistemologically authorized those who participate in each particular form of "reason." Those who best represent the "true" characteristics of "reason" thus appeared to be "true" knowers. Ontology created another type of certitude or "reality," while epistemology introduced the participation of another specific kind of knower. By defining this form of participation in that which was validated or "real," epistemology not only determined the "reasoning" characteristics of the knower, but also authorized this subject to delineate and know the specificities of "reason." "Others" that did not "speak" or did not "reason," found their ways of knowing invalidated and their characteristics marginalized. As Seth notes, this discourse used this epistemic definition of "reason" to create a hierarchical organization of "others." This specific kind of relationship of equality emerged, according to Seth, from epistemic conditions "…that enabled the thinking of difference at different historical junctures" (3).

From this epistemic construction of "reason," a number of liberal scholars in International Relations sustain yet another boundary and othering tendency. A particularly sophisticated example can be found in Alison Brysk's book *From Tribal Village to Global Village*. Brysk utilizes a Habermasian "critical approach" (Brysk 2000, 51). Habermas' understanding of language defines "reason" from the formal pragmatics of communicative actions (Habermas 1984). Unlike Hobbes, Locke, or Kant, Habermas does not claim to know "human nature" or "natural law" to define "reason," but he still universalizes the presuppositions that are supposedly found beneath the rationality of daily communicative actions. In his book *Postmetaphysical Thinking*, Habermas denies the idea of language as an objective and causally antecedent realm that acts as a structure mechanically shaping practices (Habermas 1992, 44). Instead, he seeks to understand language by participating in it; he studies the lifeworld with a footing in practices. Within this possibility of knowledge, Habermas states that language depends on "yes" or "no" options and positions, which entail actions towards validity claims. This situated empirical realm of language-related knowledge leads Habermas to the analysis of the universal presuppositions that are necessary for this type of communicative action to be possible (46). From empirical patterns of language, which are discussed by other scholars, Habermas finds the underlying conditions that make communication possible; he constructs idealizations that supposedly become "social facts" and include normative content. In other words, instead of claiming the structural or objective status of "language," Habermas finds, in the study of practices, the requirements necessary for social life to reproduce itself and then he universalizes these pragmatics as the standards that evaluate forms of communication; he finds the form of "reason" operating underneath everyday communicative practices (50). In a sense, then, Habermas implicitly uses the fact that "man" speaks, following particular patterns of communication, and then seeking to define the universalized requirements that enable this kind of "understanding."

In her work, Brysk uses this approach to understand the participation of indigenous movements in globalization and the United Nations, which empower these actors through the possibility of accessing international rights. By using communicative rationality, indigenous movements are understood as entering modernity and participating in it; they communicatively develop their transnational identity (Brysk 2000, 280). The indigenous groups that participated in communicative rationality thus appear superior to "other" voices that do not seek to be part of "our world" (5). Conversely, more radical groups are excluded because they seek to "celebrate difference without overcoming it" (72). This approach illustrates how epistemic assumptions of "reason" still lead to a possibility of empowerment and access to rights similar to old ideas of citizenship in their demand of a price of identity. Actors have to fulfill the requirements of communicative "reason" in order to access the protection of some differences, but not others. Brysk's study of indigenous movements thus hierarchicalizes "others" that do not participate in the search of a "common understanding," which was the universalized characteristic of Habermasian communicative "reason."

Moreover, since its characteristics are required to access the communicative platform of equality, "reason" often appears as the definitional basis of citizenship, which only grants rights and protections to those regarded as "rational." Habermas uses this idea, for example, in the construction of an over-arching and "civic" identity for the European Union, which has to create a form of inclusion and solidarity beyond "nationality" (Habermas 2001, 76). Additionally, the epistemological connection between communicative "reason" and its knower authorizes Habermas and other intellectuals such as Brysk to enact the specificities of "reason," which include the possibilities of further drawing the boundary of "equality" and defining the "future." Consequently, specific characteristics of citizenship, rights, and governments become attached to the validity of "reason" and they further delineate the universalized boundaries of this "self." Habermas uses this strategy not only to construct a post-national notion of citizenship, but also to define the more general features that legitimate governments. Similarly, Brysk analyzes the empowering characteristics of globalization and the United Nations, further defining notions of rights and identity politics. This epistemically legitimized enactment of specificity further determines the characteristics of the "self," which also creates stronger tendencies of marginalization in its determination of more aspects that belong to "others." As Robert Albró affirms, the specification and institutionalization of these international categories of "indigeneity" have created excluding effects against peoples in Bolivia that do not quite fit the dichotomous understanding of individual/communitarian participation (Albró 2010).

These epistemic tendencies might explain the position of other scholars of International Relations, whose work shares the tendencies of this approach as well (e.g., Posner 1994; Peang-Meth 2002; Naim 2003; Merlan 2009). Similar to Brysk's book, many scholars saw the United Nations' creation of the Working Group on Indigenous Populations in 1982 and the eventual Declaration on the Rights of Indigenous Peoples on September 13, 2007 as the empowerment of indigenous peoples and the expansion of global citizenship, which now includes "communitarian" rights (e.g., Coulter 2006; Oldham and Frank 2008; Carpenter and Riley 2014). Since the Declaration included a vast array of indigenous leaders and movements, it gained "unquestionable legitimacy in participation" (Oldham and Frank 2008, 5). As other authors have pointed out, however, the importance and the benefits of these expansions have to be emphasized while also questioning the possible continuation of underlying colonial legacies and assumptions (Cirkovic 2006; Champagne 2013).

Desire, Marxism, and the proletariat: civilizing models of equality

Before the kinds of liberalism that are related to the United Nations and a number of international discussions of indigeneity became more prominent in Bolivia, much of the country turned to a structuralist understanding of Marxism. This political project sought to overcome the segregation of non-citizen "Bolivianos" and it intended to promote "equality" in order to avoid "exploitation." The official emergence of this discourse can be traced to 1941, when the Nationalist Revolutionary Movement (Movimiento Nacionalista Revolucionario – MNR) was created. Intellectuals such as Fausto Reinaga, who would later become the "father" of Indianismo, were actively involved in the construction of this discourse. Then, between the 1952 beginning of the Nationalist Revolution and the 1964 coup d'état that ended it, much of this kind of Marxism became institutionalized in the government of Bolivia.

Once Reinaga critiqued much of his own work, moved away from Marxism, and even transformed his first definitions of Indianismo, he problematized some of the epistemic assumptions that he had made in the construction of this revolutionary movement. Reinaga found racist tendencies within the discourse that he had helped to construct for the MNR because he previously relied on "occidental" notions of "humanity," which acted as the epistemic foundations from which single ideas of truth could be erected (Reinaga 2014, 5:406). This kind of Marxism started from another definition of "reason," which was also regarded as undeniable (5:148). Because it was viewed as *the* foundational and ontological existence, "reason" was then turned into the philosophical bedrock of universal judgment (6:279). Similar to Reinaga's discussion, Foucault asserts that the notion of "man" is used as the positivity of Human Sciences, which includes Marxism. In his work, Foucault distinguishes three ontological ways of using "man:" physiology concentrated on the study of a speaking "man," biology focused on the living functions of "man," and economics prioritized the study of the ways in which "man" *desired* (Foucault 1970, 351). Together with other forms of economic studies, Marxism used this last notion of "man," which was based on the undeniability of "man's" "desire" (357). By proceeding from an assumption regarded as a universalized fact of "man's" life and a definition of what exists (i.e., desire), Marxism created a basic ontological starting point.

Since it was viewed as the way in which "humanity" satisfied its "desires" and applied its "reason," "labor" then appeared as the universal activity of "humanity." Moreover, the means to fulfill this "human" activity and the possibility of accessing its products had to belong to those who shared this very characteristic and fitted within this platform of equality. Those who "desired" thus had to have equal and free access to means of production, which could then allow them to "labor" and deploy their "reason" freely. Since all of "humanity" "desired," but not all of it had the same capacity to "labor" or the same role in social divisions of "labor," the products that were socially created had to belong to "all" based on their "needs" or "desire." "All" had to "labor" as much as possible and in whatever way they could to contribute to society and to the possibility of fulfilling their own "humanity," but everyone also had to obtain the social products of this collective endeavor of survival. Conversely, the limitation of equal access to means of production and products was regarded as "unjust" because it contradicted the "real" and universal characteristics of "humanity." The unequal control of the means of production thus enabled the unfair extraction of the product of "labor" and it created "exploitation."

Within this discourse, then, the "true" interest of "humanity" was the possibility of resisting "exploitation" and promoting equal access to means of production and products. During the 1952 Nationalist Revolution in Bolivia, the government utilized these epistemic assumptions and this notion of "equality." For example, in the document called "The Scientific Foundations of the Nationalist Revolution," the Movement stated that the people of Bolivia had a common "interest," which underlined the diversity of voices represented by the party (Nationalist Revolutionary Movement N/D, 18–19, author's translation). This "true" interest was the widespread class consciousness that interpreted the "reality" of Bolivia, understanding the colonial "structures" of feudal order, unveiling the "exploitative" relationships suffered in the mines, and creating an overarching struggle. Based on this interest, the 1953 executive order of land reform located "labor" as the basic source of rights and the only way to access land (Estenssoro 1953, 511, author's translation). Then, the constitution of 1961 institutionalized this notion of equality more broadly and it promoted rights related to the "true" interest of peoples. Here, the basis for the redistribution of land was again "labor" ("Bolivia Constitution" 1961, art. CLXVI, author's translation) and the state was the administrator of this process (art. CLXV). Moreover, "labor" was regarded as a basic duty and as the basis of economic and social order (art. CVXXIII). The constitution also unfolded a definition of national education, which continued to be centralized in the state, but now encouraged a vocational, professional, and scientific program (art. CXCIV).

This construction of a "real" form of equality, "true" interest, and general duty of "labor" explicitly opposed the liberal order of Bolivia through the notion of "exploitation," but it also invalidated other notions of equality and other struggles that appeared less "real." The ontological definition of an unquestionable idea of "man" validated the free access to means of production above other notions of justice and equality. This kind of discourse hierarchicalized indigenous political struggles of ethnic or racial equality (Ari 2014). As Reinaga emphasized at the time, this was a class-based project that was not centered on issues of race (Reinaga 2014, 1:66). Problems of racism and ethnic discrimination were thus silenced, marginalized, and governmentally repressed in several occasions of opposition. As Rivera asserts, the Revolution led to an urban, masculine, Eurocentric, and class-based project, which continued colonial forms of oppression against "others" and used governmental policies to impose its own notions more broadly (Rivera 2015, 127). Consistent with this, the land reform executive order of 1953 stated that "social systems of labor" exploited indigenous races through a semi-feudal organization, which established, for the first time in Bolivia, the "problem of the Indio and land" (Estenssoro 1953, 507). This issue was "not a pedagogical or racial problem, it was a problem essentially economic and social" (507). This class-based perspective not only relegated other struggles and equalities to the invalidated echelons of that which was not "real," but also discouraged other forms of production and social organization that did not quite fit the "just" model of social order. Clearly, this possibility of classification allowed for Marxism to judge the injustices of oligarchic liberalism in Bolivia, but this othering tendency also invalidated ayllu forms of land tenure in the country. As Rivera affirms, the Revolution discouraged indigenous forms of production and land organization such as the communitarian type of land tenure, leading to the promotion of cultural and societal homogenization (Rivera 1990, 104).

Beyond the context of the Revolution, authors of International Relations sometimes also continue to use these structuralist assumptions and still hierarchicalize diverse notions of equality by invalidating other struggles or by assimilating them under the logic of class-based equality (e.g., Petras 1989; Balibar and Wallerstein 1991; Petras and Veltmeyer 2001, 2005; Gimenez 2001; Belkhir 2001). Some of these assumptions also lead to a temporal ordering of struggles, which prioritizes class-based equality as the primary solution for all other social injustices. According to some authors, once problems of class-based exploitation are resolved, other issues such as ethnic conflict would disappear (Balibar and Wallerstein 1991, 198). This trickle-down understanding of struggles still prioritizes particular forms of oppression over "others;" it elevates a way of knowing as more urgent than "others."

From the ontological validation of a single way of knowing and a particular definition of equality, this structuralist reading of Marxism constructed in Bolivia an epistemological connection between the "proletariat" and "desire," which further solidified the boundaries of "equality" and its construction of an "other." This kind of structuralist Marxism viewed those who participated most directly in the ontologically validated notion of "labor" and its definition of equality as the authorized knowers or agents of "desire." They were the ones who knew the "real" notion of "equality," the injustices of an epoch, and the path of the future. In the Nationalist Revolution of Bolivia, the authorization of those who "labor" and thus participate in the "true" equality of "humanity" allowed for an expansion of citizenship and rights. Here, those who "labored," and not just those who "reasoned," were regarded as knowers that could access "truth" and thus successfully shape the future of the country. As the constitution of 1961 stated, citizenship now included all Bolivian persons that were older than 21, regardless of their degree of education, occupation, or income ("Bolivia Constitution" 1961, art. XL). Voting rights were made "universal, obligatory, direct, equal, and secret" for men and women (art. XLII). The same expansion was applied to the possibility of participating in elected or administrative positions in the government. According to the documents of the Revolutionary Movement, the liberal laws that previously restricted citizenship only allowed for 150,000 registered persons to participate in elections or in the government. Out of 3.5 million adults, only this minority qualified for voting and participation rights (Nationalist Revolutionary Movement N/D, 10).

As Albró points out, this important expansion of rights and democracy in Bolivia came at the cost of identity; it promoted a single way of being (Albró 2010, 74). In this context, the authorization of a labor-related knower created a hierarchy that effectively continued to silence "others" such as women and indigenous movements. As the MNR stated, the "masses" were the ones who suffered the "true" structures of oppression that previous governments had imposed or reinforced (Nationalist Revolutionary Movement N/D, 9–10). They had a deeper revolutionary sense, which was more "intuitive" and thus needed the guidance of the party. The party, its leader, and the proletariat thus had "revolutionary force and value," but they were a minority in Bolivia because labor was still structured in the country by feudal and semi-colonial forms of organization (20). Hence, the revolutionary "vanguard" had to ally with "peasant" movements, which were also "interested" in abandoning "feudal epochs" (21). At the top of this epistemological hierarchy, then, the party and its leader, Victor Paz Estenssoro, were the "vanguard that could teach everyone else the path towards liberation" (13). Moreover, only the party could create the equilibrium necessary between all the social classes that were included in the Movement and in relation to the "historical reality of Bolivia" (24). As a result of this hierarchy, the MNR was able to de-authorize and oppose the "oligarchy" and the "imperialist" classes that had previously ruled Bolivia (Estenssoro 1953, 510), but the Movement also created a tendency to silence or assimilate other voices of transformation. For example, the MNR viewed the "proletariat" as more prepared for the revolution than the "Indio" because the latter had been kept in the "past" by a semi-colonial system that excluded "him" from education, technical knowledge, and progress (510). The "Indio" had to be "incorporated into national life in his economic hierarchy and human condition." In this sense, the government of the Revolution understood education as a key tool of "integration," which helped the "Indio" to "modernize their production," promoting migration to create a "rational human distribution" and fomenting investments, scientific policies, and rural development (511).

Hence, the Revolution authorized the position of masculine and urban workers over other voices that demanded different forms of justice and transformation; it created "miserabilist" tendencies that silenced the voices of "others" such as women and indigenous peoples (Rivera 2015, 159). As several authors point out (e.g., Reinaga 2014; Ari 2014; Rivera 2015), the MNR made the "Indio problem" subservient to the "proletariat" agenda. It enacted a "civilizing" and "whitening" project, which ignored "indigenous voices" and made them fit into the urban model of the Bolivian working class (Ari 2014). As a result, indigenous peoples remained largely excluded from the government and participation even though voting rights had been universalized (Albró 2005, 434). Moreover, the MNR constructed "women" as passive and suffering "wives," who needed to be "liberated" by the masculine "heroes" of the Revolution. As other authors highlight, this notion hid the struggles, voices, and agency of important feminist movements, which mobilized in Bolivia against multiple forms of injustices (Rivera 2015, 149). Additionally, this patriarchal reading of "equality" and agency also concealed the exploitation of women. The Revolution thus exacerbated other forms of oppression while seeking to promote a specifically class-based notion of equality.

Notwithstanding renowned warnings against the othering tendencies of Marxism (e.g., Said 1978), some scholars of International Relations continue to hierarchicalize workers' movements above the diversity of voices struggling in a region. For example, Petras and Veltmeyer locate the Bolivian worker's movement as a more appropriate agent of change because they are viewed as expressing class-based goals more successfully than, for example, Evo Morales's Movement towards Socialism (Petras and Veltmeyer 2005, 218). More generally, this form of structuralist Marxism regards sociologists as intellectuals who can participate in the "desire" and "labor" that is "real." They thus seem to have access to the "objective" structures of class-based order, which allows them to examine contextual forms of "exploitation" and to judge what is "truly" necessary in order to reach a more "just" society. Thanks to this kind of epistemological authorization, "sociologists" can avoid "subjectivist" understandings of oppression, but they also sometimes silence other voices that are less "true" or "objective." This leads, for example, to the classification of indigenous struggles as "conservative" or misplaced (Balibar and Wallerstein 1991, 196).

In addition to these epistemic tendencies, the kind of Marxism that was practiced in the Bolivia of the 1950s viewed the vanguard of the proletariat, "sociologists," and Estenssoro as epistemologically authorized to use their ontological foundation as a bedrock to judge historical epochs, organizing what belonged to the "past" and enacting what needed to be achieved for the "future." Knowers could thus study each mode of production within its historical specificity, including the "reality" of the present and the "plan" for the future, but the universalized bedrock that emerged from the ontological notion of "desire" was deployed in order to compare, organize, and judge these historical "epochs." This type of Marxism thus examined how different classes occupied diverse positions in relation to the ways in which the means of production were controlled or owned over time. These forms of organization or modes of production enabled the survival of society, but they also included different degrees of "exploitation." Societies thus appeared hierarchically organized in different echelons of exploitative divisions of labor throughout space and time, and they had to be transformed into a social order of equal "desire" satisfaction. A specific form of class-based "equality" thus became a social order that was universalized in space and time; it was the topography of the "present," the history of the "past," and the destiny of the "future." Then, the "vanguard" could investigate the "structures" of the past, observe the "reality" of the present, and enact the "plans" for the future.

In the study of Bolivian society, this temporality organized the past as a series of hierarchicalized chapters that led to the present and the future of the Nationalist Revolution. The "rudimentary" Inca system, "semi-feudal" post-independence system, and lack of development thus progressed towards the "reality of the present," which "sustained a primitive system of production and excluded the indigenous race from civilized life" (Estenssoro 1953, 508). The present "reality" of Bolivia still utilized an "archaic system of exploitation of land," which prevented land from serving its social function and still sustained obstacles for "progress" (Estenssoro 1953, 508–9). In this sense, the "Indio" and the "oligarchy" appeared as remnants of the past, whereas the proletariat, the party, and Estenssoro were regarded as the present that could bring about the future. The government of the Revolution thus enacted laws and policies that were consistent with its notion of the future of "equality." Beyond the program of land redistribution that the government started in 1953, the program of literacy and education, and previous laws related to labor rights, the Constitution of 1961 instated an "economic regime." This set of policies promoted "social justice" ("Bolivia Constitution" 1961, art. CXXXVII) by protecting rights such as working hours, paid leave, disability, protest, and labor courts (art. CLXXVII, CLXXVIII), and by encouraging the formation of cooperatives (art. CLXXII). Despite the benefits of these rights, the policy of the Revolution was led by a model that emerged from an industrialist and consumerist idea of welfare. As the documents of the MNR stated, wellbeing was based on the wage-labor organization of industrialized countries, which was regarded as the "true" economic possibility of creating wealth and accessing more income (Nationalist Revolutionary Movement N/D, 16). Moreover, this idea of industrial development included a possibility of "equilibrium" between all the classes of Bolivia because they would all increase their "wellbeing" as a result of the process of transformation. The interest of "peasants" would thus be aligned with the "bourgeoisie" because "they will have money to enter the national economy and will help in the construction of the great industries of consumption" (22). Since these homogenizing notions were racialized, the model also included notions of "hygiene" and education, which only followed "Western" identities. As Reinaga later noticed, the process of civilization promoted by the Revolution also entailed the imposition of Spanish as an official language (Reinaga 2014, 5:290). In general, this linear temporality represented a "sociological law" (Nationalist Revolutionary Movement N/D, 31). Accordingly, all other experiences of history or projects of transformation were understood as less "true" or as "obstacles" against the "true" revolution.

This tendency to invalidate other projects of transformation can be found not only in the construction of history elaborated by the MNR and its Commission of History of Bolivian People, which was created by decree in 1954, but also in some of the more current intellectual productions of International Relations. As Rivera asserts, the linear understanding of history can be found in the work of Marx himself (Rivera 2018, 45), but some intellectuals continue to deploy some of the assumptions found within this kind of structuralist Marxism in their analyses of oppression, which they often relate to "indigenous" peoples. This tendency explains why renowned author Immanuel Wallerstein not only authorizes sociologists to determine the characteristics of more objective struggles, but also locates indigenous movements further into the past. As I mentioned above, the author views these voices as more "conservative" (Balibar and Wallerstein 1991, 196). Furthermore, as authors have pointed out, the Venezuelan presidencies of Hugo Chavez and Nicolás Maduro, the Bolivian presidencies of Evo Morales, and the presidency of Rafael Correa in Ecuador often deployed particular variations of Marxist ideas in order to understand the problem of "exploitation," designing policies of "equality" and framing different kinds of struggles (Petkoff 2005; Castañeda 2006; Weyland 2009; Weyland, Madrid, and Hunter 2010). These governmental applications of Marxist ideas in Latin America highlight the relevance of studying the epistemic assumptions that can potentially continue to silence and assimilate indigenous peoples, women, and many other ways of being, knowing, and enacting.

Conclusion

As the main goal of this book is to discuss various ways of dealing with difference, I begin in Chapter One with an analysis of the most salient colonial discourses that were institutionalized in Bolivia between 1825 and 1964. These formations had similar epistemic characteristics and othering tendencies as some approaches of International Relations. Since individuals, cultures, and societies are not the same as perfectly consistent discourses (Foucault 1972, 129), I analyze the meaningful patterns, rules, regularities, and convergences that emerge from practices and create discursive "atmospheres" (Rivera 2015, 23–24). This methodological focus on practices allows me to compare the meaningful regularities or "characteristics" of discourses that are similar.

An epistemic politics of colonialism

To create othering effects, colonial discourses include *conditions of possibility* (Foucault 1970, xxii). These positivities are seemingly indisputable "realities" that are constructed within each discourse to elevate the formation above "other" ways of knowing and to gain *validity*. Thus, conditions of possibility are ontological practices that create a basis of "reality;" they are a form of "alêtheia" (Foucault 2008, 66). Then, these positivities delineate the general patterns and rules of a discourse, which shine the light on the edges and boundaries of the formation. They grant intra-discursive or endogenous "reality" to a specific way of knowing while also *invalidating* and excluding "other" ways of knowing that lie beyond these boundaries. In other words, only the kind of knowledge that fits the consistency of a particular "reality" and its characteristics becomes endogenously validated. The ontological definition of what exists thus determines what lies beyond validated boundaries and cannot be "real." As Sylvia Wynter states, this endogenous monopoly of "reality" leads towards the problem of universalization because the discourse rises a singularity above everything else; it elevates a consistency that cannot be contradicted without an exclusionary, assimilating, or marginalizing effect (Wynter 1995, 25). That is, whenever a way of knowing contradicts "reality," it must be "non-real." Hence, the singularity of a particular "reality" becomes universalized upon other ways of knowing.

As the examples of liberalism and Marxism highlight, and other authors point out (e.g., Foucault 1970; Wynter 1995; Seth 2010), Western discourses often construct notions of "reality" from the anthropocentric definition of "human" characteristics. The ontological starting points of the discourses thus use the seeming indisputability of a "human" characteristic to create a foundation of "reality." Since this characteristic entails a "human" commonality, it creates a form of relationship, which grants equality to those who fit the trait. Hence, from the definition of "reality" emerges a validated conceptualization of "human" *equality*. From "desire" emerges the idea of "labor" and class-based equality, whereas the notion of "reason" leads to the construction of "rights" and "citizenship." Then, each construction invalidates other ways of knowing and other forms of equality (e.g., gender and ethnicity), which become assimilated or excluded. As I further discuss in Chapter Five, assimilation and annexation can organize "other" ways of knowing as secondary or "past" knowledges while also re-framing them within the logic of the dominant discourse (Foucault 1997, 31).

Since each notion of equality is deployed to judge the imperfections of social orders, they also determine what *struggles* are validated within each discourse. Notions of "labor" and class-based equality thus prioritize the struggle against "exploitation" and they validate the analysis of a particular axis of power. Similarly, "reason" leads to the study of rights and citizenship, which then emphasizes the oppressive characteristics of monarchies or other systems that do not respect this kind of equality. In this sense, each set of ontological practices leads to the construction of an elevated "reality," which includes a particular form of equality and prioritizes a specific kind of struggle.

In relation to these ontological functions, colonial discourses include the basic characteristics of an authorized *knower*, whose *way of being* coherently fits the general rules of a discourse and is thus regarded as the main *participant* within a way of knowing. The consistency between the characteristics of an ontology and the traits of a knower delineate an epistemological bridge of *authorization*. The positivity or condition of possibility of a discourse is epistemologically connected to the definition of an identity of a knower, which delineates a boundary of authorization for a way of being. In other words, the ontological validation of a way of knowing and the characterization of a "real" equality is used to enable an epistemological bridge between this "reality" and a knower; it creates a direct connection between someone who has the traits of "reality" and thus participates in or has access to it. Discourses thus include an authorized "self," which is constructed by practices of "êthopoiêsis" (Foucault 2008, 66). From this creation of a knowing subject, colonial discourses determine who is regarded as an inferior "other," which becomes a de-authorized, silenced, or assimilated voice. For example, the "Bolivianos" who did not fit the liberal characteristics of "active citizens" remained excluded from the public sphere or were forced to pay the price of identity in order to become "reasoning" individuals. Whenever these othering strategies were not "enough," the state was authorized to use violence. Similarly, the MNR thought that "peasants" had to learn the "true" characteristics of "labor" by following the "proletariat" in order to become worthy members of the Revolution. Only those who "knew" were thus authorized to shape the present "reality" of Bolivia and future destiny of the country. Instead, "other" voices were silenced due to their "irrational" or "traditional" ways of being. As several authors point out, the delineation of these authorized characteristics often entail gendered, racialized, and sexualized elements (e.g., Rivera and Morón 1993; Ticona 2000; Canessa 2005; Rivera 2010b; Ari 2014; Reinaga 2014; Makusaya 2014).

Beyond these philosophical platforms of validation and authorization, these discourses also include the possibility of *specifying* characterizations. They frame, specify, and include readings of social order and subjects that are more contextual and historical. The ontologically validated notion of equality thus turns into a guide that determines what elements of social reality have to be examined, transformed, and enacted. Ontology turns into a reading guide that tells knowers what aspects of history and society matter. Within this process of specification, more historical and context dependent observations then become a set of "proofs" that re-validate the discourse from below. The characteristics of "reality" appear as corresponding to a materiality that exists in particular contexts and thus becomes the proof of this very "reality." In this sense, the discourse pre-determines what is "reality," while also constructing an "objectivity" that is viewed as the proof of the discourse. The creation of civilized states and laws throughout the world thus becomes proof of "reason," whereas the "zealous" characteristics of monarchies turn into the problem that demands solution. Consistent with this, the suffering of workers is understood within Marxism as the proof of unjust exploitation and the violation of "desire." The notion of correspondence to "reality" thus connects contextualized specificities as proofs that close a circle of epistemic self-validation. Other specificities that do not quite fit "reality" appear as either unjust characteristics that ought to change or as less "real;" they are either part of the "problem" or they are "false." Hence, the production of knowledge within each colonial discourse and the specification of its ontological notions leads to more impermeable and certain boundaries against "other" ways of knowing, struggles, and equalities.

Coherently, epistemological practices specify ways of being, which become authorized as the characteristics of those who can rule. This form of self-authorization closes another epistemic circle. For example, the liberal definition of "reason" leads to notions of citizenship, which specifies the traits of an authorized way of being. The careful delineation of this way of being creates laws that determine who is authorized to participate in the government: gender, age, language skills, reading and writing skills, the capacity to stay away from "vice," property or minimum salaries, etc. Then, these specifications are deployed to judge the traits of "others," which the government ought to exclude, change, civilize, or kill. The epistemological authorization of a knower thus allows "him" to *define and enact* the specificities of a knower that is already authorized. Thus, according to liberalism, only "rational" citizens can create the boundaries of citizenship, legislation of laws, limits of policy, and even features of "peace." On the side of Marxism, only "truly" revolutionary leaders, parties, and sociologists can observe the "objective" structures of oppression in order to determine who is best located actor to guide everyone else. In this sense, the epistemological authorization of a distinct knower closes an epistemic circle of self-authorization. Colonial discourses thus construct realities, authorize knowers, specify their characteristics, and then use this authority to continue tightening boundaries. Only those who are "reality" can further enact more "reality."

As I hint throughout the chapter, the colonial constructions of validating ontologies and authorizing epistemologies are intimately related to designs of *temporalities* as well (Walker 2010). Within the colonial discourses that I study here, validated ways of knowing and authorized ways of being become foundational bedrocks, which can be deployed to judge and organize epochs and societies. Whenever there is more correspondence between an epoch in a place and "reality," the society in this location represents the "civilized," "developed," or "revolutionary" future. To the contrary, those societies and moments that contradict "reality" represent the "barbaric," "savage," "uncivilized," or "traditional" past. Hence, the future entails the present characteristics of the validated way of knowing. Furthermore, the authorized way of being appears as the voice that best knows both the path towards and the characteristics of this future. Only they can design a plan to enact this "reality" and to deal with "others." The "real" knower is thus authorized to enact and lead history by studying the past, observing the present, and designing the future. Either through a dialectical reading of temporality in the case of Marxism or through a linear notion of progress in liberalism, these colonial discourses organize the epochs of Bolivian society in relation to the "other" and they determine what needs to be done in order to enact what is "real." The differences that are not included within the boundaries of each discourse have to disappear; all "other" ways of knowing and being have to become homogenized within the validated notion of equality and the authorized traits of the model citizen. Insofar as "others" resist this pedagogical violence, they often become "threats", against which various kinds of violence are now justified.

Furthermore, since only one way of knowing and being can be used as a bedrock within each colonial discourse, all "other" plans of transformation, struggle, and notions of temporality become delegitimized. This epistemic tendency does not only cancel "previous" colonial projects, but also marginalizes "other" struggles against oppression and "other" ways to deal with difference. For example, the liberal model of the 1820s delegitimized the monarchic project of Spain, but it also excluded ideas of racial equality and it continued to silence indigenous struggles such as the rising that was led by Pablo Zárate Wilka in the 1870s (Ari 2014). Marxism sought to move away from the political segregation and economic exploitation that liberal projects had sustained in Bolivia for a century and a half, but this discourse also silenced feminist and indigenous projects in the country. Each one of these colonial discourses thus determines what needs to be done in Bolivia with "others" in relation to a "self." They try to *enact* the validated way of knowing and the authorized way of being by ignoring, killing, excluding, homogenizing, civilizing, educating, or silencing all "others." Temporality thus creates a self-enacting tendency within each colonial discourse; it legitimizes a project that consistently enacts the hierarchical organization of history, reading of the present, and destiny of the future. In this sense, the colonial relationship between ontology, epistemology, and temporality closes an *epistemic circle* of self-validation, self-definition, and self-enactment. Together, they erect the self-reinforcing boundaries of an internal possibility of thinking (Foucault 1970, xv).

The problem of difference returns

Throughout previous paragraphs, I define the regularities of discourses that are often designated as "colonial." Notwithstanding this kind of classification, much of the problem of difference remains unanswered. By following the work of many authors, I classified these liberal and Marxist discourses as "dominant" formations, "institutionalized" notions, "colonial" projects, etc. However, what exactly makes them "colonial"? Is it their epistemic characteristics and their endogenous tendencies towards universalization? Or, as Said states, is it the level of "institutionalization," "force," and power that each discourse "has"?

Insofar as I follow the work of Foucault, I renounce the possibility of deploying bedrocks of judgment that determine this kind of classification *a priori* or with some kind of criterion that I regard as previous to discourse itself. In other words, I do not claim to know the "thing" that causes, shapes, or determines the level of "power" of discourses from some kind of asset, materiality, institution, structure, or object; as if their quantity could classify what discourse is more or less "dominant." Said often uses neo-Marxist notions of structures, institutionalization, force, or hegemony to create a differentiation between colonialism and the voices that domination claims to know (Said 1978, 7). Here, a definition of "force" appears as something that shapes the level of domination of discourses from underneath. Despite this epistemic bedrock of classification, Said also states that the:

> Orient is not an inert fact of nature. It is not merely there, just as the Occident itself is not just there either. We must take seriously Vico's great observation that men make their own history, that what they can know is what they have made.
>
> Said 1978, 4–5

I take this statement seriously, and I include my own definitions of power and colonialism within this notion of construction. That is, the idea that "men" make their own definitions of power and domination should prevents us from objectifying our own ideas of power, struggle, and equality. This notion of construction is important because it allows me to study epistemic politics in a much more dynamic and complex manner, asking how ontological, epistemological, and temporal assumptions universalize particular ideas of equality and power that pre-determine politics and praxes. To the contrary, if I were to pre-settle the definition of "power" or "force" in order to determine who is "dominant" and who is "dominated," I could also fall into this colonial trap, which would pre-determine decolonial praxis *a priori* and would foreclose the possibility of studying the multiplicity of struggles voiced in different contexts. Hence, this interpretive strategy not only has an analytical advantage, but also leads to the normative possibility of avoiding the objectification of yet another "reality," which would organize all "other" struggles in a downward order of echelons. That is, the non-foundational definition of meanings and practices renounces the possibility of pre-determining its own ontology in order to avoid the creation of new othering tendencies, which would elevate its own notion of equality, power, struggle, agency, and project above "others;" it would reinforce more colonial ways of knowing, being, and enacting. As Audre Lorde states, "the master's tools will never dismantle the master's house" (Lorde 2018). Hence, "we must renounce all those themes whose function is to ensure the infinite continuity of discourse and its secret presence to itself in the interplay of a constantly recurring absence" (Foucault 1972, 129).

Notwithstanding the advantages of a non-foundational epistemic approach, now I am faced with the question of praxis and classification again. How is it possible to create an anti-oppression form of political action if I cannot separate domination from resistance? Beyond his notion of force, hegemony, and power, Said also uses the idea of *continuity* to separate colonial constructions from oppressed voices (Said 1978, 6). This notion creates, to a certain extent, a consistent possibility of classifying discourses as "colonial" without demanding an external or extra-discursive foundation. The idea of continuity leads towards the possibility of following the ways in which regularities include consistencies that emerge in different contexts and thus continuously exclude the same ways of knowing, being, and enacting. Since this approach focuses on the continuities of practiced meanings, it also renounces the study of the secret determinants that are sometimes assumed as laying underneath statements. From this study of continuity, I could thus view a particular formation as more "dominant" or "colonial." That is, the temporal and special continuity of hierarchicalizing meanings can be hereby used as the criterion that separates dominating discourses from oppressed voices of resistance. Similarly, Wynter examines the continuity of hierarchies that were put in place in the sixteenth century in Haiti (Wynter 1995, 24). These patterns create hierarchical relationships between native/settler, European/Indios, and masters/slaves, and they entail a continuity not only in this organizations of echelons, but also in the notions of reality and humanity that they include (25). In the case of Bolivia, there is a partial continuity as well. As I discuss throughout this chapter, Bolivian discourses constructed a way of knowing that validated "Western" equalities and invalidated indigenous, feminist, and "other" struggles. In this genealogy, continuity shows the dominant invalidation of other ways of knowing, which include ethnic, racial, sexualized, and gendered struggles. Despite the continuous exclusions of other forms of equality in Bolivia, the notions of justice and citizenship that the Revolution introduced in 1952 were not the same as previous notions of liberal citizenship. This modification highlights the importance of confrontation and construction. The analysis of continuity within this Bolivian genealogy thus shows the characteristics of "colonialism" in the country, but it also allows me to unveil a space for struggle and modification. The exclusion of ethnic, gender, sexual, etc. equalities is continuous, but the dominant validation of citizenship is not perfectly consistent throughout history. As the trespassing dialogue between intellectuals of "International Relations" and the Bolivian projects of civilization illustrate, the continuities of liberalism and structuralist Marxism also affect the exclusion of other "realities" within this discipline. The analysis of colonial discourses in the Bolivian genealogy also unveils a continuity in the construction of authorized ways of being, which has historically excluded "Indios" and "women." As Rivera examines, Bolivia has gone through different projects of civilization that continuously exclude and marginalize particular ways of being (Rivera 1990). The author also states that linear temporalities continue to shape the way in which the enactment of equalities create civilizing projects of development and violent policies even in the government of Evo Morales (Rivera 2018, 70).

Overall, continuity seems to provide a consistent criterion of classification, but is this criterion enough to distinguish between "colonial" and non-/anti-/de-/post-colonial formations? That is, are other discourses also continuously practiced in the Bolivian context? Do they also create different hierarchies? Do they construct their own forms of universalization? If these discourses also sustain continuous and hierarchicalizing characteristics that invalidate struggles, silence voices, and delegitimize projects, how can we separate them from "coloniality"? Are these discourses equally "colonial"? If not, what differentiates them from "colonial" projects? Insofar as foundational criteria of classification are abandoned and the idea of continuity does not create a sufficient form of classification, the problem of difference and decoloniality remains open. Overall, how is it possible to account for difference even within epistemic levels of analysis, resisting colonial tendencies and setting distinguishing boundaries at the same time?

Methodological clarifications

In order to investigate these questions, the rest of the book discusses several discourses that erect classifying boundaries to resist "colonialisms" through different epistemic strategies. However, before studying other discourses struggling in this genealogy, and before establishing dialogues with other approaches of International Relations, I would like to emphasize five methodological clarifications. First, the chapter characterizes colonial discourses as self-validating, self-authorizing, and self-enacting. This endogenous tendency can create an understanding of discourses as static and fixed within particular epochs or contexts. In order to avoid this issue, I relate the formations that I fixed above to other voices that dispute and confront their boundaries. Hence, the rest of the chapters of the book examine other discourses and they include other questions that negotiate meanings and continue to investigate the problem of difference. As Wynter affirms, particular discourses claim to be fixed and often universalize specific notions, but other practices confront these constructions and create other realities (Wynter 1995, 22).

Second, the discourses that I analyze above fix their meanings thanks to their self-validating, self-authorizing, and self-enacting epistemic tendencies, which endogenously universalize ideas. Notwithstanding this tendency, I do not generalize the *characteristics* described above as *the* attributes of all forms of liberalism or Marxism. Only the practices that I interpret and the formations that I synthesize are hereby regarded as "colonial," but the epistemic characteristics and othering tendencies of these discourses should also raise questions for other approaches with *similar traits*. That is, the relevance of this analysis lies less in the labels, names, authors, or countries taken into account, and more in the discursive *characteristics* analyzed throughout the chapter. These characteristics should problematize and unveil other colonial legacies that might marginalize "other" ways of knowing, being, and enacting.

Third, the discursive dimensions of interpretation mentioned above (i.e., ontology, epistemology, and temporality) are not the only meanings that can be used to deal with difference. For example, several scholars highlight the important role of cosmologies to examine ways of thinking that move beyond colonialism (e.g., Rivera 2010a, 2018; Reinaga 2014; Mignolo and Walsh 2018; Trownsell et al. 2019). Some even mention the dangers of staying within notions of ontology and epistemology to think about difference (e.g., Mignolo and Walsh 2018; Trownsell et al. 2019). In Chapter Six, I highlight the relevance of cosmologies and these warnings in the study of intersectional decoloniality as well.

Fourth, the epistemic dimensions of colonial discourses are often intertwined in different and complex ways. Thus, I do not assume a theoretically pre-defined chain of causality between them. As Foucault points out, the dimensions of discourses work together as systems; they are "systems of dispersion" that cannot be regarded as mechanical chains of causality (Foucault 1972, 37–38). For example, intellectual practices might not begin the construction of a discourse from its condition of possibility, they might start from experiences of oppression and possibilities of liberation. Despite the narrative that I used throughout this chapter to focus first on epistemic assumptions, I thus understand that practices might reinforce or undermine different elements of discourses from diverse fronts and dimensions. They might enter the circularity of power from diverse positions and fix the discourse from different fronts.

Fifth, the genealogy of struggles to define a way of dealing with difference in Bolivia and in International Relations showed that exogenous confrontations often transformed liberal projects and also allowed for the institutionalization of a Marxist discourse. "Others" thus confronted and transformed the fixed boundaries of particular discourses. Thanks to these exogenous or inter-discursive confrontations of endogenously universalized boundaries, together with the work of other authors (e.g., George and Campbell 1990; Shapiro 2004; Inayatullah and Blaney 2004), and due to the questions that I pose at the end of each chapter, I decided to think about this genealogical dispute as a *problem* of difference. Within each colonial discourse, difference is often not regarded as a problem. As the colonial examples that I examined above illustrated, the differences of "other" ways of knowing, being, and enacting became organized as "inferior" and the "problem" was "solved." Instead, the confrontations that emerged from othered ways of knowing, being, and enacting highlighted the othering tendencies of closed colonial discourses and it reignited the *problem* of difference. Then, my own questions entered the discussion of difference and also participated in the debate. As the following chapters illustrate, this struggle in the definition of difference leads not only to variations in liberal and Marxist discourses, but also to much more radical and innovative ways to deal with difference, some of which incorporate a possibility to think about their own boundaries, without *fixing* exclusionary tendencies or *requiring* exogenous confrontations.

Notes

1 Said explicitly used Foucault's approach to study Orientalism (Said 1978, 3), but he also asserted that he understood discourses as "superstructures" (Said 1978, 32), which retained a causal effect upon the individuals who lived under their influence. Instead, Foucault renounces this reading of discourses and he detaches discourses from structures or cultures.

2 Notice that I do not claim to "find" or "observe" a direct influence of Locke and Hobbes upon the work of Bolivar. Unlike the research of authors that focus primarily on the history of ideas, I concentrate on discursive patterns and regularities, highlighting the consistencies and connections between practices across different contexts. I borrow this differentiation between archaeological analyzes of discourses and the history of ideas from Foucault's work (Foucault 1972, 136).

References

Albró, Robert. 2005. "The Indigenous in the Plural in Bolivian Oppositional Politics." *Society for Latin American Studies* 24 (4): 433–453.

Albró, Robert. 2010. "Confounding Cultural Citizenship and Constitutional Reform in Bolivia." *Latin American Perspectives* 37 (3): 71–90.

Ari, Waskar. 2014. *Earth Politics. Religion, Decolonization, and Bolivia's Indigenous Intellectuals.* Durham, NC: Duke University Press.

Ashley, Richard. 1989. "Living on Borderlines." In *International/Intertextual Relations*, by James Der Darian and Michael J. Shapiro, 259–321. New York: Lexington Books.

Balibar, Étienne, and Immanuel Wallerstein. 1991. *Race, Nation, Class Ambiguous Identities*. London: Verso.

Belkhir, Jean Ait. 2001. "Marxism Without Apologies: Integrating Race, Gender, Class: A Working Class Approach." *Jean Ait Belkhir, Race, Gender & Class Journal* 8 (2): 142–171.

Bolivar, Simón. 2007. *Discursos y Proclamas*. Edited by Rufino Blanco Fombona. Caracas: Fundación Biblioteca Ayacucho.

"Bolivia Constitution." 1826. Biblioteca Virtual Miguel de Cervantes. http://www.cervantesvirtual.com/portales/constituciones_hispanoamericanas/bolivia_constituciones/?autor=&paginaUsuario=1&numresult=10&vista=reducida&q=&orden=fechapublicacionoriginal&paginaNavegacion=1.

"Bolivia Constitution." 1838. Biblioteca Virtual Miguel de Cervantes. http://www.cervantesvirtual.com/portales/constituciones_hispanoamericanas/bolivia_constituciones/?autor=&paginaUsuario=1&numresult=10&vista=reducida&q=&orden=fechapublicacionoriginal&paginaNavegacion=1.

"Bolivia Constitution." 1871. Biblioteca Virtual Miguel de Cervantes. http://www.cervantesvirtual.com/portales/constituciones_hispanoamericanas/bolivia_constituciones/?autor=&paginaUsuario=1&numresult=10&vista=reducida&q=&orden=fechapublicacionoriginal&paginaNavegacion=1.

"Bolivia Constitution." 1880. Biblioteca Virtual Miguel de Cervantes. http://www.cervantesvirtual.com/portales/constituciones_hispanoamericanas/bolivia_constituciones/?autor=&paginaUsuario=1&numresult=10&vista=reducida&q=&orden=fechapublicacionoriginal&paginaNavegacion=1.

"Bolivia Constitution." 1945. Biblioteca Virtual Miguel de Cervantes. http://www.cervantesvirtual.com/portales/constituciones_hispanoamericanas/bolivia_constituciones/?autor=&paginaUsuario=1&numresult=10&vista=reducida&q=&orden=fechapublicacionoriginal&paginaNavegacion=1.

"Bolivia Constitution." 1961. Biblioteca Virtual Miguel de Cervantes. http://www.cervantesvirtual.com/portales/constituciones_hispanoamericanas/bolivia_constituciones/?autor=&paginaUsuario=1&numresult=10&vista=reducida&q=&orden=fechapublicacionoriginal&paginaNavegacion=1.

Bourdieu, Pierre. 1997. *Pascalian Meditations*. Stanford: Stanford University Press.

Brysk, Alison. 2000. *From Tribal Village to Global Village: Indian Rights and International Relations in Latin America*. Stanford: Stanford University Press.

Campbell, Susanna, David Chandler, and Meera Sabaratnam. 2011. *A Liberal Peace?* London: Zed Books.

Canessa, Andrew. 2000. "Contesting Hybridity: Evangelistas and Kataristas in Highland Bolivia." *Journal of Latin American Studies* 32 (1): 115–144.

Canessa, Andrew. 2005. *Natives Making Nation: Gender, Indigeneity, and the State in the Andes*. Tucson: University of Arizona Press.

Carpenter, Kristen A., and Angela R. Riley. 2014. "Indigenous Peoples and the Jurisgenerative Moment in Human Rights." *California Law Review* 102 (1): 173–234.

Castañeda, Jorge G. 2006. "Latin America's Left Turn." *Foreign Affairs* 85 (3): 28–43.

Champagne, Duane. 2013. "UNDRIP (United Nations Declaration on the Rights of Indigenous Peoples): Human, Civil, and Indigenous Rights." *Wicazo Sa Review* 28 (1): 9–22.

Chan, Steve. 1997. "In Search of Democratic Peace: Problems and Promise." *Mershon International Studies Review* 41 (1): 59–91.

Cirkovic, Elena. 2006. "Self-Determination and Indigenous Peoples in International Law." *American Indian Law Review* 31 (2): 375–399.

Coulter, Robert T. 2006. "Using International Human Rights Mechanisms to Promote and Protect Rights of Indian Nations and Tribes in the United Nations: An Overview." *American Indian Law Review* 31 (2): 573–591.

Estenssoro, Víctor Paz. 1953. "Decreto de Reforma Agraria de Bolivia." *El Trimestre Económico* 20 (79): 507–539.

Foucault, Michel. 1970. *The Order of Things: An Archaeology of Human Sciences.* New York: Vintage Books.

Foucault, Michel. 1972. *The Archaeology of Knowledge, and The Discourse on Language.* New York: Vintage Books.

Foucault, Michel. 1986. "Nietzsche, Genealogy, History." In *The Foucault Reader*, edited by P. Rabinow. Harmondsworth: Penguin.

Foucault, Michel. 1997. *Society Must Be Defended: Lectures at the Collège de France, 1975–1976.* New York: Picador.

Foucault, Michel. 2008. *The Courage of Truth: The Government of the Self and Others II. Lectures at the Collège de France, 1983–1984.* New York: Picador.

George, Jim, and David Campbell. 1990. "Patterns of Dissent and the Celebration of Difference: Critical Social Theory and International Relations." *International Studies Quarterly* 34 (3): 269–293.

Gimenez, Martha E. 2001. "Marxism, and Class, Gender, and Race: Rethinking the Trilogy." *Jean Ait Belkhir, Race, Gender & Class Journal* 8 (2): 23–33.

Habermas, Jürgen. 1984. *The Theory of Communicative Action: Reason and the Rationalization of Society.* Boston, MA: Beacon Press.

Habermas, Jürgen. 1992. *Postmetaphysical Thinking: Philosophical Essays.* Boston, MA: Beacon Press.

Habermas, Jürgen. 2001. *The Postnational Constellation. Political Essays.* Cambridge: Polity Press.

Hobbes, Thomas. 1994. *Leviathan.* Latin Edition 1668. Cambridge, MA: Hackett Publishing.

Inayatullah, Naeem, and David L. Blaney. 2004. *International Relations and the Problem of Difference.* New York: Routledge.

Kant, Immanuel. 1952. *The Critique of Pure Reason.* Vol. 42. Great Books of the Western World. London: Encyclopedia Britannica.

Locke, John. 1980. *Second Treatise of Government.* 1690s edition. Cambridge, MA: Hackett Publishing.

Lorde, Audre. 2018. *The Master's Tools Will Never Dismantle the Master's House.* London: Penguin.

Makusaya, Carlos Cruz. 2014. *Desde El Sujeto Racializado. Consideraciones Sobre El Pensamiento Indianista de Fausto Reinaga.* Bolivia: MINKA.

Manzo, Kathryn. 1996. *Creating Boundaries, The Politics of Race and Nation.* London: Lynne Rienner Publishers.

Merlan, Francesca. 2009. "Indigeneity: Global and Local." *Current Anthropology* 50 (3): 303–333.

Mignolo, Walter. 2000. *Local Histories/Global Designs: Coloniality, Subaltern Knowledges, and Border Thinking.* Princeton Studies in Culture/Power/History. Princeton, NJ: Princeton University Press.

Mignolo, Walter. 2011. *The Darker Side of Western Modernity: Global Futures, Decolonial Options.* Latin America Otherwise. Durham, NC: Duke University Press.

Mignolo, Walter, and Catherine E.Walsh. 2018. *On Decoloniality: Concepts, Analytics, and Praxis*. Durham, NC: Duke University Press.

Mills, Charles W. 1997. *The Racial Contract*. Ithaca: Cornell University Press.

Naim, Moisés. 2003. "An Indigenous World." *Foreign Policy* 139: 95–96.

Nationalist Revolutionary Movement. N/D. "The Scientific Foundations of the Nationalist Revolution." Subsercretaria de Prensa, Informaciones y Cultura. Universidad Mayor de San Andresm Biblioteca Central.

Oldham, Paul, and Miriam Anne Frank. 2008. "'We the People…' the United Nations Declaration on the Rights of Indigenous Peoples." *Anthropology Today* 24 (2): 5–9.

Oneal, John R., Bruce Russett, and Michael Berbaum. 2003. "Causes of Peace: Democracy, Interdependence, and International Organizations, 1885–1992." *International Studies Quarterly* 47 (3): 371–393.

Parekh, Bhikhu. 1995. "Liberalism and Colonialism: A Critique of Locke and Mill." In *The Decolonization of Imagination: Critique, Knowledge and Power*, edited by Jan P. Nederveen Pieterse and Bhikhu Parekh, 81–98. London: Zed Books.

Paris, Roland. 2004. *At War's End: Building Peace After Civil Conflict*. Cambridge: Cambridge University Press.

Peang-Meth, Abdulgaffar. 2002. "The Rights of Indigenous Peoples and Their Fight for Self-Determination." *World Affairs* 164 (3): 101–114.

Petkoff, Teodoro. 2005. "Las Dos Izquierdas." *Nueva Sociedad* 197 (1): 14–29.

Petras, James. 1989. "State Terror and Social Movements in Latin America." *Journal of Politics, Culture and Society* 3 (2): 179–212.

Petras, James, and Henry Veltmeyer. 2001. "Are Latin American Peasant Movements Still a Force for Change? Some New Paradigms Revisited." *The Journal of Peasant Studies* 28 (2): 83–118.

Petras, James, and Henry Veltmeyer. 2005. *Social Movements and State Power: Argentina, Brazil, Bolivia, Ecuador*. London: Pluto Press.

Posner, Michael. 1994. "Rally Round Human Rights." *Foreign Policy* 97: 133–139.

Quijano, Aníbal, and Immanuel Wallerstein. 1992. "Americanity as a Concept, or the Americas in the Modern World-System." *International Journal of Social Sciences* 134: 583–591.

Reinaga, Fausto. 2014. *Fausto Reinaga: Obras Completas*. 10 vols. La Paz: Vicepresidencia del Estado Plurinacional.

Rivera Cusicanqui, Silvia. 1990. "Liberal Democracy and Ayllu Democracy in Bolivia: The Case of Northern Potosí." *The Journal of Development Studies* 26 (4): 97–121.

Rivera Cusicanqui, Silvia. 2010a. *Ch'ixinakax utxiwa: Una Reflexión sobre Prácticas y Discursos Decolonizadores*. Buenos Aires: Tinta Limón.

Rivera Cusicanqui, Silvia. 2010b. *Violencias (Re) Encubiertas En Bolivia*. La Paz: La Mirada Salvaje.

Rivera Cusicanqui, Silvia. 2015. *Sociología de la Imagen. Miradas Ch'ixi Desde La Historia Andina*. Buenos Aires: Tinta Limón.

Rivera Cusicanqui, Silvia. 2018. *El Mundo Ch'ixi Es Posible: Ensayos Desde Un Presente En Crisis*. Buenos Aires: Tinta Limón.

Rivera Cusicanqui, Silvia, and Raúl Barrios Morón. 1993. *Violencias Encubiertas En Bolivia: Cultura y Política*. La Paz: Talleres Gráficos Hisbol.

Russett, Bruce. 2013. "Liberalism." In *International Relations Theories: Discipline and Diversity*, edited by Tim Dunne, Milja Kurki, and Steve Smith, 94–114. Oxford: Oxford University Press.

Said, Edward W. 1978. *Orientalism*. New York: Vintage Books.
Seth, Vanita. 2010. *Europe's Indians: Producing Racial Difference, 1500–1900*. Durham, NC: Duke University Press.
Shapiro, Michael J. 2004. *Methods and Nations. Cultural Governance and the Indigenous Subject*. New York: Routledge.
Shesko, Elizabeth. 2010. "Hijos Del Inca y e La Patria: Presentaciones Del Indígena Durante El Congreso Indígena de 1945." *Fuentes, Revista de La Biblioteca y Archivo Histórico de La Asamblea Legislativa Plurinacional* 4 (6): 5–10.
Ticona, Esteban Alejo. 2000. *Organización y Liderazgo Aymara, La Experiencia Indígena En La Política Boliviana, 1979–1996*. Cochabamba: AGRUCO, Agroecología Universidad Cochabamba, Universidad de la Cordillera.
Todorov, Tzvetan. 1982. *The Conquest of America: The Question of the Other*. Norman: University of Oklahoma Press.
Trownsell, Tamara, Amaya Querejazu Escobari, Giorgio Shani, Navnita Chadha Behera, Jarrad Reddekop, and Arlene B. Tickner. 2019. "Recrafting International Relations through Relationality." *E-International Relations* (blog). January 8, 2019. https://www.e-ir.info/2019/01/08/recrafting-international-relations-through-relationality.
Walker, R. B. J. 1993. *Inside/Outside: International Relations as Political Theory*. Cambridge: Cambridge University Press.
Walker, R. B. J. 2006. "The Double Outside of the Modern International." *Ephemera* 6 (1): 56–69.
Walker, R. B. J. 2010. *After the Globe, Before the World*. New York: Routledge.
Walzer, Michael. 1990. "The Communitarian Critique of Liberalism." *Political Theory* 18 (1): 6–23.
Weber, Cynthia. 2016. *Queer International Relations: Sovereignty, Sexuality and the Will to Knowledge*. Oxford: Oxford University Press.
Weyland, Kurt. 2009. "The Rise of Latin America's Two Lefts: Insights from Rentier State Theory." *Comparative Politics* 41 (2): 145–164.
Weyland, Kurt, Raúl L. Madrid, and Wendy Hunter, eds. 2010. *Leftist Successes and Shortcomings*. New York: Cambridge University Press.
Wynter, Sylvia. 1995. "The Pope Must Have Been Drunk, The King of Castile a Madman: Culture as Actuality, and the Caribbean Rethinking Modernity." In *Reordering of Culture: Latin America, the Caribbean and Canada in the Hood*, by Alvina Ruprecht, 17–42. Ottawa: Carleton University Press.

2 Revolutionary Indianismo and the universalization of an "Other"

Despite the promotion and institutionalization of colonial discourses in Bolivia and the continent, Latin America has a rich history of resistance against processes of "Westernization" (Todorov 1982; Mignolo 2000; Canessa 2005; Albró 2005; Rivera 2010c, 2010a, 2012; Escobar 2010; Reinaga 2014b; Ari 2014; Mignolo and Walsh 2018). Movements and intellectuals often reignited the problem of difference, constructing other ways of knowing, being, and enacting. According to a number of authors, Andean indigenous movements such as the various branches of Indianismo have had particularly relevant rebellions and intellectual productions (Thomson 2002; Escobar 2010; Rivera 2015, 2010a; Ticona 2011, 2013, 2000; Assies 2009; Ari 2014; Mignolo 2012). As Silvia Rivera Cusicanqui highlights, Indianismo includes several branches and diverse intellectual productions (Rivera 1990, 107). In order to analyze another way to deal with the problem of difference while also moving along the genealogy of struggles centered in Bolivia, I focus throughout this chapter on the analysis of a particular kind of Indianismo between 1962 and 2017.[1]

As intellectuals from Bolivia have pointed out, liberalism and Marxism sought to assimilate and/or "kill the Indio" (Reinaga 2014b, 5:321, author's translation). The emergence of the independent Republic of Bolivia in 1825 included an oligarchic form of liberalism, which introduced an exclusionary delineation of citizenship and negated the "humanity" of indigenous peoples and women. As the Nationalist Revolutionary Movement gained power and became governmentally institutionalized in 1952, Marxist ideas were used both to transform the governmental notion of citizenship and to include women and indigenous peoples in a different manner. Instead of sustaining a relationship of segregation, the Revolution sought to include indigenous peoples and women by using a homogenizing idea of "mestizaje" and class. This notion of equality and assimilation avoided explicit segregation, but it still entailed a civilizing model, which continued to reinforce older oligarchic hierarchies (Rivera 2015, 105). The Marxist project led towards a pedagogical system of Europeanization, which "… made Indios hate their skin, their gods, their language, their race, and themselves" (Reinaga 2014b, 5:288). Additionally, women and indigenous peoples appeared as passive persons who only had to accompany or support the "true" agents of transformation. Similar to liberalism, these Marxist ideas and their implications continued to reinforce hierarchies that regarded "other" struggles as less valid, other voices as less authorized, and other projects as less legitimate.

Against these ideas and the violent policies that governments used in Bolivia to enact the "real" destiny of the country, several indigenous intellectuals and activists signed in 1962 the founding document of the Indio Party of Aymaras and Quechuas (PIAK for its initials in Spanish), which later became the Indio Party of Bolivia (PIB for its initials in Spanish). In Peñas, the place where the indigenous leader Tupaj Katari had been dismembered 181 years earlier for his anti-colonial struggle and the siege of La Paz, this party was the first organization that explicitly deployed Indianismo. These activists and intellectuals sought to oppose the colonial tendencies of liberal and Marxist models of civilization by constructing a different discourse, which was designed to validate their struggle, authorize their voice, and legitimize their revolution. Since then, Fausto Reinaga, Armando Choque, Raymundo Tambo, Tania Cruz, Ramiro Reinaga, Felipe Quispe, Virgilio Roel, Ayar Quispe, Hernán Arroyo, Rosa Tito, Cristina Choque and many others have constructed a revolutionary project of Indianismo, which has been promoted within movements, parties, and unions such as the PIAK, PIB, Unified Syndical Confederation of Rural Workers of Bolivia (CSUTCB for its initials in Spanish), Indianista Tupakatarista Movement (MITKA for its initials in Spanish), Indianista Movement, and the Katarista Guerrilla Army (EGTK for its initials in Spanish). They have constructed a different locus of enunciation, introducing it into the struggle for the definition of difference in Bolivia and the world.

Of course Andean indigenous struggles have a long history of rebellions, which goes as far as the 1500s in South America, but only in the 1960s did intellectuals explicitly synthetize the project called Indianismo. In order to create this new project, Fausto Reinaga, one of the most prominent Indianista intellectuals of Bolivia, participated in the foundation of the PIAK in 1962. Although Reinaga used the name "Indio" to begin his Marxist analysis of exploitation in the 1940s, the notion took a different meaning in 1962, when it was used as the name of a party that sought to oppose the Marxist agenda of the Nationalist Revolution. In his new intellectual phase, Reinaga sought to move away from his previous conception of the "Indio problem," which entailed class-based ideas of exploitation. Instead, he moved towards the examination of racial issues of colonialism. Reinaga explicitly defined the meaning of Indianismo and its roots in 1970, when he wrote the *Manifesto of the Indianista Party* (Reinaga 2014a). In his work, the author mentioned that Christopher Columbus mistakenly named the peoples that he encountered as "Indians" because he thought that he had arrived in India. Reinaga asserted that this was the moment that marked the beginning of the European process of identity imposition in the now-called Americas. This event began the imposition of the historical contradiction of colonialism

(Reinaga 2014b, 5:361). To the author, the name "Indianismo" carried the very tension of a history that had to be transformed, in a dialectical sense, through revolution. The word "Indio" was an incorrect label imposed by colonialism, but it was now used by Reinaga to show the arbitrary contradiction of history, which often remained hidden under erroneous ideologies. Once he could resolve this contradiction through revolution, the "Indio" would become "Inca" again (5:361).[2] Until he could achieve his liberation, then, the "Indio" would carry the weight of colonialism and the name that it gave him. As Ayar Quispe asserted, this definition of Indianismo turned Reinaga into the founding "father" and main ideologue of the movement (A. Quispe 2009, 17). Moreover, the name of "Indianismo" has been used in this manner by several movements, parties, and unions that consider themselves close to the ideas first promoted by Reinaga. For example, the political proposal of the CSUTCB in 1989 explicitly followed this definition (CSUTCB 2009a, 164).

Additionally, I decided to emphasize the revolutionary principles of the various organizations composing the movement in order to distinguish their intellectual production from other forms of Indianismo. This particular set of actors often sought revolutionary strategies of transformation due to their disillusion with institutional paths after the failure of the 1952 government, which lasted until 1964. As the founding document of the PIAK stated, the "Indio" could seek power through democracy, but revolution was often necessary (PIAK 2014, 5:341). Some Indianista intellectuals even dismissed the path of democracy altogether. They asserted that the only possible path to liberate the "Indio" was through revolution and guerrilla warfare (A. Quispe 2009, 14; F. Quispe 1988, 149).

By combining these names, I aim to distinguish a consistent discourse from other Indianista constructions such as the idea of Indianismo Amáutico that Reinaga later elaborates, the Marxist understanding of Indianismo by Álvaro García Linera, and the neoliberal view of Indianismo by Victor Hugo Cárdenas. Throughout this chapter, I analyze "Revolutionary Indianismo" as a separate stance or discursive locus in the struggle to define a way to deal with difference in Bolivia and beyond. How does Revolutionary Indianismo include an alternative way of knowing, being, and enacting? Does this kind of Indianismo include epistemic boundaries that marginalize "others" as well? How is Revolutionary Indianismo different to colonial discourses? In order to answer these questions, I first describe the ontological assumptions built by Revolutionary Indianistas who oppose Marxism and liberalism, while also validating their own struggle and way of knowing. Second, I connect this epistemic dimension to the epistemological authorization of the "Indio." Third, I turn towards the Indianista notion of history and liberation that emerges from these assumptions. Finally, I examine some of the limitations that other Indianistas and intellectuals highlight in Revolutionary Indianismo to construct the other loci of enunciation and projects described in the following chapters.

Revolutionary Indianismo is reality: Validity and equality

By the 1960s in Bolivia, it had become clear to Reinaga and other intellectuals that problems of racial and ethnic inequality were not going to be solved by the policies of the Nationalist Revolution or by the liberal projects that had continued colonial hierarchies since 1825. In this context, Indianistas defined an ontology of their own. Their definition of what is regarded as "real" is related to a particular conceptualization of "humanity." Similar to Marxism and liberalism, Indianismo uses a seemingly undeniable fact of "humanity's" empirical life as a starting foundation from which it can create a discourse beyond doubt. Unlike the assumption of "desire" used by Marxism or the notion of "reason" that liberalism deployed, however, the definition of this Indianista foundation begins from the *fact of inheritance*. Indianismo constructs its discourse from the fact that all human beings are born into families or relationships with guardians and tutors. In turn, these relationships inevitably connect persons to the past because each child appears molded by the previous generation, who was also molded by a previous generation and so on. This connection with the past is viewed as the basic and undeniable fact of the discourse; it is the ontological "reality" that acts as a foundational "truth" and validates the rest of the discourse.

For example, Reinaga begins his definition of race by asserting, "inheritance is a fact related to the somatological part of man" (Reinaga 2014b, 5:104).[3] Because "inheritance" appears as a hard and biological foundation, which connects the "Indio" to his past, Reinaga is able to develop the rest of his edifice from this very fact. Similarly, Virgilio Roel claims, in the Indianista document that resulted from the First Conference of the South American Indio in Peru, 1980, that the difference between peoples throughout the world emerges because each one of them is connected to a particular past through their relationship with previous generations (Roel 1980, 5). According to Roel, this is the fact that still connects the "Indio" with his genuine and "true" past, even though this history is often concealed or partially erased by the foreign oppression of colonialism. Iván Apaza Calle similarly asserts, in a more current publication in the magazine produced by the Indianista-Katarista Movement, *Pukara*, that Indianismo begins from the fact of colonialism (Calle 2016). According to the author, this phenomenon can only be understood from the fact that the "Indio" is still connected to his pre-colonial past through the "long chain of generations" (17, author's translation). The founding document of the PIAK also claims that the "Indio" can liberate himself from his enemies thanks to the rebirth of the millenary Inca culture, which can free the power and spirit of the indigenous race by realizing its "universal and humanist inheritance" (PIAK 2014, 5:341).

The usage of this seemingly undeniable ontological assumption thus acts as a foundation, which includes important epistemic implications, affecting the rest of the project and creating some of the discursive tendencies that intellectuals later critique. First, Revolutionary Indianismo uses the "reality" of the fact of inheritance to validate its own way of knowing, equality, and struggle. The level of certainty that emerges from this strong condition of reality acts as a status that is then transferred to the rest of the discourse. Since it constructs the connection with its genuine past as "true," for example, Revolutionary Indianismo creates a strong idealization of an identity that is then deployed as a basis for politics. The validity that Revolutionary Indianismo grants to its own way of knowing the past is discussed and analyzed by Carlos Makusaya (2014, 320). In his work, the author asserts that Indianismo creates much of its political potential from the validity that is granted to the myth of its own past. In other words, Revolutionary Indianismo uses the "reality" of its inheritance and the connection to a pre-conquest past to construct the legitimacy of its political project. Ontological validation and political legitimation are thus intertwined throughout the discourse.

Second, Revolutionary Indianismo not only validates its way of knowing, but also constructs its knowledge as a *superior* form of "truth." Within this ontology, the undeniability and reality of one way of knowing logically denies the existence of whatever contradicts it. Hence, the epistemic assumptions used by Indianismo begin to create a hierarchy that orders other ways of knowing. Thanks to this epistemic tendency, Revolutionary Indianismo is able to confront Marxism and liberalism, while also endogenously determining its own ideas as a "superior degree of truth" (Reinaga 2014b, 5:473).

Third, since the existence of inheritance appears undeniable and hierarchically higher than other ways of knowing, the elements that are consistently connected to this platform acquire a status of truth that travels beyond the discursive boundaries of Indianismo. The fact of inheritance thus includes a universalizing tendency, which extrapolates a particular notion of reality, equality, struggle, access to knowledge, and historical path towards liberation upon other discourses. The "Indio's" connection with the past, situation of the present, and destiny of the future represents the universal, singular, and dialectical history of all human beings (Reinaga 2014b, 5:93). This tendency universalizes a single experience of struggle and equality, which then enables the construction of a global idea of Indianista order. Reinaga asserts, "We will use our strength in the struggle to conquer power. Power to construct a new society, a new human nature, a new man, better than the one made by occident" (5:348).

Fourth, the characteristics of this ontological foundation begin to create the classifying and organizing logic of the discourse, which articulates, assimilates, and orders different realms of knowledge. For example, Reinaga asserts that the inheritance of the "Indio" is transcendental and "cosmic" (Reinaga 2014a, 5:402). Then, the cosmic notions of Indianismo are viewed as consistent with "science" (5:103). Hence, science has to be used as a tool (e.g., archaeology, history, gene-based studies, etc.) that can help Revolutionary Indianismo to rediscover the "true" past of "humanity" and to reconstruct the destiny of the "Indio" (5:352). The "Indio's" science thus fits within the notion of the connection to the past and it becomes organized as a consistent part of the

Indianista "dogma" (5:345). To the contrary, "colonialism" appears to contradict the fact of inheritance and it is classified as an "arbitrary" lie. Reinaga thus separates Revolutionary Indianismo from the "colonial" and "occidental" usage of science, which utilizes a "lie" to create technologies for war, nuclear bombs, concentration of food, etc. (5:93). Unlike the colonial form of "secularism" found in "occidental" science (5:341), Reinaga asserts that scientific knowledge has to be re-deployed by Indianismo in order to liberate humanity. Only then "the light of science shall illuminate our path" (5:351).

Finally, by utilizing the fact of inheritance as an ontological foundation, Indianismo locates its notion of "humanity" and equality as an anthropocentric bedrock of universal judgement. The fact of inheritance thus pre-shapes Indianismo as a particular form of "humanism" (Reinaga 2014b, 5:92; A. Quispe 2009, 18). Here, "humanity" is located at the pinnacle of the hierarchy of entities in the universe. In turn, this placement prioritizes the necessities of "humanity" above all else. As the 1978 political declaration of the Indianista Tupakatarista Movement states, "the human person, whatever its race or condition may be, is the most important creation of nature" (F. Quispe 1999, 19, author's translation). This shapes Revolutionary Indianismo primarily as a response to the problems of a "humanity" (CSUTCB 2005). As I further discuss in the conclusion, this humanist tendency of Indianismo contradicts some of the notions of Pachamama (Mother Nature) often used by indigenous peoples in the Andes.

Inheritance becomes race and/or nation: The characteristics of an ontology

Indianista intellectuals consistently substantiate the ontological notion of the fact of inheritance and its epistemic tendencies by defining the characteristics of that which exists. They achieve this goal by constructing ideas of race and/or nation, which define the generational connections that the fact of inheritance validates. Although they often appear intertwined within the oeuvre of different Indianista intellectuals, the notions of race and nation tend to lead the discourse closer to two different ends of a spectrum. To discuss these trends, I analytically contrast race and nation, exploring how each tendency unfolds and produces different theoretical consequences. Specifically, I analyze how the notion of race has particular problems, which are often solved by intellectuals who focus more prominently on the idea of nation.

On one side, the notion of *race* moves closer to biological explanations of the fact that there are connections with past generations. The undeniable links with the past are possible thanks to inter-generational relationships of blood and endogamy. For example, much of the work by Reinaga uses UNESCO's definition of race from 1967. This definition understands race as a "natural group of people," which have historically inherited physical characteristics due to the genes that they retain (Reinaga 2014b, 5:103). These genes can be historically continuous thanks to the predominance of endogamy over exogamy.

Hence, Reinaga defines and establishes the undeniable connection with generational pasts through a biological notion of race. This explains why

Reinaga often asserts that the "Indio" is Inca "blood" and race, still resisting the colonial oppression brought into the Americas (Reinaga 2014b 5:150). Other Indianista intellectuals have followed this definition as well. For example, Felipe Quispe asserts that the blood of grandparents and ancestors still runs in the veins of "Indios" and it calls for the revival of the revolution (F. Quispe 1988, 28). Moreover:

> To their twenty-first century children, (grandparents) are the communitarian model that is present in our Aymara and Quechua minds and hearts. That is why we have awakened our own history and raised the same flag of the revolutionary and armed Indio struggle.
>
> F. Quispe 1988, 28, author's translation

This racial definition of the fact of inheritance explains the importance of family descendancy in relation to the "Indio's" struggle. Direct descendants of important heroes sometimes enjoy higher levels of legitimacy in relation to the current positions of agency and action in the possibility of revolution. They have closer racial ties to the "real" past of the "Indio," which unveils his "true" identity and shapes his future. Reinaga, for example, traces his descendancy to Tupaj Katari and Bertolina Sisa, who led in the 1780s one of the most important and famous anti-colonial uprisings in South American history (Reinaga 2014b, 5:47); he signs his explanation of the Indianista Revolution in 1970 as Rupaj Katari (Reinaga 2014c, 5:410). Felipe Quispe also asserts that he is a direct descendent of Diego Quispi, who was a high ranked officer in Tupak Amaru's army in Peru and a Colonel in Tupak Katari's army in La Paz (F. Quispe 1988, 13).

Unlike "European forms of racism," however, Reinaga denies the organization of racial differences into "Western" hierarchies (Reinaga 2014b, 5:107). According to him, the scientific study of race by UNESCO shows that there are no pure races throughout the world (5:104). Biology falsifies the "grotesque notion of racism" (5:107). Despite our racial differences as peoples, then, there is always at least a small degree of mixture in the common origin of the homo-sapience specie. These inter-racial connections give everyone a minimum basis of commonality and equality within "humanity;" it creates an "ontic unity," which destroys "Occidental" racism (5:67).

On the other side of the spectrum, the notion of *nation* is more often related to the "color of ideas" (Reinaga 2014b, 5:473) and the *meanings* that are shared by the different forms of pedagogical relationships established through inter-generational education, socialization, guardianship, etc. For example, Felipe Quispe Huanca, Hernán Arroyo, Rosa Tito, Cristina Choque, and other Indianista intellectuals published in 2005 a proposal presented by the CSUTCB. Within this proposal, the authors promote the "Warisata" school system that is based on a form of education autonomously led by indigenous communities of Bolivia between 1931 and 1940 (CSUTCB 2005, 44, author's translation). This experience is viewed as the momentary revival of Tupaj

Katari's mission of liberation (41). These events of the "Indio's" past are thus conceived as two historical moments from which the contemporary "Indio" can understand his present and design his future. They are pedagogical moments connecting the past and creating a possibility of passing on "true" meanings. Here, inheritance is regarded as meaningful connections with the past, which can be revived through inter-generational teachings.

Indianista intellectuals thus substantiate the characteristics of "inheritance" through ideas of race and/or nation. Because these connections to the past form the equally validated characteristics of the ontological fact of inheritance, all races and/or nations have to be regarded as equal as well. They are all equally "real" in their biological or pedagogical inheritance. In the substantiation of their characteristics, epistemic assumptions of ontological reality thus consistently unfold into notions of equality. The characterization of that which is "real" constructs the validated boundaries of "human" commonality. In the case of race, equality is defined through the idea of "human" mixture and common origin. For the idea of nation, intellectuals focus more prominently on the notion of a commonality in origin, which can be found more clearly in the Indianista organization of history. The notion of nation divides history between validated epochs of "equality," invalidated epochs of "colonialism," and transitional times of "revolution." The epoch of "equality" corresponds to "humanity's" *common origin*. For example, Roel claims that Pachamama created all human beings; she is the "common mother" of all of "humanity" (Roel 1980, 5, author's translation). However, since they were created in different parts of Pachamama, each people has its own nation and is equally different. Through the notion of race or the idea of nation, the "real" connections to the past thus lead to the shared origin and commonality that equalizes all peoples. The characterization of that which is "real" thus defines the commonality that constructs a validated and consistent notion of equally.

These ideas of a common origin are then epistemologically connected to the "Indio," who gains direct access to the "real" past of a common origin and is hereby authorized to know "equality." How does Revolutionary Indianismo, however, construct this epistemological form of authorization for its own agent? Moreover, how does the idea of inheritance establish this link between a common origin and the current "Indio" after 500 years of colonialism?

Who knows "equality:" Authorization and enemies

To authorize a knower and agent of transformation, Revolutionary Indianismo creates an epistemological connection between the current "Indio" and the validated notion of equality, which is attached to the idea of undeniable inheritance. The "Indio" has to be able to access that which is "real" in order to know the "truth" and to re-establish equality. The ontological definition of a way of knowing is thus epistemologically connected to the construction of a way of being. Someone, with particular characteristics, knows equality better than others.

The idea of *nation* connects the "Indio" to a tradition and cosmology that views "humanity" as equal due to its common origin in Pachamama. From this origin on, each generation shared the knowledge that was acquired by the founders who saw the process of original creation (Roel 1980, 5). On the other side, the idea of *race* uses a more "scientific" connection with the past. For Reinaga, race always entails a common origin for the specie and a degree of mixture through exogamy, which bounds "human" differences within the broader category of "homo sapiens" (Reinaga 2014b, 5:67). Due to their blood ties and past, some people remember this equality and seek to practice it in their social order.

Despite these possibilities of epistemological connection with a common origin of equality, Revolutionary Indianismo also needs to show that there is a *continuous* link between these ideas and the current agent of transformation. In other words, Revolutionary Indianismo needs to prove that the "Indio" has been able to retain this genuine knowledge of a common origin throughout the epoch that contradicts it, namely colonialism. Within the nation-based definition of the fact of inheritance, Revolutionary Indianismo has to prove that teachings have in fact been passed on and have thus *resisted* the process of colonialism that began in 1492. This possibility is established by emphasizing historical moments and actions of epistemic resistance. For example, according to the political declaration of the CSUTCB in 1989, religion is passed on to current "Indios" thanks to the resistance of Indianista "priests," whom the Catholic Church sought to kill (CSUTCB 2009a, 157, author's translation). The political proposal also claims that the communitarian form of social organization called ayllu is the wisdom that currently lives thanks to actions of resistance against Spanish colonialism (141). One of these key moments of resistance is Tupak Katari's rebellion and the communitarian system that he established for a short period of time in the 1780s. From these fractions of recovered memory, Indianista intellectuals such as Felipe Quispe seek to construct a similar form of confederation (F. Quispe 1988, 21). This system would entail an aggregate of communitarian and autonomous governments (23). Similarly, Ayar Quispe claims that the most important moment that the "Indio" has to remember is the revolt of Tupaj Katari (A. Quispe 2009, 48–49). These inherited ideas lead Ayar Quispe, Felipe Quispe, Álvaro García Linera, and others towards the foundation of the Katarista Guerrilla Army (EGTK) in 1986. Others also use the history of Tupaj Katari as the past that needs to be recovered and enacted (MITKA 1977). Many of these intellectuals also attribute great importance to Bertolina Sisa. For example, the Clandestine Manifesto of the MITKA describes her position of commander, which she gained once Tupaj Katari left the siege in La Paz to go to other battles. Felipe Quispe also dedicates several pages to the discussion of her role in the rebellion and the way in which she was later betrayed (F. Quispe 1988, 83). Current intellectuals similarly claim Reinaga and his work as a more contemporaneous moment of pedagogical linkage with the past of the "Indio" (A. Quispe 2011).

Thanks to these moments of resistance, teaching, and revival of memories, the "Indio" is constructed as the one who has a privileged access to the ontologically validated notion of equality. His nation-based resistance is related to the heroism of ancestors, who were able to share their wisdom through stories, rebellions, and written documents (A. Quispe 2009, 14). To the contrary, "others" appear more disconnected from the equality of common origins. They do not know the "truth," but can learn from the "Indio." Since "others" can learn about "real" equality, they have a possibility of making decisions about their levels of colonialism and liberation.

> Everyone, absolutely everyone, can be an Indio or Indian, as long as they fulfill the requisites of respecting the values of the Indio, the will to promote his own people and locality, the solidarity with his community, the defense of nature, the constant effort towards personal perfection, and the adhesion to the morality of the Indio.
>
> Roel 1980, 30

On the other side and in order to define a *racial* possibility to know equality, Reinaga asserts that the link between the current "Indio" and his "true" past of equality remains strong because he still has an endogamic and genetic connection with previous generations. Here, ideologies ultimately belong to people and people are often assumed as biologically connected to different pasts. Despite several of his efforts to counter the problems that emerge from biological understandings of race and notwithstanding the modification of his work in later years, Reinaga asserts:

> Ideologies are not just in the air like clouds. They are embodied in people, in their bodies and bones. Each ideology classifies people within the right, the left, or the center. The relationship between each ideology is inter-generational. Liberals and nationalists are thus the progenitors of communists. In this way, the liberals, nationalists, and communists of the Bolivian "cholage"[4] all come from the same flesh and the same blood.
>
> Reinaga 2014b, 5:487

Race-based resistance against the influence of colonial centuries is thus possible thanks to the idea of endogamy, which partially, and only partially, still separates the "Indio" from colonial "whites." This explains why Reinaga asserts that the "Indio" has never been fully mixed; he is not like the "mestizo" (Reinaga 2014b, 5:396). The possibility of knowing a genuine past and regain knowledge of a "true" equality thus emerges from the "blood" of the "Indio." His "blood" and "spirit" have this epistemological capacity because they are connected to the pre-colonial past of the Inca, who had a society of "love and work" (5:49). Instead, the "mestizo" is regarded as the result of the rape and violation of "Indio" women by Spanish men. According to Reinaga, this act of violence explains the ideological proximity between "mestizos" and "whites" (i.e., colonialism). This also explains, however, the "mestizo's" connection with the "Indio's" past, which represents a possibility of alliance. "Mestizos" can return to their "true" roots by acknowledging the blood connections established by their mothers, grandmothers, and great grandmothers (5:487).

These kinds of epistemological connections thus couple the ontologically validated notion of equality and the characteristics of a knower. They link a validated way of knowing and a consistently authorized way of being, which constructs the main agent of "human" equality and transformation. Hence, the "Indio" appears as "the only true nation that has existed in Bolivia and that now needs to be liberated" (Reinaga 2014b, 5:496). He is regarded as the "subject of history" whose "true interest" and "historical right" makes him the "demiurge of the socialist era" (5:347). For the "Indio," this kind of liberation is his "cosmic mandate" and the general "force of reason" (5:476–477).

Colonialism and the enemy: The anti-thesis of history

From their construction of an ontologically validated way of knowing and an epistemologically authorized way of being, Indianista intellectuals can then classify different epochs and determine who are the agents responsible for colonial oppression. Pre-colonial and pre-conquest times represent the thesis of history, which is epistemologically connected to the "Indio." This past of "equality" is regarded as history's original moment in a dialectical sense and the "Indio" is understood as the authorized knower of this epoch. Conversely, Indianismo views the racialized hierarchicalization of "humanity" as the anti-thesis and colonial epoch of history. According to the manifesto of the Tupakatarista Guerrilla Army, "colonialism" began the cycle of the 500-year-old "Arum Pacha" (time of night) (ERTK 2009, 171, author's translation). During this time, Europeans imposed a hierarchical separation between peoples and reconstructed the identity of the "Indio" as an inferior object, which had to be civilized, assimilated, or, if all else failed, annihilated through genocide (Reinaga 2014b, 5:467). This form of racism constructed the "Indio" as "sad," "slow," "acquiescent," "timid," "lazy," "childish," and "melancholic" (5:121). Europeans used these qualifications as "proofs" of the inferiority, "sub-humanity," and "monkey-like characteristics" of this group of people (5:106).

According to Reinaga, this idea has been imposed in the Americas by "white" people born in Europe and by their descendants (Reinaga 2014b, 5:487). Felipe Quispe similarly asserts that "white" Bolivian elites are descendants of Europeans who have continuously imposed, for the last 500 years, their notion of superiority (F. Quispe 1988, 18). From Christopher Columbus and Francisco Pizarro to contemporaneous politicians, such as former Bolivian presidents Jaime Paz Zamora or Hugo Banzer Suárez, "white" people have sustained "colonialism" and its racist ideology. They are the agents of "colonialism." For example, current streams of liberalism and Marxism still sustained this re-construction of the "Indio" during the 1970s. Communism and Marxism are thus viewed as promoting ideas of class struggles, which still see the "Indio" as inferior (Reinaga 2014b, 5:474). Within this ideology, the "Indio" had to follow the proletariat or he had to disappear because he was regarded as an obstacle for progress (5:131).

Since the Indianista idea of "equality" emerges from the seemingly undeniable ontology that can be epistemologically known by the "Indio," racism cannot be "true" and racist people cannot be "right." Revolutionary Indianismo thus regards colonial racism and colonial agents as its "enemy," which cannot fit the ontologically validated and epistemologically known platform of equality. On the side of *race*, the idea of a universal commonality in "human" origin and mixture classifies colonial hierarchies as arbitrary "lies." To achieve this goal, Reinaga invokes the legitimacy of sciences and uses anthropological studies, which show that there is no evidence of biologically hierarchical relationships between races (Reinaga 2014b, 5:105). Then, those who carry colonial ideologies appear as liars who construct arbitrary notions in order to benefit themselves. For example, Europeans are regarded as "a hypnotized people who live trapped within illusions" due to their role in the construction of hierarchies and violence (5:483). Their ideologies of liberalism, nationalism, and Marxism are thus understood as tools of alienation, which are based on fictitious ideologies (5:485). Felipe Quispe also asserts, in a similar sense, that "colonialism" constructed a fake ideology, which distorted the past in order to impose European domination (F. Quispe 1988, 9–10).

On the side of *nation*, the inter-generational connection between "colonialism" and a European past makes racism appear as a "foreign" idea, which is imported into the Americas. For example, the Indianista Manifesto of Tiahuanaco claimed, in 1973, that "colonialism" is a fictitious ideology imported from Europe (Movimiento Indianista 1973, author's translation). Additionally, the "reality" of a common origin of nations makes colonial hierarchies appear as "lies." In the creation of Pachamama, all notions of peoplehood emerged from a common creation. Thus, they are regarded as equal. Contradicting the characteristics of this "reality" leads towards invalidation. For example, the educational project of the CSUTCB seeks to create a "pedagogy of liberation," which proclaims that the "Indio" has to look back in order to recover his "true" memory and unveil the "reality" that has been hidden under the lie of colonialism (CSUTCB 2005, 4). In their hierarchicalizing effects and their contradiction against "equality," the ideologies that accompany "colonialism" thus appear as "propaganda" (24). They are "… de-contextualized colonial ideologies about our first nations and they use traditional methods of demobilization, which fortify cultural alienation and strengthen the hate oriented towards our ancestral cultures" (31).

In other words, the Indianista discourse uses its own ontology and epistemology to judge and classify what is "real" and who is "right." Since it is classified as a "lie," an "arbitrary ideology," or a "foreign propaganda," "colonialism" is hereby invalidated as the "enemy." Accordingly, Felipe Quispe, together with other intellectuals, asserts that Indianismo has a clear and identifiable "enemy," which represents invasion and colonialism (F. Quispe 1988, 67). In 1989, the political declaration of the CSUTCB also stated:

> Because Occident has occupied with arrogance and arbitrariness our land Qollasuyu-Tawantinsuyu for over 500 years, we can no longer tolerate colonialism. It is time to expel and sweep off of our lands their ideas, principles and laws, codes, science, philosophy, religion, capitalist individualism, oppression and exploitation, class-based hierarchicalization, their raw racism against the Indio, and their drunken complex of superiority. It is time to destroy their authorities, burn their symbols and flags, their corrupt and prostitute morale, ...
>
> CSUTCB 2009a, 166

A way of enactment: Specifying enmity and constructing liberation

How does Revolutionary Indianismo use this invalidation of "colonial" hierarchies and de-authorization of "colonial" agents to judge social *relationships*? How does this kind of Indianismo define "oppression" and "injustice"? Since they emerge from "lies," the social relationships that are created from or consistent with "colonialism" appear as unjust forms of oppression. In their contradiction of "real" equality, "colonial" forms of social relationships appear as oppressive and unjust. The ontological "reality" of "equality" and the epistemological authority of the "Indio" thus lead to a basis of normative judgement. To achieve this goal of classification while following its epistemic assumptions consistently, Revolutionary Indianismo prioritizes racism as the most important form of injustice. Indianismo constructs its own way of knowing, which views inheritance as the fundamental "reality" of "humanity." Then, the substantiation of this ontological notion includes the definition of race and/or nation, which characterizes a "real" commonality and a platform of equality. Since "humanity" is, first and foremost, ethnic and/or racial equality, racism is then viewed as the "fundamental" contradiction from which the "Indio" and "humanity" have to be liberated (MITKA 1977, author's translation). According to the 1978 political declaration of the MITKA, racism is the basic contradiction imposed upon humanity's history (F. Quispe 1999, 19). Others claim that fighting racism is the genuine interest of the "Indio" (Reinaga 2014b, 5:344) or the basic struggle against colonial domination (F. Quispe 1988, 45). Hence, the Indianista ontology validates a particular kind of "equality," which elevates a distinct kind of injustice above other struggles.

The most direct consequence of this fundamental contradiction of equality is *discrimination*, which entails the devaluation of identities and peoples based on cultural or physical stereotypes. According to Roel, this form of injustice creates fictitious stereotypes that re-construct the "Indio" in negative terms (Roel 1980, 30). Reinaga discusses this colonial construction of the "Indio," affirming that peoples in the Andes have often been classified as "savages," "primitives," "naturals," "indigenous," and other notions that entail inferiority and sub-humanity (Reinaga 2014b, 5:81).

The author also cites the works of Gabriel René Moreno, Mariano Baptista, Franz Tamayo, Alcides Arguedas, Porfirio Diaz Machiado, Fernando Diez de Medina, Regis Debray and other intellectuals as examples of the continuation of colonial ideologies in the works of Bolivian nationals since the declaration of independence (Reinaga 2014b, 5:427). For example, he quotes Gabriel René Moreno, who promoted oligarchic notions of liberalism, toyed with the idea of genocide, and asserted that:

> … the stupidity of the Inca Indio and the "cholage" are molded for despotism. The brains of indigenous peoples and the brains of "cholos" are molecularly incapable of conceiving republican liberty and republican civility. On average, these brains weigh between 5 and 10 ounces less than the brain of the pure white race.
>
> Reinaga 2014b, 5:428[5].

This form of discrimination has led to political, social, and geographical *segregation* (Reinaga 2014b, 5:161–164). These stereotypes have also led to colonial policies of *assimilationism*, which are civilizational processes of homogenization based on the characteristics of those who are located at the top of the hierarchy. In Bolivia and much of Latin America, liberal projects of assimilation have entailed racial policies of "mestizaje," which seek to bring the "Indio" closer to "white" people through the biological mixture of races. Other strategies of assimilationism have included educational systems, which erase the "Indio's" history, language, values, heroes, etc. (Movimiento Indianista 1973). "Mestizaje" is also used as a colonial strategy of national "unification," but Revolutionary Indianismo unveils the ways in which these policies seek to erase the "Indio" even through Marxist ideas of class-based equality (Reinaga 2014b, 5:158). Assimilation has been widely used in Bolivia and Latin America, but, according to Reinaga, the "Indio" has always been viewed as a "beast of burden" for work or as "cannon fodder" for war (5:164). According to Revolutionary Indianismo, *genocide* or *extermination* appear as the other policies that are used if the previously mentioned forms of assimilationism or segregation fail (MITKA 1977).

The colonial hierarchy of races appears as coherently enabling or justifying relationships of *exploitation* as well. Racism justifies or enables the possibility of exploiting the bodies of those regarded as "inferior," "uncivilized," "barbaric," etc. In Bolivia, this form of injustice entails using the bodily strength or the very life of the "Indio" in order to gain wealth. As the Clandestine Manifesto of the MITKA stated in 1977, exploitation has been the reality suffered by the "Indio" for five centuries (MITKA 1977). In another document, the MITKA also states that the racial and economic problems suffered by the "Indio" are part of the same phenomenon (F. Quispe 1999, 19).

Within the earlier colonial ideologies of Spanish conquest, exploitation entailed the complete ownership of the "Indio." "White" Europeans appeared to be the owners and masters of the "Indio." The hierarchy imposed by this Eurocentric ideology constructed the "Indio" as a non-human "commodity," which could be owned and used as a slave by a master (Reinaga 2014b, 5:49; F. Quispe 1988, 17). After the declaration of independence in 1825, this way of using and owning the "Indio" was continued by the "mita" and the "pongage," which were systems of forced labor (CSUTCB 2005, 29). In this context of oligarchic liberalism, "Indios" were viewed as inferior "beasts of burden" and they were often obligated to work without wages. Because the colonial notion of hierarchy constructed the "Indio" as non-human beings that could not participate in rights of property and ownership, this form of liberal racism also included the possibility of extracting material resources from the Americas and stealing land from the people who inhabited these territories (Reinaga 2014b, 5:195; F. Quispe 1988, 17; MovimientoIndianista 1973). Several intellectuals and documents emphasize the importance of the extraction and exploitation of "resources" such as gold, silver, and land. For example, the 1989 political proposal of the CSUTCB asserted:

> We, the small agricultural producers, do not know any kind of economic help, have been excluded from national life, and have been viewed as simple beasts of burden, treated as foreigners in our own ancestral lands; as farm workers who, from generation to generation, are forced to declare publicly that we cannot develop our own coherent agricultural program and will never be able to modernize our own lands. Since Francisco Pizarro set foot on our lands and until the current chicken-face white Jaime Paz Zamora, no one has returned our stolen dear Pachamama, which is still under the control of white q'aras to enjoy the products of exploitation like pigs.
>
> CSUTCB 2009a, 160[6]

Between the declaration of independence and the Nationalist Revolution, "Indios" were regarded in Bolivia as objects. The oligarchic liberal ideas of citizenship and law promoted throughout this period did not include "Indios" as full subjects of rights and they enabled "white" citizens to exploit the bodies and lands of indigenous peoples. After the 1952 Nationalist Revolution, the exploitation suffered by "Indios" in the Andean region of Latin America became more closely related to the private ownership of land and other means of production. Since the "Indio" was now conceived as a class-based ally, who needed to be liberated by the urban worker's movement, the Revolution sought to dismantle oligarchic systems of forced labor and it brought the "Indio" closer to its own notion of "humanity." Within this form of Marxism, the "Indio" was no longer viewed as a commodity or an object. Instead, he was reconstructed as a "peasant." Despite the benefits gained by indigenous peoples during this period, the Revolutionary re-construction of the "Indio" still sustained a Eurocentric hierarchicalization, which shallowly modified the system of exploitation and continued to oppress the "Indio" in a different way (Movimiento Indianista 1973).

Hence, "colonial" hierarchies contradict the validated idea of "human" equality and they appear as "arbitrary" constructions. Then, their social relations are classified as "unjust" forms of oppression and those who benefited from these kinds of injustices are regarded as oppressors. Discrimination, violence, exploitation, expropriation, assimilation, and genocide are thus related to the hierarchicalizing effects of "colonialism," which attach less value to the life of the "Indio" and privilege the agents of civilizational order. Revolutionary Indianismo thus invalidates these hierarchies, de-authorizes these oppressors, and delegitimizes these social relations. It classifies the colonial ways of knowing, being, and enacting that create the continuous suffering of indigenous peoples in Bolivia. As the political declaration of the CSUTCB claimed in 1988:

> The Indio has lived through 500 years under the bloodthirsty whip of oppression; exploitation; and the racial, cultural, social, spiritual, economic, and political discrimination that comes from a colonial minority, which has withheld power and still does. In the past, they were "Pizarristas" or "Almagristas." In the republic, they were "conservatives" or "liberals." In the present, they are "rightists" or "leftists," but, at the end, they are all the same: bosses, bourgeoise, businessmen, landowners, etc.
>
> CSUTCB 2009b, 124

Enacting a just social order

On the other side of the Indianista boundary of classification, "equality" is understood as the ontological "reality" and the "Indio" is regarded as the epistemologically authorized way of being. The "Indio" knows "reality" because he can still access his "inherited" past of "equality." His bloodline or his generational relationship separates him from the "oppressor." Additionally, these connections give him access to a pre-conquest past that is "true" and that opposes coloniality: "Indianity is the contrary of Occident. This culture will replace the old Hellenic-Christian culture that today succumbs in the midst of nihilism, hanger, and the horrific thunder of atomic war" (Reinaga 2014b, 5:151). Hence, this epistemological classification of ways of being authorizes the "Indio" to *enact* "equality," which entails two analytically distinct possibilities. On one side, this epistemological authorization includes a possibility of rescuing a social order that emerges from the "Indio's" past and is consistent with the validated idea of "equality." As I analyze in this section, the "Indio" can further specify "equality" by intellectually recuperating the characteristics of his pre-conquest social order. On the other side, the authorization of the "Indio" constructs him as the legitimate agent of the revolution. As I further elaborate in the following section, the "Indio" hereby becomes the one who can define and rule the strategy of transformation that leads to "equality."

In order to rescue the specificities of a social order of "equality," the "Indio" has to recover and re-draw his "genuine" past, which has resisted the last 500 years of injustices. Since this social order is consistent with racial or nation-based "equality," the "Indio's" past includes "fraternal love" for all peoples (Reinaga 2014b, 5:55). According to Reinaga, Indianista notions of love and equality emerge from the Inca philosophy of "ama suwa, ama llulla, ama qhilla" (do not steal, do not lie, do not be lazy) (5:216). This idea entails a form of collective cooperation that permeates all the dimensions of daily life. According to Revolutionary Indianismo, the Inca had put this notion into practice in their socialist system, which was based on the "ayllu" form of communitarianism (5:433). They created a type of organization in which hunger and exploitation were inexistent (5:123). Similar to Reinaga, Felipe Quispe views the 1780s struggle of Tupaj Katari and Bertolina Sisa as a rebellion that was oriented to the re-establishment of the ayllu system. Quispe states, "our natural and communitarian laws are not to enslave or to discriminate foreign white q'aras, mestizos, etc. Instead, we will promote the communitarian law of equality for all who live and work within the dignity of Qullasuyu (Bolivia)" (F. Quispe 1988, 149). Other Revolutionary Indianistas also view the ayllu social order as the "true" past of the "Indio" and as the possibility of a future of equality (CSUTCB 2005, 42).

In this system, the basic unit of social order is the community, which results from integrating the boundaries of race or nation together with dynamic delineations of territories (Reinaga 2014b, 5:89). Either through a racial or nation-based connection to a validated past, the "Indio" thus appears rightfully linked to the land of the Americas. His genuine past constructs a territorialized idea of identity, which gives the "Indio" land-related rights. On one side, this idea constructs the community as the basic unit of production, where all its members have to work and collectively help each other (5:358). On the other side, this connection between the land and the community enables a geographical separation between peoples that can sustain some level of autonomy and difference. In turn, this geographically delineated unit constructs the community as the basis of statehood or political organization (5:316). The aggregate of communities forms a confederation of free peoples (5:433), creating the Inca Empire and Tawantinsuyu (realm of the four parts) (5:433). Roel similarly attributes the fraternal principle of "tinkuy" to the Inca Empire and its system of confederated nations (Roel 1980, 8).

As Reinaga states, this kind of system is the universal synthesis of history, the global liberation from oppression, and the last revolution for all peoples (Reinaga 2014b, 5:405). All the characteristics of this social order re-constructs the "true nation" of the "Indio" (5:496). They form the "millenary national being," which was hidden under the lie of "colonialism" (5:502). They are the flashes of memory that are in danger of disappearing when the "Indio" does not recover them to liberate himself and humanity (Mollinedo 1988). Here, a way of knowing and being is consistently connected to a way of enacting, which includes a dialectical temporality. Ontology, epistemology, and temporality thus became coherent dimensions of the Indianista discursive formation.

The Indio's revolution: Enacting the strategy of transformation

As I mention above, the Indianista epistemological authorization of the "Indio" allows him to enact "equality" by defining how transformation is possible, which includes discussions of who is the legitimate leader, who the revolution opposes, how "equality" can be institutionalized, and how liberation can be universal. In other words, Indianismo seeks to define how the "Indio's" past of "equality" can be reinstated in the near future. According to a number of Indianista intellectuals, the possibility of liberation can be fulfilled through a revolutionary process called "Pachakuti" (the return to what was before) (CSUTCB 2005, 69). This is the war and revolution of the "Indio," which begins by transforming Bolivian society, but then has to expand globally (69). Whenever institutionalized contexts of political participation remain open for the "Indio," the path towards the reconstruction of this past of "equality" can include "democracy." For example, the foundational document of the Indianista Party states that "Indios" can reach power through "democratic reason" (PIAK 2014, 5:341, author's translation). Conversely, if "colonialism" continues to exclude and oppress "Indios," they have to take up arms and begin a "total war" (Reinaga 2014b, 5:337). This action is understood as a "... holy war against everything that is and that represents the white race" (5:337). Here, the notion of "war" is not used as a mere metaphor for harsh political struggle; it is understood as a "long, ferocious, and bloody path towards liberation" (5:451). According to the foundational document of the Indianista Party, this revolution does not spare the sacrifice of life (PIAK 2014, 5:342).

The level of "exploitation" and "oppression" suffered by the "Indio" for centuries often justifies the violence and potential death that can emerge from war and revolution. Accordingly, Reinaga asserts, "we are more dangerous than that force, more dangerous than nuclear power. We are moved by hunger and hate. We will be victorious" (Reinaga 2014b, 5:345). The manifesto of the Tupakatarista Guerrilla Army similarly asserts that they seek "... to close the drama of the 500 years of colonialism by inaugurating the war of the Indio" (ERTK 2009, 175). The failures, betrayals, and treasons experienced during the processes of transformation that sought to utilize established institutionalized paths, also push towards more radical notions of revolution and war. In this regard, Ayar Quispe affirms that pacifist ways of transformation often go against history and common sense (A. Quispe 2009, 24). In 1988, the political declaration of the CSUTCB also claimed that "pacifism and legalism have failed and have only resulted in the death of our brothers" (CSUTCB 2009b, 134, author's translation). The declaration added:

> Companions ("compañeros"), our fight ought to be armed and violent, we have to affect the interests of the rich; sack, burn their cars, break the windows of their skyscrapers, until we make our oppressors feel … that this is our style of radical and communitarian struggle, the same struggle our grandparents fought against Spaniards, republicans, and liberals.
>
> CSUTCB 2009b, 135

Despite internal divisions and discussions about the different strategies that can be used for transformation, the discourse also makes violence possible against "colonial" people, "whites," "Occident," "mestizos," and "traitors" through the hierarchy that it constructs from its own ontological validation of an "equality" and epistemological authorization of an agent. These epistemic dimensions create or sustain a condition of possibility for violence. The hierarchical differentiation between the "reality" of the "Indio" and the "lies" of "whites" creates the possibility of "othering" everything that is "colonial." The ontological correspondence between "reality" and "equality" invalidates "colonial" hierarchies while the epistemological connection between the "Indio" and his "truth" devalues "colonial" "oppressors." This epistemic invalidation of "colonial" knowledge and deauthorization of "colonial" agents then enables political or even military action against those who participate in "coloniality." This position entails the firm identification of the "enemy" (CSUTCB 2005, 67). Accordingly, Reinaga asserts that the revolution of the "Indio" represents a "total war against everything that is and represents the white race" (Reinaga 2014b, 5:337). Similarly, Felipe Quispe writes that the Indianista war would "put all European whites on their way back to their territory" (F. Quispe 1988, 58).

Insofar as Revolutionary Indianismo consistently follows the *racial* definition of the fact of inheritance, "colonialism" becomes attached to biological and physical sets of characteristics of European "whites." In turn, these characteristics cannot be abandoned, liberated, or changed. The epistemological construction of a biological way of being "white" and "colonial" thus creates a problem for Indianismo. For example, Reinaga asserts that "the white man of occident has his own essential substance as an innate characteristic of his being: lie, robbery, exploitation, and fratricide" (Reinaga 2014b, 5:83). This essentialized and biological construction attaches the notion of "colonialism" to the very biological characteristics of "white" people that have few options of transformation or liberation. Similar to the notions of "mestizaje," the biological characteristics of "colonialism" can only be modified through racial mixture, but the results of such policies always entail lower positions for those classified as "hybrid" or "impure." The other solution can be separation, segregation, or exclusion, but if a particular group of people were to be biologically oriented towards domination, they could be viewed as biologically inconsistent with the capacity to live in a world where racial differences were respected. In the racial extreme of the spectrum that this analysis delineates for the fact of inheritance, a particular set of physical or biological characteristics can thus be rigidly linked to "colonialism" and they can locate a particular set of people in an invariably low position.

Despite this endogenous discursive coherence, it is important to note that Indianista intellectuals resist these implications. They often oppose this tendency and they view this racialized construction of "white" people as a problem. For example, Reinaga asserts:

> Between white racism and the Indio there is an abyss, while whites impose slavery, the Indio fights for liberation. Its revolution is liberating, it is not enslavement of anyone. The Indio does not seek the death of the "cholage;" what it ardently wants is for them to understand the reason of the Indio's liberation. The Indio is not the "Jew-killing" Nazi or the "anti-black" Yankee.
>
> Reinaga 2014b, 5:122

Moreover, Revolutionary Indianismo includes the possibility of alliance with and liberation for the "white" person. Even Reinaga asserts that Indianismo is not a new form of racism: "we do not judge man based on his skin color, we judge him based on the degree of truth that his spirit has. For us, race is not the color of flesh, it is the color of ideas" (Reinaga 2014b, 5:473).

To include this possibility of universalized liberation, racial understandings of "colonialism" had to be abandoned. They introduce into Indianismo an inconsistency that can only be solved by prioritizing the idea of nation. In its definition of a colonial "enemy," Indianismo has to explain how some knowledges and peoples *deviate* from the equality that is regarded as universal "reality." Insofar as race connects European people to a present and past of "colonialism," the explanation of their "colonial" deviation from the validated notion of "equality" leads either to the complete and unchangeable separation of the "white" European person from "humanity" or it undermines the very possibility of defining the fact of inheritance through the idea of race. In its discursive coherence, race delineates "colonialism" as deeply engraved in the very nature of European people. Their biological violation of the "true" characteristic of "humanity" thus makes them "non-humans." They are not "real" human beings. They have a different "nature," which does not fit the original characteristics of "equality," granted to the homo sapiens. This classification contradicts the Indianista universality of original "equality" and the possibility of re-including everyone within a universal form of liberation. Hence, the differences between peoples cannot be understood as biologically and naturally fixed. The hierarchicalization of "colonial" people thus has to be ultimately closer to the notion of nation. This explains why, after the 1990s, much of Revolutionary Indianismo pivots towards notions of nation, which construct the agents of "colonialism" as the ones who *intellectually* contradict their own "humanity." Because the deviation of the oppressor from the "true" characteristics of "humanity" is ideological, the idea of nation allows for "colonial" people to participate in the synthesis of history whenever they pedagogically liberate or change themselves. This understanding of deviation also gives oppressors a degree of "responsibility" in the decisions that they make about their own "coloniality."

The two sides of the fact of inheritance used by Revolutionary Indianismo thus create two separate tendencies, which enable intellectuals to discuss the role and place of "white" people more contextually. The notions of race and nation allow the discourse to retain internal ambiguity and diversity, which produce discussions about how much can be accepted from "white" people. However, even in the harsh historical context of dictatorships during the 1970s in Latin America, Reinaga asserts, "we are all born with different skin colors that we do not choose; this is no one's fault. The human being is, however, *responsible* for the ideas that he carries in his brain" (Reinaga 2014b, 5:473).

Despite this ambiguity and internal discussion, the concept of nation enables the discourse to have a more consistent logic, which can follow the epistemic tendency of universalization in all its dimensions, including liberation and transformation. The "Indio" hereby invokes the return to a past that deconstructs every "colonial," "unjust," "foreign," and "arbitrary" aspect of life. He seeks to enact the true "equality" of "humanity" that he has inherited. This political action of transformation is understood as the general liberation of "humanity" (MITKA 1977), but to achieve this level of universality Revolutionary Indianismo has to avoid the construction of another form of racism (Reinaga 2014b, 5:122). The revolution of the "Indio" thus has to enable a possibility for "white" Europeans to liberate themselves or to be liberated. Oppressors themselves have to be included in the last revolution and synthesis of history (5:426). Revolutionary Indianistas thus construct a single and universalized organization of history, which leads towards the Indianista revolution in a dialectical manner, finally enacting true human "equality." As Roel asserts, the cyclical notion of time often used by indigenous peoples is consistent with the idea of dialectics because the latter entails a return to the past, "but with a superior level of synthesis" (Roel 1980, 7). Reinaga also explicitly uses the notion of dialectics in much of his work during the early 1970s (Reinaga 2014b, 5:348).

Conclusion

Similar to the Marxist and liberal projects that are practiced in/for Bolivia and in/for International Relations, Revolutionary Indianismo universalizes a particular notion of equality and way of knowing, authorizes a specific kind of agent and way of being, and legitimizes a single type of political project and way of enacting. Despite the differences between these formations, both sets of discourses reinforce similar *epistemic tendencies*. Both kinds of discourses epistemically marginalize "other" ways of knowing, being, and enacting; they both tend to grant equality to some while also excluding "others." This similarity highlights the risks of using the master's tools to undo the master's house (Lorde 2018). The prioritization of a particular axis of power and struggle, authorization of a specific agent, and enactment of a single project creates "single-axis thinking," which limits the possibility of dialogue or ally-ship between different ways of knowing, being, and enacting social justice (Cho, Crenshaw, and McCall 2013, 787). This tendency towards the universalization of a particular experience is related to the epistemic assumptions that elevate the way of knowing, being, and enacting that is more "true" or more "real" than "others." Epistemic assumptions thus play important roles in the construction of more inequalities and the limitation of struggles (Mann 2013; Cho, Crenshaw, and McCall 2013; Collins 2015; Rivera 2015; Méndez 2018). Within its discursive boundaries, Revolutionary Indianismo reinforces these epistemic tendencies in several ways.

First, the Indianista utilization of a universalized *ontology* leads to the invalidation of other ways of knowing, equalities, struggles, and axes. Revolutionary Indianismo uses an ontological assumption that emerges from the fact of inheritance, validating a different form of equality and creating a distinct bedrock of classification. This definition of that which exists helps Revolutionary Indianismo to construct the hierarchy of knowledges that opposes "colonialism," liberalism, and Marxism; it allows for Indianistas to validate their own struggle against colonial projects of civilization, violence, inequality, oppression, and privilege. Despite the importance of this epistemic possibility, the single, superior, and universalized definition of "equality" also hierarchicalizes all other notions of equality and struggle. Revolutionary Indianismo excludes the possibility of respecting other forms of difference that do not quite fit its racial or nation-based equality. Notwithstanding its own goal of validating a hidden and silenced form of struggle, Revolutionary Indianismo promotes similar epistemic tendencies as Marxist and liberal projects for Bolivia and the world. This does not classify Indianismo as a moral equivalent to Marxism and liberalism, but it does show how *epistemic tendencies* create biases that regard other experiences of oppression as "obstacles" or as ideas that are "untrue" and therefore irrelevant.

Second, Indianismo universalizes its own *epistemological* form of authorization for the "Indio." Epistemology is a bridge that connects ontology and the definition of an authorized way of being. Thus, the epistemological connection between the ontology of the fact of inheritance, its validated idea of equality, and the "Indio" authorizes only this particular knower to be or to represent "equality," to define its specificities in the construction of a legitimate social order, and to draw the strategy that can lead to it. Within Revolutionary Indianismo, then, this universalized definition of a way of being creates three interrelated epistemic tendencies. On one side, the universalized authorization of the "Indio" creates a hierarchy not only against colonial "oppressors," but also organizing other voices into descending echelons. As I discuss in following chapters, other movements and demands of social or environmental justice become silenced by this kind of Indianismo.

The notion of a racial or nation-based connection between the "Indio" and a "true" past of "equality" is constructed by the idea of inter-generational relationships. By participating in this epistemological connection and by having the way of being that characterizes those who participate in "reality," the "Indio" appears as a superior agent of knowledge, liberation, and equality; whereas, "others" are viewed as wrong, lying, or oppressive. As the clandestine political manifesto of the MITKA asserts, this hierarchy prevents the "Indio" from relying on "representation" (MITKA 1977). Moreover, "only the Indio frees the Indio" (Reinaga 2014b, 5:495). Revolutionary Indianismo thus locates those who truly know "equality" as superior agents, separated from colonial actors and those who do not know the "truth" (5:476).

On the other side, this kind of authorization consistently helps Indianistas to universalize their way of enacting "equality." Here, the "Indio" becomes authorized to judge, organize, and classify history, constructing a dialectical temporality that is based on the ways in which epochs fit or contradict "equality." Then, the pre-conquest thesis of history is regarded as corresponding to the ontologically real "equality" of humanity and the inheritance of the "Indio." In the reconstruction of this epoch, the "Indio" can recover the social order that represents "equality." The epistemological authorization of a knower thus enables him to define the specificity of validated "equality." Then, the "Indio" can use this social order as a model to shape the synthesis of the future that will undo the contradiction of colonialism. Since he knows best, the "Indio" can also determine how this future can come to be. He can define the legitimate strategy of transformation. Here, a specific memory of a past, particular experience of an oppression, and consistent imaginaries of a revolution become a universalized reading of history, colonialism, and transformation. As the 1962 foundational document of the PIAK asserts, the "Indio" is the one who has to claim power and with it he has to liberate all of humanity (PIAK 2014, 5:342). As I further illustrate in other chapters, this epistemic tendency classifies other memories of the past, readings of the present, and imaginaries of the future as illegitimate ways of enacting "untrue" histories.

Finally, the universalized epistemological authorization of a particular knower enables him to determine the *level of specificity* that is required to enact the elevated way of being and knowing. The "Indio" can thus continue drawing the characteristics of "equality" and specifying his boundary of classification. In turn, this process of specification leads towards the marginalization of more characteristics attached to "colonialism," "enemies," and "oppressors." Revolutionary Indianismo thus ends up universalizing its communitarian social order as the global solution against "colonialism." This form of equality is based on the ideas of the ayllu, the collective organization of economic production, the confederate international system, etc. The epistemological connection between the "Indio" and his "true" past thus enables him to define the specificity of national or racial equality, which is hereby based on the Inca experience of communitarian organization. Then, intellectuals such as Reinaga organize all the characteristics that do not fit these specificities as parts of an "enemy." In this sense, Reinaga asserts that Indianismo is "… a war against everything that signifies the culture of Occident" (Reinaga 2014b, 5:338).

Revolutionary Indianismo thus ends up creating boundaries of classification that impose a specific form of "Indianista" civilization and nation. This tendency begs the question of how much "Occidental cultures" need to be transformed in order to avoid colonialism. Moreover, are there other experiences of ethnicity and social order that do not quite fit the specificities of this project? For example, much of the Indianismo Katarista that successfully took control of the CSUTCB in Bolivia often marginalized other forms of ayllu communitarianism and ethnic struggle (CSUTCB 1990, 109). Furthermore, the specification and epistemic elevation of a particular form of equality and social order leads towards two different ideas of liberation, which create homogenizing tendencies of territorialized social order. On one side, Revolutionary Indianismo seeks to construct a division between two Bolivias. This separatist movement aims to create a territory for the "Indio" and another territory dedicated to everything that represents "colonialism." Here, the "Indio" is separated from the internal colonialism that Bolivian "whites" or "mestizos" have imposed since the wars of independence (Reinaga 2014b, 5:159). The idea of two Bolivias thus separates the "Indio," who has inherited the glorious past of the Inca Empire and the ayllu system, from the "ridiculous republic, sad and unhappy parody of France" (5:168). This project continued to be an important goal of Revolutionary Indianismo until the early 2000s, when Felipe Quispe sought to construct a more separatist solution against the problems of neoliberalism and the crisis of Bolivia (Albró 2005, 434). On the other side, Fausto Reinaga states that this separation can only be an initial moment, which will then lead towards a universal solution against "colonialism." Occident thus has to be transformed to fit the global way of Indianista life. Because this kind of epistemology authorizes the "Indio" to define the specificities of "equality," only his way of being and knowing can prevail in the universal and global synthesis of history. To the contrary, everything that represents the "enemy" has to be transformed and abandoned.

Beyond these ontological, epistemological, and temporal tendencies, Revolutionary Indianismo includes another epistemic implication. The combination of these epistemic assumptions creates a tendency to constrain *reflexivity*. Indianismo includes its notions of equality, social order, "Indio," inequality, oppressor, revolution, and liberation as parts of a self-validated, self-authorized, and self-enacted formation. Revolutionary Indianismo is thus explicitly understood as a "dogma" and a harmonic form of unity (Reinaga 2014b, 5:345). "The Indio is racial unity, historic unity, religious unity, linguistic unity, economic unity, and the national subject. His past and present are factors of cohesion. And his future only posts one problem: his liberation" (5:158). This endogenous sedimentation and foreclosure of the discourse also explains why Felipe Quispe and the other intellectuals who participate in the development of the Indianista definition of the Warisata program of education assert that this political form of liberation entails a "solid basis of principles" (CSUTCB 2005, 65). Indianismo is thus regarded as "harmonious" and "perfect" (51). It is a coherent logic that creates an "a priori" and a clear mission (67–68). Similarly, Roel claims that Indianismo entails the "great unity" that organizes time and space (Roel 1980, 6–7). This philosophy, passed on to the "Indio" of the present by his "elderly," entails the equilibrium of "tinkuy" (24), which allows for some differences, but also dictates its own laws (27). The combination of high levels of epistemic certainty, authorization, legitimation, universalization, and this notion of "harmony" tends to foreclose the endogenous or intra-discursive possibility of discussing the boundaries of Indianismo and its limitations.

Of course this is only one synthetization of a movement that is highly disputed and constantly negotiated even by the same intellectuals that I cite in this chapter. To show some of the other approaches of the movement, I expand the discussion of Indianista resistance throughout the rest of the book. In Chapter Two, however, my goal is to examine the internal epistemic tendencies of this particular discourse and its anti-colonial opposition. In this sense, I illustrate the epistemic proximity between Revolutionary Indianismo and colonial discourses such as Marxism and liberalism. Similar to coloniality, Revolutionary Indianismo deploys a set of epistemic assumptions that tend to validate a single struggle, authorize a single voice, enact a single form of equality, and foreclose reflexive possibilities of questioning inadvertent tendencies. Notwithstanding these similarities, I refuse to equate colonial and anti-colonial ways of knowing, being, and enacting. That is, I do not claim that Revolutionary Indianismo, Marxism, and liberalism are equally colonial. This separation then begs the question of how they are in fact different. What separates colonial and anti-colonial discourses? This possibility of classification is a key condition of possibility for decolonial praxis, but how is it possible to construct such judgement while also avoiding epistemically colonial tendencies? How is it possible to separate colonial and anti-colonial discourses without sedimenting another definition of reality, equality, and power struggle?

Revolutionary Indianismo constructs this possibility of classification by erecting a foundation of "reality," authority, and legitimacy, but this epidemic strategy leads towards the marginalization of other "others." Another way of distinguishing Indianismo from colonial projects is to focus on the levels of violence, institutionalization, or "force" that each discourse acquires throughout history (Said 1978). It is obvious and undeniable that colonial projects both in Bolivia and other countries have had enormous consequences, whereas Revolutionary Indianismo has never been a fully governmental project. Despite this difference between colonial and anti-colonial projects, the utilization of extra-discursive elements such as the level of "force" or violence assumes particular bedrocks or foundations that exceed the realm of self-inquiry and reflexivity. The externalization, structuralization, or extra-discursive understanding of power assumes a materiality or foundation for practices, which can lead once again towards the universalization of a particular way of knowing, being, and enacting. That is, the notion of "force" pre-determines the definition of power and equality that appears to cause meaning from underneath. Then, this structure classifies practices even before they settle particular discourses. As approaches deploy this kind of bedrock of judgement, they tend to generalize their own definitions of struggle, voice, and project; they generalize and universalize their own praxis. Of course I do not deny colonial genocide, violence, oppression, and privilege; instead, I ask how colonialism can be resisted without creating yet more coloniality. I question the universalizing tendency that emerges when particular experiences are structuralized, single forms of classification are generalized, and colonial discourses are deployed irreflexively. I aim to avoid the construction of other forms of violence against other "others," questioning the possibility of using the master's tools to undo the master's house (Lorde 2018). Hence, how is it possible to avoid ignoring demands for transformation while also resisting more coloniality?

Another way to create a differentiation between Revolutionary Indianismo and colonial discourses could emerge through the study of the historical continuity of discourses. Insofar as coloniality entails practices that continuously marginalize similar characteristics of "others," it is possible to assert that liberalism and Marxism are different to Revolutionary Indianismo. In other words, Revolutionary Indianismo authorizes the "Indio" as an agent, creates a notion of racial or ethnic equality, and enacts a form of liberation that contradicts the continuous hierarchies of colonialism in Bolivia. In this sense, Indianismo validates, authorizes, and legitimizes another way of knowing, being, and enacting, which is different to the "Western" characteristics that have been validated, authorized, and enacted by discourses for centuries. Here, the *characteristics* of Indianismo differentiate the discourse from the "Western" constructions that actively invalidate racial equality, de-authorizing the "Indio" and enacting homogenizing projects. As Said asserts, colonialism entails a continuous reinforcement of "Western" characteristics as superior (Said 1978, 7). In the case of Bolivia, colonial discourses have continuously excluded indigenous ways of knowing, being, and enacting, but the Revolutionary form of Indianismo seeks to construct an anti-colonial project that aims to achieve the opposite. Despite this possibility of classification and separation, does Indianismo not claim a long history of struggles against colonialism? Does this antecedent not entail continuity? Does Revolutionary Indianismo not include practices that emerged at least in the 1960s? Moreover, if this continuity also includes silencing and marginalizing tendencies, is it not similar to colonialism? At this point, I often find myself tempted to say that colonial continuity entails institutionalization and "force," but this strategy of classification re-introduces solidifying bedrocks and universalizing tendencies; it returns to the epistemic problems of coloniality. Hence, continuity might not be a sufficient form of classification between colonial and anti-colonial discourses whenever epistemic politics are examined.

Again, I do not deny the experience of struggle of indigenous peoples in the Andes. Instead, I question the universalizing tendency that can be found in this particular construction of Revolutionary Indianismo. Additionally, I examine how it might be possible to sustain the validity of Revolutionary Indianismo while also listening to other "others." Here, the problem of difference re-emerges once more. How is it possible to classify "coloniality" and listen to anti-colonial struggles without universalizing a particular experience? If elevated assumptions of "reality," settled definition of equality, and fixed ideas of struggle lead towards universalization, how is it possible to move beyond that tendency while also creating a separation between those who "dominate" and those who "resist"? Here, the question of difference continues to confront the possibility of settling classifications, but decoloniality prevents us from abandoning separations as well. This is the tension of the problem of difference.

These questions are difficult to ask. Throughout this chapter, I seem to deconstruct and critique a project that is already marginalized and silenced in much of International Relations. Despite this appearance, I do not seek to invalidate Revolutionary Indianismo; instead, I question its universalizing tendency in order to investigate how we can further move beyond colonialism. This is how I enter the genealogical discussion of the problem of difference, trespassing geographic and disciplinary boundaries. More importantly, a number of Indianista intellectuals have tackled these epistemic questions and have successfully constructed other projects. For example, Reinaga continued his own work after 1974, investigating some of these epistemic problems and creating a less anthropocentric notion of ecological equality. Especially after 1978, the author examined epistemic politics, unveiling the problems of universalizing a particular form of humanism and seeking a possibility of constructing another way of knowing, being, and enacting. In order to achieve this goal, Reinaga constructed another anti-colonial project called Indianismo Amáutico, which I discuss in Chapter Three. Similarly, Evo Morales Ayma and Álvaro García Linera sought to move beyond some of these Revolutionary tendencies of epistemic totalization and they created another anti-colonial discourse. As I discuss in Chapter Four, they constructed a project of "plurinationality," which sought to avoid the homogenizing social order that Revolutionary Indianismo ended up universalizing. In an attempt to move beyond the epistemic limitations of colonial and anti-colonial discourses, some intellectuals in Bolivia also turned to post-structuralist notions. As I further discuss in Chapter Five, these intellectuals sought more radical possibilities of respecting differences, but post-structuralism was seldom able to create or distinguish decolonial alternatives. To the contrary, another set of discussions about the limitations and contributions of Revolutionary Indianismo emerged from feminist scholars, who pointed out that this branch of the movement often erased women's agency and ignored gendered experiences of ethnicity (Rivera 2010b, 218). To move beyond this problem, Rivera constructed a more intersectional form of decoloniality, which I discuss in Chapter Six. The legacies and limitations of Revolutionary Indianismo thus opened several doors in this genealogical struggle to define difference, enabling very important discussions. The following chapters engage these projects and their ideas, examining their epistemic assumptions, the benefits of intersectional decoloniality, and the implications for that emerge for International Relations.

Notes

1 "Indianismo" is the proper noun used to name the movement itself, "Indianista" is the adjective linking the movement to other elements, actors, or concepts, and "Indianistas" is the attributive noun denoting the bearer of the quality or attribute of the subject of Indianismo.
2 The Revolutionary branch of Indianismo retained a patriarchal tendency in its masculine construction of ethnicity and in its implicit relegation of gender-based injustices to secondary positions. Perhaps as a result of this issue, many intellectuals used the pronoun "he" to describe the "Indio" and the "man" ("hombre") of "humanity." In order to illustrate these biases, I decided to continue using the pronoun "he" throughout this chapter.
3 Somatology is understood as the part of anthropology that studies the human body. It is often connected to the study of the physical, anatomical, and physiological characteristics of the body.
4 "Cholage" is a pejorative way to describe people whose lineage entails a mixture of European and indigenous descendancy. They are also called "mestizos."
5 As I mentioned above, "cholage" is often used as a pejorative term that classifies "mestizos" or people who have a mixed descendancy of indigenous and European origin. In this case, Gabriel René Moreno uses the term to describe the "problems" of mixture and the "inferiority" of people who are not purely white. "Cholos" are thus the individuals who belong to the race of "cholage."
6 The word "q'ara" is a pejorative adjective used to describe "white" people of European descent.

References

Albró, Robert. 2005. "The Indigenous in the Plural in Bolivian Oppositional Politics." *Society for Latin American Studies* 24 (4): 433–453.

Ari, Waskar. 2014. *Earth Politics. Religion, Decolonization, and Bolivia's Indigenous Intellectuals*. Durham, NC: Duke University Press.

Assies, Willem. 2009. "Pueblos Indígenas y Sus Demandas En Los Sistemas Políticos." *Revista CIBOB d'Afers Internacionals*85: 89–107.

Calle, Iván Apaza. 2016. "Sobre Dos Axiomas Del Indianismo." *Pukara: Cultura, Sociedad y Política de Los Pueblos Originarios*, October 2016.Accessed April 27, 2020. https://drive.google.com/file/d/0B3a1FQjVcLZVWC1Td2ZYUEZpWTA/view.

Canessa, Andrew. 2005. *Natives Making Nation: Gender, Indigeneity, and the State in the Andes*. Tucson: University of Arizona Press.

Cho, Sumi, Kimberlé W. Crenshaw, and Leslie McCall. 2013. "Toward a Field of Intersectionality Studies, Applications, and Praxis." *Signs* 38 (4): 785–810.

Collins, Patricia Hill. 2015. "Intersectionality's Definitional Dilemmas." *Annual Review of Sociology* 41 (1): 1–20.

CSUTCB. 2005. *Pachakuti Educativo: Propuesta de La CSUTCB al II Congreso Nacional de Educación, Basada En El Modelo de Ayllu*. Bolivia: Artes Gráficas Abril.

CSUTCB. 2009a. "Propuesta de Declaración Política al IV Congreso Extraordinario de La CSUTCB (1989)." In *Los Tupakataristas Revolucionarios*, by Ayar Quispe. La Paz: Ediciones Pachakuti.

CSUTCB. 2009b. "Propuesta de Declaración Política al Primer Congreso Extraordinario de La CSUTCB (1988)." In *Los Tupakataristas Revolucionarios*, by Ayar Quispe. La Paz: Ediciones Pachakuti.

ERTK. 2009. "Manifiesto." In *Los Tupakataristas Revolucionarios*, edited by Ayar Quispe. La Paz: Ediciones Pachakuti.

Escobar, Arturo. 2010. "Latin America at a Crossroads: Alternative Modernizations, Post-Liberalism, or Post-Development?" *Cultural Studies* 24 (1): 1–65. https://doi.org/10.1080/09502380903424208.

Lorde, Audre. 2018. *The Master's Tools Will Never Dismantle the Master's House*. London: Penguin.

Makusaya, Carlos Cruz. 2014. *Desde El Sujeto Racializado. Consideraciones Sobre El Pensamiento Indianista de Fausto Reinaga*. Bolivia: MINKA.

Mann, Susan Archer. 2013. "Third Wave Feminism's Unhappy Marriage of Poststructuralism and Intersectionality Theory." *Journal of Feminist Scholarship* 4 (4): 54–73.

Méndez, María José. 2018. "'The River Told Me': Rethinking Intersectionality from the World of Berta Cáceres." *Capitalism Nature Socialism* 29 (1): 7–24.

Mignolo, Walter. 2000. *Local Histories/Global Designs: Coloniality, Subaltern Knowledges, and Border Thinking*. Princeton Studies in Culture/Power/History. Princeton, NJ: Princeton University Press.

Mignolo, Walter. 2012. "Decolonizing Western Epistemology/Building Decolonial Epistemologies." In *Decolonizing Epistemologies, Latina/o Theology and Philosophy*, edited by Ada María Isasi-Díaz and Eduardo Mendieta, 19–44. New York: Fordham University Press.

Mignolo, Walter, and Catherine E. Walsh. 2018. *On Decoloniality: Concepts, Analytics, and Praxis*. Durham, NC: Duke University Press.

MITKA. 1977. "Manifiesto Clandestino del MITKA." https://www.slideshare.net/wilmichu/mnifiestio-clandestino-del-mitka.

MITKA. 1978. "La Ideología de Indianismo II." Pukara: Cultura, Sociedad y Política de los Pueblos Originarions.

Mollinedo, Pedro Portugal. 1988. "Prologue." In *Tupak Katari Vive y Vuelve… Carajo*, by Felipe Quispe. La Paz: Ediciones Pachakuti.

MovimientoIndianista. 1973. "Primer Manifesto de Tiahuanaco." http://marianabruce.blogspot.com/2010/06/primer-manifiesto-de-tiahuanaco-1973.html.

PIAK. 2014. "Acta de Fundación." In *Fausto Reinaga: Obras Completas*, 5:341. Bolivia: Vicepresidencia del Estado Plurinacional.

Quispe, Ayar. 2009. *Los Tupakataristas Revolucionarios*. La Paz: Ediciones Pachakuti.

Quispe, Ayar. 2011. Entrevista a Ayar Quispe: Antropólogo y Militante IndianistaInternet. https://soundcloud.com/llajtainsurgente/entrevista-a-ayar-quispe-antropologo-y-militante-indianista.

Quispe, Felipe. 1988. *Tupak Katari Vive y Vuelve… Carajo*. La Paz: Ediciones Pachakuti.

Quispe, Felipe. 1999. *El Indio En Escena*. La Paz: Ediciones Pachakuti.

Reinaga, Fausto. 2014a. "El Manifiesto del Partido Indio de Bolivia." In *Fausto Reinaga: Obras Completas*, 5, by Fausto Reinaga, 337–408. La Paz: Vicepresidencia del Estado Plurinacional.

Reinaga, Fausto. 2014b. *Fausto Reinaga: Obras Completas*. 10 vols. La Paz: Vicepresidencia del Estado Plurinacional.
Reinaga, Fausto. 2014c. "Revolución India." In *Fausto Reinaga: Obras Completas*, 5, by Fausto Reinaga, 405–410. La Paz: Vicepresidencia del Estado Plurinacional.
Rivera Cusicanqui, Silvia. 1990. "Liberal Democracy and Ayllu Democracy in Bolivia: The Case of Northern Potosí." *The Journal of Development Studies* 26 (4): 97–121.
Rivera Cusicanqui, Silvia. 2010a. *Oprimidos Pero No Vencidos. Luchas Del Campesinado Aymara y Quechua, 1900–1980*. La Paz: La Mirada Salvaje.
Rivera Cusicanqui, Silvia. 2010b. *Violencias (Re) Encubiertas En Bolivia*. La Paz: La Mirada Salvaje.
Rivera Cusicanqui, Silvia. 2010c. "The Notion of 'Rights' and the Paradoxes of Postcolonial Modernity: Indigenous Peoples and Women in Bolivia." *Qui Parle: Critical Humanities and Social Sciences* 18 (2): 29–54. doi:10.5250/quiparle.18.2.29.
Rivera Cusicanqui, Silvia. 2012. "Ch'ixinakax Utxiwa: A Reflection on the Practices and Discourses of Decolonization." *South Atlantic Quarterly* 111 (1): 95–109. doi:10.1215/00382876-1472612.
Rivera Cusicanqui, Silvia. 2015. *Sociología de la Imagen. Miradas Ch'ixi Desde La Historia Andina*. Buenos Aires: Tinta Limón.
Roel, Virgilio. 1980. "Indianidad y Revolución: Raíz y Vigencia de la Indianidad." London: Editorial Alfa, S.A. https://catalog.hathitrust.org/Record/006004509.
Said, Edward W. 1978. *Orientalism*. New York: Vintage Books.
Thomson, Sinclair. 2002. *We Alone Will Rule: Native Andean Politics in the Age of Insurgency* (Living in Latin America). Madison: University of Wisconsin Press.
Ticona, Esteban Alejo. 2000. *Organización y Liderazgo Aymara, La Experiencia Indígena En La Política Boliviana, 1979–1996*. Cochabamba: AGRUCO, Agroecologia Universidad Cochabamba, Universidad de la Cordillera.
Ticona, Esteban Alejo. 2011. *Bolivia En El Inicio Del Pachakuti: La Larga Lucha Anticolonial de Los Pueblos Aimara y Quechua*. La Paz: Akal Ediciones S.A.
Ticona, Esteban Alejo. 2013. *El Indianismo de Fausto Reinaga: Orígenes, Desarrollo y Experiencia En Qullasuyu-Bolivia*. Ecuador: Universidad Andina Simón Bolívar.
Todorov, Tzvetan. 1982. *The Conquest of America: The Question of the Other*. Norman: University of Oklahoma Press.

3 Indianismo Amáutico and the universalization of an "Other"

Revolutionary Indianismo has been practiced in public debates and collective political settings primarily in Bolivia, but also in other countries of the Andes. By contrast, the intellectual construction of Indianismo Amáutico implied a less collective endeavor. The emergence of this anti-colonial and systematically defined approach can be traced more specifically to the later books of Fausto Reinaga and some of the ideas found in the work of his son, Ramiro Reynaga.[1] Both Fausto Reinaga and Ramiro Reynaga claim that their intellectual production emerges from a widely shared set of "indigenous" notions (Reinaga 2014, 6:171, author's translation). Despite the potentially shared characteristics of these Andean notions, Fausto Reinaga and Ramiro Reynaga synthetize them in a particular way, which shows that anti-colonial approaches can expand their respect for difference; they can include other struggles such as ecological concerns.

Despite their shared anti-colonial stance, the main differences between Revolutionary Indianismo and Indianismo Amáutico are their ontological foundations, the degree to which they critique anthropocentrism, their focus on ecological equality, and their discussions of cosmology. Even before his father, Ramiro Reynaga began emphasizing the cosmological notions of the "religion of the Indio" and he sought to oppose anthropocentrism. In 1972, R. Reynaga asserted:

> The Indio's conception of life and of the universe continues to be naturalist and cosmological. The Indio does not feel like a master of nature, he does not label himself the king of creation because he still feels like the son of earth and of the sun. The Indio is located in the middle of a dynamic and vital harmony, where stars, plants, animals, and everything that exists have the right to be.
>
> Reynaga 1972, 45, author's translation[2]

Fausto Reinaga began focusing on these ideas in his book *América India y Occidente* (Indian America and Occident) in 1974, when the author engaged with cosmological notions and discussions of anthropocentrism to push his own intellectual production deeper into the examination of the epistemic roots of Occidental colonialism. F. Reinaga found the cause of this problem in the Occidental notion of "reason," which was considered to be universal, but often located a single form of European "humanity" as above nature and other peoples (Reinaga 2014, 6:51). Against these colonial tendencies and the forms of violence that unfolded from them, F. Reinaga saw a liberating possibility in the cosmology of the "Indio" (6:171).

In 1978, F. Reinaga further synthesized, systematized, and defined the ramifications of these ideas in his book *La Razón y el Indio* (Reason and the Indio), which thoroughly inaugurated his Amáutico phase.[3] As Esteban Alejo Ticona asserts, this is the third intellectual phase of F. Reinaga and it "is a search for the possibility of life in the world" (Ticona 2013, 209, author's translation). After 1978, F. Reinaga continued writing until 1991, three years before he passed away, and he expanded his work with 15 more books and essays. Throughout this set of discussions, the author noticed that the universalization of an anthropocentric, humanist, and Occidental ontology led towards ecocide and racism. Consequently, F. Reinaga followed cosmological notions from the Andes to denounce colonialism and to construct a possibility of equality for all the other entities coexisting within the Cosmos (Reinaga 2014, 5:227). This cosmological notion has important implications for the construction of the institutionalized project of plurinationality in Bolivia, which I discuss in Chapter Four, and it highlights the possibility of expanding anti-colonial projects beyond "humanism." Despite these ramifications, Indianismo Amáutico uses an essentialist and universalizing ontology, authorizing a single anti-colonial voice and marginalizing other experiences of struggle; it sustains the epistemic tendencies of colonialisms by marginalizing other "others."

Indianismo Amáutico is cosmic reality: Validity and equality

As F. Reinaga states, Occidental assumptions of anthropocentric knowledge, technology, and progress lead towards the construction of nuclear weapons (Reinaga 2014, 5:93) and the destruction of the environment (6:176). Some of the ecological and cosmological concerns that are discussed by F. Reinaga in his Amáutico phase are also taken into account by Revolutionary Indianistas. For example, the collective works of several intellectuals in the CSUTCB claim that the possibility of reconstructing the educational system of Bolivia emerges from the wisdom shared by their ancestors (CSUTCB 2005, 41). This inheritance authorizes the "Indio" to be connected to the communitarian system of the ayllu, which includes equality among nations and with nature. The ontology of the fact of inheritance thus authorizes a subject to organize and assimilate a possibility of ecological equality, but it also reinforces its own "humanism" and it prioritizes national or racial equality above other struggles. As a result, even though some Revolutionary authors try to locate Pachamama above "humanity" (e.g., Roel 1980, 4), they often contradict this notion and they end up prioritizing "human" struggles.

While trying to avoid humanist ontologies, F. Reinaga builds a foundation and basis of commonality that equalizes "humans" and other entities. He moves beyond the ontological notion of inheritance to discuss broader characteristics of what is "real," validating the equality of all entities. In order to create this foundation, F. Reinaga locates the Cosmos first. He understands the undeniable "reality" of the Cosmos as the foundation that validates the rest of the discourse. "To think is to know. To know what? To know what is, how is, and what it is for: to be that is. And what is that is? The Cosmos is that is" (Reinaga 2014, 6:403). Or, in other words, "What exists? The Cosmos exists" (6:225). From this ontological status of "reality," F. Reinaga grants existence and validity to a relationship of equality among all the elements of the Cosmos.

Hence, consistent with some Andean understandings of Pachamama, F. Reinaga substantiates this ontology through the discussion of the cosmological coexistence between all the different entities of the universe; he defines that which is "real."

> Every planet of each system, every system of each galaxy exists inside laws of cohesion and interdependence. From their joined work, or, better yet, from their solidary movement emerges the being and the existence of each galaxy, each system, each planet, each man.
>
> Reinaga 2014, 6:234

For F. Reinaga, this relationship of coexistence presupposes a cosmological and non-anthropocentric form of equality in difference:

> The Mayan thinker had reached the conclusion that man was created by the same creators of earth and that he was not *an* exceptional being inside of nature; he is only one part in it. He realized that man, just like nature, had to obey the laws of nature, just like plants, beasts, birds, insects.
>
> Reinaga 2014, 6:227

This ontologically validated relationship of equality in difference surges from the universally shared "co-substantiation" of all entities (Reinaga 2014, 6:33). The essence of all the entities of the universe appears to be connecting everything through a basis of commonality and a relationship that entails different combinations of matter and/or energy. Every different entity exists as a particular combination of shared elements of nature. This possibility of sharing the elements of the Cosmos provides a basis of commonality for every existence. F. Reinaga illustrates this notion through the description of Mayan ideas, which Itzá intellectuals proposed (6:227). Whether the basic elements of entities are water, fire, matter, energy, the sun, or earth, is a secondary issue. The main purpose of this idea is to demonstrate that the components that make up every entity form a basis of universal and cosmological commonality. The shared co-substantiation of every being thus creates a positive platform of commonality, which grants equality to every entity, erecting one of the principles that constitutes Amáutico coexistence.

Additionally, F. Reinaga defines cosmic coexistence as based on difference. Since the Cosmos results from the infinite aggregation of every entity or thing in it, all differences equally compose the complex relationship of cosmic coexistence. The fact that each entity is different and is a distinct part of the complex aggregate that makes up Pachamama grants equal status to every live or inert existence. Since it is based on the idea that entities are separate and missing something vis-à-vis each other, difference appears as a negative principle of equality.

Notwithstanding the analytical separation between the positive and negative principles of cosmic equality, every combination of the shared elements of the universe is different and it makes up a distinct entity. Hence the positive and negative principles of equality are hereby combined consistently into a notion of equality in difference. In the combination of these two principles, F. Reinaga constructs coexistence as a relationship of interdependence and solidarity. The positive commonality of everything provides a connection between all entities, while the negative notion of difference allows for their distinction. On one side, difference draws a Cosmos constituted by entities that can be divergent things and can have separate roles. On the other side, these entities are connected in their co-substantiation and they are parts of an overarching relationship of solidarity and interdependence. "Between all the parts and the whole there is an interrelation, community, and solidarity. From the common effort of all emerges a collective and harmonic action" (Reinaga 2014, 6:223).

Epistemically contradicting equality in difference

Within F. Reinaga's notion of equality in difference, no single entity appears as superior and the role of each being is viewed as equally important. Therefore, "man" loses his authority to control or dominate the universe; he becomes an equal element within cosmic coexistence. "Man outside of the Cosmos is nothing, he does not exist" (Reinaga 2014, 6:387). This idea often pushes F. Reinaga to question the epistemological superiority and authority of "humanity." "For the Amáutico mentality, man thinks, ants think, and trees think too. From somewhere emerges the possibility of thinking. Neither man, nor the ant, nor the tree can think without the Sun." (6:403). Here, the Sun is the energy that enables the experience of coexistence, but each entity has the equal capacity to access and experience the light of the Sun. The underlying equality of coexistence thus pushes F. Reinaga to grant equal epistemological authority to other entities found in "nature."

Despite this possibility of following the ontological notion of equality in difference consistently towards epistemological equality, F. Reinaga avoids the relativism that can emerge from authorizing several or contradictory knowers at the same time. For example, he vehemently rejects the paralyzing relativism that Occidental notions construct from nihilist ideas of knowledge. To him, this is another consequence of the "darkness of reason" (Reinaga 2014, 6:225). Similarly, Ramiro Reynaga affirms that Indianismo has to be able to define a possibility of struggling against colonialism, domination, and oppression. Indianismo needs to be able to determine its "enemy" (Reynaga 1972, 103). In order to achieve these goals, F. Reinaga uses an essentialist understanding of ontology, which constructs the possibility of a single "reality" from the inner characteristics or essence of separate entities. In this Amáutico cosmology, every entity is regarded as equal, but their relationship of coexistence emerges from the "real" characteristics of difference and co-substantiation, which each entity shares in its very essence.

Regardless the cosmological idea of equality in difference, F. Reinaga thus utilizes a notion of single "reality" to authorize those who can access this truth above others who ignore it. Then, the author deploys this essentialist notion of ontology to grant epistemological superiority to "humanity." He uses the idea of co-substantiation to say that "humanity" is directly connected to the essence of all other entities. This connection epistemologically enables a "humanity" to experience the single "reality" of the Cosmos. "Man, with an even greater right, must make his instinct into mentality, his mentality into reason, his reason into consciousness, his consciousness into liberty" (Reinaga 2014, 6:382). Here, "man" appears as superior in his epistemological access of "reality," which gives him the greater right to define the objective relationship between all the entities of the universe. "Man" is regarded as an equal entity in his co-substantiation and his own difference, but he also appears as superior in his authority to define the Cosmos for everything and everyone else. F. Reinaga thus constructs a non-anthropocentric ontology, but he then follows the essentialist understanding of the Cosmos to build an anthropocentric epistemology that authorizes a particular "humanity" or way of being. Here, "the Amáutico man, unlike the Socratic man of Occident, is the consciousness of the Cosmos. He is the Cosmos made Amáutico consciousness" (6:405).

Who is and knows the Cosmos?: The "Indio" and cosmological equality

By emphasizing an essentialist reading of ontology, then, F. Reinga contradicts the cosmological notion of equality in difference and he epistemologically authorizes a particular entity above others. To achieve this goal, the author begins by claiming that "humanity" is part of the Cosmos because it is also "co-substantiated." "Humanity" is matter and energy as is everything else (Reinaga 2014, 6:33). In this essential connection with the Cosmos, however, "humanity" appears as an "antenna," which receives and transmits messages from the universe (6:33). This notion conceives "humanity" as capable of understanding and knowing the logic of coexistence that emerges from the characteristics of the entities of the Cosmos. According to F. Reinaga, this epistemological capacity to know the Cosmos is found in "human" thought, which is the mechanism that organizes all the "signals" received by "man" when he acts as the co-substantiated "antenna." This is how F. Reinaga is able to claim that the mentality of the "Indio" Amáutico corresponds to the laws of the Cosmos (6:356).

The shared essence of all entities is thus used by F. Reinaga to authorize the thoughts of those who belong in the Cosmos. This creates a connection between "humanity" and the Cosmos in an epistemological commonality between the energy of human thought and cosmic "reality." In other words, "humanity" is one with the Cosmos because it shares its energy in the possibility of "real" thought. Then, the author asserts that language directly expresses thought, and thought is only possible through language. This interconnection or correspondance between language and thought explains why F. Reinaga asserts that "the quality of a mentality and a thought is included in the quality of a language. There are no thoughts without words, and there are no words without thoughts" (Reinaga 2014, 6:235). Since language and thought are connected to each other and they correspond to the objective characteristics of the Cosmos, F. Reinaga then chooses to study expressed meanings in order to find "man's" thought of the Cosmos. Language hereby becomes the empirical datum or indicator that represents thought and the Cosmos. In other words, the Cosmos is co-substantiation, co-substantiation includes energy, thought is energy, thought corresponds to language, and language-related meanings represent thought.

This epistemological bridge gives "humanity" its "special right" to know the Cosmos. In turn, those who practice meanings and languages that are consistent with the positive and negative principles of equality appear as authorized ways of being. That is, ontology determines what is "real," epistemology creates a possibility of a connection with "reality," and the meanings that are consistent with "reality" begin to draw the characteristics of those who have "real" thoughts. F. Reinaga thus seeks to study the "real" meanings and thoughts that correspond to the Cosmos. Since the "religion of the Indio" is consistent with the "reality" of the Cosmos, F. Reinaga studies the possibility of cosmic coexistence from the language of the "Indio" and the meanings that still resist the influence of colonialism (Reinaga 2014, 6:235). In other words, the "Indio" has the epistemological connection and the characteristics of cosmic "reality;" he has superior observational capacities (6:234). Then, the author interprets the ways in which stories, documents, and monuments attribute certain characteristics to indigenous societies. To him, the Mayan calendar, the ayllu of the Andean world, the Pop Vuh of Guatemala, and the Calpulli of Mexico contain the meanings that are consistent with cosmic coexistence and can help him to construct the Amauta community (6:237). The epistemological chain of connections between a language and a "reality" delineates the characteristics of a way of being that is authorized as the one who accesses or is the Cosmos.

Enacting "reality:" The "Indio" and ecological equality

Since a particular set of "thoughts" and a single kind of "reality" are hereby epistemologically connected, the study of "real" meanings leads to the specification of the Cosmos and the "Indio." Meanings further enact a way of being that corresponds to "reality." For example, F. Reinaga claims that "indigenous" children in the Andean region of Latin America often grow up socialized by teachings that are consistent with the laws of the Cosmos (Reinaga 2014, 6:34). According to these stories, even a tiny plant of corn becomes an entity that is equal to the child growing up and to "humanity" more in general. In their co-substantiation, the shared elements that make up both entities display their equality within the Cosmos. Their difference shows the value that each one of them gains as a complementary part of aggregated coexistence. Here, the very existence of the child only becomes possible thanks to the solidarity and interdependence of the Cosmos.

F. Reinaga affirms that the specificities of the Cosmos can also be found in the meanings that shape current forms of "indigenous" social order. Accordingly, the author asserts that Sak'abamba is an example of a society that explicitly regards "humanity" as an equal entity in the Cosmos. Here, "humanity" only takes from Mother Earth what it needs and it avoids the individualist accumulation of natural resources (Reinaga 2014, 6:206). Sak'abamba has a relationship of complementarity and solidarity with nature and it prevents the anthropocentric accumulation of everything. As this example shows, the specification of cosmic coexistence leads to a notion of ecological equality with "nature."

F. Reinaga finds another possibility of specifying "reality" and the "Indio's" way of being in the Inca principle of "ama llulla, ama suwa, ama qhilla" (do not lie, do not steal, and do not be lazy), which hereby acquires a different meaning than it has within the Revolutionary branch of Indianismo. To the Amauta, this precept is related to the laws of the Cosmos. Hence, lies entail contradictions against Amáutico "reality." Stealing is the violation of the equality between "man" and "nature." Since, accumulation is regarded as stealing from Mother Earth and from other entities of the Cosmos, the accumulation and depletion of nature is understood as inconsistent with the cosmic equality of co-substantiation and difference (Reinaga 2014, 6:179). Finally, laziness is viewed as a possibility that emerges from private property. According to F. Reinaga, private property is the mechanism that allows owners to exploit others, avoiding work and renouncing their participation in the cosmic requirement of solidarity.

Overall, then, F. Reinaga constructs an ontological definition of coexistence; he builds an idea of equality with nature, which includes a notion of commonality and leads to the possibility of connecting "reality" to particular meanings. In turn, these meanings belong to the "Indio," who knows and accesses the Cosmos. Hence, the study of these meanings is the simultaneous specification of the Cosmos and the "Indio." In this discourse, a way of knowing becomes a specified way of being. Ontology and epistemology are intertwined in the construction of the Cosmos and the "Indio."

Who is and knows humanity: The "Indio" and nation

Despite this epistemological possibility of having a direct connection to "reality" and being one with the Cosmos, "humanity" has a thought-related commonality that is shared only by "humans;" it has a distinguishing characteristic, essence, and difference. That is, the Amáutico cosmology entails the commonality and equality that connects "humanity" and the rest of the Cosmos. The positive cosmological equality, epistemological connection, specification of ecological equality, and authorization of the "Indio" construct the oneness of a singular and universal "reality." On the other side, the Amáutico cosmology includes the negative principle of equality in difference, which separates each entity. Hence, F. Reinaga examines how "humanity" is an entity in itself; he investigates the "essence" of "humanity," determining what separates or distinguishes it from the rest of the Cosmos.

To achieve this goal, the author finds the commonality or characteristic that can be understood as the essence of "humanity." Unlike Revolutionary Indianismo, the F. Reinaga of Indianismo Amáutico cannot seek the characteristic that defines "humanity" in a common origin of a specie; he cannot distinguish "humanity" by using notions of "creation" and "inheritance." Instead, the author finds this separation in the particularity of "human" thought; he distinguishes "humanity" by defining how the "energy" of the Cosmos adapts into a bounded commonality that makes up the "human" entity itself. In other words, F. Reinaga uses the same epistemological connection that he establishes between cosmic "reality" and a way of being to find the distinguishing characteristic that constructs "humanity" as a particular kind of commonality and equality. To construct cosmological coexistence and to specify the ecological equality of the "Indio," he emphasizes the positive principle of equality and creates the epistemological connection between thought and "reality." Instead, the author emphasizes the negative principle of equality to construct "humanity," and he creates an epistemological possibility of distinctness.

As a result of his epistemological connection between "reality" and thought, F. Reinaga can study the meanings and languages that are "real," or consistent with the Cosmos, and he can separate "humanity." "Real" thoughts and meanings thus ought to show the essence and bounded commonality of "humanity." According to the author, this boundary can be initially illustrated by the traces of Mayan language that can be found in other languages of the world (Reinaga 2014, 6:228). These traces exemplify the possibility of an underlying commonality in the thought that is shared only by "humanity." Despite this linguistic proximity, F. Reinaga does not find the distinguishing essence of "humanity" in the hypothesis of a Mayan etymological origin for all languages. Instead, he determines the essence of this entity by re-incorporating and assimilating the notion of "nation" into the Amáutico discourse. Here, "nation" is the thought that distinguishes "humanity" from other entities. "Nation" is the "human" aspect of cosmic energy; it is the thought that includes "humanity" as a distinct entity of the Cosmos; it is the relationship of equality that separates this entity in its own difference.

To F. Reinaga, the idea of "nation" is the essence of "humanity" in the Cosmos because it respects the laws of the Cosmos. In other words, the definition of the essence of "humanity" is hereby regarded as "real" because it corresponds to the "reality" of the Cosmos. In order to be the "real" essence of "humanity," then, "nation" has to follow coherently the positive and negative principles of equality. Thus, F. Reinaga understands each "nation" as equal because they are all co-substantiated by the essence or thought of "humanity." On the other side, each "nation" is also different because they entail distinct combinations of this essence. In other words, "nations" are all different combinations of the essence, energy, or thought of "humanity." Then, each person is valued because they are also parts of "humanity" and "nation." They are discrete entities within broader relationships of commonalities. "Nation" thus turns "humanity" into a different and unique entity, but it also makes it "real." The epistemological connection between the "reality" of the Cosmos and the difference of a "human" way of being thus authorizes the particularity of a distinct set of thoughts and meanings. Then, "real" meanings can be used to specify the commonality and equality that make up the essence of "humanity." F. Reinaga can then study the "real" meanings of "nation."

Enacting "humanity:" The "Indio" and cosmic socialism

Similar to the notion of cosmological and ecological equality, F. Reinaga specifies "human" equality by studying the "real" meanings and thoughts that are found in the language of the "Indio." The epistemological connection between "reality" and the "Indio" thus authorizes the meanings that are consistent to the Cosmos as "real;" they are the nation-based essence of "humanity" in the Cosmos. The thought of the "Indio" is thus the "reality" of the Cosmos and the "reality" of "humanity." For example, the author views Sak'abamba as a community where peoples from different nations and races coexist in accordance to the laws of the Cosmos (Reinaga 2014, 6:510). This idea of national equality in difference entails the possibility of relationships of solidarity, where each people and each individual is viewed as a key component of a complementary relationship of communal or "human" production (6:237).

Additionally, F. Reinaga specifies this "human" possibility of equality in the study of "cosmic socialism," which puts the ayllu community as the basic unit of equality (Reinaga 2014, 6:177). Here, each ayllu, nation, or shared thought creates a flexible community, which is equal to other communities in its shared "humanity" and different in its national distinctiveness. Each ayllu thus becomes a unit of organization and equality.

Epistemic implications: Assimilation, universalization, and enemies

The singular, universal, and ontological "reality" of the Cosmos, together with the epistemological attachment of this "reality" to a particular way of being and the enactment of specificities, creates at least four epistemic implications. First, the ontological "reality" of the "Cosmos" constructs the "certainty" of the Amáutico mentality (Reinaga 2014, 6:388). Second, F. Reinaga uses the epistemological connection between "reality" and the "Indio's" ways of being to open a field of knowledge, which seeks to delineate the specificities of the Cosmos. Insofar as "sciences" can be used to understand and then follow the laws of the Cosmos, they can be regarded as authorized forms of knowledge, which can help the "Indio" Amáutico. Accordingly, F. Reinaga asserts that the mission of "humanity" is the expansion of cosmic knowledge towards the comprehension of the inner characteristics of "humanity" and towards the study of the laws of the cosmos as they relate to the environment, galaxy, etc. (6:356). Different forms of sciences, such as biology, astronomy, medicine, physics, etc., thus become reoriented towards the study of cosmic coexistence. This explains why F. Reinaga claims that the possibility of transformation that emerges with the Amáutico mentality is "scientific" (8:42).

By using sciences, F. Reinaga aims at specifying the laws of the Cosmos and the essence of entities. To achieve this goal, the author defines the "reality" of the Cosmos as the articulating and assimilating logic that unites two levels of equality. He uses the idea of difference in equality as the general principle that assimilates other relationships of commonalities and equality such as "humanity" and "nation." The overarching "reality" of coexistence (i.e., the negative and positive principles of equality) thus becomes the "harmonious" logic that assimilates the bounded commonality (i.e., essence) and intra-entity equality of "humanity" (Reinaga 2014, 6:197).

To achieve this construction of oneness and assimilation, the specificities of cosmological equality and the specificities of "human" equality have to meet each other in "real" thoughts and a "real" social order; they have to be consistent. Hence, F. Reinaga uses the notion of the ayllu as the core of his social and ecological organization. The ayllu becomes the harmonious and "real" way to relate peoples among themselves and with the rest of the Cosmos. According to the author, each one of the communities sharing particular meanings can form equally different ayllus. Each ayllu is thus constituted by a communitarian thought that identifies each people. Since they are all parts of "humanity" and they share the thought of "nation," each ayllu is equally different. Then, the territory that is used by each ayllu becomes a part of their shared meanings. This connection between land and thought authorizes the communal utilization of a land for the satisfaction of needs; it creates the possibility of an ecological relationship with nature (Reinaga 2014, 6:237).

This form of social and ecological organization does not allow for accumulation and competition in communal or individualist terms. Since each community is an equally different part of "humanity," they have to recognize each other, and they also have to sustain porous boundaries. In other words, ayllus have to remain open because they belong to broader commonalities; they are all nations, which are "human" thoughts and energy of the Cosmos. Moreover, the notion of the ayllu prevents material accumulation, which is the source of inequality, exploitation, hunger, and the destruction of the environment (Reinaga 2014, 6:364). Instead, this communal form of organization satisfies the needs of all its members while also respecting the equality of Mother Earth.

According to F. Reinaga, this form of social order is perfect because it is in harmony with the laws of the Cosmos. "The mentality of the New World, the Mentality of the Indio, builds a perfect society; a society unique in history" (Reinaga 2014, 6:185). Here, the Tawantinsuyu represents an overarching confederation that unites all the ayllus and communities of "humanity." F. Reinaga thus proposes a single and global organization that respects equally different nations and promotes their communal balance with nature (6:199). This global unity is the universalized oneness of the Cosmos and the Indio, which becomes a single unity in his mentality, language, and Amáutico government (6:235). "The universe of the Indio will return to be one single ayllu" (6:185). As other authors have pointed out, this tendency universalizes a particular form of social order and identity within each territory and even globally (Viaña, Claros, and Sarzuri-Lima 2010, 18).

Third, these specificities of "reality" authorize the way of being of the "Indio" and they construct him as the main knower or agent of the Cosmos. Unlike Revolutionary Indianismo, the Amáutico authorization of the "Indio" is no longer possible thanks to an epistemological connection to an authentic and pre-colonial past. Instead, authorization hereby emerges from the language of the "Indio" (Reinaga 2014, 6:236). The epistemological connection between "reality" and the language of the "Indio," explains how his consistency with the Cosmos emerges from his possibility to know cosmic truth. This elucidates why F. Reinaga insists that he is the one re-constructing the Amáutico mentality from "indigenous" meanings and languages (6:424). Moreover, F. Reinaga asserts that the Inca's consciousness is the Cosmos; it is the consciousness of "truth" and "liberty" (6:211). From this epistemological authorization, F. Reinaga creates a hierarchy. The different levels of proximity between diverse ways of being and the Cosmos organize the echelons that every mentality occupies. Here, the "Indio" is understood as a total unity with the Cosmos; his universe and his "self" are a single and absolute identity (6:234). Thus, the "Indio" appears a superior subject in his mentality, participation in the Cosmos, and proximity to "reality." Within the definition of the "Indio's" way of being, moreover, F. Reinaga points out that Amautas are the masters who study and discover the laws of the Cosmos (6:376). Since they are the true representatives of the Sun on earth, they are owed respect, obedience, and love

(6:377). F. Reinaga thus uses the epistemological connection between "reality" and the Amautas to authorize this main agent to rule. This authority entitles the Amauta to protect and regulate the equality between different nations and their relationships with the rest of the Cosmos. In the global organization of a confederate system, Amautas protect cosmic coexistence as it is specified through the notions of "human" and ecological equality. Those who know the Cosmos thus become legitimate rulers. This explains why F. Reinaga asserts that the World Amáutico Community requires the rule and government of an Amáutico Council. "The government of the world can only be integrated by geniuses or by a single genius, an Amáutico genius who, together with his Sun-brain, has a cosmic heart. The authority and jurisdiction of the Amáutico Government is global" (8:159).

To a certain extent, F. Reinaga still seeks to be consistent with the non-anthropocentric equality of cosmic coexistence and he claims that the Cosmos rules over "humanity." He states, for example, that the control of population and the usage of nature depends on the capacity of production of earth. People have to decrease or increase procreation based on the laws of the Cosmos and their relationship with a finite earth (Reinaga 2014, 6:368). F. Reinaga thus tries to locate the Cosmos above "humanity." To him, universal order emerges from the universe itself. "Man is the Cosmos. Man has not created the Cosmos. It is the other way around" (6:381).

Despite the supremacy initially granted to the Cosmos, the possibility of accessing and knowing the law of the Cosmos gives "humanity" its throne back. In its knowledge of universal "reality," "humanity" becomes re-authorized to specify and rule ecological and "human" relations. Since he knows the "real" laws of the Cosmos, the "Indio" can represent the Cosmos and rule on its behalf. The way of being of the "Indio" thus becomes the universal "reality" of coexistence for every other entity. As a consequence of this epistemological authorization, F. Reinaga is able not only to legitimize who ought to rule over the global Tawantinsuyu, but also to classify other ways of being that are not in harmony with "reality." He authorizes the way of being that is closest to "reality" while also de-authorizing the characteristics of those who are epistemologically farther; he defines the "enemy" of Indianismo Amáutico.

Fourth, F. Reinaga uses this delineation of an "enemy" to shape the temporality of Indianismo Amáutico. Unlike Revolutionary Indianismo, the Amáutico reconstruction of history cannot emerge from a direct and "inherited" connection with previous times. Instead, the meanings found in the languages and social experiences of "indigenous" peoples currently contain memories that are consistent with cosmic "reality." "Unlike the things that fallacious statements of European chroniclers and scientists say, the mentality and thought of the Indio is currently alive" (Reinaga 2014, 6:36). History thus becomes a construction that emerges from presently shared meanings. The concurrent correspondence between meanings and cosmic "reality" thus validates specific memories and invalidates other thoughts. Through this kind of validation, F. Reinaga separates history from the rectilinear possibility of accessing a genuine or objective past as a thesis or basis from which the "Indio" can judge the present and construct a liberated future. Instead, F. Reinaga revises his previous ideas of dialectics and he introduces a notion of circular temporality, which views life as an integral part of the eternal time of the Cosmos, without beginning or end (6:387).

Despite the way in which F. Reinaga opens the door to understanding temporality in a different way, he also finds, in presently shared meanings, a bedrock of universal judgment. He claims to have an epistemological access to the "reality" of coexistence, which he can then use to judge the thoughts and mentalities that are erroneous and "unreal." From the living "reality" of the "Indio's" thought, F. Reinaga can judge the "enemy" and he can seek the construction of an alternative future. Liberation is thus regarded as the salvation of "humanity" and life on Earth (Reinaga 2014, 6:215). In order to achieve the goal of salvation from the potential destruction of the nuclear era, the Amáutico mentality proposes to free man so that he may integrate the Cosmos again (6:377). In other words, liberation entails the possibility of enacting a social and ecological order that respects the laws of the Cosmos while also opposing the enemy of the "Indio."

The Enemy: "Reason" is not "reality"

Through the validation of a single, universalized, and ontological idea of the Cosmos, F. Reinaga can elevate a particular "reality" above other mentalities. In order to define "colonialism," F. Reinaga can thus analyze the characteristics and the genealogy of the mentalities that contradict the Amáutico notion of the Cosmos. According to the author, "reason" is the core notion of this unreal or false ontology. The first discussion of "reason" appears in the intellectual work of Socrates, who defines "humanity" as a being whose superior characteristic is the non-emotional capacity to think logically (Reinaga 2014, 6:279). Here, the "reason-based" knowledge of "humanity" emerges as a bedrock from which everything else can be judged. Since it is the superior capacity of "humanity," Socrates uses "reason" as the philosophical foundation that sets the standard for universal judgment and he regards it as more "real" than anything else. "Man becomes the measurement of everything" (6:279).

According to F. Reinaga, Socrates was one of the fathers of Occidental "reason," but this idea evolved and changed throughout history. For example, Descartes further develops this notion, guaranteeing the very existence of the universe from the undeniability of his own doubt (Reinaga 2014, 6:287). Here, "reason" becomes the ontological foundation of Occidental "reality" (6:288). Unlike F. Reinaga's ontology of the Cosmos, Descartes begins from "reason;" he uses a "human" characteristic as the undeniably "real" starting point of the Occidental mentality. Then, Kant completes this relationship between "reason" and the transcendental foundation of philosophy by detaching "reason" from everything that is empirical. According to F. Reinaga, Kant makes "reason" completely sovereign and he constructs this idea as an absolute; he regards the human world of ideas as God and the universe (6:289). Following these notions, Hegel puts "reason" into history and he constructs an idea of dialectical progression (6:290). Here, temporality becomes a teleology, which dialectically leads to the philosophically logical expression of the rational state.

Unlike this intellectual line, Marx breaks away from the "idealist" definition of "reason" (Reinaga 2014, 6:57). According to F. Reinaga, Marx reintegrates "reason" into the relationship between "humanity" and nature. He studies "reason" in the materialist activities of human beings (6:293) and the social organization of labor, which can now be explored empirically throughout history (6:148). Marx attaches "reason" to the ways in which "humanity" uses nature as a "resource" or a force of production that is necessary to survive and progress. This Marxist idea hierarchicalizes forms of social order based on their levels of consistency with "rational" relationships of production. Instead of organizing history towards the "rational" state, Marx constructs a temporality that judges social order based on their mode of production.

Despite the "reality" that Occidental intellectuals treasure in their ontologies of "reason," F. Reinaga points out that Nietzsche unveils the arbitrariness of this notion, while also falling into nihilism. Since they draw the foundation of the universe from constructions that change based on the creative capacity of intellectuals, idealists and Marxist philosophers alike chase an ontology that is an arbitrary legislation. Nietzsche concludes that there is no bedrock or ontological basis, denouncing the arbitrariness of "reason-based" epistemic foundations. However, Nietzsche fails to move beyond "reason" and he falls into a philosophical nihilism that is based solely on the possibility of power struggles. According to F. Reinaga, Nietzsche finds the solution to the arbitrariness of "reason" in the power of ideas and their victories. In other words, F. Reinaga regards Nietzsche's work as a justification of the wars of ideas, which is another form of "reason." To the author, the Occidental "man is a being that emerges from nature and then rushes towards the abyss of nothingness" (6:293).

Beyond these idealist, Marxist, and nihilist notions, F. Reinaga finds a parallel and sometimes conflicting path in the construction of Occident. In this intellectual line, Jesus Christ and his disciples promote a single notion of God and truth (Reinaga 2014, 6:248). Then, Saint Thomas Aquinas uses the story of Moses to prove God's existence (6:253). He asserts that God "is that is" and he turns the possibility of faith in God's existence into the ontological moment of undeniable "reality." Then, Aquinas uses "reason" to prove God's existence and to determine some of his characteristics. According to F. Reinaga, this strategy puts "man" and his rationality as the guarantee and creation of God (6:350). God is hereby regarded as an ontological foundation that can be epistemologically accessed by those who "reason." This form of anthropocentric rationality is then embodied in the Pope and the Church, which have power over kings (6:253). In turn, this notion leads Christopher Columbus and Queen Isabella I of Castile to justify the conquest of the Americas, the extraction of resources, the enslavement of peoples, etc. (6:255). The idea of a single truth attached to God and known by the Church thus authorizes Occident in its colonial endeavors. It also authorizes Europeans to fight against each other in the wars that begin during the Reformation. Christianity is thus regarded as a history of wars against other "reasons," religions, and nations (6:262). It is the violent search for the definition of a single ontology, which can only be accessed by those who "reason."

F. Reinaga views all these intellectuals as struggling between secular and faith-based definitions of "reason" to construct a single and Occidental mentality. Despite these differences, the author affirms that Descartes connects "faith" and "reason;" he converts these traditions into "sisters" (Reinaga 2014, 6:350). These ideas were thus philosophically united and fused into the construction of the Occidental "man" (6:352). In the work of Descartes, "reason" conceives faith and God. Then, those who "reason" become God or fully sovereign rulers (6:247).

In order to classify Occident as the "fallacy" that leads to lies, oppression, and injustice, F. Reinaga highlights how "reason" contradicts the ontological "reality" of the Cosmos. He elevates his own ontology over the foundations used by Occidental idealism, Marxism, nihilism, and faith. According to F. Reinaga, the main ontological contradiction against the "reality" of the Cosmos emerges from the anthropocentric characteristics of "reason." In its ontological dimension, the Occidental way of knowing begins from the undeniability of "reason," which prioritizes the "reality" of a "human" essence as the bedrock of universal judgement (Reinaga 2014, 6:378). Due to this ontological utilization of a "human" characteristic, the Occidental mentality constructs "reason" as the "real" and universal criterion that can be deployed to judge and rule everything else. Even the Cosmos is assimilated within the anthropocentric idea of "reason" (Reinaga 2014, 6:290).

Said differently, the anthropocentric utilization of a "human" foundation contradicts the utilization of a cosmic "realty." F. Reinaga views the Cosmos as an undeniable "reality" that comes before everything else. From the essence of this "reality" (i.e., the positive and negative principles of equality), the author constructs the laws of the Cosmos, which include a non-anthropocentric equality for all entities. The specification of the cosmic ontology thus leads, first, to the construction of an ecological form of equality and, second, to a consistent delineation of a "human" form of social order. To the contrary, Occident uses the "reality" of "reason" to establish an ontology that begins from a "human" characteristic and then ignores the equality of other entities. Occident puts "man" first and then it ignores the laws of the Cosmos and their "reality."

Who is the enemy: Occidental anthropocentrism

To continue studying this Occidental and anthropocentric mentality, F. Reinaga uses a notion of epistemological disconnection, which defines who is the incorrect agent of oppression. He describes how the Occidental way of being corresponds to the arbitrary or false ontology of "reason." Notwithstanding the epistemological connection between "reality" and the "Indio," F. Reinaga explains how other ways of being are not epistemologically connected to "reality." To achieve this goal, the author asserts that "man" is generally driven by thought (Reinaga 2014, 6:224). In his creative capacity, however, "man" sometimes stops listening to the Cosmos and he creates his own thoughts, which then shape everything he does (6:243). Despite the epistemological connection to "reality" that some "humans" enjoy, others fabricate arbitrary ideas that deviate from the kind of thought that corresponds to the Cosmos. This possibility enables F. Reinaga to construct a boundary of classification, which de-authorizes and hierarchicalizes other ways of being. "There are two kinds of mentalities: the Amáutico mentality and the mentality of Occident" (Reinaga 2014, 6:378).

Specifying anthropocentrism: Environmental exploitation and progress

Based on this possibility of epistemological disconnection, F. Reinaga can study and specify the characteristics of those who ignore "reality." In other words, the anthropocentric ontology of Occident leads to an anthropocentric way of being, which F. Reinaga specifies through the study of environmentally destructive social orders. To the author, the Occidental notion of "reason" leads to a society that is based on environmental exploitation. Since "reason" organizes nature below "humanity," the environment hereby loses its status of cosmic equality and it becomes a depletable "resource." This hierarchy can be illustrated through the Occidental idea of "labor." Occidental mentalities often understand "labor" as the application of "reason" upon nature. In turn, this application grants rights of property because the outcomes of "labor" are the results of universal "reality." As F. Reinaga asserts, "reason" becomes, for Occident, the universalized "reality" that judges everything; it becomes universalized law. Hence, the application, deployment, or outcomes of "reason" are understood as legitimate laws. The application of "reason" upon nature thus justifies "humanity's" possession and endless accumulation of everything else; it justifies the exploitation of Mother Earth and it leads towards ecocide (Reinaga 2014, 6:215). This explains why F. Reinaga asserts that "reason," together with property, is the accumulation of gold (6: 331). Since "reason" is not cosmic "reality," however, Occident is an unjust way of being, private property is an illegitimate form of social order, and accumulation is the exploitation of nature. Private property and accumulation entail unjust "robbery," created by the "error" of anthropocentrism (6:201).

Relatedly, the "reason-based" notions of "labor" turns nature into a "means" or a "resource" for future progress; it creates a linear notion of temporality that bases progress on ideas of endless accumulation and the control of nature. Occidental societies thus grant to "humanity" an infinite right to manipulate "nature." Additionally, sciences and technologies hereby become instruments of exploitation, utilized to deplete nature and destroy the world. In 1974, F. Reinaga had already denounced this ecological problem, together with the overutilization of oxygen, which has become so evident and prominent in more current decades (Reinaga 2014, 6:176). Moreover, this "scientific craze" explains how the study of nuclear physics led to the discovery of the structure of atoms and their manipulation towards the creation of nuclear energy, which was the basis of the nuclear bomb (6:176). The certainty of anthropocentric "reason" thus leads to the arrogance that blinds "humanity" even while facing its own annihilation. To F. Reinaga, the invalidated ontology of "reason" constructs the de-authorized way of being of Occident, which leads to an illegitimate social order of exploitation and the potential destruction of the world.

Who is the enemy: Occidental racism

Besides the epistemological connection between the anthropocentric ontology of "reason" and Occident, F. Reinaga shows that this way of being contradicts the essence of a particular entity of the Cosmos as well. The author demonstrates that Occidental notions of "man" clash with the essence of "humanity" because they create racism and oppressive social orders. In other words, F. Reinaga asserts that Occident contradicts the "reality" of national equality, which the "Indio" represents in his ayllu-based system of social order.

According to the author, Occident views those who "reason" as the masters of universal knowledge. Their proximity to the Occidental ontology of "reason" authorizes them and hierarchicalizes everyone and everything else. As F. Reinaga shows in his genealogical study of "reason," this hierarchy continuously assumes an egocentric and Occidental scale, which authorizes a racialized European "man" above other peoples and nature. "(Occident) establishes the value of people based on skin color, economic range, cultural monopoly, etc. It divides humanity into slaves and free peoples" (Reinaga 2014, 6:403). Moreover, Occident uses this hierarchy to classify the "Indio" as an "other" that is inferior and "uncivilized." Here, the "Indio" has to convert himself into "reason" or he has to be removed from society for the sake of "progress" (6:474). As F. Reinaga highlights, these Occidental hierarchies of peoples contradict the cosmic authorization of the "Indio" and his way of being; they oppose national equality and the "real" essence of "humanity."

Moreover, as F. Reinaga discusses, the Occidental source of its hierarchicalizing authority is the "myth" of "reason." "The European mentality, its time, life, death, pain, and its entire value scale is nothing but an anti-Amáutico and anti-cosmic lie" (Reinaga 2014, 6:378). An invalidated way of knowing thus entails a de-authorized way of being. Here, the man of Occident becomes the representative of falsehood, error, lies, enslavement, and crime (6:388).

Specifying oppression: An Occidental social order

This Occidental hierarchicalization against the "Indio" leads to a social order of "human" oppression and exploitation. According to F. Reinaga, the hierarchicalizing mentality that emerges from the epistemological authorization of the Occidental "man" is the cause of a homogenizing process of civilization. This process presupposes a linear understanding of time. In his solitude, "man" constructs time from his own and isolated life; in his separation from the Cosmos, "man" defines time as a line with a beginning and an end (Reinaga 2014, 6:378). When Occidental intellectuals annex the notion of time to the idea of "reason," they convert history into a hierarchical line of beginning and end. Here, "reason" becomes a bedrock, which has to measure the past and design the future. Time itself thus appears as a hierarchy based on the different degrees of proximity that each epoch has with "reason" (Reinaga 2014, 6:233). Then, this notion of time appears as the basis from which Occident can apply colonial violence against "others" that do not fit "reason." History ought to move closer to "reason" and undo whatever obstacles lie in its way. The past and the future thus appear as a line that goes from "uncivilized" or "irrational" obstacles to more pure and perfect "reason." The violence of the past is thus regarded as necessary against the irrationality of the "other." The violence of the future is justified as the protection or development of "reason." To F. Reinaga, this construction is a "lie," which erases the colonial violence of the "past" and enables the "future" violence of "progress" (6:231).

Since "reason" is based on "lies" and "errors," whatever actions the temporal ideas of civilization promote and justify appear as injustices; the social order that it creates is colonial oppression. For example, F. Reinaga denounces the erasure of indigenous peoples. According to the author, Occidental thought categorizes the "Indio" as an inferior way of being from a past that is far from "reason." For "humanity" to progress towards "reason," the "Indio" thus has to disappear. To achieve this goal, states have applied policies of "mestizaje" (Reinaga 2014, 6:464–466). "Mestizaje" changes throughout time and it is debated by Latin American intellectuals and politicians who redefine "reason" within their contexts. Throughout history, however, all these intellectuals and politicians have hierarchicalized whoever is farther down from "reason" than they are (6:395). This hierarchicalizing tendency denies the "Indio" his "human" condition and it excludes him from rights or from political agency. Then, states and intellectuals seek to mold the "Indio" based on the racialized way of being of "reason." Whenever molding "others" seems impossible for Occidental states and intellectuals, these policies of homogenization lead to segregation or genocide (9:209).

According to F. Reinaga, genocide continues to be a possibility through the threat of nuclear war. Moreover, the author asserts that Occidental states contemporaneously commit genocide through the killings of non-Occidental peoples in, for example, the Cold War (Reinaga 2014, 6:508). Finally, genocide is also a crime that affects Europeans themselves. This is not only due to the threat of suicide in nuclear wars, but also to the definition of "reason," which always entails a specific, yet universalized, way of being. For example, the USSR used a Marxist idea of "reason" that contradicted the liberal notion promoted by the United States. Both of these notions also contradicted the Nazi idea of "reason" and they all went to war against each other. Each one of them fought anyone who appeared as inferior and did not follow the "real" characteristics of "reason." Furthermore, when Occident does not directly fight against its "other," it often imposes domestic governments that follow its instructions and violently seeks the same process of homogenization. This is how F. Reinaga explains the Occidental support of dictatorships by both communist and capitalist states. He points out that the USSR imposed revolutions based on its own Marxist definition of "reason" (Reinaga 2014, 6:495). Similarly, the United States strongly supported dictatorships throughout the world to promote its own liberal and capitalist notion of "reason" (6:496).

F. Reinaga also connects the definition of "reason" to the notion of private property, which is a condition of possibility for the capitalist exploitation of nature and peoples. The "human" application of "reason" through "labor" is the main Occidental justification for the right to appropriate and accumulate "resources." The individual applies his "reason" to nature through his "labor" and then he appropriates it to survive. This notion enables the accumulation of "resources" and it restricts the possibility of freely accessing nature. Since those who "reason" are Occident, those who "labor" and accumulate "resources" are "European." The racialized and Occidental definition of "labor" thus entitles "Europeans" to be the owners of earth (Reinaga 2014, 9:124). To the contrary, "other" peoples often find themselves excluded from their lands and exploited by those who control means of production because their relationship with nature and their labor is not quite "rational." According to F. Reinaga, this is the Occidental root of hunger and economic inequality (6:169).[4] Additionally, this is how the "Indio" was removed from his lands.

Liberation: The return to the Cosmos

Since F. Reinaga invalidates "reason," de-authorizes Occident, and delegitimizes environmental exploitation and racism, he calls for the Amáutico liberation of the world. To the author, the "Indio" has to free earth and "humanity" from falsehood, tyranny, and oppression. To him, "reason," Occident, and oppression represent the global problem of colonialism and the enemy of the "Indio." "To this end has Occident arrived thanks to reason; thanks to the stupidity of reason" (Reinaga 2014, 6:348).

The Occidental erasure, genocide, exploitation, and homogenization of all "others" are regarded as the effects of "lies" from which the Cosmos has to be liberated. Since thoughts shape societies, liberation has to begin from the transformation of mentalities and languages. That is, F. Reinaga uses his understanding of the epistemological connection between an erroneous ontology of "reason" and the Occidental way of being to discuss the possibility of transformation and liberation. Here, thought becomes the dimension that has to be changed in order to bring "humanity" closer to the "reality" of the Cosmos (Reinaga 2014, 8:39).

Since it creates lies, injustices, and death, "reason" cannot be the root of the new order; instead, liberation has to emerge from "another mentality" (Reinaga 2014, 6:373). F. Reinaga asserts that liberation is only possible through a mentality that opposes the error of Occident. Only a thought capable of fixing the Occidental myths that cause exploitation, homogenization, destruction, genocide, and ecocide, can liberate "humanity" and the rest of the Cosmos from its current path. As a mentality that respects the cosmic principles of equality in difference, Indianismo Amáutico appears as the solution (8:43). "Thought, and only thought, can change the world and men" (6:402).

On one side, F. Reinaga uses his epistemological classification to authorize those who are or choose to be "Indios." Since he knows the laws of the Cosmos better than anyone, the Revolution first begins with the "Indio" Amáutico as its main agent. This authority makes the "Indio" the leader of a strategic unification, which connects the countries of the "South" in a broader political platform (Reinaga 2014, 8:28). F. Reinaga also asserts that all the oppressed peoples of the world, who have suffered the consequences of anthropocentric and Occidental hierarchicalizations, have to unite and struggle together for liberation. For example, F. Reinaga asserts that the "Indio" ought to ally with other racial movements such as the struggles of black power (6:192). Then, this notion of an authorized way of being includes anyone who agrees with and lives by F. Reinaga's definition of cosmological and "human" coexistence. In relation to the Revolution, this notion emphasizes the strategic need to unite as "Indios."

On the other side of his epistemological classification, F. Reinaga calls for the opposition of Occidental thought and its manifestations throughout history. The possibility of removing Socrates, Kant, Marx, and Jesus Christ from the Occidental brain thus becomes the first task for liberation (Reinaga 2014, 8:43). Here, the duty of liberation not only includes the possibility of freeing those peoples, animals, plants, things, etc. that have been discriminated, erased, silenced, exploited, killed, and enslaved throughout colonialism, but also entails the liberation of the Occidental mind. Therefore, changing the Occidental mentality is a key aspect and part of a process of liberation designed to include all (6:368). In this sense, F. Reinaga seeks to avoid the biological understanding of race and the reconstruction of another form of racism against "whites" or "mestizos." He creates the possibility of a universal liberation by including the oppressor itself. The "Indio" is thus a mentality; he is not a skin color (6:399). Insofar as Europeans become "Indios" and learn to respect the form of Amáutico coexistence, they can be included in this liberation and its resulting order. To the contrary, the individuals who promote and impose Occidental thought, while also opposing the possibility of Amáutico liberation, are regarded as enemies. Their "mentality" thus classifies them as the agents of colonialism.

Hence, the Amáutico mentality includes a clear delineation of the enemy that contradicts the "reality" of the Cosmos in his thoughts, mentalities, and actions. Their distance to "reality" thus classifies them as ways of being that ought to change. This boundary strongly separates anyone who acts as an agent or defender of the "lies," "errors," and "injustices" of Occidental thought. Because thought comes first, these colonial agents have to be liberated through a pedagogical action of transformation. However, if the opposition against the Amáutico liberation turns to violence and it aggressively resists the creation of an order based on ecological and "human" equality, the "Indio" becomes justified in raising arms and struggling through war. F. Reinaga thus asserts that the "Indio" has the right to begin a "holy war" because he has suffered hundreds of years of oppression and because Occidental resistance against transformation often includes violent ways of silencing peoples or exterminating them (Reinaga 2014, 6:196). F. Reinaga affirms that "if Occident insists in its stupidity and crime, then my mentality will unchain and generate a cosmic war; a war like no other in the universe. Through Amáutico persuasion or through nuclear incineration, at the end, I will defeat Occident" (6:424).

As this citation illustrates, F. Reinaga grants a high level of validity to his own way of knowing, which authorizes his way of being and legitimizes his process of enactment even when it leads to violence and war. However, F. Reinaga realizes that this tendency towards war and even using nuclear power unveils a problematic contradiction in his own work. He thus asserts that war and democracy are the products of the Occidental mentality of "reason." By contrast, the "Indio" has to create something different based on his own mentality, which has to lead to a deeper level of transformation (Reinaga 2014, 6:400). Unfortunately, F. Reinaga does not develop this argument and he does not follow the discussion that this contradiction could have begun. Instead, the author prioritizes his self-validating, self-authorizing, and self-enacting notion of Amáutico mentality, which reaffirmed his end goal of liberation. Here, an ontology, epistemology, and temporality create a condition of possibility for anti-colonial violence.

Conclusion: Assimilation and universalization

Overall, the Indianismo that R. Reynaga discusses in 1972 and F. Reinaga synthesizes after 1974 entails a partial contradiction between its cosmological equalization and its epistemological hierarchicalization. At the level of the Cosmos, all entities appear as equal and different simultaneously. Then, the ontological essentialization and epistemological accessibility of "reality" leads towards another hierarchy, which authorizes a subject to enact the "real" order of the universe. An elevated and intelligible way of knowing thus authorizes a single way of being, which then legitimizes a particular way of enacting. In turn, this way of enacting includes the specification of the characteristics of a legitimate social order, a construction of the strategic path towards it, and a determination of the traits of the main ruling subject.

This contradiction brings the Amáutico project closer to colonial epistemics. F. Reinaga uses a set of epistemic assumptions that elevate and universalize a particular kind of reality, identity, social order, and transformation. As Said states, this kind of epistemic tendency emerges from essentialist understandings that assume a possibility of accessing the real, objective, and singular essence of the objects of the universe (Said 1978, 32). For F. Reinaga, the universal and single "reality" of the Cosmos is the general law of coexistence; the positive and negative principles of equality. Hence, the author asserts that the law of the Cosmos entails a threefold principle (Reinaga 2014, 6:405). First, the Amáutico mentality entails "truth" as a single source of human wisdom. The "reality" of the Cosmos is the single truth of the universe. Second, the Amáutico mentality seeks "liberty" as the source of "human" dignity. Here, "liberty" entails the possibility of following the laws of the Cosmos and constructing a single form of "harmonious" coexistence. To F. Reinaga, "humanity" can only be free when it respects the general principles of the Cosmos and when it applies these principles to its own social order. Finally, the Amáutico mentality seeks "good" as the cosmic imperative of "human" existence. Here, "good" entails the solidarity of peoples among themselves and in the Cosmos.

As I show throughout the chapter, this universalized and validated singularity unfolds as the "Indio's" way of being, which is then specified as the ecological and "human" equality of the ayllu and the Tawantinsuyu. Despite the different understandings of ayllus in Andean cosmologies (Rivera 1990), F. Reinaga uses an epistemological connection that turns the singularity of his Cosmos into a legitimate and universalizable social order. Here, F. Reinaga constructs the Cosmos, "Indio," national and ecological equality, ayllu, and World Amáutico Community as different elements that correspond to each other in the epistemological connection of "real" thought or "cosmic energy." This connection extrapolates the "reality" of the Cosmos onto the other discursive elements that substantiate it. "Reality" is thus characterized into a form of equality and social order. Then, the author uses this epistemological possibility of accessing the very essence of the Cosmos and "humanity" to authorize those who are, know, and represent "reality" itself. The "Indio" thus becomes the representative of the Cosmos on earth; he knows cosmic law and he can legitimately rule. Notwithstanding the possibility of equality in difference between multiple kinds of entities, the singularity of the discourse and the epistemological possibility of specifying this "reality" become a homogenizing logic that assimilates or excludes other ways of knowing, being, and enacting; it hierarchicalizes other "others."

Similar to the Kantian notion of "reason" that F. Reinaga denounces, the Cosmos becomes a single and universal "reality" that organizes, assimilates, and annexes everything else. Then, this universal "reality" becomes knowable by those who are epistemologically connected to it in a particular kind of thought and way of being. As I discuss in Chapter One, Kant decouples "reason" from all empirical conditions of possibility. Then, he grants the epistemological possibility of accessing "reason" to those who appear as "civilized." Similarly, F. Reinaga decouples the Cosmos from the genuine past of Revolutionary Indianismo, and then he grants the access of cosmic laws to the "Indio." Moreover, Kant regards "reason" as above "man" and his inclinations, but those who "reason" can access this kind of thought to become free (Kant 1952). Consistent with this, F. Reinaga regards the ontological "reality" of the Cosmos as above "man," but then the "Indio" accesses the Cosmos and rules on its behalf. Thus, F. Reinaga calls for a removal of Kant from the Occidental brain, but he also sustains the epistemic notion of a single ontological "reality" that can be epistemologically accessed by some and not "others."

In addition to these questions, Indianismo sustains other epistemic continuities with colonialism. For example, the epistemic assumptions used by F. Reinaga lead to the universalization of a particular experience of ecological exploitation. Then, the author generalizes a single understanding of the ayllu as the universal solution to this colonial problem. To the contrary, Rivera discusses a different understanding of ecology, which includes deeper critiques of anthropocentrism. In much of her work, Rivera follows the notions of cosmological equality to problematize epistemological hierarchicalizations as well. This idea locates humanity in a much more egalitarian relationship with nature. Despite the benefits of Rivera's discussions, the universalization of a single idea of ecology prevents a dialogue between the two experiences of oppression and transformation. Rivera's approach thus appears less "real" and the universalization of a particular definition of the Cosmos silences her voice. Moreover, F. Reinaga's assumption of an epistemological connection between the Cosmos and the "Indio" re-anthropomorphizes the control of nature. As a direct representative of the Sun, the "Indio" becomes the one who knows the laws of the Cosmos. He can thus determine how to relate with nature. This kind of assumption often leads to a high level of certainty vis-à-vis the manipulation of nature. Despite the equality among all cosmic entities, then, F. Reinaga authorizes the "Indio" to determine, for example, how much environmental exploitation is "equality" or is respectful of cosmic laws. In a way, then, "nature" still becomes an object of human knowledge. The "Indio" knows it and therefore controls it. This entails still a form of faith in science and its control of the universe. In turn, this anthropocentric certainty contradicts the possibility of listening to nature more carefully, which Rivera emphasizes in Andean cosmologies.

Another colonial continuity can be found in F. Reinaga's universalization of a single notion of "human" equality, which he also attaches to a particular idea of the ayllu. Once F. Reinaga grants the status of cosmic "reality" to "national" equality, he is able to oppose colonial hierarchies, but he also invalidates all other experiences of racism, discrimination, exploitation, oppression, etc. As Rivera demonstrates, these masculine readings of ethnicity often ignore gendered experiences of racism and exploitation (Rivera 2015, 41). Since these struggles are less "real," their voices are silenced and their experiences erased. Moreover, the agency of feminist movements often becomes hidden under the legitimized actions of the "Indio." Other struggles, voices, and projects thus become less "real" and they are sometimes even viewed as obstacles against "true" revolutions.

This epistemic tendency to marginalize other "others" becomes particularly pernicious when temporality is understood in linear terms. When essentialized "reality" becomes the bedrock of universal judgment, change or transformation always opposes the enemy and the characteristics that do not fit whatever is epistemically elevated. Despite F. Reinaga's aim of understanding temporality in a circular way, his work turns "reality" into a condition of possibility for assimilation, transformation, or violence against everything that is epistemically inferior. Throughout this process, violence against violent "others" is justified even to the point of "nuclear incineration," but the construction of "others" includes not only a murderous or genocidal Occident, it also entails every way of being that does not quite fit the characteristics of the "Indio." Other ways of being and voices can thus become assimilated or silenced through violence. The epistemic othering that emerges from the elevation of singularity thus acts as a condition of possibility for violence against explicit and implicit "others." This highlights the importance of analyzing epistemic politics. These continuities between F. Reinaga's work and colonial epistemics illustrate how particular definitions of "reality" elevate specific definitions of power, equality, and agency. Based on these ideas, the discourse enables an endogenous form of classification, but it also leads to a universalization that ends up marginalizing other "others." In this sense, anti-colonial discourses use colonial epistemics to erect bedrocks of judgment against "colonialism," but they also lead to the exclusion of other struggles and voices.

These epistemic similarities between colonial and anti-colonial discourses highlight again the risks of utilizing the "master's tools" (Lorde 2018). By using epistemically fixed and elevated bedrocks to classify colonialism, Revolutionary Indianismo and Indianismo Amáutico tend to exclude other "others." In this sense, the utilization of strong bedrocks can enable a clear definition of the "enemy," but it can also create a downward hierarchy of echelons that organize multiple kinds of "others." Hence, epistemic bedrocks, foundations, and extra-discursive structures can enable a distinct kind of anti-colonial praxis, but they might also elevate a single discourse, voice, and project, creating yet another form of oppression, inequality, and colonialism. Here, the problem of difference confronts the discussion of coloniality and decoloniality again. On one side, decoloniality aims to move beyond colonialism and it seeks "epistemic disobedience" (Mignolo 2009). To achieve this goal, decolonial praxes ought to refuse the epistemic tendencies of colonialisms and their othering effects. On the other side, decoloniality should also avoid the assimilation of Indianismo through a framework that regards it as equally colonial as Western projects of civilization. Personally, I refuse to fall into the paralyzing relativism that undoes bedrocks of judgment only to undo all possibilities of decolonial praxis. However, this position begs the question of how it might be possible to classify "colonialism" while also avoiding yet more othering tendencies.

As I mention in Chapter Two, several authors often point out that some discourses have been practiced more *continuously* throughout history (Said 1978; Todorov 1982; Rivera 1990; Wynter 1995; Reinaga 2014). Similarly, my genealogical account of Bolivian colonialism can attest to the continuity of liberalism since at least 1825 and Marxism since 1941. These colonial practices have reinforced, often through violence and death, a continuous set of discursive characteristics in Bolivia and beyond. As the work of other authors shows, some of these notions have deeper roots in Spanish colonialism as well (Todorov 1982; Rivera and Morón 1993; Mignolo 2000, 2011; Rivera 2010, 2015; Reinaga 2014). Hence, much decolonial and post-colonial work emphasizes the continuity of particular meanings that can be consistently followed in practices of different historical moments and spaces. Against this continuity, Indianismo Amáutico seeks to change some of the characteristics that have been validated, authorized, and legitimized throughout the history of Bolivia and the world. F. Reinaga aims to elevate a way of knowing, being, and enacting that contradicts "reason," Occident, and anthropocentric racism; he validates the Cosmos, authorizes the "Indio," and legitimatizes ecological and ethnic equality. Hence, the author proposes the possibility of elevating different characteristics, which construct an opposing way of knowing, being, and enacting; he resists the continuity and elevation of particular characteristics, and his approach of anti-coloniality seeks to turn the colonial universe "up-side-down." In order to achieve this goal, F. Reinaga uses a set of epistemic assumptions that function similarly to "Occidental" discourses of colonialism, but the characteristics that the author elevates change. He uses the same epistemic strategies as colonialism, but he also validates a different reality, authorizes a different subject, and enacts a different social order.

How is it possible, then, to determine that these anti-colonial characteristics are in fact "different" to "coloniality" and "domination"? If they also create a tendency to invalidate other ways of knowing, silence other voices, and destroy other projects, how are they separate from oppression? The notion of continuity seems to help, but is continuity a sufficient condition of possibility to distinguish between colonialisms and anti-colonialisms? As F. Reinaga and other Indianista intellectuals claim, many of their anti-colonial notions can be traced back hundreds of years and they can be connected to memories of events such as the 1780s siege of La Paz. Additionally, Indianismo officially emerged in the 1960s, which means that it has a continuous history of several decades. Indianismo has become a history of Bolivia and the Andes. Similar to colonial discourses, Indianismo has its own continuity. Hence, continuity does not seem to provide a sufficient criterion of classification when it is utilized by itself to determine what is "colonial" and what is "resisting." In other words, both sets of discourses entail a degree of continuity, they both elevate particular realities, agents, and projects, and they both universalize their own notions which end up othering "others." Therefore, continuity often demands the utilization of an extra-discursive bedrock such as "force," level of institutionalization, levels of violence, or power to construct a separation between a discourse that is "dominant" and one that is "oppressed." Again, the possibility of classification and decolonial praxis demands the re-introduction of an external structure, extra-discursive criterion, or elevated bedrock to measure the level of "dominance" of a discourse and to grant "reality" to particular experiences of oppression. Continuity begs the utilization of an underlying notion of power to determine which discourse appears the more "official" or "dominant" history of a place, which can be resisted by the ones that are understood as anti-colonial "others."

In turn, would this foundational or elevated understanding of power universalize another kind of "reality"? Would this possibility of classification presuppose another pre-definition of power, equality, struggle, and justice? Would this bedrock of classification marginalize other voices yet again? Additionally, what authorizes me or any other interpreter to grant validity to our own construction of power above "others"? How and why do interpreters acquire the epistemic authority that is required to classify the discourses that are interpreted? How and why are we allowed to put our own discourses above other discourses? How does this epistemic elevation prevent us from thinking about our own boundaries and the tendencies that emerge from them to marginalize other "others"?

Overall, the analysis of Indianismo Amáutico highlights the epistemic problems that emerge when intellectuals deploy strong bedrocks, but the discussion also emphasizes the limitations that surge when notions of continuity are deployed without bedrocks. Despite these epistemic issues, a decolonial approach and endeavor ought to listen to voices such as Indianismo in order to create localized possibilities of praxis against colonialisms. The denunciation of the form of oppression that is illuminated by F. Reinaga has important insights about epistemic politics and Occidental injustices. Furthermore, many of these problems of epistemic superiority, racism, and anthropocentrism continue to plague international politics and International Relations. My question is, however, are these injustices the only or even the most important problems in domestic, international, or global politics? Are these Amáutico ideas the only or most legitimate projects of transformation? Are they above other struggles and voices? In other words, how can we listen to Revolutionary Indianismo and Indianismo Amáutico while also being aware of their epistemic limitations? How is it possible to listen to Indianismos and other struggles at the same time, preventing the universalization of particular singularities?

All these questions are related to the possibility of creating praxis while also listening to multiplicity; they are linked to the problem of difference. Decolonial praxes require the possibility of classifying "colonialisms" while also undoing foundational bedrocks that create universalizing and totalizing effects. Decolonialities demand the possibility of listening to Indianismo while also taking other voices into account. As I discuss in Chapter Six, other Andean intellectuals have taken Indianismo into account while also moving far into these decolonial questions. For example, Rivera proposes a different way of thinking about Andean cosmologies. She uses some of the insights from F. Reinaga while also moving beyond the epistemic universalization of singularity. In this sense, Rivera allows us to respect Indianismo Amáutico and Revolutionary Indianismo, while still seeing other struggles, listening to other voices, and walking with other projects.

Despite the benefits of Rivera's work, the most salient critique of F. Reinaga's singularity and universalization emerged in Bolivia from a different perspective. In the early 2000s, Juán Evo Morales Ayma and Álvaro García Linera sought to construct a platform of political transformation that included "indigenous" and "Occidental" ways of being as equal identities of a single and plurinational territory. In their approach, Evo Morales and García Linera created a form of equality between liberal notions of citizenship and communitarian ideas of rights. Here, plurinationality included "reason" and the Cosmos, the individual and the ayllu, and development and Pachamama all at the same time. Evo Morales and García Linera thus avoided generalizing the "Indio" as the only kind of legitimate social order in Bolivia. Their approach showed, moreover, how an anti-colonial struggle could aim to construct a space where equality entailed a mutual limitation between different identities. Despite these advantages, the anti-colonial approach of plurinationalism also sustained the epistemic strategies of colonial discourses. As the next chapter shows, the project assimilated and violently silenced other voices.

Notes

1 Since last names were sometimes written in Spanish despite their original language, they often changed the ways in which they were spelled. Additionally, indigenous intellectuals and leaders often changed their last names in order to avoid persecution. These phenomenon might explain why Ramiro Reynaga chose to spell his last name differently than his father Fausto Reinaga, but there might be other reasons as well.

2 Similar to much of Revolutionary Indianismo, the works of Ramiro Reynaga and Fausto Reinaga still express a masculine bias in their implications and in their linguistic styles. Consistent with this, I follow the usage of the pronoun "he" and the noun "man" when referring to the "Indio" and "humanity" in this chapter.

3 "Amauta" means "wise one" or "master" in Quechua. This was a title given to the teachers of noble children in the Inca Empire. F. Reinaga uses this name in order to describe those who know the laws of the Cosmos and can guide the rest of humanity towards liberation. In this sense, "Amáutico" is the adjective used to classify objects or subjects that fit this kind of knowledge.

4 Of course Marxism disagrees with the individualistic definition of "reason" and "labor," but it still creates an anthropocentric hierarchy that locates "humanity" above nature. In turn, this idea also views nature as a resource and it constructs progress as the industrialized development of the forces of production. This tendency of anthropocentrism classifies Marxism as another form of colonial and Occidental mentality (Reinaga 2014, 6:88).

References

CSUTCB. 2005. *Pachakuti Educativo: Propuesta de La CSUTCB al II Congreso Nacional de Educación, Basada En El Modelo de Ayllu.* Bolivia: Artes Gráficas Abril.

Kant, Immanuel. 1952. *The Critique of Pure Reason.* Vol. 42. Great Books of the Western World. London: Encyclopedia Britannica.

Lorde, Audre. 2018. *The Master's Tools Will Never Dismantle the Master's House.* London: Penguin.

Mignolo, Walter. 2000. *Local Histories/Global Designs: Coloniality, Subaltern Knowledges, and Border Thinking.* Princeton Studies in Culture/Power/History. Princeton, NJ: Princeton University Press.

Mignolo, Walter. 2009. "Epistemic Disobedience, Independent Thought and Decolonial Freedom." *Theory, Culture & Society* 26 (7–8): 159–181. doi:10.1177/0263276409349275.

Mignolo, Walter. 2011. *The Darker Side of Western Modernity: Global Futures, Decolonial Options.* Latin America Otherwise. Durham, NC: Duke University Press.

Reinaga, Fausto. 2014. *Fausto Reinaga: Obras Completas.* 10 vols. La Paz: Vicepresidencia del Estado Plurinacional.

Reynaga, Ramiro. 1972. *Ideología y Raza En América Latina.* La Paz: Ediciones Future.

Rivera Cusicanqui, Silvia. 1990. "Liberal Democracy and Ayllu Democracy in Bolivia: The Case of Northern Potosí." *The Journal of Development Studies* 26 (4): 97–121.

Rivera Cusicanqui, Silvia. 2010. *Violencias (Re) Encubiertas En Bolivia.* La Paz: La Mirada Salvaje.

Rivera Cusicanqui, Silvia. 2015. *Sociología de la Imagen. Miradas Ch'ixi Desde La Historia Andina.* Buenos Aires: Tinta Limón.

Rivera Cusicanqui, Silvia, and Raúl Barrios Morón. 1993. *Violencias Encubiertas En Bolivia: Cultura y Política.* La Paz: Talleres Gráficos Hisbol.

Roel, Virgilio. 1980. "Indianidad y Revolución: Raíz y Vigencia de la Indianidad." Editorial Alfa, S.A. https://catalog.hathitrust.org/Record/006004509.

Said, Edward W. 1978. *Orientalism.* New York: Vintage Books.

Ticona, Esteban Alejo. 2013. *El Indianismo de Fausto Reinaga: Orígenes, Desarrollo y Experiencia En Qullasuyu-Bolivia.* Ecuador: Universidad Andina Simón Bolívar.

Todorov, Tzvetan. 1982. *The Conquest of America: The Question of the Other.* Norman: University of Oklahoma Press.

Viaña, Jorge, Luis Claros, and Marcelo Sarzuri-Lima. 2010. "La Condición Colonial y Los Laberintos de La Descolonización." *Revista Integra Educativa* 3 (1): 13–36.

Wynter, Sylvia. 1995. "The Pope Must Have Been Drunk, The King of Castile a Madman: Culture as Actuality, and the Caribbean Rethinking Modernity." In *Reordering of Culture: Latin America, the Caribbean and Canada in the Hood*, by Alvina Ruprecht, 17–42. Ottawa: Carleton University Press.

4 The universalization of Evo Morales and plurinationality

Throughout much of their political careers in Bolivia and abroad, Juán Evo Morales Ayma and Álvaro García Linera have critiqued and effectively opposed colonialism together with other leaders and organizations that often act under the umbrella of the Movement Towards Socialism (MAS). They have disrupted some of the "Western" injustices that have excluded "indigenous" peoples for 500 years.[1] As scholars have pointed out, their governmental administrations struggled between 2005 and 2019 in multiple domestic dimensions and international arenas to promote respect for the identities of "indigenous" peoples, expand democracy, decrease inequality, contribute to a world of peaceful coexistence, and advocate for decolonization (e.g., Kohl 2010; Ticona 2011; Filho, Gonçalves, and Dalla Déa 2010). Evo Morales and García Linera's control of the Bolivian government ended when a conservative coup d'état forced both leaders into exile in 2019, but, prior to those events, Morales and Linera enacted rights and benefits for some of the most marginalized sectors of the country (Albró 2010, 72). Rosaleen Howard stated in 2010 that "we are witnessing in Bolivia the gradual evolution of the structural conditions necessary for previously marginalized voices to be heard" (Howard 2010, 191). In order to tackle issues of colonialism, discrimination, and inequality, this government also created the Vice Ministry of Decolonization under the umbrella of the Ministry of Culture. As former Vice-Minister Félix Cárdenas Aguilar stated, "the challenge now is for Bolivia, under the presidency of Evo Morales, to decolonize itself, reconstruct its past and identity, and build a plurinational country, where many indigenous nations can thrive" (Cárdenas Aguilar 2015, author's translation). Morales and Linera sought to promote this project not only in Bolivia, but also in, for example, the Union of South American Nations (UNASUR), the United Nations General Assembly, the World People's Conference on Climate Change and the Rights of Mother Earth, and many other international forums.

In the construction of their discourse and project, Morales and Linera use several notions that can be connected to other forms of Indianismo, but they also seek to move beyond the universalization of a single "indigenous" identity. As other authors note, some of the leaders and intellectuals of Revolutionary Indianismo universalize a single way of knowing, being, and enacting, which often excludes and hierarchicalizes other identities. While discussing this issue, Robert Albró, the former Minister of Ethnic and Indigenous Affairs in Bolivia, points out that Ricardo Calla even categorizes the Revolutionary Indianismo of Felipe Quispe as "fundamentalist" and "ethnocentric" (Albró 2005, 449). In order to avoid this problem, Morales and Linera seek to include "non-indigenous" identities within their political platform and project (434). They aim to avoid exclusivist and separatist notions of the "Indio," while elaborating a broader platform that includes urban sectors and converges multiple experiences of struggle against neoliberalism (436). Morales and Linera achieve this goal by using notions of heritage, which expand the epistemic ideas used by Revolutionary Indianismo, building a more pluralistic platform of equality. They construct notions of heritage that do not focus only on the glorious past of the Inca (449).

Hence, the discourse of plurinationality creates another form of anti-colonialism, which aims to undo colonial oppressions while also expanding the respect for differences in Bolivia and the world. Despite the expansion of rights and the partial redistribution of political and economic power that Morales and Linera had achieved during their governments, scholars and activists have noticed important limitations in this project. For example, many denounce the governmental promotion of extraction-based economic activities, which often had deleterious effects for indigenous peoples and the environment (e.g., Kaup 2010; Calla 2012; Pellegrini and Arismendi 2012). Silvia Rivera Cusicanqui asserts that many of these extractive activities undermined communities, destroyed forests, and weakened internal markets (Rivera 2018, 105). The author claims that the economic program of the government entailed a new form of colonialism, which no longer followed the United Sates. Instead, the government was influenced now by Chinese, Brazilian, and Russian companies (98). Others also critique the governmental concentration of power (Canessa 2005; Albró 2005, 2010). In cases of opposition against extractive and developmental projects, the MAS government of Bolivia often ignored social movements or other popular sectors. Despite the democratization of Bolivia, then, the government continued to concentrate and centralize power (Bebbington 2012; Tockman and Cameron 2014). Since 2016, Morales also sought to reform his own constitution to legalize endless re-elections (Landau 2018). In general, this concentration of power allowed Morales to silence other voices such as feminist movements (Rivera 2010b) and to invalidate other struggles such as environmentalist demands (Rivera 2018).

By analyzing public speeches, documents, conferences, books, interviews, the 2009 Constitution, policies, and official reports, I examine the epistemic roots of these problems. The chapter highlights the universalizing tendency that emerges from yet another anti-colonial discourse and its usage of an elevated foundation or bedrock. This construction aims to avoid the problems of Amáutico and Revolutionary Indianismo, but it still elevates a single way of knowing, being, and enacting above all "others;" it deploys a single bedrock, universalizing a particular discourse and marginalizing other "others."

However, my interpretation of these limitations does not aim to undermine the entirety of the Bolivian project, nor does it indirectly legitimize neoliberal discourses or the conservative and often racist tendencies of the government that has taken power in the country since the coup d'état of 2019. As I state in relation to the Revolutionary and Amáutico forms of Indianismo, the relevance of this investigation lies in the opportunity of contributing towards a kind of decolonial construction that can take into account multiple struggles simultaneously. Instead, Morales and Linera end up silencing, ignoring, or assimilating other decolonialities, actors, and projects by granting a superior epistemic status to a single discourse. The universalization of a particular way of knowing, authorization of a single kind of knower, and legitimation of a distinct way of enacting lead towards the hierarchicalization of other struggles, voices, and projects, which then become subjected to annexation or marginalization. As Rivera points out, this epistemic tendency explains the "miserabilist" construction of "others" whose struggle and voice disappear under official projects of civilization (Rivera 2015, 151).

In order to achieve this goal, the first section examines how Morales and Linera construct their ontological foundation and basic idea of equality. Second, the chapter describes how the discourse invalidates the neoliberal inequality that represents colonial injustice. Third, the chapter discusses how the formation includes a particular way of being, which authorizes "indigenous" and "liberal" voices. Fourth, the chapter describes the enactment of these identities and the implications of this process, which expands the political participation of "indigenous" communities, but also creates silencing tendencies against "others." Fifth, the chapter resumes the discussion of equality, examining the way in which the discourse enacts a form of economic transformation that hierarchicalizes and assimilates other struggles. Finally, the conclusion conceptualizes the relationship between the different epistemic dimensions of the discourse, emphasizing broader implications for other projects of anti-colonial transformation and laying out some of the questions that post-structuralist approaches seek to answer in relation to the problem of difference.

Evismo is reality: Validity and equality

Evismo, the discourse that Evo Morales and García Linera promote together with other intellectuals, movements, and politicians, uses some of the epistemic notions constructed by Indianismo. As one of the most prominent intellectuals of the movement, Fausto Reinaga constructs the epistemic foundation of Revolutionary Indianismo by using a seemingly undeniable fact of "humanity's" life. Then, this ontological existence and seeming undeniability validates other dimensions of the discourse. Specifically, Revolutionary Indianismo emerges as "real" by using the fact that all human beings are born into families or relationships with guardians or tutors, which help infants to grow old enough to survive independently. Since each child appears differently molded by the previous generation that takes care of them, this seemingly undeniable relationship connects "humanity" to its past. Reinaga thus constructs his ontological foundation by asserting, "inheritance is a fact related to the somatological part of man" (Reinaga 2014, 5:104, author's translation).

Similar to Revolutionary Indianismo, Evismo deploys the undeniability of inheritance or "heritage" to construct its project. Despite this Indianista legacy, Evismo uses a more pluralistic idea of "indigeneity," which deploys a contemporary social fact of indigenous heritage as a rallying point in response to the exhaustion of the modern neoliberal state (Albró 2005, 449). To achieve this goal, Morales and Linera mix Indianista notions with more liberal ideas of citizenship and equality (Linera 2015, 304). In their construction of a unifying governmental project, which has to include different sectors of Bolivian society, Morales and Linera, neither of them liberals in background or belief, seek to fuse liberal notions of individual rights together with Indianista philosophy and communitarian rights (314). Since it introduces liberal notions, Evismo takes a turn away from Indianismo, but both discourses deploy the idea of an indisputable connection throughout time as a positivity and condition of "reality."

From this "reality," Linera draws a particular definition of identity and equality. According to the author, who published his book *Identidad Boliviana* (Bolivian Identity) through the Vice-presidency Press, identity is the basis of the consciousness and affirmation of oneself (Linera 2014, 9). In the construction of an identity, people create a relationship with others through the definition of commonalities, but they also differentiate themselves in the erection of boundaries and categories, which separate groupings from each other. The process of identity construction is made possible thanks to meanings that are *inherited* from a social space of reference (10). In other words, the inclusion and participation of individuals in social spaces connects them to meanings of affirmation and categorization. These meanings are passed on from social pasts to participating individuals or actors in contemporaneous interactions. Hence, the basic ontological existence of inheritance or heritage is defined as a social, pedagogical, and intergenerational relationship, which enables peoples to know categories of identification. Heritage thus entails a process of socialization, which shares or imposes identities in particular moments of interaction, enabling knowledge and meaning. For the construction of each identity to be possible, then, Evismo presupposes a past background of meanings, which is socially re-shared, re-actualized, and re-deployed within concurrent interactions. Since these meanings are deployed in interactions, the fact of heritage hereby enables the knower to reconstruct the long chain of past meanings, which acts as the basis of actualized possibilities of peoplehood. In other words, each moment of diachronically organized interaction entails meanings that are connected throughout time. This assumption enables the possibility of tracing the continuity of meanings backwards.

The Evista definition of heritage and past connections is different to the idea of "nation" and identity often emphasized by Revolutionary Indianismo and the earlier works of Reinaga. Evismo builds its fact of heritage as a broad connection to a *social* past of meanings, which becomes repeatedly revived and re-actualized in different kinds of interactions. An individual or an actor can thus inherit valid meanings from social spaces beyond the family and the community. Additionally, the possibility of a variety of interactions turns identities into a "situational" phenomenon, which also means that individuals can often change their identities based on the characteristics of the interactions that they have (Linera 2014, 12). Hence, identities can be reconstructed and modified throughout time. They can be either "assigned" or "assumed" in each context of interaction (12). Assigned identities are inherited and imposed within particular social contexts of interaction, which means that they are difficult to resist or renounce. Assumed identities entail the creative possibility of modifying inherited identities in different directions. Despite this flexibility, the possibility of knowing categories still depends on the moments of meaning inheritance, which socially limit the means used by actors to reconstruct identities. Since identities become re-activated in social interactions, the possibility of creativity is also limited by the confrontations that take place within these moments. Evismo thus views the inheritance of meaning as flexible and dynamic, but also limited.

Consistent with the possibility of flexibility, creativity, and confrontation, Linera asserts that identities result from long processes of struggle and domination, which can modify different notions or can even erase particular identities (Linera 2014, 28). The idea of struggle and negotiation emerges not only in relation to confrontations, which can take place within a series of moments of identity re-deployment, assumption, and assignment, but also in connection to the very nature of identities. According to the author, identities are inevitably hierarchicalizing because they entail differentiating and valuing boundaries. These lines create a sense of belonging and simultaneously exclude "others" who do not quite fit the delineated commonalities of that group (13). This exclusion entails a hierarchicalization, which creates politics of force and power (14).

As a result, Linera asserts that certain identities can become hegemonic. Some notions achieve this status through power struggles and by homogenizing or excluding other identities. They impose a single notion of identity as the official definition of a nation, "committing ethnocide" against all the other identities sharing the territory (Linera 2014, 75, author's translation). To the contrary, other forms of hegemony build more encompassing and accepting ideas, which can successfully articulate and accommodate many identities together. Some notions thus entail more *complex* ideas, which are capable of integrating a diversity of identities (18). Both homogenizing and complex constructions of nations need to impose themselves throughout time and struggles in order to become dominant, institutionalized, and territorialized (18). These nations can thus reach historical points of hegemony, which accommodate or homogenize many identities within a single territory, common origin, common future, and common set of institutions (19).

Equality and validation

Despite these possibilities of struggle, domination, and creativity, Linera sustains the notion of meaning inheritance and he creates an epistemic possibility of knowing the historical chains of meanings. In other words, diachronic connections can show the struggles and modifications of meanings, but they can also display the historical *continuity* and the connections of some elements and identities. Hence, creativity and struggle do not obstruct the epistemic validation that emerges whenever an interpreter can establish the long chain of connections and inheritance. This capacity to know the historical continuity of identities can be proved and empirically examined by taking into account events that include the deployment, re-actualization, and dispute of national identities. From this way of knowing, which creates an objectified capacity of drawing maps of continuous identities, Evismo constructs the boundaries that enable a form of classification and validation. In order to achieve this goal, Evismo uses two interconnected notions, which consistently unfold from the fact of meaning inheritance.

On one side, Evismo deploys the idea of a pre-conquest commonality in origin. The notion of identity and meaning inheritance leads towards the possibility of reconstructing the history and map of concurrent identities. This epistemic strategy presupposes the possibility of knowing the continuous path of identities since their moment of inception. However, the assumption of origins is epistemically warranted even when the original creation of an identity might be empirically untraceable. The notion of origins is a philosophical principle of classification that is warranted by the idea of inheritance; it is the ontologically "real" characteristic of identities. Hence, continuity hereby appears as an epistemic justification of a philosophical bedrock of classification. To define this criterion, Linera claims that identities always result from the "will (voluntad) and the national construction, which existed prior to the conquest or the real nationalization of each one of them" (Linera 2014, 23).[2] The notions of "will" and "construction" validate identities that can be assumed as having an initial moment of creation and a collective decision to gather under a single category. The "reality" of inheritance thus becomes the validation of identities that can be regarded as having their own "will" and "construction." Here, ontology becomes a boundary of validation that defines the characteristics of a way of knowing. This notion of a commonality in origin equally validates the national identities that share "will" and "construction" as their characteristics, creating a space of coexistence for multiple nations. The epistemic definition of inheritance thus leads Linera to use a philosophical idea of common origin as a basis of commonality and a boundary of equality between identities. Insofar as a state, society, and territory coincide in the creation of such a boundary, they can construct the form of equality called "plurinationality" (Linera 2014, 75).

Despite its capacity to include several national identities as equally valid within a defined realm, this notion of a commonality in origin also creates an exclusionary boundary. On one side, different identities can entail the original characteristic of nations (i.e., "will" and "construction"), which classifies them as equally validated. The Evista version of the fact of inheritance thus leads to a notion of equality that validates the very heterogeneity of original identities. Through this form of validation, the discourse constructs a form of complex identity, which can encompass a diversity of nations within a single territory, society, and state. On the other side, all processes of homogenization, conquest, exclusion, ethnocide, and domination become invalidated. Their disrespect of equally validated identities leads towards invalidation.

Insofar as it only includes the notion of a commonality in origin to determine a criterion of classification, however, Evismo cannot determine the difference between, on one side, a moment of "will" and "construction" and, on the other side, a moment of conquest. How can Evismo determine that a "homogenizing" identity does not emerge from a new, widespread, and shared moment of "will" and "construction"? To answer this question, Linera and Morales introduce a second criterion of classification, which is consistently attached to the fact of inheritance. They use the notion of meaning *continuity*, which enables the possibility of tracing an identity before and after a moment of conquest. This continuation proves the resistance of a "will" and a "construction" throughout time. Moreover, the analysis of a map of identities requires an examination of the continuity of identities over time all the way until the moment of present charting. Insofar as identities have resisted conflicts and have continued towards the concurrent moment of mapping, they become validated against the possibility of their contemporaneous homogenization or exclusion. The continuity of an identity thus requires the possibility of respecting its differences. To the contrary, the processes of homogenization and/or hierarchicalization of those differences become invalidated. Their disrespect of identities that have continuously sustained their own "will" and "construction" turns them into colonial "others" (Linera 2014, 75).

As a result of this criteria of classification, Evismo aims to separate itself from the tendency of Revolutionary Indianismo towards another form of homogenization. Evismo does not construct the possibility of liberation from the reconstruction of a genuine past, found specifically in the Inca Empire or in previous Tiwanaku civilizations. Here, national diversity is not a single and unchanging form of communitarian equality. Instead, the reconstruction of the respect of national differences has to take into account the modifications that have been assumed throughout time and it has to respect the inclusion of new "wills" and "constructions." The "indigenous" struggle in Bolivia thus becomes a broader fight against the universalization of monoculture, homogenization, and conquest.

Inequality: Colonialism, ethnocide, and oppression

In this particular discourse of anti-colonialism, the ontological construction of an intelligible "reality" leads to a boundary of classification, which regards whatever contradicts the principles of validation as less "real." Accordingly, Evismo understands "colonialism" as the processes that aim to disrupt the continuity of validated identities, disrespecting the differences that should coexist in a particular territory. These colonial projects are partially invalidated because they violate the original "will" and "construction" of "indigenous" identities through the imposition of their own ideas of nation. Hence, European nations overstep their epistemic validity by expanding their own identities upon other "wills" and "constructions." By doing so, they disrespect the diversity of nations that pre-existed in the Americas before conquest; they disrupt the continuity of "wills" and "constructions," which explains why Evismo classifies colonialism as a "lie" and as the main cause of injustices in the world.

Enacting colonialism: Dialectical history and neoliberalism

Based on the principles of classification that emerge from the ontological understanding of "reality," Linera and Morales contribute to a reconstruction of history, which organizes epochs dialectically. They deploy the notions of "will," "construction," and continuity to classify epochs, using their own bedrock to organize temporality. Based on the ways in which they respect or disrespect identities that appear as "real" within the boundaries of the discourse, epochs are classified as "reality," contradictions of "reality," or transformations towards "reality." As the 2009 Constitution of Bolivia narrates, pre-colonial epochs are regarded as respectful of identity diversity ("Bolivia Constitution" 2009). Due to its consistency with ontological "reality," this epoch is viewed as the thesis of history. To the contrary, the beginning of European conquest marks the opening of the antithesis of history and the continuous resistance of "indigenous" nations. Hierarchy, falsehood, injustice, and resistance thus characterizes the 500 years of colonialism (Linera 2014, 56). This civilizing project not only takes place in terms of identity, but also includes institutionalized and economic forms of exclusion (281). That is, the hierarchicalization of identities leads to material effects of inequality, segregation, discrimination, exploitation, etc. Additionally, the erasure of identities includes different kinds of violence against the peoples who represent these ways of being. To disrupt the continuity of "indigenous" identities, colonialism thus uses genocide, repression, military service, tools of citizenship, education, etc. (210). Beyond their physical and cultural erasure, this process also seeks to silence "indigenous" agency and struggle throughout history. Colonialism thus entails a "miserabilist" reading of "indigenous" struggles and historical participation (211).

This epoch of injustices and historical contradiction began with the conquest of the Americas and, in the case of the Andean region, the Inca Empire. The independence of Bolivia in 1825 only continued this process by denying "indigenous" peoples their rights (Linera 2014, 35). The oligarchic state that emerged at the time constructed a notion of citizenship that excluded "indigenous peoples" and regarded everything "Indio" as a non-nation (30). Then, the 1952 Nationalist Revolution modified the civilizing project of Bolivia by using class-based ideas of equality, but it also continued the exclusion of everything that was regarded as "indigenous." During the years of the Revolution, the government solidified a hegemonic notion of common identity, nationalized hydrocarbons, and began a program of land redistribution (37). Through these policies, as well as other strategies, the Revolution sought to impose a single notion of nation and it aimed to homogenize the identity differences that existed in the Bolivian territory (40). The fourth colonial moment of Bolivian history began with the rise of neoliberalism during Hugo Banzer Suárez's dictatorship in 1971 and it ended with the election of Morales and Linera in 2005.

The Evista re-organization of history is not very different to the narrations created by other forms of Indianismo, but Linera and Morales emphasize the importance of identity diversity and they also highlight the relevance of studying the neoliberal decades that emerged in Bolivia and the world in the 1970s. Within this narration, Evismo views neoliberalism as the last moment of colonialism and resistance. According to Morales, this neoliberal agenda corresponds to new imperialist tactics, used to control the "South" and all marginalized peoples (Morales 2015a). Linera adds that neoliberalism is a form of capitalism, purely oriented towards the increase of profit through wars, the destruction of nature, and the erasure of all nations (Linera 2015, 320). The neoliberal epoch in Bolivia, the Americas, and the world thus entails its own homogenizing and conquering identity.

According to Morales and Linera, neoliberalism elevates a model citizen and identity through a universalized idea of "rationality." Instead of a "mestizo" identity or a segregation-based idea of nation, neoliberalism constructs its notion of "humanity" by proceeding from the universalized idea of a profit-seeking individual (Linera 2015, 323). This notion of "humanity" claims universality, but it also hierarchicalizes other identities, homogenizing other nations and disproportionally benefiting some peoples over others. According to Evismo, the neoliberal scale of judgment entails a system of classification that is based on the levels of "rationality" of different nations and their degrees of competitive capacity to accumulate power, resources, wealth, etc. Morales calls this classification the "hierarchy of the market" (Morales 2012, author's translation). The lower levels of "development" entail inferior capacities of competition and individual "rationality." "Other" nations and identities thus appear as inferior, less "rational," "under-developed," or "developing" cultures that have to modernize or disappear from the path of progress. Moreover, the responsibility of "progress" depends on the capacity of each individual, which transforms notions of solidarity and more collective ideas of organization into "irrationalities."

In relation to the domestic application of neoliberalism in Bolivia, Evismo views this period as the colonial continuation of nation-based hierarchies and homogenizing policies (Linera 2014, 57). In this country, neoliberalism tried to pacify the continuation and increasing resistance of "indigenous" movements by "protecting" their "ancestral" identities, but, beneath this form of "multiculturalism," the state excluded "indigenous" peoples from political power and it hierarchicalized their identity as an inferior nation, inevitably disappearing under the superior forces of globalization.

By contrast, the neoliberal state enabled and empowered those individuals who were regarded as the "rational" agents of progress and "development." The Bolivian state followed policies promoted by the International Monetary Fund, World Bank, and its own elites, which pushed the government towards a wide range of privatizations, labor market deregulations, financial market deregulations, etc. Those who were regarded as "rational" were given leeway to civilize the rest of the country. The state granted a disproportionate amount of privilege to those who fitted the universalized idea of profit-seeking rationality. Hence, the neoliberal form of citizenship allowed for the concentration of capital and wealth in the hands of the few who could in fact access contracts of privatization. On the other side, the individuals that were regarded as less "rational" due to their incapacity to accumulate wealth could work for someone else. Exploitation was thus justified for those who were hierarchically lower in the scale of individualist "rationality" (Linera 2015, 320, author's translation). According to Evismo, this hierarchicalization of identities and the prioritization of capitalist individualism led Bolivia to an unsustainable increase in poverty and inequality, which eventually resulted in economic crises, weakened productive bases, unemployment, fragmentation of institutions, political crises, deaths, and the collapse of the traditional state (Linera 2015, 307–308). Within these crises, which took place in Bolivia throughout the 1990s and early 2000s, the Aymara movement was the main actor continuously resisting the homogenizing, yet hierarchicalizing and immiserating tendencies of neoliberalism. They were the ones who resisted against the privatizations of water, gas, and other resources. They opposed the neoliberal interventions of the International Monetary Fund, the World Bank, and foreign direct investments. They were the ones denouncing the general exclusion and marginalization of "indigenous" peoples (235). They represented the continuity of "indigenous" resistance throughout this last epoch of colonialism.

Throughout the neoliberal moment of Bolivian history, then, the main contradiction and injustice was the exclusion of national diversity and equality. This colonial form of hierarchicalization entailed the monocultural imposition of a particular form of citizenship and social order, which included racialized classifications of individuals based on their skin color, practices, clothing, traditions, etc. Due to the ideational connection that neoliberalism established between "whiteness" and official notions of "rational" identity, this colonial ordering of nations appeared as a racial hierarchicalization of individuals. Accordingly, "whiteness" was regarded throughout time as "social capital," which was required in order to access institutional power, economic power, certified education, and military positions (Linera 2014, 51).

Beyond these domestic issues, Evismo constructs neoliberalism as the main form of global hierarchicalization and racism. Immigrants, for example, are viewed as less "rational" individuals from less "rational" societies, which have not developed due to their own "irrational" choices. This perspective entails a hierarchicalization of capitalist businessmen over the populations that they affect with their individualist profit-seeking actions (Morales 2015a). Moreover, this hierarchy appears to be justifying wars and invasions whenever profits or "rationality" are threatened (Linera 2015, 320); it pushes towards violent policies whenever nations or states become obstacles against the continuation of profit accumulation, but then it excludes those affected by violent policies because their misery appears to be caused by their own "irrationality." This neoliberal hierarchicalization of peoples and the increase of global inequality are also regarded by Evismo as the main causes of terrorism. The exclusion and marginalization of peoples, imposition of colonial forms of homogenization, wars against other identities, extraction of resources from all over the world, and disproportionate accumulation of wealth in the "North" are the causes of the frustration that leads to the insurgent usage of violence (Morales 2016).

According to Evismo, the neoliberal hierarchy described above not only organized other "human" identities based on their degree of "rationality," but also arranged all other "natural" entities and objects. At the summit of this vertical arrangement of echelons, the profit-seeking individual successfully accumulated wealth and income. At its bottom, all other entities become "resources," "assets," or "tools" that are used in the development of the faculty hereby elevated as the universal identity of "humanity." Even some peoples become usable "resources" or "cheap labor." They become means in the accumulation of wealth and profit; the achievement of the essence of "humanity." Furthermore, as Morales stated in the Peoples' World Conference of Climate Change and the Rights of Mother Earth, this neoliberal form of "progress" entails an endless or limitless search of accumulation because it universalizes its profit-seeking rationality above all else (Morales 2010b, author's translation). The elevation of the neoliberal identity locates profit-seeking as the universal bedrock of historical judgment. Profit-seeking arranges the past and "knows" the future. The past appears as the lack of "development;" whereas the future is viewed as the continuous increase of accumulation and economic growth.

Since it disrespects other nations and it threatens other peoples, the anthropocentrism of neoliberalism also becomes invalidated. Evismo undermines this vertical organization because it imposes an identity upon other "wills" and "constructions," threatening their historical continuity and claiming to be superior. The neoliberal contradiction of the "reality" of identities thus becomes the main factor of invalidation. As a result, the violation of the equality among identities leads to the invalidation of the anthropocentric tendencies of neoliberalism. The epistemically unwarranted universalization of a profit-seeking rationality is understood as the unjust cause of unequal accumulation and the destruction of the environment. One of the main problems of neoliberal anthropocentrism is thus the disproportionately greater utilization of natural resources in the countries of the "North." The unequal accumulation of wealth and higher standards of living in developed countries appear possible only through the abusive usage of oxygen, fossil fuels, oceanic fishery, mining products, etc. Moreover, the countries of the "South," which are the ones polluting the least, often pay the highest costs of environmental degradation and climate change. Finally, the unequal relationship between peoples that emerges from neoliberalism also affects future generations, which are regarded as equal identities within Evismo. In its profit-seeking endeavor, neoliberalism universalizes consumption as the standard of epochal judgement and it creates a dichotomy between developed and developing nations. To the contrary, Evismo views the universalization of this identity as a threat for future generations and the continuity of humanity (Linera 2015, 318).

Re-authorizing "indigenous" peoples: A way of being

As previous sections show, ontology validates a way of knowing, which emerges from the "reality" of meaningful heritage and then creates a platform of equality for the identities that fit the principles of classification of the discourse. As a result, the ontological "reality" of the continuous identities that emerge from a "will" and a "construction" invalidates the universality of neoliberalism and other monocultural forms of colonialism. The antithesis of history thus appears as a contradiction against the "reality" of continuously resisting identities. To plan, construct, and implement a solution for the historical problem of colonialism, Evismo epistemologically authorizes a way of being that has access to "reality" and can thus enact it in a new epoch. That is, the ontological dimension of the discourse determines what is "reality," but epistemology dictates who can access it to rule on its behalf. Only those who know "reality" gain the authority that is necessary to reshape an epoch and, in this case, bring about the synthesis of history.

Since "indigenous" identities are regarded as connected to a continuous, resistant, and pre-conquest "will" and "construction," which also respects the plurality of other identities, Evismo authorizes them as the knowers of the "reality" that will bring about liberation. On one side, "indigenous" identities are viewed as consistent with the principle of equality in common origin. They entail a moment of "will" and "construction," which makes them equal to all other validated nations. In order to ensure this original moment, these forms of identity appear connected to pre-colonial times. This link does not mean that "indigenous" identities neatly correspond in all their characteristics to a specific way of life such as the Inca Empire. Instead, Evismo establishes a form of complex continuity to show that some indigenous notions do not belong to conquest. Indigenous identities are thus regarded as having some kind of pre-conquest moment of original agreement from which they create a form of "brotherhood." These identities also include a historical continuation throughout the rest of the colonial epoch. Some of their aspects have resisted colonialism and still sustain a degree of continuity in the present. Finally, "indigenous" identities entail a form of respect for other nations, which are regarded as equally validated forms of "will" and "construction." This respect for national differences appears as the most important part of the original and pre-conquest form of "indigenous" identity, which has resisted colonialism ("Bolivia Constitution" 2009, Preamble, author's translation); this is the main characteristic of an identity continuously treasured by "indigenous" peoples through 500 years of resistance (Linera 2014, 44). Sociologists, intellectuals, social movements, politicians, and other actors can trace the continuous path of "indigenous" heritage from pre-conquest periods to contemporary Bolivia. Many things might have changed throughout the path of historical inheritance and dispute that affected these meanings, but intellectuals and political actors claim to know the "indigenous" continuation of a search for the respect of national differences.

"Indigenous" pre-colonial histories show the congruency between their knowledge and the basis of equality that is validated by the fact of inheritance. For example, their pre-colonial communitarian systems illustrate how their ways of being were consistent with the originary moment of identities and with the notion of national equality used by Evismo. Through these systems, "indigenous" peoples allowed for a plurality of originary "wills" and "constructions" to coexist. Additionally, "Indios" are the ones who have resisted homogenization throughout time in Bolivia, which makes them the ones consistently authorized as the main agents of this process of anti-colonialism. Their epistemological possibility of accessing the ontological "reality" of inheritance makes them true agents of plurinationality. "Indios" are epistemically authorized knowers (Linera 2014, 58). The proximity between "indigenous" identities and "reality" thus demands that Bolivia "Indianizes" its state, territory, and government (50–51).

Enacting rule: Participation, rule, and Evo Morales

In order to enact the synthesis of history, Evismo epistemologically authorizes "indigenous" peoples as agents who can rule on behalf of a "reality" of identity pluralism and equality. Then, in 2005, Morales and Linera won the presidential elections of Bolivia.[3] From this position, Morales and Linera further enacted their epistemological notion of authorization, which specified the characteristics and rights of "citizens," the authority of the government, and the legitimacy of representatives. In other words, the enactment of

Evismo includes epistemological notions of authorization, which were used to define how a particular way of being could participate in the state, rule in the government, and represent in the party.

Since Morales and Linera are the leaders of the "indigenous" movement, which has historically carried the form of identity that is attached to the notion of "reality," they are regarded as the main authorized agents of Evismo. They appear within the discourse as the legitimate representatives of "indigeneity" and the ones who can rule in the government of Bolivia. Here, the epistemic authority of an "indigenous" way of being legitimizes the position of Morales and Linera in the government. On one side, this authority emerges from the constructions of "indigeneity" as the identity that represents the resistant continuation of inherited meanings. Here, Morales and Linera become the embodiment of the long-term memory of the "Indio" (Linera 2015, 316). On the other side, this authorization transforms them into the agents who can open a new era by enacting the equality that emerges from the continuous resistance against monocultural forms of civilization in Bolivia. Accordingly, Morales affirms that his government and social movements begin a "… Pachakuti, an awakening of life, the culture of life, and a transition away from capitalism (which is violence between human beings and against nature) to the time of the totality of the Cosmos" (Morales 2012). Morales and, to a lesser extent, Linera thus appear as the personifications of "indigenous" struggles, which are now unified under a single reading of history and a single notion of a future in "plurinationality."

Beyond the legitimation of a leader and representative in the government, Evismo also includes the important possibility of popular participation, which redistributes political power in Bolivia and significantly democratizes the definition of citizenship in the state. The discourse thus epistemologically authorizes Morales and Linera as the main representatives of "reality" in the government, but this "reality" is also more generally connected to the identities that correspond to the principles of equality. In other words, all those peoples who are "will," "construction," and "respect" become authorized knowers of "plurinationality." Morales and Linera thus appear as the leaders and representatives of "reality," but the discourse also turns its epistemological authorization into a notion of active citizenship and a basis of democratic participation, which moves beyond some of the limitations of neoliberalism.

In order to democratize citizenship in Bolivia, Morales and Linera promote the idea of "vivir bien" or "buen vivir," which is translated as "live well" (*sumak kawsay* in Quechua or *suma quamaña* in Aymara).[4] This project uses notions of complementarity and reciprocity to think about political and economic equality. In this section, I discuss the process of political democratization, which unfolds neatly from epistemic authorization. In the next segment of the chapter, I concentrate on the idea of economic equality that can be more easily connected to the dimension of ontological "reality."

Within Evismo, complementarity is the possibility of valuing the differences of the validated national identities that are mapped in a particular territory.

In order to implement this form of respect, Morales and Linera reshaped the Bolivian state through a new Constitution, which was approved in 2009. This constitution includes several rights and mechanisms, which are designed to ensure the respect of "indigenous" and "liberal" differences, while also redistributing political power. In relation to the equal respect of differences, "indigenous" peoples gained rights that are designed to protect "their" institutions, autonomy, and self-government ("Bolivia Constitution" 2009, art. II). Additionally, the Constitution grants "indigenous" peoples the right to have an "indigenous jurisdiction," separated from an "ordinary jurisdiction" and an "agro-environmental jurisdiction" (art. CXIC, § 1). The judicial system of Bolivia thus includes juridical pluralism (art. CLXXIX). Even the education system is broadly delineated within the Constitution to avoid homogenizing pedagogies of mono-nationalism (art. LXXVIII, § 2). Together, these rights enable "indigenous" peoples to sustain a degree of separation from the rest of "liberal" society.

On the other side, the Evista project includes the notion of reciprocity, which promotes the connection of solidarity and equality that can emerge among these different nations within a realm of "plurinationality." This connection requires that all nations equally contribute to and participate in the general possibility of "living well." Buen vivir thus entails the respect of differences between nations, but it also demands a more equal, solidary, and overarching form of relationship among them. The usage of these notions together leads to a respect for differences that does not entail separatism or secessionism. Here, the notions of "plurinational" equality and reciprocity connect all the different nations coexisting within a single territory and state.

By promoting this form of relationship, buen vivir opposes the universalization of capitalist and neoliberal identities, which result in systems of nation-based hierarchies and exploitation (Linera 2015, 318). Accordingly, buen vivir entails an economic, social, and political transformation; it includes a series of "commandments to confront capitalism and construct the culture of life" (Morales 2012). That is, Evismo de-authorizes the disproportionally high status of liberal identities in previous state constructions of citizenship and it aims to remedy the marginalization of "indigenous" identities. Morales and Linera seek to "Indianize" Bolivia, "… for example, with the constitutional coexistence of representative and communitarian democracy, ordinary and indigenous-originary justice, the control of the state by social organizations, etc." (Linera 2014, 50). By including communitarian forms of participation, the state can avoid the "mono-organizational" characteristics of liberal states and it can expand its construction of citizenship (Linera 2006, 71). The Evista project thus aims to include the sectors of Bolivian society that have been excluded until recently (71). The inclusion of communitarian subjects of citizenship leads to the destruction of the monopoly of state power that was held in Bolivia by a single ethnic group (72). In order to institutionalize this possibility, the 2009 Constitution of Bolivia delineates a complex system of participation for "indigenous" peoples. The Constitution includes not only representative democracy for individuals, but also integrates communitarian and direct forms of democracy, which are systems regarded as more consistent with "indigenous" practices and identities ("Bolivia Constitution" 2009, art. XI, § 1).

In the case of Bolivia, the enactment of "plurinationality" concentrates primarily on the possibility of empowering "indigenous" identities due to their historical marginalization, but the notion of equality that emerges from this discourse seeks to avoid the exclusion of "urban" or "liberal" identities. Morales and Linera thus propose an encompassing idea of national equality, which seeks to build a space where different identities can coexist not only by following a communitarian or "indigenous" ways of life, but also by respecting other "Western" identities. Hence, Evismo includes "Occidental" identities as a parallel nation, which also coexists within the country. Their "liberal" "will" and "construction" did not originate in the pre-colonial Americas, but it has a legitimate moment of creation and a historical continuation among certain peoples who also live in Bolivia today. The originary creation and continuation of "liberal" identities thus prevents Evismo from completely cancelling them as invalid, foreign, or false identities. Instead, both of these identities are validated as equal nations once liberalism loses its privileges and dominating tendencies.

Moreover, "liberalism" has become a part of the state, society, and territory of Bolivia. Insofar as it entails a complete isomorphism among the entire society, state, and territory of Bolivia, "plurinationality" has to include them as well. Hence, the "liberal" idea of justice was included as a separate jurisdiction called "ordinary" justice, whereas the possibility of "indigenous" autonomy was called "indigenous jurisdiction" ("Bolivia Constitution" 2009, art. CXIC, § 1). Additionally, individual voting rights and representative forms of governance are guaranteed by the Constitution. The inclusion of "liberalism" within Evismo does not, however, come free of epistemic costs and redistributive measures. While still granting it a space within the Bolivian territory, state, and society, the Evista notion of national equality strips "liberalism" of its claim of superiority and universality, which previously enabled it to act as the source of mono-nationality within Bolivia. Plurinationalism thus entails a space of national diversity and equality, which allows for two contradicting identities to coexist; it settles the "colonial" contradiction by avoiding yet another form of mono-nationality.

The dual inclusion of "liberalism" and "indigeneity" in the formation of a new state for Bolivia leads to a process of democratization because the state expands the possibility of participation beyond individual voting and representation. Despite this expansion, Evismo pre-defines how a specific set of differences can be heard by the state. Notwithstanding the redistribution of political power that Morales and Linera achieved during their administrations, then, the reconstruction of the state assumes that the "real" identities of a territory are intelligible. From this possibility of knowing, Evismo draws who is a validated identity and it establishes how they are authorized to speak in the state; it constructs another form of citizenship. As a result, the state entails the characterization of the "real" national identities that are inherited within a territory. In the case of Bolivia, this specification includes a separation between "liberal" rights, granted to all "individuals," and "communitarian" or "indigenous" rights, which are granted to specific peoples. Despite the right to "self-identify," the Constitution then delineates a criterion to classify "indigenous" peoples or nations. Consistent with the fact of inheritance, Evismo institutionalizes the requirement of pre-conquest existence and continuity throughout history to classify who is a "real" "indigenous" community ("Bolivia Constitution" 2009, art. XXX). As other authors have also pointed out, the new constitution of Bolivia reserves for the state the authority to define what differences can be protected and heard; it creates a particular definition of "indigeneity" (Albró 2010, 79). Then, the protection or safeguarding of "indigenous" identities is defined in equally specific terms, which include "the patrimony of peasant originary indigenous peoples and nations, cosmic visions, myths, oral history, dances, cultural practices, knowledges, and traditional technologies. This patrimony is part of the identity and expression of the State" ("Bolivia Constitution" 2009, art. CI, § 1).

Since buen vivir includes both complementarity and reciprocity, the state not only entails a definition of who is an authorized difference within plurinational citizenship, but also determines the overarching connection between these identities. That is, plurinational citizenship respects some differences through ideas of complementarity, but it also demands equality by promoting notions of solidarity and reciprocity. Hence, the constitutional law of Bolivia explicitly enacts the overarching definition of a single logic of "plurinationality." For example, the new constitution appears as the superior set of norms that regulates the "differences" found in the territory. Moreover, the Constitutional Court of Bolivia regulates over all the separate jurisdictions of the state ("Bolivia Constitution" 2009, art. CLXXX, § 3). As a result, the separate and autonomous jurisdiction of "indigenous" peoples has to respect the overarching logic of plurinationality (art. CXIC, § 2). Similarly, the education system of Bolivia seeks to respect national differences while also promoting a unifying notion of "plurinationality." The state thus respects a group of national identities and autonomies, but it also centralizes the education system by promoting an overarching notion of equality, which seeks to include all the pre-existing and continuous identities of Bolivia. The state educates all the different nations of Bolivia into "plurinationality" (art. LXXX, § 2).

Implications: The government of Morales and the citizenship of some differences

Within the epistemic functions of the discourse, the epistemological possibility of accessing "reality" leads towards the authorization of particular identities, which are defined in the Constitution as the citizens of the state. Distinct kinds of "liberal" individuals and "indigenous" communities thus become authorized to participate in the state and access its rights. Since citizens can acquire active roles in the government or they can elect people on their behalf, their epistemological authority is transferred to the government. Thus, the government is regarded as the functioning body of the state. From this epistemically authorized position, the government can determine the specificities of those who have to be heard in particular contexts; it can define the mechanisms and limits of participation as long as they fit the general understanding of citizenship. Finally, the epistemological authorization of those who best fit the characteristics of "reality" leads towards the legitimation of the representatives in office. Morales, Linera, and the members of the MAS thus become the "real" leaders of "plurinationality." This epistemic authorization of a citizenry, government, and set of representatives has important implications.

On one side, the definition of citizenship delineates who is a "real" "indigenous" community. This centralized definition of an authorized "indigenous" way of being requires the pre-conquest and continuous principles of "plurinationality." According to Albró, this notion authorizes particular voices and privileges a more Aymara-centric definition of indigeneity, which silences "others" in Bolivia (Albró 2010, 73). The new constitution and state thus draw a "well intentioned" notion of plurinationality, which expands liberal democracy while still excluding the diversity of peoples that coexist in the Bolivian territory (73). According to the author, other forms of association and other voices, which do not quite fit the binary model of communitarian/individual participation, remain excluded from the state. For example, Quillacollo communities have forms of complex association that are often marginalized in Bolivia because they do not square with the collective/individual distinction of citizenship (82).

Furthermore, the state-centered definition of the validated identities that fit "reality" dictates who can access the guarantees and rights that are granted to citizens. In the case of "indigenous" rights, this is particularly important because peoples cannot just self-identify within the classification. In the current state of Bolivia, to be "indigenous" means that a "plurinational," pre-conquest, and originary identity enjoys an intelligible continuity throughout colonial history. This criterion can create obstacles for smaller communities that have suffered more colonial violence and erasure. Additionally, the process of recognition that allows for communities to access rights ultimately depends on the governmental apparatus of daily decision-making. As the functioning body of the state, the government enjoys an unequal epistemic authority to define who is "indigenous" enough to access "indigenous" rights. For example, an open letter of international support recently denounced the governmental exclusion of Qhara Qhara communities from rights of autonomy and from the protection of their lands in the regions of Potosí and Chuquisaca, Bolivia (Observatorio del Cambio Rural 2019). According to the letter, this community found it particularly difficult to access autonomy because the former government of Morales and Linera continuously postponed their applications. Moreover, the Quara Qhara community is located in territories that were related to governmental projects of infrastructure and the extraction of hydrocarbons. The letter thus denounced that the petition of the community had been largely ignored due to the economic interests of the government and international corporations. In relation to this case, the Regional Movement for Land denounced Morales as "neocolonial and monocultural" (Movimiento Regional por la Tierra y el Territorio 2019, author's translation).

The state-centered definition of citizenship thus delineates a general criterion that determines who is a true "indigenous" voice, worthy of participation and rights. As Rivera states, this is the problem that emerges from official delineations of an "Indio," which utilize colonial and masculine ideas of "nation" to demarcate bounded, fixed, territorialized, excluding, and essentialized identities (Rivera 2018, 128). Since the state transfers its epistemic authority to the government, different offices and ministries become authorized to define the context-dependent specifies of participation as well. That is, the government is authorized not only to scrutinize the applications to access rights such as autonomy, but also to determine the daily limits of participation that are required in relation to particular policies. For example, the government can define, within the limits of the constitution, who has to be heard in relation to specific projects of development. Since the democratization of the state authorizes certain voices, the Constitution demands the participation of certain peoples within the decision-making processes that affect the environment ("Bolivia Constitution" 2009, art. CCCXLIII), but the government enjoys a disproportional authority to classify peoples and to determine the mechanisms of participation.

During the well-known case of the Isiboro Secure National Park and Indigenous Territory (TIPNIS for its initials in Spanish), the government of Morales began constructing a road through "ancestral" lands, which belonged to "indigenous" communities. In 2011, hundreds of peoples planned to march on foot for 375 miles from the region to La Paz, where they were going to stage a protest against the project. The police intervened on September 25, using force to suppress the protest. Additionally, indigenous movements expressed in a manifesto in 2012 that the government and its supporters had discriminated and violently opposed their demands (Semanario Aqui 2012). As a result of strong opposition, the Morales government decided to postpone the project. Despite this delay, the government re-started the project in 2017. On August 13, Morales signed a law that took away the protection and autonomy of these "indigenous" territories. At this time, he claimed that 58 of the 68 "indigenous" communities inhabiting the region had agreed to the construction of the road. These communities and the government were the "true indigenous" peoples of Bolivia (Morales 2017, author's translation). By contrast, all those opposing the project were classified as "enemies," who worked for international corporations or the right-wing politicians of Bolivia. These peoples were not "indigenous." Morales asserted, "we consulted them. The ones opposing this are enemies. They are enemies of the indigenous movement. They want us to live like we did 200 or 300 years ago. They do not want us to develop" (Morales 2017). The very participation of some communities and the possibility of silencing others was thus used as part of a self-authorizing strategy, which allowed for the government to ignore rights previously granted by the same structure of laws.

Finally, the epistemological authorization of those who best fit the characteristics of "reality" leads to the legitimation of particular representatives. The legitimation of Morales as the true "indigenous" leader creates the arrogance of thinking that he can speak for everyone else, defining all struggles and situations in Bolivia and beyond (Rivera 2018, 111). According to Rivera, Morales uses "magic words" such as "indigenous" or "social movements" to create an "epistemological blockade," which subjugates rebellions and oppositions of different kinds (114, author's translation). As the main representative of "indigeneity," Morales has even claimed that he can classify in specific moments who is a true "indigenous" people, or whether their demands are legitimate (Morales 2015a). Since Morales appears within the discourse as the true knower of "reality," moreover, he gains the legitimacy that is necessary to continue enacting this "reality." Hence, the discourse locates Morales as the main representative and agent of "plurinationality," which justifies his continuous role in the government. Consequently, Morales sought to run for a fourth term as president of Bolivia. The 2009 Constitution of Bolivia barres him from doing so and Morales lost the referendum that he proposed in order to reform that law. Notwithstanding these obstacles, the Supreme Court of Bolivia argued that the limitations of presidential terms was a violation of human rights (Casey 2018). Hence, Morales and Linera ran for another term in 2019 and then suffered the coup d'état that exiled them in Argentina.

The authorization of a citizenry, government, and leader thus emerges from the epistemological possibility of accessing an ontological "reality." Throughout the enactment and institutionalization of this way of being, the delineation of more specific characteristics further determines who is a citizen, a government, and a leader; it creates stronger and more impermeable boundaries of classification. Since the Evista "reality" of heritage is regarded as an unquestionable ontology, which is elevated above other realities, the epistemological authority of those who can access "reality" also becomes universalized above other voices. As a result, Morales, the state, and the government become the authorized voices of all other equalities, struggles, movements, and projects. They can assimilate or marginalize other experiences of ethnicity, race, gender, class, ability, sexuality, etc. In this sense, Rivera asserts that Morales often deforms or transforms all other demands (Rivera 2018, 111), truncating or silencing the networks that seek to construct meaning from below or that aim to have power to "do," which is not the same as power to dominate (101). As I illustrate throughout this section, this form of authorization silences other experiences of ethnicity, but Morales has also marginalized other kinds of struggles and voices. For example, Morales tried to assimilate gender-related demands. As the President of Bolivia, Morales created a special cabinet against women's violence and for women's rights (TeleSur 2018). Despite this governmental initiative, feminist movements marched in La Paz in 2014, denouncing the misogynist phrases of Morales and other functionaries of the government, as well as demanding more action against gendered violence and femicides (Pan y Rosas 2014). Additionally, the government has silenced other feminist voices during cases of opposition. For example, by ignoring them in the judicial system and creating disproportionate obstacles against their demands, the government silences the voices of women who denounce gender violence. In relation to the murder of María Isabel Pillco, the movement called Mujeres Creando has repeatedly critiqued this kind of impunity (Comisión de Justicia, Constitucion y Regimen Electoral 2018). The problem of impunity is also related to the way in which the legal system of Bolivia provides women with very little legal recourses and often imposes several kinds of obstacles (Salmón, Elías, and Portugal n.d., 220). As Rivera affirms, the masculine authority of Morales and the government also erases the agentic role of women in different moments of resistance (Rivera 2010b). The assimilation and silencing of other voices draws a historical narration that only highlights those who are closest to "reality." Hence, the agency of women in the uprisings that took place in Bolivia between 2000 and 2005 often becomes erased from official accounts of history (Rivera 2018, 141).

Of course social movements, communities, individuals, and unions can participate thanks to the democratization of Bolivia. However, these subjects can speak when they already fit the categories of authorization, which are pre-determined in the state-centered definition of citizenry, re-deployed by the government, and contextually re-specified by representatives. In a sense, then, these voices often act as a form of self-authorization; they act as a support for already authorized voices, further solidifying the exclusion of "others."

Enacting equality: Plurinationalism and the economic systems

Throughout previous sections, I discuss the enactment of the epistemological authority that emerges by connecting a way of being to "reality." On the other side, the ontology of the discourse consistently unfolds as the "real" definition of equality and justice in Bolivia, which demands an economic and environmentalist transformation of the country. In order to achieve this goal, Evismo assimilates a relationship between "nature" and "humanity" into its own "reality," which primarily concentrates on the principles of identity equality. Hence, the epistemic prioritization of "plurinational" equality between specific identities leads to the articulation and annexation of notions of ecological equality and economic production within Evismo.

To be able to create this possibility, the two dimensions of "plurinationality" (i.e., complementarity and reciprocity) are often intertwined as parts of the "harmonic" balance between nations, and also with nature. The logic of these two ideas thus re-shapes and accommodates economic and ecological relationships within the discourse.

In relation to the notion of complementarity and the respect of national differences, "plurinationality" creates a constrained possibility of separation and autonomy for those who are "real." This form of respect is reapplied to the understanding of *production*, which is called "economic pluralism" or "pluralistic economy" ("Bolivia Constitution" 2009, art. CCCVIII, § 1, 2, and 3). Consistent with the mapping of validated identities in Bolivia, the respect of national differences is granted to the two main forms of composed identities that are recognized within the country, namely "liberalism" and "indigeneity." This form of respect validates "their" practices of production as parts of "their" identities. For example, the notion of a "pluralist economy" gives "indigenous" peoples the rights of self-government and autonomy, which include the possibility of respecting "their" form of relationship with nature. Through the validation of "indigenous" nations, Evismo validates "their" conceptions of ecology, which is regarded as "communitarian" and in "harmony" with nature (Linera 2015, 328). This protection of differences not only includes the historically demanded rights of communal property and territorial integrity, but also entails political, economic, and legal protections for communitarian forms of economic organizations ("Bolivia Constitution" 2009, art. CCCVIII). Article CCCLII of the 2009 Constitution even affirms that the state needs to consult the people affected by developmental or economic projects whenever it seeks to utilize natural resources found in their regions.

Since it is also an identity included in the citizenry of Bolivia, "liberalism" appears to be an equally respected difference. Morales and Linera often critique the "neoliberal" or "capitalist" form of production, but they also include, protect, and validate several "neoliberal" economic practices within their constitution. The respect of this "liberal" identity requires the constitutional recognition of its form of relationship with nature. Accordingly, the 2009 Constitution recognizes and protects individual property rights ("Bolivia Constitution" 2009, art. LVI, § 1, 2, and 3). Additionally, the state guarantees the respect and promotion of private businesses within the Bolivian territory (art. CCCIX, § 1 and 2).

On the other side, the idea of reciprocity leads to the limitation of "liberalism" because it creates a shared connection between the validated identities of Bolivia. The equality between nations demands this kind of transformation because "liberalism" has promoted a historically dominant form of mononationality in Bolivia, which excludes "indigenous" notions from the state, government, and even territory of the country. The national equality of "indigenous" identities thus requires the inclusion and recuperation of "their" economic ideas at the overarching level of the state and the government (Morales 2012). One of the most salient "indigenous" notions of ecology and production is the idea of Pachamama (Mother Earth), which entails a form of equality among all the entities of the Cosmos. This notion is regarded as the part of Evismo that leads towards a more ecological from of equality between "humanity" and "nature" (Morales 2010a). Then, the inclusion of this idea is enacted within the definitions of a state, government, and representative for Bolivia. For example, the Bolivian state includes this notion of ecological equality in the creation of another legal jurisdiction, dedicated exclusively to environmental matters. This jurisdiction appears as an equal branch of the judicial system ("Bolivia Constitution" 2009, art. CLXXXVII). The Constitution of 2009 thus grants independence from the "ordinary" and the "indigenous" jurisdictions to the environmental and agricultural court. Moreover, the Constitution creates special environmental rights, which any citizen can exercise by presenting cases in the events of their violation (art. XXXIV). Other legal forms of ecological equality include the requirement of independent studies of environmental impact whenever developmental projects take place (art. CCCXLVI, § 1 and § 2).

The inclusion of these "indigenous" notions into the overarching equality of the state not only constructs a space for Pachamama, but also directly limits the previously universalized ideas of "liberal" development. Evismo thus constrains the "liberal" tendency to impose its own relationship of production as a universal program that justifies limitless growth, individualist rationality, inequality, and exploitation (Morales 2010b). The limitation of the universalizing tendencies of neoliberalism takes into account future generations. Since future generations appear as part of the continuity of currently validated identities, Evismo rejects the endless form of economic growth that threatens their survival. The limitation of economic growth and development is thus connected to the equality among present and future peoples ("Bolivia Constitution" 2009, art. IX, § 6). This notion pushes Evismo towards a "humanist" relationship with nature, which uses the satisfaction of the necessities of the present and future peoples as the main criterion of growth limitation. The Bolivian Constitution of 2009 stipulates that "the state has as its highest value the human being and it will ensure its development through the equal re-distribution of income from social, medical, educational, and cultural policies as well as from re-investment in economic and productive development" (art. IX, § 6). This brings Evismo closer to the ideas of "sustainable development." Indeed, the 2009 Constitution explicitly mentions and promotes the notion of "sustainable development" (art. CCCXII, § 2). Here, the state of Bolivia has to find ways to industrialize in order to satisfy current needs, but it also has to avoid depleting resources for future generations. In order to achieve this goal of industrialization, the construction of infrastructure becomes a strategic economic dimension, which facilitates all other economic activities (art. CCCXVIII, § 3).

To achieve the limitation of neoliberalism at an international level, Evismo also uses the notion of reciprocity, which promotes economic solidarity among foreign nations. This notion demands a form of historical reparation between the "North" and the "South;" it requires that those who have been able to develop through an unjust over-utilization of resources pay back and help the rest of humanity to satisfy its needs (Morales 2012). Additionally, Bolivia, as well as other countries of the "South," hereby appear justified to re-appropriate their resources and redistribute their wealth among their own peoples. Morales and Linera thus promote the nationalization of strategic resources such as hydrocarbons and mines, which return some of the wealth to its peoples. Beyond the possibility of nationalizing resources, the Constitution also limits the foreign administration, ownership, and exploitation of key national resources ("Bolivia Constitution" 2009, art. CCCLI, § 1, § 2, and § 3). By law, foreign companies can only utilize or exploit some resources in association with the Bolivian government or under its strict regulation and control.

Implications: Assimilation and hierarchy of equalities

Since reciprocity connects the validated identities of Bolivia by establishing an overarching relationship of equality and solidarity, Evismo not only limits "liberalism," but also constrains "indigenous" notions of Pachamama. That is, the logic of the "reality" that is deployed by the discourse respects some of the differences of the two identities, but it also assimilates and articulates a reading of "liberalism" and an understanding of "indigeneity." In turn, the discourse tames and limits the ecological notions of Pachamama that it first sought to protect. This assimilating tendency emerges from the epistemic elevation of a particular "reality" above "other" ways of knowing. Evismo deploys the ontological "reality" of heritage to validate the identities that fit the principles of "will," "construction," and pre-conquest continuity. This foundation creates and elevates a platform of equality that bounds particular identities together. Since this kind of national equality comes first, the ecological elements of "indigenous" identities have to negotiate their meanings with the other identities, or nations, that are regarded as equal members of the Bolivian state. The separated and independent jurisdiction of agro-environmental matters, for example, is annexed within the overarching supremacy of the Constitution and its law. Agro-environmental law thus has to follow not only ecological equality, but also private property rights, "humanist" notions of social welfare, polices of industrialization, sustainable development, and other anthropocentric forms of economic relationships with nature. The logic of Evista "reality" thus assimilates other forms of equality within its own principles, taming their implications in order to integrate "liberal" ideas of rationality.

As a result of the articulation of multiple equalities, Evismo deforms "other" ways of knowing. For example, Evismo reintroduces anthropocentric assumptions into the idea of Pachamama. The idea of ecological equality is thus re-shaped into the notion of "sustainable development," which limits economic growth, industrialization, and environmental exploitation based primarily on the needs of "human" generations of the future. The rights of nature are thus designed to create a healthy environment for peoples ("Bolivia Constitution" 2009, art. XXXIII). Even when ecosystems appear as the objects of legal protection, the state assures their "normal" and "permanent" continuation by using national equality as its main criterion. All natural resources can thus be used and exploited as long as economic activities do not completely destroy ecosystems that are necessary for the future of "humanity" (art. CCCLXXX, § 1).

The articulation of the "indigenous" notion of Pachamama into Evismo leads to the prioritization of "human" development and welfare, which can take place insofar as it does not completely destroy the environment. Then, the government is authorized to design the context-dependent specificities of "sustainable" strategies of development and economic growth. For example, the government of Morales passed the Law of Mining and Metallurgy in 2014. This law justified mining for development, but The National Council of Ayllus and Markars of Qullasuyu (CONAMAQ for its initials in Spanish) denounced the capitalist and dangerous aspects of the project. According to the organization, the law threatened the survival of indigenous peoples, criminalized protests, consolidated capitalism, and exacerbated the colonialism of the Evista government (CONAMAQ 2014). Other voices also denounced that development continued to destroy the environment and the livelihood of their communities during the Evista administrations. For example, the Uru people often fought to keep their lake, whereas, the government aimed to divert its waters towards damming systems (Casey 2018). Similarly, the Tacanas resisted a hydroelectric dam near their homes. As Rivera asserts, the Morales government often reinforced neoliberal legacies that were based on consumerist, modernist, capitalist, and progressive ideas (Rivera 2018, 98).

Furthermore, the epistemic elevation of a particular kind of equality means that the discourse validates its own definition of struggle and justice above "other" ways of knowing. Evismo regards the nation-based struggle of "plurinationality" as the most "real" form of equality. This explains why the 2009 Constitution locates "humanity" above all else ("Bolivia Constitution" 2009, art. CCCVII, § 5). Additionally, Morales often organizes "human" buen vivir above "nature." When the tension between the two equalities emerges, Morales regards the relationship of ecological equality as secondary (Morales 2017). Other social movements have denounced similar issues in relation to other struggles beyond ecology as well. As Rivera discusses, feminist struggles are often invalidated in Bolivia due to the elevation of masculine readings of ethnicity (Rivera 2010a, 218). For example, after the governmental announcement of the special cabinet that was created in 2018 to deal with the problem of violence against women, María Galindo, one of the leaders of Mujeres Creando, denounced the demagogical usage of women for electoral purposes (La Sexta 2018). According to Galindo, the Morales government used false promises while also charging women the legal fees that were required to denounce cases of violence. Moreover, a number of authors who analyze this problem in three cities in Bolivia reported an increase of violence against women in the last 20 years (Salmón, Elías, and Portugal n.d., 218) As Farthing states, in 2016, after 10 years of Evista governments, Bolivia was the country with the highest rate of violence against women in Latin America (Farthing 2016).

The problem of assimilating and hierarchicalizing "other" forms of equality becomes even more salient when the main "reality" of a discourse is used to authorize the government and representatives. That is, the combination of a validating ontology and an authorizing epistemology elevates a particular "reality" and a single voice simultaneously. Throughout the chapter, I analytically separated these epistemic dimensions in order to highlight the implications that unfold from the enactment of each one of them, but practices often include the authorization of a voice and the validation of a "reality" at the same time. For example, the Bolivian state includes a constitutional definition of environmentalism and development, but the government is then authorized to deal with the specificities of each economic situation and context ("Bolivia Constitution" 2009, art. CCCXII, § 1; and art. LXXIII, cl. 10). Hence, the Constitution draws the main criterion of limitation for development, which is based on the equality of future generations, but the government is still entitled to define when each project actually reaches that point. This authorization over environmental knowledge enables the destruction of forests and ecosystems as much as the government deems "sustainable" or in "equilibrium." In the case of the TIPNIS, for example, the Morales government regarded the road as necessary for the development of Bolivia and for the buen vivir of its peoples. The government viewed the impact of the project as minimal. Then, those who opposed the road appeared as de-authorized voices whose knowledge of the environment was silenced. They were the "enemies" or the agents of "colonial environmentalism" that were telling lies only to undermine the government (Morales 2017).

This epistemic authority to define the specificities of policies within constitutional boundaries not only includes the possibility of ignoring the opposition of "others," but also entails a certainty or arrogance that travels temporally. The "reality" of plurinationality is thus temporally universalized as the future of Bolivia. This temporal certainty can be found in notions of development, sustainable economic growth, and equality, which first design the future of the country in the Constitution of 2009. Then, the government becomes the embodiment of the state, which is authorized to define the more context-dependent aspects of the near future. Hence, Morales presented developmental reports and plans in 2015, which assumed a high level of certainty in their utilization of nature and its future exploitation (Morales 2015b). Within these plans, the "others" who oppose the project appear again as "obstacles" against the "real" process of transformation and the "real" knower.

Conclusion

Overall, the project of "plurinationality" creates epistemic hierarchies that continue to exclude "other" struggles, voices, and projects; it marginalizes other "others." By using the "master's tools" (Lorde 2018), Evismo aims to expand inclusion in Bolivia, but it still forecloses yet another form of boundary. On one side, the elevation of a single kind of "reality" leads to the hierarchical organization of "other" ways of knowing, which include other forms of equality, justice, and struggle. As the discourse becomes further enacted, details and specificities construct more rigid boundaries, which either marginalize or assimilate other struggles such as the notions of ecological equality and Pachamama. The chapter focuses on a particular definition of ecology to illustrate this epistemic implication, but the elevation of a "reality" can affect other definitions of axes such as gender, ethnicity, race, sexuality, ability, etc. In this sense, the Evista ontological foundation still creates a tendency of "single-axis thinking" (Cho, Crenshaw, and McCall 2013, 787).

On the other side, the epistemological definition of a possibility of accessing "reality" hierarchicalizes "other" ways of being, which do not quite fit the characteristics of "indigenous" or "liberal" peoples. Evismo thus defines and elevates a particular knower, which can participate in the state, rule the government, and represent society. Hence, the "plurinational" state includes a particular definition of "indigeneity" in order to define who can participate in politics and who can access rights. Then, the government is authorized to determine the specific characteristics of "indigenous" peoples in policy-related contexts. Finally, Morales, Linera, and the members of the MAS are constructed as the main representatives of "indigeneity" in Bolivia. This kind of authorization silences "other" voices that do not know "reality." "Other" ways of being that do not fit the characteristics of the authorized knower are thus marginalized because they are an "enemy" or they are not quite "indigenous." This tendency silences "other" experiences of ethnicity and it de-authorizes "other" voices that might appear as even further from "reality."

As a number of authors have pointed out, the Evista project of "plurinationality" limits the diversity of struggles and voices that coexist in Bolivia (Albró 2005, 2010; Canessa 2005). The discourse forecloses the problem of difference from above and it silences the voices that confront colonial legacies from below (Rivera 2018). This epistemic tendency is particularly problematic because the discourse creates a closed circle of self-validation, self-authorization, and self-enactment. In other words, Evismo not only regards "other" struggles as less "real" and other voices as less "true," but also forecloses an epistemic circle that reaffirms its own certainty, authority, and characteristics. The reading of historical events, analysis of the present, and enactment of the future thus become the evidence of "reality" itself. A way of enacting returns to the ontological platform of the discourse and it reaffirms its "reality." Thus, the epoch of pre-conquest becomes the thesis of "reality," colonialism is turned into the contradiction of "reality," and the synthesis is the revival of "reality." Similarly, the form of participation that is authorized as the citizenry of Bolivia becomes the support for the authority of an Evista voice. The participation of "indigenous" communities in the referendum that was related to the construction of the road in the TIPNIS was turned into a form of re-authorization for the state, the government, and Morales himself. In this discourse, authorized voices thus re-authorize themselves. Finally, the enactment of specificities and policies further characterizes the equality, voice, and project of Evismo, drawing careful delineations that are consistent with the more abstract philosophical notions of the discourse. Here, the epistemic tools of the master become specified into impermeable boundaries that substantiate a way of knowing, being, and enacting, further marginalizing other "others." Similarly to other chapters, this discussion highlights the importance of epistemic politics.

Overall, the intra-discursive and endogenous functions of Evista epistemics tend to invalidate "other" realities, assimilate "other" struggles, silence "other" voices, prove its own "reality," support its own authority, and make impermeable its boundaries. This endogenous circle of self-validation, self-authorization, and self-enactment allows for many intellectuals of Evismo to speak about a perfect "harmony," "balance," or "equilibrium" between peoples and with nature (e.g., Morales 2010b; Linera 2015, 328; Choquehuanca 2012, author's translation), but it also forecloses the possibility of self-reflexivity. Comparably to Revolutionary Indianismo and Indianismo Amáutico, Evismo seldom allows for a possibility of questioning its own boundaries. Additionally, these epistemic limitations prevent more egalitarian dialogues between different struggles, voices, and projects.

Similar to other discourses of anti-colonialism, Evismo illustrates the problems that emerge from using epistemic bedrocks that enable a possibility of political praxis against colonialism while also elevating a single way of knowing, being, and enacting. Evismo shows how the utilization of a particular definition of "reality" leads to certain ideas of power and equality, which enable the classification of oppression and injustice, but also erects the kind of universalization that ends up marginalizing other "others." Similar to colonial epistemics, the elevation of another form of equality and power leads to another form of othering. How is it possible, then, to classify "oppression" while also listening to multiple voices and sustaining self-reflexivity?

An interesting aspect of Evismo is that the discourse deploys the idea of continuity as part of its bedrock. In previous chapters, I ask whether this criterion could provide a different kind of classification between "colonial" and "resisting" discourses. The case of plurinationality and Evismo shows that a discourse can cleverly avoid the epistemic utilization of "human nature," "human essence," or some kind of "human" characteristic; it unveils a way of classifying that renounces "empirico-transcendental" foundations (Foucault 1970, 386). Unlike other anti-colonial and colonial discourses, Evismo aims to expand its respect of difference by staying within the consistency of identity politics and nation. This platform of equality allows for two contradictory identities to coexist and limit each other in a shared territory. The epistemic accomplishment of a more plurinational way of thinking is important, but the discourse then assumes a possibility of actually accessing and mapping the "real" continuities of Bolivia, generalizing the logic of a relationship that partially respects only two differences. The possibility of accessing "reality" re-essentializes the bedrock of classification and the specificities that characterize it, sedimenting, generalizing, and universalizing a particular kind of equality, struggle, voice, and project. That is, the assumption of correspondence between an epistemic bedrock and two continuities elevates a particular equality, voice, and project above others, creating yet another form of universalization. Here, the Evista utilization of continuity illustrates again the problem of essentialized bedrocks of classification, which tend to create more universalization on behalf of praxis. Similar to Revolutionary Indianismo and Indianismo Amáutico, Evismo provides fruitful discussions and it denounces important forms of injustice, but the epistemic limitations of the discourse become more apparent whenever its universalizing tendencies are confronted with the question of difference and multiplicity.

If epistemically essentialized bedrocks of classification and assumptions of correspondence are the master's tools that create this tendency towards marginalizing other "others," should decoloniality move beyond them in order to think about multiplicity? However, how could decoloniality achieve this goal without falling into paralyzing forms of relativism that undo possibilities of praxis? In order to continue investigating this question, I move beyond anti-colonialism in the following chapters, engaging first with post-structuralist discussions of multiplicity and desubjugation.

Notes

1 In Evismo, "indigenous" and "indigeneity" are notions that become associated with particular ideas of heritage and to specific epistemic assumptions. Similar to other cases in other chapters, I thus use quotation marks to emphasize the specific meaning that a word acquires in the context of a discourse. To the contrary, I do not use quotation marks when the words "indigeneity" and "indigenous" have other meanings, which are related to the work of other authors, intellectuals, or movements.

2 This notion of "will" and "construction" is not far from liberal ideas of social contract and voluntary association such as the ones constructed by John Locke (1980).

3 Of course I am not stating that the epistemic authorization that emerges from a discourse automatically leads to winning elections and taking over powerful positions. Clearly, many of the alliances, negotiations, struggles, and connections that involved Morales, Linera, and the Movement Towards Socialism took place before the elections. Despite the complexity of historical events and alliances that led to the presidency of Morales, however, I focus primarily on the description of the discursive characteristics of this project in order to highlight its internal limitations.

4 Notice that I do not translate "buen vivir" as "good life" because I aim to avoid a liberal understanding of consumerism or endless preference satisfaction.

References

Albró, Robert. 2005. "The Indigenous in the Plural in Bolivian Oppositional Politics." *Society for Latin American Studies* 24 (4): 433–453.

Albró, Robert. 2010. "Confounding Cultural Citizenship and Constitutional Reform in Bolivia." *Latin American Perspectives* 37 (3): 71–90.

Bebbington, Denise Humphreys. 2012. "Consultation, Compensation and Conflict: Natural Gas Extraction in Weenhayek Territory, Bolivia." *Journal of Latin American Geography* 11 (2): 49–71.

"Bolivia Constitution." 2009. Biblioteca Virtual Miguel de Cervantes. https://www.oas.org/dil/esp/Constitucion_Bolivia.pdf.

Calla, Ricardo. 2012. "TIPNIS y Amazonia: Contradicciones En La Agenda Ecológica de Bolivia." *European Review of Latin American and Caribbean Studies* 92: 77–83.

Canessa, Andrew. 2005. *Natives Making Nation: Gender, Indigeneity, and the State in the Andes.* Tucson: University of Arizona Press.

Cárdenas Aguilar, Félix. 2015. "Bolivia's Decolonization Mission Interview by Alexandra Valiente." Internet Blog. https://libya360.wordpress.com/2015/03/16/bolivias-decolonization-mission.

Casey, Nicholas. 2018. "In Bolivia, Morales's Indigenous Base Backtracks on Support." *New York Times*, December 8, 2018. https://www.nytimes.com/2018/12/08/world/americas/bolivia-evo-reelection.html.

Cho, Sumi, Kimberlé W. Crenshaw, and Leslie McCall. 2013. "Toward a Field of Intersectionality Studies, Applications, and Praxis." *Signs* 38 (4): 785–810.

Choquehuanca, David. 2012. "Tiempo del Pachakuti: Ten Commandments to confront capitalism and construct the culture of life" (speech). Celebration of Summer solstice on the Island of the Sun, Titikaka, BoliviaInternet. https://youtu.be/E8H2Zfuy3ug.

Comisión de Justicia, Constitucion y Regimen Electoral. 2018. "Auditoria Jurídica Del Caso de Feminicidio de Isabel Pillco Elaborada Por La Comisión de Justicia, Constitucion y Regimen Electoral de La Cámara de Diputados." Accessed April 27, 2020. http://mujerescreando.com/index.php/component/content/article/89-justicia/99-auditoria-juridica-del-caso-de-feminicidio-de-isabel-pillco-elaborada-por-la-comision-de-justicia-constitucion-y-regimen-electoral-de-la-camara-de-diputados?Itemid=437.

CONAMAQ. 2014. "Pronunciamiento Ante la Promulgación de la Ley de Minería y Metalurgia." CONAMAQ. https://www.ocmal.org/pronunciamiento-ante-la-promulgacion-de-la-ley-de-mineria-y-metalurgia.

Farthing, Linda. 2016. "Despite Legal Protections, Violence Against Women Is Spiking in Bolivia." *World Politics Review*. December 2016. https://www.worldpoliticsreview.com/articles/20720/despite-legal-protections-violence-against-women-is-spiking-in-bolivia.

Filho, Clayton Mendonça Cunha, Rodrigo Santaella Gonçalves, and Ariane Dalla Déa. 2010. "The National Development Plan as a Political Economic Strategy in Evo Morales's Bolivia: Accomplishments and Limitations." *Latin American Perspectives* 37 (4): 177–196.

Foucault, Michel. 1970. *The Order of Things: An Archaeology of Human Sciences.* New York: Vintage Books.

Howard, Rosaleen. 2010. "Language, Signs, and the Performance of Power: The Discursive Struggle over Decolonization in the Bolivia of Evo Morales." *Latin American Perspectives* 37 (3): 176–194.

Kaup, Brent. 2010. "A Neoliberal Nationalization? The Constraints on Natural-Gas-Led Development in Bolivia." *Latin American Perspectives* 37 (3): 123–138.

Kohl, Benjamin. 2010. "Bolivia under Morales: A Work in Progress." *Latin American Perspectives* 37 (3): 107–122.

Landau, David. 2018. "Populist Constitutions." *The University of Chicago Law Review* 85 (2): 521–544.

La Sexta. 2018. "Feministas de 'Mujeres Creando' Lanzan Pintura Roja Contra la Sede del Ejecutivo en Bolivia para Protestar Contra el Machismo." La Sexta. https://www.lasexta.com/noticias/sociedad/feministas-mujeres-creando-lanzan-pintura-roja-sede-ejecutivo-bolivia-protestar-machismo_201811275bfdc9a90cf2ae0c60f9d133.html.

Linera, Álvaro García. 2006. "Democracia Liberal Vs. Democracia Comunitaria." In *Interculturalidad, Decolonización Del Estado y Del Conocimiento*, by Walter Mignolo and Catherine E. Walsh, 71–82. Buenos Aires: Ediciones del Signo.

Linera, Álvaro García. 2014. *Identidad Boliviana. Nación, Mestizaje y Plurinacionalidad.* La Paz: Vicepresidencia del Estado. Presidencia de la Asamblea Legislativa Plurinacional.

Linera, Álvaro García. 2015. *Hacia El Gran Ayllu Universal. Pensar El Mundo Desde Los Andes.* Edited by Álvaro Huayta Zárate. México: Altepetl Editores, Biblioteca Indígena.

Locke, John. 1980. *Second Treatise of Government*. 1690s edition. Cambridge, MA: Hackett Publishing.

Lorde, Audre. 2018. *The Master's Tools Will Never Dismantle the Master's House.* London: Penguin.

Morales Ayma, Juán Evo. 2010a. Conferencia Mundial de los Pueblos sobre el Cambio Climático y los Derechos de la Madre Tierra: Causas Estructurales del Cambio Climático. DVD from Ministerio de Relaciones Exteriores, Estado Plurinacional de Bolivia.

Morales Ayma, Juán Evo. 2010b. Conferencia Mundial de los Pueblos sobre el Cambio Climático y los Derechos de la Madre Tierra: Inauguration. https://youtu.be/p-IeSRONqyA, https://youtu.be/YGXxkfFWBCI and https://youtu.be/8vka-0TudJY.

Morales Ayma, Juán Evo. 2012. Tiempo del Pachakuti: Ten Commandments to confront capitalism and construct the culture of life" (speech). Celebration of Summer solstice on the Island of the Sun, Titikaka, Bolivia. https://youtu.be/E8H2Zfuy3ug.

Morales Ayma, Juán Evo. 2015a. 70th Session of the United Nations General Assembly: Discurso del presidente Evo Morales Ayma. https://youtu.be/OR4wfTCn7E4.

Morales Ayma, Juán Evo. 2015b. Presidente Morales presenta el Plan de Desarrollo Económico Social 2016–2020. https://youtu.be/hF5cSLq35Nk.

Morales Ayma, Juán Evo. 2016. 71st Session of the United Nations General Assembly: Discurso del presidente Evo Morales Ayma. https://youtu.be/jH2mLIiNhRI.

Morales Ayma, Juán Evo. 2017. Promulgation of the Law of the Integral Development of TIPNIS. https://youtu.be/S4s9AisyBL8.

Movimiento Regional por la Tierra y el Territorio. 2019. "Estado Boliviano no Escucha ni Responde a Demandas de Naciones Indígenas Originarias." January 31, 2019. https://porlatierra.org/novedades/post/287.

Observatorio del Cambio Rural. 2019. "Carta Internacional de Respaldo a la Marcha de Naciones Originarias y Pueblos Indígenas de Bolivia." Observatorio del Cambio Rural. http://ocaru.org.ec/index.php/comunicamos/noticias/item/8876-carta-internacional-de-respaldo-a-la-marcha-de-naciones-originarias-y-pueblos-pueblos-indigenas-de-bolivia.

Pan y Rosas. 2014. "Protesta de Organizaciones Feministas y Socialistas." http://www.estrategiainternacional.org/Organizaciones-feministas-y-socialistas-protestan-contra-la-creciente-violencia?lang=es.

Pellegrini, Lorenzo, and Marco Octavio Ribera Arismendi. 2012. "Consultation and Extraction in Bolivia after the 'Left Turn': The Case of Oil Exploration in the North of La Paz Department." *Journal of Latin American Geography* 11 (2): 103–120.

Reinaga, Fausto. 2014. *Fausto Reinaga: Obras Completas.* 10 vols. La Paz: Vicepresidencia del Estado Plurinacional.

Rivera Cusicanqui, Silvia. 2010a. *Violencias (Re) Encubiertas En Bolivia.* La Paz: La Mirada Salvaje.

Rivera Cusicanqui, Silvia. 2010b. "The Notion of 'Rights' and the Paradoxes of Postcolonial Modernity: Indigenous Peoples and Women in Bolivia." *Qui Parle: Critical Humanities and Social Sciences* 18 (2): 29–54. doi:10.5250/quiparle.18.2.29.

Rivera Cusicanqui, Silvia. 2015. *Sociología de la Imagen. Miradas Ch'ixi Desde La Historia Andina.* Buenos Aires: Tinta Limón.

Rivera Cusicanqui, Silvia. 2018. *El Mundo Ch'ixi Es Posible: Ensayos Desde Un Presente En Crisis.* Buenos Aires: Tinta Limón.

Salmón, Carmen Elena Sanabria, Daniela A. Elías, and Yenny Portugal. n.d. "Violencia Contras Las Mujeres. Entre Avances y Resistencias. Estudio En 3 Ciudades." OXFAM and Colectivo Rebeldía. Accessed April 29, 2019. https://www.academia.edu/27222103/Violencia_contras_las_mujeres._Entre_avances_y_resistencias._Estudio_en_3_ciudades.pdf.

Semanario Aqui. 2012. "Manifiesto Público de la IX Marcha Indígena Originaria." *Semanario Aqui.* http://www.semanarioaqui.com/index.php/nuestra-tierra/701-manifiesto-publico-de-la-ix-marcha-indigena-originaria.

TeleSur. 2018. "Bolivia Announces Special Cabinet to Eradicate Violence Against Women." TeleSur. November 27, 2018. https://www.telesurenglish.net/news/Bolivia-Announces-Special-Cabinet-to-Eradicate-Gender-Violence-20181127-0011.html.

Ticona, Esteban Alejo. 2011. *Bolivia En El Inicio Del Pachakuti: La Larga Lucha Anticolonial de Los Pueblos Aimara y Quechua.* La Paz: Akal Ediciones S.A.

Tockman, Jason, and John Cameron. 2014. "Indigenous Autonomy and the Contradiction of Plurinationalism in Bolivia." *Latin American Politics and Society* 56 (3): 46–69.

5 Post-structuralism as a limited Western ally

The work of Michel Foucault is often deployed in debates that are related to the problem of difference and othering (e.g., Said 1978; George and Campbell 1990; Milliken 1999; Mignolo 2000; Campbell 2013; Rivera 2015; Weber 2016). In the genealogy that I discuss, Foucault's work enters the struggle to define the problem of difference from at least three different but interconnected locations. First, and most importantly, several authors that focus on the problem of difference in/for Bolivia have discussed some of the benefits and limitations of Foucault's work (e.g., Estermann 2006; Escobar 2010; Viaña, Claros, and Sarzuri-Lima 2010; Alcoreza 2014; Rivera 2015). Hence, much of the genealogical relevance of Foucault's work comes from its relationship with other intellectuals who either use his approach to understand Andean constructions of difference or discuss the limitations of his work within this context. For example, Josef Estermann uses archaeology to think about the epistemic assumptions of occidental philosophies. Then, the author highlights the epistemic ways in which Andean philosophies move beyond these anthropocentric assumptions (Estermann 2006, 211). Estermann also asserts that post-structuralist authors such as Foucault create a possibility of deconstructing the universality of Occident (30). He asserts that Foucault's work enables a possibility of relativizing these occidental structures. While studying Andean philosophies and their approaches to the problem of the "other," Estermann points out that this deconstructing effect aims to revalue non-occidental cultures (Estermann 2006, 31). Similarly, Viaña, Claros, and Sarzuri-Lima affirm that Foucault wishes to locate the intellectual as someone who can create spaces to allow the oppressed to speak for themselves (Viaña, Claros, and Sarzuri-Lima 2010, 30). Additionally, Silvia Rivera Cusicanqui states that Foucault's work unveils the structures of domination that locate different subjects in hierarchized echelons (Rivera 2015, 27).

Notwithstanding these benefits, many of these authors highlight the limitations that emerge when Foucauldian notions are deployed to understand the problem of difference beyond the "West." For example, Rivera points out that Foucault's work constrains Andean discussions of decoloniality (Rivera 2015, 27). According to the author, Foucault focuses primarily on singular discourses and their totalizing effects, but colonialism often entails complex contexts, which overlap multiple and dynamic projects simultaneously (28).

Estermann also adds that post-structuralism does not overcome occidental paradigms because it tends to generalize a form of deconstruction that leads to indifference (Estermann 2006, 30). From a different perspective, Viaña, Claros, and Sarzuri-Lima also state that Foucault's work does not commit to the voices of "others" because it still analyzes them as equally colonial. In this sense, the authors assert that Foucault reinforces a representationist tendency, which tries to enable "others" to speak, but also prevents interpreters from listening because "others" appear as identities that are equally trapped within the colonial power that they denounce (Viaña, Claros, and Sarzuri-Lima 2010, 32). Similarly, Alcoreza affirms that Foucault does not take the step that Andean cosmologies enable when they recognize and re-affirm the heterogeneity of knowledges disqualified by official notions of science (Alcoreza 2014, 17). This possibility of committing to the heterogeneity of "others" leads to decolonial projects (18), which Foucault does not reach. Hence, the benefits of this kind of post-structuralism seem to create possibilities that encompass differences beyond the epistemic tendencies of liberal, Marxist, Indianista, and plurinationalist discourses, but its constraints also suggest a degree of difficulty in relation to decolonial praxis. Hence, how does Foucault create an epistemic condition of possibility that is designed to know, be, and enact more difference? How do these epistemic assumptions create limitations in relation to decolonial praxes?

Second, Foucault's work is also relevant here because many authors of International Relations deploy his approach to study international politics and the problem of difference (e.g., Ashley and Walker 1990; George and Campbell 1990; Walker 1993; Stoler 1995; Walker 2010; Brincat, Lima, and Nunes 2012; Campbell 2013; Weber 2016). In this chapter, I thus emphasize a genealogical possibility of connecting arbitrarily separated discussions, which are often hidden behind colonial boundaries of territoriality and disciplinarity. This connection and dialogue illustrates again how the analysis of the problem of difference can trespass borders, enabling more open and egalitarian debates of politics. Joining authors of "International Relations" and scholars "from Bolivia" in a discussion of Foucault's work contributes to the analysis of the benefits and limitations of his approach, undoing the artificial and Eurocentric borders that often marginalize scholars of the "Global South" in the discipline. As the work of the authors mentioned above illustrates, Foucauldian notions are often utilized to critique universalized discourses of International Relations and international politics. Some of these scholars have sought to denounce the hierarchicalizing tendencies of discourses, interpreting the fluidity of dominant formations, celebrating difference, and creating more epistemically egalitarian spaces for marginalized voices. Despite these benefits, Rivera, Estermann, Viaña, Sarzuri-Lima, and others often call for epistemic moves that lay beyond post-structuralism. Together with other authors of decoloniality (e.g., Mignolo 2000), these intellectuals assert that Foucault's approach sustains "Western" limitations. Thus, how does Foucault create an epistemic possibility of encompassing more multiplicity and difference? How does he move beyond the tendencies of colonial epistemics? Additionally, what limitations does this approach sustain in relation to possibilities of decolonial praxis?

Third, my own utilization of archaeology and genealogy introduces some aspects of Foucault's work as part of an approach that is designed to study the problem of difference. Similar to other authors concerned with this discussion, I utilize some of the benefits provided by Foucault's work while also finding some of its limitations. This process enables me to move beyond Foucault's work, learning from scholars such as Rivera about the possibility of constructing yet another position in the struggle to define the problem of difference (Rivera 1990, 2010, 2012, 2015, 2018). To achieve this goal, I follow interpretivist and feminist understandings of methodology, which remind us that approaches are never neutral or innocent in the processes of synthetization and narration that take place throughout interpretation (Cox 1981; Tickner 1992; Zehfuss 2002; Ackerly, Stern, and True 2006; Ackerly and True 2008; Schwartz-Shea and Yanow 2012; Yanow and Schwartz-Shea 2014; Lynch 2014). Then, I explicitly locate Foucault's work as a locus of enunciation in the struggle to define the problem of difference. This introduction of methodological discussions as another position in a genealogical struggle highlights the benefits and limitations of Foucauldian epistemic assumptions in relation to the problem of difference. Similar to other intellectuals that discuss the problem of difference, I find in Foucault's work a possibility of investigating the epistemic assumptions of multiple discourses. Then, I follow the ways in which these formations confront each other. This endogenous study of each discourse and exogenous examination of their relationships enables the possibility of interpreting how liberal, Marxist, Indianista, and plurinationalist discourses have solved the problem of difference in Bolivia since 1825 and in current debates of International Relations. Moreover, this kind of study highlights the ways in which each discourse universalizes its own way of knowing, being, and enacting, which then creates tendencies to marginalize other "others." In this sense, the Foucauldian approach provides a fruitful way to study *epistemic politics* and their effects. However, how is it possible to classify colonialism and domination if all structures and bedrocks are abandoned? Does Foucault focus on the epistemic tendencies of discourses and their effects of universalization to distinguish "domination"? If so, how is it possible to determine a difference between colonial discourses and anti-colonial voices? How is Indianismo different than liberalism and Marxism if both sets of discourses equally universalize their own ways of knowing, being, and enacting? Insofar as I sustain an epistemically open form of interpretation by renouncing all foundations and conditions of classification, discourses such as liberalism, Marxism, Indianismo, and plurinationality appear equally othering; they become equally "colonial." This epistemically open perspective prevents us from making a more decolonial commitment to othered voices. As several authors affirm, Foucault's work includes a form of critique and action (George and Campbell 1990; Hoy 2005; Campbell 2013; Lynch 2014), but how does the author construct a field of inquiry that is capable of studying multiple epistemic formations while also creating a possibility of "desubjugation" or "diversification"? Why do authors of decoloniality claim that Foucault's work does not commit to "other" voices?

In order to answer these questions, I examine the conditions of "reality" that Foucault utilizes to create his own field of enquiry. The characteristics of this epistemic starting point show the potential benefits of archaeology and genealogy. Then, I discuss how the author creates a way of being, which authorizes interpreters to act politically. This form of authorization tends to generalize another approach to the problem of difference, which raises some of the limitations that are often denounced by scholars of decoloniality. The complexity of Foucault's work includes epistemic openings that could have moved beyond these limitations, but his "Western" generalization of domination and deconstruction often prevents him from taking the extra step towards decolonmialities. As I discuss in Chapter Six, Rivera fruitfully crosses that line and she moves beyond Foucault's "Western" constraints by listening to Andean voices and by engaging with multiple struggles simultaneously.

Conditions of "reality:" An incomplete post-structuralist positivity

In order to proceed with the definition of this approach and its limitations, I begin by analyzing the ontological assumptions that validate Foucault's field of inquiry. In *The Archaeology of Knowledge,* Foucault asserts that his methodology begins from the very "fact of discourse" (Foucault 1972, 22). Here, the author uses an epistemic assumption of "reality," which appears as an empirically undeniable possibility of existence to establish a starting point beyond doubt. Foucault aims to reject the signified and the signifier in order to focus on the fact that, "here and there," there is language (111). To define this condition of "reality," Foucault deploys two interrelated epistemic constructions. On one side, the "fact of discourse" is further analyzed through the discussion of its characteristics. Here, Foucault asserts that the "statement" is a function that makes sense of otherwise disaggregated signs (79); it is the meaningful functioning of discourse, which bounds signs together into some kind of "sense." The statement is, then, the very unit and characteristic of discourse; it is the element that creates a possibility of "making sense." As Foucault asserts, the statement "… is a function of existence that properly belongs to signs and on the basis of which one may then decide, through analysis or intuition, whether or not they make sense …" (86). However, Foucault does not seek to pre-determine the nature or ontological essence of discourse. Instead, the essence of the statement appears unintelligible. The statement is something that "does," not something that "is" (80). Thus, the constitutive element of discourse is not the intelligible essence of language or its foundation; it is not the proposition, sentence, inter-subjectivity, speech act, or structure of language itself (80–85); it is an undetermined and complex functioning that makes sense of signs.

On the other side, Foucault defines how the statement is "real." In order to grant the status of "knowledge" to his kind of interpretation, not only does Foucault need an epistemic possibility of "making sense," but he also requires the possibility of granting some kind of validation to these senses. Therefore, Foucault reminds us that "senses" can often be "… repeated, known, forgotten, transformed, utterly erased, and hidden, far from all view, in the dust of books" (Foucault 1972, 25). The fact that particular senses can be *repeated*, and thus *shared* in different ways, is the epistemic aspect that gives these senses the possibility of belonging to a form of understanding that is more than an arbitrary and/or isolated moment of meaningful irruption. Through this epistemic operation, Foucault is able to assume that senses are "non-arbitrary" (29). This assumption of non-arbitrariness presupposes a commonality or sharedness in relation to the "sense" that is momentarily fixed in a group of signs.[1] This notion explains why Foucault affirms that the enunciative function of the statement cannot operate without the existence of an associated domain or field (97). According to the author, this "complex web" is not a structural context; it is a background made up of formulations within which the statement appears (98). Additionally, this idea explains why Foucault asserts that archaeology describes practices that are specified in the elements of the *archive*, which is the common system that makes enunciability possible (129). Here, the archive appears to be the assumption of a shared background of meaning, which connects the senses that emerge in multiple moments of irruption and practice.

Despite this condition of "reality" and possibility of validation, Foucault delineates his own epistemic assumptions with important differences to other ontological ways of knowing. Instead of proceeding from a solid and completely defined ontological foundation of "reality," the author constructs archaeology as an approach that analyzes meaning from the undetermined "fact of discourse." Here, archaeology emerges as a field of inquiry that avoids seeking the secret or hidden bedrock that shapes discourse transcendentally, foundationally, or from underneath (Foucault 1972, 109). Foucault stops at the moment of sense making:

> We must be ready to receive every moment of discourse in its *sudden irruption*; in its punctuality in which it appears, and in that temporal dispersion that enables it to be repeated, known, forgotten, transformed, utterly erased, and hidden, far from all view, in the dust of books.
>
> Foucault 1972, 25, italic by author

Hence, the author uses a possibility of producing knowledge while also renouncing the ontological determination of that which makes it "real." In other words, he uses the assumption of sharedness without claiming to know its essentialized and universalized characteristics. "We must renounce all those themes whose function is to ensure the infinite continuity of discourse and its secret presence to itself in the interplay of a constantly recurring absence" (Foucault 1972, 129). As a result, Foucault avoids pre-defining the archive, its logic, or its essence.

> It is obvious that the archive of a society, a culture, or a civilization cannot be described exhaustively; or even, no doubt, the archive of a whole period. On the other hand, it is not possible for us to describe our own archive, since it is from within these rules that we speak.
>
> Foucault 1972, 130

In order to construct an archaeological field of inquiry and to discuss the problem of difference, Foucault thus creates an approach that begins from an epistemic assumption designed to be understood as an undetermined and infinitely complex possibility of granting sharedness and validation to meanings. This epistemic starting point affects the way in which Foucault defines power relations and genealogy. Although archaeology and genealogy have several differences, I argue that the undetermined assumption of sharedness acts as the condition of "reality" that validates both of these methodologies. In other words, I understand genealogy as using the "fact of discourse" to build a field of knowledge that focuses on the dynamic, diachronic, confronting, and inter-relating aspects of discourse analysis. This explains why Foucault asserts that he studies the power effects of discourses themselves (Foucault 1997, 10).

In order to construct a genealogical field of inquiry, Foucault discusses the notion of power. Here, power does not acquire its epistemic status of "reality" from a correspondence to extra-discursive structures or objects. Power is not understood as some kind of commodity, asset, or something that can be possessed (Foucault 1997, 14). This is an important difference between Foucault's work and Edward Said's notion of "force," which I discuss in Chapter One. Foucault does not define power as a previous structure beneath senses and discourses; he does not regard it as a material element that shapes discourse exogenously. Instead, genealogy stays within discourse to create a possibility of grasping the complex patterns or dynamics of power effects. Here, power circulates; it is a function that can be exercised (Foucault 1997, 14). Similar to the undetermined definition of the statement, then, power is understood as momentary functionings that annex materiality within discourses and construct power relations. Despite the genealogical emphasis on "life" and power, then, post-structuralism does not understand the idea of senses as structurally or exogenously caused by something outside of discourse. Foucault often mentions institutions, actors, weapons, instruments of torture, bodies, states, prisons, etc., but this materiality of power is still studied as an epistemically intrinsic part of discourses that annex elements of the world, constructing power relations and demanding specific applications of assimilating, disciplining, segregating, or colonizing strategies. Hence, disciplining practices are understood as the moments in which bodies and objects become related to senses and power effects; it is in this "flash" of signification where "intentions" and "senses" settle momentarily, annexing, shaping, and organizing materiality.

Foucault is not interested in the objectivity or independent existence of "objects." Instead, he focuses on how discourses make them "our" objects by embedding them within discourses and by constituting them as something to "us." Hence, the functioning of practices momentarily fixes and constitutes the object by annexing it and colonizing it (Foucault 1997, 30). As a result of this epistemic prioritization of discourse, power is:

> analyzed as something that *circulates*, or rather as something that *functions* only when it is part of a chain. It is never localized here or there, it is never in the hands of some, and it is never appropriated in the way that wealth or a commodity can be appropriated. Power *functions.* Power is *exercised* through networks, and individuals do not simply circulate in those networks; they are in a position to both submit and exercise this power.
>
> Foucault 1997, 28, italics by author

Since power hereby appears epistemically intertwined with the complexity of functioning statements, Foucault unsettles the study of power. Similar to the archaeological characteristic of senses, power loses pre-determined, essentialist, and ontological boundaries. Instead, power becomes whatever effects are practiced within chains of temporal dispersion. Despite this possibility of studying multiple kinds of power effects and relations, Foucault does not conceive power as an arbitrary, isolated, and free moment of annexation. He does not regard power as effects that anyone can practice freely or in an unconstrained manner. Instead, power becomes "real" because it also presupposes an epistemically undetermined form of sharedness. This explains why Foucault asserts that individuals "do not simply circulate in those networks" (Foucault 1997, 28). Additionally, these epistemic notions helps us to understand why the author asserts that power functions "only when it is part of a chain." Power includes an epistemic element that lies beyond the isolated moment of power-related effects; it is more than the moment of functioning that Foucault uses to study it, but the author also renounces the epistemic pre-determination and pre-definition of such "networks." To the contrary, genealogy studies power in its "real effects" (Foucault 1997, 28), while also abandoning the possibility of assuming that those patterns are the characteristics of an essentialized and universalized ontology. Unlike Juan Evo Morales Ayma and Álvaro García Linera, Foucault does not assume that the continuities analyzed by his work correspond to the "real" characteristics of the social background of meanings in a particular territory. Finally, this notion explains the sharedness that is presupposed in the possibility of domination, violent segregation, colonization, normalization, and annexation. These relationships impose meanings and disciplining moments upon "others." Hence, they presuppose two separated moments of construction that become connected, annexed, and assimilated within the logic of one discourse. Here, the assumption of sharedness acts as the epistemic possibility of connecting meanings that are practiced in different moments but become colonized or annexed by a particular formation. For example, this epistemic condition of "reality" enables Foucault to establish connections between bodies and the forms of knowledge that claim to know them in order to discipline them (Foucault 1978, 1995).

To establish a possibility of studying difference, while also validating the multiple expressions of meaningful moments of irruption, Foucault thus constructs an epistemic tension. He uses a condition of "reality" while renouncing its pre-determination and *a priori* definition. In turn, this epistemic strategy allows him to acknowledge the non-arbitrariness of meanings, while also allowing for meanings to remain untamed, dynamic, and complex. Here, meaning and power become dynamic, but not free; "real," but not fixed. Foucault uses an idea of "reality" that emerges from an undeterminable assumption of sharedness; he uses an ontology to validate the dynamics of power and meaning beyond isolation and arbitrariness, but he also avoids determining the characteristics of this construction.

Accessing irruptions of senses and power effects

In order to access these undeterminably "real" senses and power effects, Foucault locates interpreters in "proximity" to discourse (Foucault 1972, 111). Foucault thus aims to construct an epistemological bridge or connection between interpreters and meanings. To achieve this goal, the ontological notion of undetermined sharedness becomes an epistemological connection between the meanings that are interpreted and the meanings that are practiced by others. In other words, the possibility of "repeating" meanings creates an epistemological condition of authorization because the work of interpreters appears *connected* to the "real" irruptions that are practiced by others.

In the case of archaeology, Foucault asserts that interpreters can grasp the functioning moments of the statement when discourses are practiced. Here, interpreters appear authorized to produce knowledge by describing practices and their regularities (Foucault 1972, 87). In turn, the analysis of these practices is regarded as non-arbitrary because the senses that are analyzed are potentially shared (29). Interpretation is thus more than the isolated and subjectivist understanding of a particular individual. Despite this enabling and epistemological form of authorization, Foucault also reminds us that he renounced the possibility of determining the ontological characteristics of sharedness. As a result of this definitional deficit, the author cannot consistently construct a fixed and strong form of epistemological authorization. That is, Foucault uses the notion of sharedness again in order to authorize a form of interpretation and a knower, but he also avoids settling the characteristics of this connection between practiced and interpreted meanings. Hence, Foucault asserts that the possibility of "making sense" can be grasped in the inexplicable "flash" that takes place when experiencing some form of discursive occurrence (112). This moment is not the transcendental or anthropological description of meaning; it is not the essence of language; instead, it is the operational domain of enunciative functions (112).

In the case of genealogy, Foucault proceeds to construct his possibility of interpretation from the fact of a power-related effect, which can only be settled and grasped in the very moment that a practice fixes the "circularity" of power (Foucault 1997, 29). Similar to archaeology, the interpreter accesses these practices thanks to her/his proximity. Here, the undetermined notion of a "reality" that is not "free," constructs an epistemological possibility of connecting processes of interpretation and power effects. In other words, the inexplicable connection that is presupposed in the notion of annexation and colonialization of materiality epistemically authorizes interpreters to study the complex irruptions of power that are not free, but are also not structures. This form of authorization enables interpreters to study power in its sudden irruptions or in practices.

> To study power at the point where his intentions – if, that is, any intention is involved – are completely invested in real and effective *practices*; to study power by looking, as it were, at its external face, at the point where it relates directly and immediately to what we might, very provisionally, call its object, its target, its field of application, or, in other words, the places where it implants itself and produces real effects.
>
> Foucault 1997, 28, italics by author

Epistemic implications and methodological benefits

This undetermined condition of "reality" and possibility of interpretation lead towards several methodological implications that are related to the problem of difference. First, Foucault creates a separation between analyzed discourses and his possibilities as an interpreter. The author validates his fields of inquiry, while also leaving a definitional deficit, which avoids complete epistemic assumptions of "reality" and knowing subjects. To achieve this goal, Foucault renounces the possibility of accessing "reality" and he stays at the level of discourse and practices; he sustains his field of inquiry only at the moment of sudden irruptions, without digging underneath them for some kind of structure, foundational totality, force, archive, essence, cause, etc. This decoupling moment appears as an epistemic deficit only if we assume that truth correspondence is a necessary construction. That is, if we assume the need to determine the essence of our ontological foundation and our epistemological capacity to access such "reality," we would regard Foucault's epistemic starting point as lacking definition or leaving a void. To the contrary, the author explicitly abandons the possibility and need of fixing his condition of "reality."

> We are not linking these exclusions to a repression; we do not presuppose that beneath manifest statements something remains hidden and subjacent. We are analyzing statements, not as being in the place of other statements that have fallen below the line of possible emergence, but as being always in their own place.
>
> Foucault 1972, 119

As a result of this epistemic decoupling and purposeful deficit, Foucault creates a moment of separation between his possibilities as an interpreter and the epistemic strategies of the discourses that he analyzes. On one side, discourses claim epistemic access to foundations that often become fixed, determined, and characterized within each formation. Despite genealogical confrontations and transformations, each discourse often determines the status of "reality" that enables its universalization upon "others." Moreover, discourses frequently include definitions of who can access this "reality." Hence, these interpreted formations appear as foundationalist or at least structuralist ways of knowing, being, and enacting, which then universalize their own patterns upon "others." On the other side, Foucault renounces the possibility of fully determining an ontology and an epistemology. As I further discuss below, this separation between Foucault's practices of interpretation and the discourses that he interprets enables a particular form of praxis and political action. Since Foucault renounces the possibility of fixing an ontology and an epistemology, he distinguishes himself from the discourses that do so. This differentiation enables him to transform discourses throughout his work of interpretation; it allows him to unveil the epistemic arbitrariness that hides underneath foundationalist claims of universality.

Second, the notion of an epistemic tension partially cautions post-structuralist interpreters against considering their own theoretical productions as reflections of the archive itself. Since knowledge production emerges from the interpretation of the "senses" that are grasped in particular sets of practices, and since interpreters do not know the characteristics of the epistemological connection between these "senses" and the archive, they cannot assume their own knowledge as directly corresponding to the very structure or foundation of senses. They cannot assume their interpretations as directly representing the underlying sharedness of meaning itself. Unlike authors who regard their interpretations as representing the characteristics of social structures (e.g., Giddens 1979; Bourdieu 1980; Wendt 1999; Adler 2008), scholars who view meaning as an accessible "social reality" of intersubjectivity (e.g., Schwartz-Shea and Yanow 2012; Yanow and Schwartz-Shea 2014), or intellectuals who elevate particular identities as the "real" continuities of Bolivian history, Foucault sustains an epistemic deficit or definitional void, which allows him to avoid the prioritization of a particular set of epistemic assumptions. As a result, Foucault does not replace foundationalist epistemics with new notions of intersubjectivity, continuity, or structures. Instead, he sustains a void that enables the deeper study of epistemic politics; he creates a possibility of studying how different discourses construct their own ontologies and epistemologies. In this manner, Foucault moves beyond the universalization of singular epistemic notions and he enables the possibility of encompassing a broader field of difference.

Third, this possibility of broadening differences not only enables the study and interpretation of epistemic politics, but also expands the understanding of power relations. Since the characteristics of "reality" and sharedness are left undetermined, Foucault does not ontologically elevate a single kind of relationship to connect the dispersion of sense-making irruptions. The author does not use a particular kind of essentialized relationship between meanings as the only shape of "reality." Instead, he enables a field of inquiry that seeks to interpret how discourses construct their own "realities." In these constructions, discourses that sustain universalizing tendencies regard, through different kinds of epistemic strategies, particular relationships as the connections that make meanings "real." The construction of epistemic connections between meanings and, for example, "human nature," "reason," "desire," "inheritance," "Cosmos," or "heritage" lead to the determination and elevation of the relationship that is "real." Through this strategy, universalizing discourses construct their own possibility of moving beyond the arbitrariness and isolation of particular meanings and they assume the characteristics of these connections as "reality" itself. Since these discursive definitions of "realities" include the characterization of a connection and a relationship, they pre-determine the commonality and sameness that appears more "real;" they define an epistemically elevated form of equality. That is, the construction of ontological relationships that connect some meanings to a "reality" include notions of equality. This determination creates a boundary between the "real" relationship of equality and the social orders that contradict it; it defines the inequality and struggle that appears elevated above other kinds of oppression. In this sense, each universalizing discourse tends to validate and elevate a particular kind of power relation. To the contrary, Foucault leaves the definition of the characteristic of sharedness as an open question, which allows for the possibility of studying how discourses construct their own "real" relationships. In turn, this enables a field of enquiry that can study multiple forms of power relations, without epistemically prioritizing any of them.

This possibility is related to a fourth implication, which highlights how the notion of an epistemic tension opens a possibility of studying multiple temporalities. Since he uses a condition of "reality" while also trying to avoid a pre-determined characterization of a single ontology, Foucault does not create a fixed bedrock or foundation from which a particular form of judgment can be deployed to narrate history and to construct a single form of future. In other words, Foucault uses an incomplete definition of a possibility of repeating statements as his condition of "reality;" he does not settle a single relationship of "reality." This strategy helps him to avoid the elevation of a particular conceptualization of equality. Within this epistemic deficit, no single bedrock of equality can be deployed to judge epochs or societies. Moreover, since Foucault's work leaves a void in his epistemic starting point, genealogy and archaeology can study how each discourse constructs its own idea of "reality," which then judges how it might be historically contradicted in particular epochs and potentially enacted in a near future. Similar to meanings and power effects, temporality hereby also becomes untamed.

Finally, the fifth implication of following the epistemic notion of a tension is that the possibility of generalization becomes partially undermined, allowing for Foucault to expand the study of multiplicity and change. Since the tension does not include a determined definition of sharedness, the connection between interpreted discourses and the archive itself cannot be known. Hence, interpreted discourses cannot be regarded as objective, socially real, or structural. In turn, this strategy cautions interpreters against the generalizability of the discourses that they analyze. Each discourse does not necessarily represent "reality" itself. As Foucault asserts, discourses are not the totalitarian forms of society that determine all meanings in a particular epoch (Foucault 1972, 148). Rather, there can be other formations, practices, modifications, and variations coexisting in particular contexts. In this sense, Foucault emphasizes the enabling side of his epistemic deficit, which reminds interpreters about the complexity of meanings and the possibilities of variation.

Enacting discourses

From the notions of a tension and a possibility of proximity, Foucault creates a field of inquiry that is designed to enact the specificities of discourses and their relationships, while also avoiding the epistemic generalization of these characteristics. In other words, the author interprets discourses, but he does not theorize them as *the* characteristics of the archive itself. In the case of archaeology, interpreters can achieve this goal by finding synchronic regularities or patterns from moments of meaningful irruption that are grasped in a particular context; they can reconstruct connections that form discourses. Foucault interprets the different patterns or regularities that can be grasped in the practices that momentarily stabilize the functioning of statements (Foucault 1972, 144). From these regularities, the author analyzes the endogenous commonalities and meaningful connections that make up each discourse. At a general and broad level, discourses include positivities (127). These kinds of rules are conditions of "reality," which bound each discourse under a particular set of characteristics, validating whatever fits within their boundaries. In a sense, a positivity is a fully defined ontology and epistemology; it is a determined "reality" that is also assumed as accessible in a particular way and by a specific kind of knower. Thus, discourses are groups of statements that belong to the same conditions of existence (117). The characterization of this "reality" and the possibility of knowing it creates boundaries against whatever is not "real" and whoever cannot access it. Hence, positivities determine the point at which each discourse creates a rupture, which separates the formation from other discourses (157).

For example, in *The Order of Things*, Foucault examines the boundaries between the Renaissance, the Classical Era, Modernity, and the re-emergence of language in multiplicity (Foucault 1970). Each one of these discourses includes its own condition of "reality" and they also define how they are accessible by particular knowers. The Renaissance is based on notions of resemblance, the classical era includes notions of representation, and modernity constructs ideas of "man," which then become partially abandoned in the re-emergence of language in multiplicity. In Chapter One, I also analyze the construction of colonial discourses that include their own conditions of "reality" and epistemological forms of authorization. Nineteenth-century liberal ideas in Bolivia proceed from a notion of "reason" that appears "real" because it is a God-given human nature. Then, the discourse includes a characterization of this kind of "reality," which leads to notions of equality, rights, and civilization. Additionally, the people who fit the characteristics of "reality" and embody "reason" are authorized as the knowers of this equality; they are the "active citizens" that can rule and shape Bolivia. As these examples illustrate, each discourse includes boundaries that exclude other "realities" and knowers. Discourses entail ruptures and separations that emerge from these conditions of "reality" and lead towards othering tendencies.

Beyond the endogenous tendencies of each discourse, Foucault mentions different types of inter-discursive relationships, such as archaeological isomorphism, archaeological isotopia, archaeological shifts, and archaeological correlation, which can entail subordination (Foucault 1972, 160–161). As this possibility of studying different inter-discursive relationships shows, archaeology not only defines the boundaries of each formation, but also studies the ways in which discourses can precede, include, colonize, annex, articulate, or organize their "others." These relationships can lead to a politics of domination and articulation, which can be grasped empirically in the juxtapositions between different discursive formations. As Foucault asserts, discourses expose the forms of unification that they create for other formations (167). Moreover, ruptures and articulations between different discourses are the main concerns of archaeology (146).

The study of discursive relationships thus entails an examination of how practices not only construct their own boundaries, but also annex or reorganize "others." This is possible because boundaries can coexist in the senses that are settled in practices. A particular set of practiced senses can organize othered discourses. They can, for example, include "other" ways of knowing through a notion of succession or perhaps through subjugation. The very patterns of practices thus define relationships of otherness because they organize "others" through the attachment of senses. Throughout *The Order of Things*, for example, Foucault focuses his interpretation on the analysis of unifying ideas of succession, which connect different discourses as parts of a linear and cumulative form of knowledge progress (Foucault 1970).

In the case of genealogy, Foucault studies how practices diachronically erect and construct matrixes of knowledge, which include boundaries and establish different kinds of relationships with other discourses. Genealogy focuses on messy processes of struggle and meaning contestation; it analyzes the disputed paths of transformation that lead towards different kinds of discourses, boundaries, and relationships; it examines "histories of struggle" (Foucault 1997, 8). Unlike archaeology, this field of enquiry focuses less on the settled boundaries and relationships of neatly formed discourses and it prioritizes the possibility of following how practices transform them throughout time and space.

This methodology introduces into the analysis of discourses the diachronic messiness of interaction, transformation, and world constitution, which draws politics of struggles. Despite the introduction of "life" into the analysis of discourses, genealogy can still be understood as consistent with Foucault's epistemic assumptions. By using the fact of discourse and its epistemic tension, genealogy appears to focus primarily on the ways in which *practices* momentarily settle the circularity of power (Foucault 1997, 28). These moments are the multiple and complex ways in which power functions, annexing and organizing different elements into a matrix of knowledge. From the moments in which power produces "real effects," Foucault thus derives a possibility of analyzing the links historically established between discourses and particular actors, the annexation of certain institutional conformations, the violence attached to these processes, and the ways in which discourses constitute particular objects, worlds, and even bodies. Hence, genealogy entails a possibility of understanding the much more complex and diachronic relationships that are created among actors, matrixes of intelligibility (i.e., knowledges or discourses), institutional settings, processes of transformation, and politics; it entails a combination of knowledge production, history, and life in the comprehension of temporally organized relationships of struggle (172).

This methodological analysis of processes that annex materiality within a particular matrix of knowledge also examines hierarchical organizations that classify whatever is less "real." Genealogy thus follows the ways in which struggles lead towards the colonization of "other" ways of knowing and being; it studies diachronic processes of assimilation, articulation, unification, organization, colonization, and domination. The boundaries of "reality" that are constructed in messy disputes and wars act as the condition of possibility for the definition of "others" as "inferior," "barbaric," "antecedent," "deviant," etc. As a result, the analyzed patterns of the dynamic functioning of power shows how particular discourses can become transformed and re-organized as internal "others." These genealogical processes of hierarchicalization include ways of knowing and also entail the violent deauthorization of "other" ways of being. In order to study these possibilities of othering, genealogy includes the analysis of institutions, forms of governmentality, strategies of discipline, and the role of war. For example, Foucault shows how a particular form of juridical knowledge created the rights of kings and the nobility to rule in seventeenth-century Europe (Foucault 1997, 130). Despite this form of knowledge, rule, and institutionalization, Foucault also highlights how other matrixes of power confronted these discourses, constructing the history of the nobility as a history of robbery and ruin (132). This new form of knowledge constructed a different subject of history, notion of rights, idea of land, etc. (133). Despite the degree of transformation that these struggles entailed, Foucault clarified that new discourses did not necessarily entail a form of liberation; rather, these notions often became re-colonized by states that sought to sustain order (137).

These kinds of unifying, annexing, organizing, colonizing, articulating, and dominating processes are the central focus of Foucault's genealogical work, which often shows how the emergence of newer discourses do not entail a possibility of liberation. Instead, they often create broader politics of organization and unification, which include newer boundaries and forms of othering. The central root of this problem of domination emerges from the epistemic assumptions of discourses that universalize a particular form of "reality" and a consistent way of being. This explains why Foucault asserts that power cannot be exercised unless it has an economy of truth functioning as a basis that enables power (Foucault 1997, 24). Of course power effects and economies of truth enable each other. For example, Foucault states that power effects define particular matrixes of truth throughout the genealogical process of struggle, but these notions also create the possibility of thinking about power and politics (165). In this sense, Foucault does not define a causal direction in the study of genealogical processes. Instead the author studies how power effects and economies of truths create universalized discourses that hierarchicalize, colonize, discipline, and kill "other" validities, authorizations, and projects; other ways of knowing, being, and enacting; other matrixes of knowledge, actors, and bodies. As a result, Foucault asserts that "Western" forms of knowledge often universalize their own discourse, creating colonial forms of organization and exclusion for all "others" (Foucault 1971).

In his work, then, Foucault often emphasizes how processes of transformations lead to new forms of domination. For example, Foucault shows how the Victorian regime of sexuality was replaced by the discourse of power as repression (Foucault 1978, 10). Similarly, juridico-political notions of sovereignty from roman times were transformed to a discourse that understood power in ways that could be applied directly to the body (Foucault 1997, 35). This notion of power enabled a better extraction of time and labor, which concealed the possibility of domination and hid the coercive power of the sovereign (37). Finally, Foucault also analyzed the transformation of the discourse on punishment over to a scientifico-legal discourse of discipline (Foucault 1995, 23). This transformation allowed for the carceral system to encompass broader dimensions of life and society, expanding the possibility of disciplining bodies beyond specific moments of torture and spectacle (297).

A Foucauldian way of being

Foucault often tries to avoid the fixed definition of a basic subject; he rejects the epistemological construction of a connection between a determined form of "reality" and a particular knower. Instead, the author seeks to understand a:

> field of regularity for various positions of subjectivity. Thus conceived, discourse is not the majestically unfolding of a thinking, knowing, speaking subject, but, on the contrary, a totality, in which the dispersion of the subject and his discontinuity with himself may be determined.
>
> Foucault 1972, 55

In this sense, archaeology and genealogy create a possibility of analyzing how discourses construct their own basic subjects and ways of being. As I stated above, the Foucauldian interpretation of discourses includes, among other patterns, the examination of conditions of "reality" and the study of the epistemological bridges that connect these ontologies with particular knowers. The field of inquiry thus untames meaning to enable the analysis of how *interpreted* discourses authorize particular subjects. This possibility emerges consistently from the epistemic tension that Foucault uses to construct archaeology and genealogy. The idea of an undetermined sharedness creates an undetermined possibility of accessing statements; it constructs a notion of proximity between interpreters and discourses while avoiding its definition. As a result, interpreters are precariously authorized, but the characteristics of knowers are only settled within discourses and their epistemic claims of "reality."

Despite this dynamic and untamed understanding of meaning, Foucault enables a second level in his methodological relationship with discourses. The author creates an epistemic authorization of interpreters that can move beyond the internal logic of particular discourses. That is, discourses entail ontological definitions of "reality" and epistemological constructions of fixed ways of being, but interpreters can move beyond the epistemic tendencies of discourses themselves. They can study epistemic politics, showing the variation of assumptions, unveiling the arbitrariness of each formation, and examining the limitations of each set of boundaries. This form of authorization creates a Foucauldian possibility of praxis, which is directly connected to the problem of difference.

In order to create this possibility of praxis, Foucault locates interpreters in *proximity* to discourse (Foucault 1972, 111). Here, interpreters become the epistemic tension between sharedness and deficit; the condition of possibility becomes a way of being. Since they are somehow connected to the moments of irruption, which are somehow shared, interpreters can access the discursive patterns of discourses, but they can also know that these discourses are not direct representations of "reality" itself. This epistemic decoupling highlights the foundational incompleteness of analyzed discourses; it emphasizes the complexity and dynamic aspects of meaning and power. In turn, this means that the boundaries of each discourse limit a complexity that could potentially enable other forms of "real" meanings and power; other ways of knowing, being, and enacting. Hence, Foucauldian interpreters know that practiced meanings and power effects are somehow socially "real," but they also know that these irruptions might be limiting the complexity of statements or the circularity of power because they are not *the* sole characteristics of sharedness itself; they are not society or social reality itself. Here, interpreters become the tension or, better yet, the tension becomes a way of being that authorizes a Foucauldian subject above the foundationalist discourses that they analyze. In other words, Foucault constructs interpreters as the separation that he creates between himself and discourses when he renounces the epistemic search of foundations.

Foucault thus builds the interpreter as an authorized voice, locating her/him above the foundational tendencies of discourses that do not include sharedness and deficit simultaneously. This epistemic form of authorization allows for interpreters to understand a set of epistemic notions as above the internal or endogenous patterns of discourses. In other words, the undetermined notion of sharedness becomes an elevated meta-discourse that can be used to judge and transform other discourses. Then, Foucauldian interpreters emerge as the authorized knowers of this possibility. The epistemic tension of Foucault thus creates its own practice and knower; it creates its own unifying logic and possibility of praxis.

In the case of archaeology, this form of authorization enables interpreters to map different discourses, finding the boundaries and ruptures that separate them. By describing these ruptures, Foucault unveils how certain unifying logics belong within the boundaries of particular discourses that claim universality and thus annex other formations. Then, the author is authorized to undo the endogenous claims of universality that discourses often include in their own notions of ontology and epistemology, breaking the continuity and annexation that colonizes other formations. In this sense, interpreters are authorized to show discontinuity (Foucault 1970, 50). For example, Foucault critiques the notion of "chronological succession" that is often used to organize all thought into a meta-relationship of history and hierarchy (Foucault 1972, 148). Instead, Foucault asserts that this notion belongs to a particular discourse and field of inquiry; it belongs to the "history of ideas" and its tendency to search for the secret or foundational unity that creates principles of cohesion between discourses (149). This "diversifying effect" is the main critical praxis of archaeology (175).

In the case of genealogy, Foucault aims to expose the diachronic processes in which dominant discourses become the boundaries that organize, hierarchicalize, assimilate, and/or exclude "other" ways of knowing, being, and enacting. These discourses construct "economies of truth" that validate particular kinds of social order and authorize specific subjects (Foucault 1997, 24). To the contrary, "others" often appear as "threats," "barbarians," "objects of science," "manipulable bodies," "deviants," etc. Despite this endogenous characteristic of interpreted discourses, genealogy allows for interpreters to locate themselves above the dominating tendencies of these formations. Thus, they can show that the "economy of truth" enabling particular discourses to become universalized and dominant is not necessarily the sole "reality" of sharedness itself or the only power effects settling the circularity of power. This explains why Foucault seeks to "release power" from assumptions of unity, subjects, and law. By achieving this goal, the author is able to focus on "power relations."

> This means that rather than starting with the subject (or even subjects) and elements that exist prior to the relationship and that can be localized, we begin with the power relationship itself, with the actual effective

> relationship of domination, and see how that relationship itself determines the elements to which it is applied.
>
> Foucault 1997, 45

Similar to archaeology, then, genealogy undoes the determined foundations from which particular discourses claim the authority and validity that they need to annex "others;" it unveils how discourses are both "real" and in deficit. Here, interpreters can study how discourses claim "reality" and a possibility to access it, while also remembering the epistemic deficit of discourses, which demands the deconstruction of universalizing tendencies. As a result, the author opens up a possibility of analyzing the multiple forms of power effects that often become excluded by dominant discourses. In this regard, Foucault asks: "What theoretico-political vanguard are you trying to put on the throne in order to detach it from all the massive, circulating, and discontinuous forms that knowledge can take?" (Foucault 1997, 10). Through this form of praxis, genealogy aims to deconstruct the colonial boundaries and relationships that are practiced in institutionalize settings such as prisons, states, psychiatric institutions, universities, etc. Foucault calls this possibility of praxis "desubjugation" (10).

Throughout much of his genealogical work, Foucault plays the differences that are annexed in dominant discourses off against the universalized boundaries of these matrixes of knowledge. As an interpreter, Foucault plays an actively desubjugating role by de-universalizing the discourses that claim to know and organize "others." This praxis deconstructs the homogenizing tendencies that emerge in processes of annexation and "othering." For example, Foucault shows how the struggle between the Victorian regime of sexuality and the discourse of power as repression does not lead towards the liberation of sexuality (Foucault 1978, 10). Instead, this diachronic process of emergence leads towards newer and broader ways of unification and domination. Despite the power effects that are related to these matrixes of knowledge, Foucault de-universalizes both discourses, unveiling their notions of truth and re-opening the possibility of complexity for "others." Similarly, Foucault shows how the transformation of the discourse on punishment over to a scientifico-legal discourse of discipline does not entail a more benevolent or liberating way of controlling conduct (Foucault 1995, 23). Notwithstanding the continuation of domination among interpreted discourses, the effects of Foucault's praxis uncover the possibilities of complexity that lie beyond the claims of universality of each formation.

Conclusion

Overall, archaeology and genealogy enable a possibility of knowing, being, and enacting more difference. The construction of an epistemic tension between an assumption of sharedness and a definitional void creates a possibility of studying epistemic politics; it erects a field of inquiry that is designed to understand multiple ways of knowing, being, and enacting at the same time. Moreover, Foucault enables more difference by moving beyond the othering tendencies that emerge from universalized, essentializing, and foundationalist ideas of "reality," subjects, and history. As Said states, essentialist knowledges often assume that "others" are intelligible objects whose nature can be known, controlled, and dominated (Said 1978, 38). Instead, Foucault stays at the level of discourse, analyzing the relationships that are established by interpreted practices. In this sense, Foucault creates a relational approach to knowing, being, and enacting difference; he constructs a distinct position in the struggle to define the problem of difference.

Several authors involved in the context of Bolivian discussions of the problem of difference deploy this methodological possibility to study Andean indigenous movements, contributing in the construction of more respectful forms of coexistence (e.g., Estermann 2006; Viaña, Claros, and Sarzuri-Lima 2010; Alcoreza 2014). Similarly, authors involved in the dispute of the problem of difference in International Relations use post-structuralist insights to study the epistemic assumptions of theories and policies (e.g., George and Campbell 1990; Ashley and Walker 1990; Walker 1993; Stoler 1995; Walker 2010; Campbell 2013; Weber 2016). Others emphasize the ways in which Foucault creates more dynamic and complex understandings of meaning (e.g., Schwartz-Shea and Yanow 2012; Lynch 2014; Yanow and Schwartz-Shea 2014). Several of these authors also deploy these methodological possibilities to undo universalized discourses and to desubjugate marginalized voices; they explicitly utilize the possibility of praxis that emerges from this way of knowing, being, and enacting difference (e.g., Ashley 1989; George and Campbell 1990; Walker 1993; Campbell 2013; Yanow and Schwartz-Shea 2014; Weber 2016). This kind of praxis is a consistent aspect of the epistemic tension between sharedness and deficit. Foucault renounces structures and foundations; he avoids searching for the essence or true object of language, but he then turns this epistemic stance into another possibility of authorizing interpreters above interpreted discourses. Interpreters know the deficit of discourses even when particular formations include universalized and determined epistemic assumptions. Hence, interpreters are hereby authorized to deconstruct the universality that emerges from these epistemic assumptions; they can claim the authority that is required to act upon discourses and demand their transformation.

> Archaeology is the method specific to the analysis of local discursivities, and genealogy is the tactic which, once it has described these local discursivities, brings into play the desubjugated knowledges that have been released from them. That just about sums up the overall project.
>
> Foucault 1997, 11

Despite these praxical and methodological advantages, several of the intellectuals involved in the Bolivian locus of discussion of the problem of difference emphasize the limitations of this approach (e.g., Estermann 2006; Viaña, Claros, and Sarzuri-Lima 2010; Alcoreza 2014; Rivera 2015). These scholars point out that Foucault's work still imposes its own kind of Western tendency, generalizing the single coherence of a discourse within a context, overly deploying deconstruction, and avoiding the possibility of committing to the struggle of "others." These limitations consistently unfold from the epistemic notions that Foucault uses.

From the tension that emerges by utilizing a form of "reality" that cannot be ontologically determined or fixed, Foucault authorizes interpreters as the knowers that can access this epistemic indeterminacy. Thanks to their "proximity," they enjoy an indeterminate epistemological connection to the tension between sharedness and deficit. On one side, this epistemic notion precariously authorizes knowers to interpret discourses. On the other side, it locates knowers above discourses because these formations contain universalized foundations that limit statements and power effects. Here, knowers can practice a deconstructive praxis, which unveils the epistemic assumptions included in discourses themselves. This praxis entails a possibility of diversification and desubjugation. Notwithstanding the advantages that emerge when "Western" discourses become de-universalized, Foucault tends to generalize the deficit of discourses and he focuses more prominently on the possibility of deconstruction (Mignolo 2000, 70).

Foucault focuses primarily on colonial discourses that claim universality. Here, discourses appear more oriented towards processes of annexation, homogenization, and colonialism. Hence, archaeology shows the fractures that are hidden under settled philosophical ideas of succession often practiced by the history of ideas (Foucault 1972, 149). Then, genealogy is a:

> way of playing local, discontinuous, disqualified, or nonlegitimized knowledges off against the unitary theoretical instance that claims to be able to filter them, organize them into a hierarchy, organize them in the name of a true body of knowledge, in the name of the rights of a science that is in the hands of the few.
>
> Foucault 1997, 9

Even when Foucault listens to the insurrection of subjugated knowledges, he does so to push towards the diachronic or synchronic discovery of the deficit of dominant discourses. The process of interpretation thus appears to resist the repressiveness of colonial claims in order to allow for more multiplicity and difference; it creates a negative value of difference, which constantly demands deconstruction from all universalized discourses.

This tendency to generalize dominating characteristics in discourses and to deploy interpretation to deconstruct universalities emerges consistently from the emphasis that Foucault places in the possibility of renouncing epistemic structures and foundations. Given his locus of interpretation, which primarily concentrates on Western, dominating, universalizing, and epistemically foundationalist discourses, the author often aims to unveil discontinuities, boundaries, limitations, oppressions, and coercions that emerge from epistemic assumptions of single "realities." Due to this tendency, Foucault prioritizes the epistemic void over his notion of sharedness; he undermines the usage of epistemic foundations and bedrocks due to their tendencies to create othering boundaries and oppressive marginalization. The undoing of all bedrocks leads the author towards shining light on the oppressive aspects of ontologies, epistemologies, and temporalities. This is in fact consistent with the notion of an epistemic tension. Foucault hereby becomes the indeterminacy that emerges from using sharedness without defining it. However, Foucault elevates the deficit of this tension over the enabling side of his condition of possibility when he interprets practiced discourses. In International Relations, several authors follow this tendency to generalize domination, also emphasizing deconstruction. For example, Richard Ashley and R. B. J. Walker investigate a possibility of staying in a constantly dynamic form of exile. This epistemic space only allows for momentary and dynamic constructions, which have to deconstruct themselves continuously in order to question their own boundaries (Ashley and Walker 1990). Additionally, Walker often generalizes his critiques against constructions of political projects because they create conditions of possibility for violence and othering (Walker 1993, 2010).

As Mignolo asserts, this generalization of deconstruction and domination enables a fruitful position for "Western allies" (Mignolo 2000, 70). Despite this possibility in relation to the problem of difference, Foucault's approach still sustains limitations that become clearer when we think about "anti-colonial" and/or "non-Western" ways of knowing, being, and enacting. Specifically, how does this approach categorize "anti-colonial" discourses that also tend towards a universality of their own? How can Foucault select, classify, or distinguish "dominant" discourses from those that are "oppressed" and "subjugated" if their epistemic tendencies are the same? Insofar as a Foucauldian way of being only creates a separation between foundationalist discourses and the meta-discourse of the tension, all foundational notions of "reality," knowers, and temporality become homogenized. Insofar as genealogy and archaeology become epistemically elevated only by a separation against epistemically determined bedrocks, all universalizing discourses become equally "colonial," "dominant," "oppressive," "marginalizing," "subjugating," etc. Here, struggles, voices, and projects such as Indianismo become as colonial as liberalism and Marxism.

In some cases, Foucault seeks to create a possibility of distinguishing between dominant and subjugated discourses by focusing on the ways in which *practices* settle the circularity of power and the functioning of the statement. The author concentrates on interpreting how practices fix moments of annexation, colonizing and disciplining "others." Then, Foucault epistemically assumes that the practices that he selects for interpretation include meanings that are somehow shared in the indeterminate background of the archive and the complex circularity of power. As a result of this notion, domination appears as a phenomenon that takes place within the ways in which practices shape and construct worlds. However, how can we distinguish "anti-colonial" or "non-Western" discourses that are practiced as forms of resistance but also entail similar practices of othering? If they have the same kind of practices, how can we distinguish oppressed voices from dominant discourses? For example, how is it possible to distinguish between, on one side, the forms of liberalism and Marxism that I analyze in Chapter One and, on the other side, Revolutionary or Amáutico forms of Indianismo? Both types of discourses entail strong ontological definitions that validate single "realities," epistemological forms that authorize specific knowers, and political projects that enact linear temporalities. From these notions, both sets of discourses tend to organize and annex "others." How, then, are liberalism and Marxism more "colonial"? How is Indianismo more "anti-colonial"?

Another strategy to distinguish between "colonial" and "anti-colonial" discourses is to focus on the genealogical *continuity* of dominant ways of knowing, being, and enacting. For example, Said states that colonialism entails a continuous reinforcement of "Western" characteristics as superior (Said 1978, 7). Similarly, Sylvia Wynter talks about the continuity of the hierarchies that were put in place in the sixteenth century in Haiti and the world system (Wynter 1995, 24). Nevertheless, Foucault explicitly seeks to deconstruct notions of continuity and he often highlights the differences that are hidden under claims of historical succession (Foucault 1997, 120). Additionally, Foucault shows the historical presence of counter-histories and voices of resistance that sometimes become victorious (74). Similarly, I show the transformations that are practiced in Bolivia to construct different kinds of liberal and Marxist discourses. On the other side, several intellectuals highlight the continuity of indigenous struggles in the region (Rivera and Morón 1993; Rivera 1990, 2018; Reinaga 2014; Ari 2014; Linera 2015). As I discuss in previous chapters, Indianismo also entails a degree of continuity at least since the moment it officially became a party in 1962. Insofar as "colonial" and "anti-colonial" discourses include continuities and discontinuities, how is it possible to distinguish them?

A third strategy to separate "colonial" and "anti-colonial" discourses can emerge by using *levels of institutionalization* as a factor of differentiation. For example, Foucault affirms that states intervene to annex knowledges and generalize a particular discourse (Foucault 1997, 180). This intervention enables the "disciplinary power" that selects, normalizes, centralizes, and hierarchicalizes knowledges, creating disciplines and official notions of "science" (182). In turn, this form of organization and order entails a "dogmatism" that constrains the possibilities of voices, creating an "orthodoxy of statements" (184) and erecting a new relationship between power and knowledge (185). This notion of institutionalization can be understood in two different ways. Sometimes institutions seem to appear as "non-discursive" systems (Foucault 1972, 162). In some cases, Foucault seems to construct institutions as an exogenous element that settles discourses and generalizes them in a particular epoch or society. In *Discipline and Punish*, for example, Foucault attaches a discourse to the very context in which it is practiced. Hence, genealogy sometimes appears as "… an insurrection against the centralizing power-effects that are bound up with the institutionalization and workings of any scientific discourse organized in a *society* such as ours" (Foucault 1997, 9, italics by author).

By using an extra-discursive notion of institutions, Foucault seems to re-introduce another bedrock into his field of enquiry; he re-deploys another notion of power that causes discourses exogenously. This tendency is particularly prevalent whenever Foucault generalizes some discourses of domination. For example, Foucault studies the kind of domination that emerges when discourses of discipline transform into a carceral system (Foucault 1995). Here, the author appears to assume a high level of institutionalization for a particular matrix of knowledge, which then locates the discourse as affecting society itself. In other words, Foucault seems to create an ontological separation between discourses and the "reality" of institutions and society.

> The frontiers between confinement, judicial punishment and institutions of discipline, which were already blurred in the classical age, tended to disappear and to constitute a great carceral continuum that diffused penitentiary techniques into the most innocent disciplines, transmitting disciplinary norms into the very heart of the penal system and placing over the slightest illegality, the smallest irregularity, deviation or anomaly, the threat of delinquency.
>
> Foucault 1995, 296

In turn, "the carceral archipelago transported this technique from the penal institution to the *entire social body*" (Foucault 1995, 297, italics by author). Within this tendency, Foucault's work sediments particular discourses as corresponding to society itself, which then re-authorizes him to generalize the characteristics of domination upon an entire context or epoch. By generalizing domination, Foucault emphasizes that transformations often lead to more concealed and invasive forms of domination, which interpreters ought to continue deconstructing.

Despite this tendency to structuralize discourses by re-introducing ontologically exogenous notions of institutions and states, Foucault affirms that:

> this institutionalization of scientific discourse is embodied in a university or, in general terms, a pedagogical apparatus, that this institutionalization of scientific discourses is embodied in theoretico-commercial networks such as psychoanalysis, or in a political apparatus – with everything that implies – is largely irrelevant.
>
> Foucault 1997, 9

Notwithstanding the possibility of bringing institutions into archaeology and genealogy as an ontologically exogenous element that empowers discourses and makes them "dominant," Foucault thus reminds us that his field of inquiry focuses on discourses themselves. "Genealogy has to fight the power-effects characteristic of any discourse that is regarded as scientific" (Foucault 1997, 9). This reminder highlights the consistency of the tension and its notion of the epistemic deficit. In other words, bringing institutions as something ontologically external to discourse in order to separate and distinguish domination is inconsistent with the epistemic possibility of renouncing the foundational continuity of discourse, the essence of language, or the assets of power. Moreover, the utilization of structures often leads to unwarranted generalizations that silence voices of resistance and change.

A fourth strategy to separate "anti-colonial" voices from dominant discourses could be created by regarding institutions as *distinct sets of practices*. One could say that practices annex materiality, constructing our worlds, bodies, institutions, etc. This idea conceptualizes institutions as sets of practices and annexed materialities. Here, states, governments, universities, mental health institutions, etc., become parts of discourses that can be interpreted within the logic of the tension. Insofar as this is the case, however, intra-discursive analyses of institutions do not construct a possibility of separating or classifying the levels of power of different institutions. Hence, those practices that create universalizing tendencies and construct institutions cannot be distinguished among each other in relation to their levels of domination. For example, is the Evista discourse of plurinationality equally as colonial as neoliberalism? Many authors would separate the two (Albró 2005, 2010; Ticona 2011; Ari 2014) and even assert that plurinationality is a decolonial project that increases equality (Kohl 2010; Filho, Gonçalves, and Dalla Déa 2010; Howard 2010; Ticona 2011), but the possibility of abandoning bedrocks undermines this type of classification in Foucault's work.

A fifth strategy entails concentrating on the level of enactment and specificity that universalizing discourses include. For example, Foucault claims that states hierarchicalize and organize all knowledges into disciplines, policing otherness in order to classify even the smallest details of knowledge (Foucault 1997, 182). This form of specification entails an expanding and colonizing possibility, which emerges from epistemic notions of "reason" and the logic of universities (182). Despite this possibility, "anti-colonial" discourses such as Revolutionary Indianismo and Indianismo Amáutico include high levels of enactment and specification. Moreover, the plurinational project of Morales, Linera, and the MAS has expanded to all kinds of realms. Given their high levels of specificity, "colonial" and "anti-colonial" discourses still appear as equally dominating formations. Hence, how can interpreters determine what discourse needs to be deconstructed first or more deeply in order to enable difference and decoloniality? What discourse is more "dominant," "colonial," "oppressive," etc.?

Due to these issues, Foucault does not seem to construct a condition of possibility to distinguishing between "colonial" and "anti-colonial" discourses. One could argue that the author in fact avoided creating this separation on purpose, but that is precisely the problem. Foucault might have renounced foundational ontologies, epistemologies, and temporalities in order to expand the possibility of knowing, being, and enacting difference, but he also created a homogenizing tendency that generalizes domination and deconstruction. Within this tendency, archaeology and genealogy do not provide ways to determine the point at which deconstruction can momentarily stop to enable enunciation and sharedness. The lack of a set criterion of classification, together with the elevation of the possibility to renounce foundations, leads to the homogenization of all foundationalist discourses, indiscriminately demanding their deconstruction. This tendency explains why it is so important to differentiate "anti-colonial" discourses from "colonial" formations. On one side, "anti-colonial" discourses denounce and fracture the privilege of dominant formations. Hence, they require some kind of prioritization if undoing privilege and domination is our main normative and methodological goal. On the other side, their prioritization is a condition of possibility to create momentary opportunities of enunciation, construction, creation, sharedness, and enablement. They can provide a complex, dynamic, and bottom up possibility to stop momentarily the demand of deconstruction that the problem of difference poses. "Their" voices of confrontation can become a criterion to deconstruct universalities and enable multiplicity simultaneously. Many of the intellectuals that are involved in the discussion of the problem of difference in and for Bolivia, but also in and for the world, aim to move beyond the generalization of domination and deconstruction in this sense (e.g., Estermann 2006; Escobar 2010; Viaña, Claros, and Sarzuri-Lima 2010; Alcoreza 2014; Rivera 2015). Other decolonial scholars that are slowly entering the struggle of the problem of difference within International Relations seek to move beyond Foucault in this same way as well. For example, Mignolo states that Foucault does not perceive exteriority; he does not investigate outside of modern and colonial borders (Mignolo 2000, 37). According to the author, Foucault overlooks the differences of "other" voices; he is blinded to colonial difference (38).

Notwithstanding this problematic tendency in Foucault's work, the author sometimes warns us against generalization and pure deconstruction. For example, Foucault explores the possibility of thinking about a different kind of politics by following the emergence of "language in multiplicity" (Foucault 1970, 386). Additionally, Foucault asserts that the analysis of discourse is based on the principle of deficit because never can everything be said (Foucault 1972, 118).

> However, we are not linking these exclusions to a repression; we do not presuppose that beneath manifest statements something remains hidden and subjacent. We are analyzing statements, not as being in the place of

> other statements that have fallen below the line of possible emergence, but as being always in their own place
>
> Foucault 1972, 119

Here, the author avoids the epistemic generalization of deficit, emphasizing the role of sharedness and preventing us from finding repression everywhere. From this perspective, Foucault could have explored how it may be possible to stay and coexist in both sides of the tension at the same time. In other words, how is it possible to respect and limit the epistemic assumptions of discourses simultaneously?

This possibility could have unfolded also from Foucault's separation between power and domination (Foucault 1995, 35). The author even asserts that interpreters should be weary of defining power as pure repressiveness (Foucault 1997, 18). In some of his later lectures at the Collège de France, Foucault also emphasizes the enabling possibilities of "truths" (Foucault 2008). By highlighting the indeterminate notion of sharedness and by separating power from domination, Foucault could have shed light on the enabling side of discourses and he could have avoided some of the generalizations that he often included in his conclusions. Consistent with this, some authors involved in the discussion of the problem of difference in International Relations deploy Foucault's work while also emphasizing the possibility of moving beyond domination and deconstruction (e.g., Epstein 2008; Agathangelou and Ling 2009; Schwartz-Shea and Yanow 2012; Lynch 2014; Weber 2016).

Finally, Foucault could have followed the implications that unfold from applying the epistemic notion of tension to genealogical and archaeological interpreters themselves. Since interpreters enjoy a precarious form of authorization in indeterminate proximity, they also need to sustain higher levels of reflexivity about their positionalities and against generalizations. That is, the epistemological precarity that Foucault uses to create his own praxis should have warned him against the generalization of domination and deconstruction. Many feminist and interpretive authors of International Relations emphasize this demand for reflexivity (Tickner 1992; Sylvester 1994; Milliken 1999; Ackerly, Stern, and True 2006; Ackerly and True 2008; Schwartz-Shea and Yanow 2012; Lynch 2014).

Despite these opportunities and warnings, Foucault did not develop a clear commitment to "others" and a more precise form of decoloniality; he did not venture into the construction of the condition of possibility that is necessary to stop deconstruction and to listen to "others." Due to the risks of domination and violence that emerge from elevated ways of knowing, being, and enacting, he kept away from differentiating "others;" due to the risks that surge from any boundary, he stayed as a limited "ally" from the "West," but he did not seek a possibility of walking alongside multiple "others." To the contrary, Rivera provides a fruitful way of moving beyond this generalization of deconstruction. She creates a way of walking the here/now. In this sense, she constructs another locus of enunciation (Rivera 1990, 2012, 2015, 2018).

Note

1 I derive the word "sharedness" from the possibility of repeating a sense that is grasped from a group of signs, but the word was not used by Foucault.

References

Ackerly, Brooke A., Maria Stern, and Jacqui True. 2006. *Feminist Methodologies for International Relations*. Cambridge: Cambridge University Press.

Ackerly, Brooke A., and Jacqui True. 2008. "Reflexivity in Practice: Power and Ethics in Feminist Research on International Relations." *International Studies Review* 10 (4): 693–707.

Adler, Emanuel. 2008. "The Spread of Security Communities: Communities of Practice, Self-Restraint, and NATO's Post-Cold War Transformation." *European Journal of International Relations* 14 (2): 195–230.

Agathangelou, Anna M., and L. H. M. Ling. 2009. *Transforming World Politics: From Empire to Multiple Worlds*. New York: Routledge.

Albró, Robert. 2005. "The Indigenous in the Plural in Bolivian Oppositional Politics." *Society for Latin American Studies* 24 (4): 433–453.

Albró, Robert. 2010. "Confounding Cultural Citizenship and Constitutional Reform in Bolivia." *Latin American Perspectives* 37 (3): 71–90.

Alcoreza, Raúl Prada. 2014. "Epistemología Pluralista." In *Pluralismo Epistemológico*, edited by Amílcar B. Zambrana, 13–55. Cochabamba: FUNPROEIB Andes. https://es.scribd.com/doc/296610165/Pluralismo-Epistemologico.

Ari, Waskar. 2014. *Earth Politics. Religion, Decolonization, and Bolivia's Indigenous Intellectuals*. Durham, NC: Duke University Press.

Ashley, Richard. 1989. "Living on Borderlines." In *International/Intertextual Relations*, by James Der Darian and Michael J. Shapiro, 259–321. New York: Lexington Books.

Ashley, Richard, and R. B. J. Walker. 1990. "Speaking the Language of Exile: Dissent Thought in International Studies." *International Studies Quarterly* 34 (3): 259–268.

Bourdieu, Pierre. 1980. *The Logic of Practices*. Stanford, CA: Stanford University Press.

Brincat, Shannon, Laura Lima, and João Nunes, eds. 2012. *Critical Theory in International Relations and Security Studies: Interviews and Reflections*. 1 edition. Abingdon; New York: Routledge.

Campbell, David. 2013. "Post-Structuralism." In *International Relations Theories: Discipline and Diversity*, edited by Tim Dunne, Milja Kurki, and Steve Smith, 223–247. Oxford: Oxford University Press.

Cox, Robert W. 1981. "Social Forces, States and World Orders: Beyond International Relations Theory." *Millennium: Journal of International Studies* 10 (2): 126–155. doi:10.1177/03058298810100020501.

Epstein, Charlotte. 2008. *The Power of Words in International Relations: Birth of an Anti-Whaling Discourse*. Cambridge, MA: MIT Press.

Escobar, Arturo. 2010. "Latin America at a Crossroads: Alternative Modernizations, Post-Liberalism, or Post-Development?" *Cultural Studies* 24 (1): 1–65. doi:10.1080/09502380903424208.

Estermann, Josef. 2006. *Filosofía Andina: Sabiduría Indígena Para Un Mundo Nuevo*. 2nd ed.La Paz: Instituto Superior Ecuménico Andino de Teología.

Filho, Clayton Mendonça Cunha, Rodrigo Santaella Gonçalves, and Ariane Dalla Déa. 2010. "The National Development Plan as a Political Economic Strategy in

Evo Morales's Bolivia: Accomplishments and Limitations." *Latin American Perspectives* 37 (4): 177–196.

Foucault, Michel. 1970. *The Order of Things: An Archaeology of Human Sciences.* New York: Vintage Books.

Foucault, Michel. 1971. Michel Foucault Interview by Elders Fons. Dutch Television. November 28. https://youtu.be/qzoOhhh4aJg.

Foucault, Michel. 1972. *The Archaeology of Knowledge, and The Discourse on Language.* New York: Vintage Books.

Foucault, Michel. 1978. *The History of Sexuality.* New York: Vintage Books.

Foucault, Michel. 1995. *Discipline and Punish: The Birth of the Prison.* New York: Vintage Books.

Foucault, Michel. 1997. *Society Must Be Defended: Lectures at the Collége de France, 1975–1976.* New York: Picador.

Foucault, Michel. 2008. *The Courage of Truth: The Government of the Self and Others II. Lectures at the Collège de France, 1983–1984.* New York: Picador.

George, Jim, and David Campbell. 1990. "Patterns of Dissent and the Celebration of Difference: Critical Social Theory and International Relations." *International Studies Quarterly* 34 (3): 269–293.

Giddens, Anthony. 1979. *Central Problems in Social Theory: Action, Structure, and Contradiction in Social Analysis.* Berkley; Los Angeles: University of California Press.

Howard, Rosaleen. 2010. "Language, Signs, and the Performance of Power: The Discursive Struggle over Decolonization in the Bolivia of Evo Morales." *Latin American Perspectives* 37 (3): 176–194.

Hoy, David Couzens. 2005. *Critical Resistance: From Poststructuralism to Post-Critique.* Cambridge, MA: MIT Press.

Kohl, Benjamin. 2010. "Bolivia under Morales: A Work in Progress." *Latin American Perspectives* 37 (3): 107–122.

Linera, Álvaro García. 2015. *Hacia El Gran Ayllu Universal. Pensar El Mundo Desde Los Andes.* Edited by Álvaro Huayta Zárate. México: Altepetl Editores, Biblioteca Indígena.

Lynch, Cecelia. 2014. *Interpreting International Politics.* New York: Routledge.

Mignolo, Walter. 2000. *Local Histories/Global Designs: Coloniality, Subaltern Knowledges, and Border Thinking.* Princeton Studies in Culture/Power/History. Princeton, NJ: Princeton University Press.

Milliken, Jennifer. 1999. "The Study of Discourse in International Relations: A Critique of Research and Methods." *European Journal of International Relations* 5 (2): 225–254.

Reinaga, Fausto. 2014. *Fausto Reinaga: Obras Completas.* 10 vols. La Paz: Vicepresidencia del Estado Plurinacional.

Rivera Cusicanqui, Silvia. 1990. "Liberal Democracy and Ayllu Democracy in Bolivia: The Case of Northern Potosí." *The Journal of Development Studies* 26 (4): 97–121.

Rivera Cusicanqui, Silvia. 2010. "The Notion of 'Rights' and the Paradoxes of Postcolonial Modernity: Indigenous Peoples and Women in Bolivia." *Qui Parle: Critical Humanities and Social Sciences* 18 (2): 29–54. doi:10.5250/quiparle.18.2.29.

Rivera Cusicanqui, Silvia. 2012. "Ch'ixinakax Utxiwa: A Reflection on the Practices and Discourses of Decolonization." *South Atlantic Quarterly* 111 (1): 95–109. doi:10.1215/00382876-1472612.

Rivera Cusicanqui, Silvia. 2015. *Sociología de la Imagen. Miradas Ch'ixi Desde La Historia Andina*. Buenos Aires: Tinta Limón.

Rivera Cusicanqui, Silvia. 2018. *El Mundo Ch'ixi Es Posible: Ensayos Desde Un Presente En Crisis*. Buenos Aires: Tinta Limón.

Rivera Cusicanqui, Silvia, and Raúl Barrios Morón. 1993. *Violencias Encubiertas En Bolivia: Cultura y Política*. La Paz: Talleres Gráficos Hisbol.

Said, Edward W. 1978. *Orientalism*. New York: Vintage Books.

Schwartz-Shea, Peregrine, and Dvora Yanow. 2012. *Interpretive Research Design: Concepts and Processes*. New York: Routledge.

Stoler, Ann Laura. 1995. *Race and Education of Desire: Foucault's History of Sexuality and the Colonial Order of Things*. Durham, NC: Duke University Press.

Sylvester, Christine. 1994. *Feminist Theory and International Relations in a Postmodern Era*. Cambridge: Cambridge University Press.

Tickner, J. Ann. 1992. *Gender in International Relations: Feminist Perspectives on Achieving Global Security*. New York: Columbia University Press.

Ticona, Esteban Alejo. 2011. *Bolivia En El Inicio Del Pachakuti: La Larga Lucha Anticolonial de Los Pueblos Aimara y Quechua*. La Paz: Akal Ediciones S.A.

Viaña, Jorge, Luis Claros, and Marcelo Sarzuri-Lima. 2010. "La Condición Colonial y Los Laberintos de La Descolonización." *Revista Integra Educativa* 3 (1): 13–36.

Walker, R. B. J. 1993. *Inside/Outside: International Relations as Political Theory*. Cambridge: Cambridge University Press.

Walker, R. B. J. 2010. *After the Globe, Before the World*. New York: Routledge.

Weber, Cynthia. 2016. *Queer International Relations: Sovereignty, Sexuality and the Will to Knowledge*. Oxford: Oxford University Press.

Wendt, Alexander. 1999. *Social Theory of International Politics*. Cambridge; New York: Cambridge University Press.

Wynter, Sylvia. 1995. "The Pope Must Have Been Drunk, The King of Castile a Madman: Culture as Actuality, and the Caribbean Rethinking Modernity." In *Reordering of Culture: Latin America, the Caribbean and Canada in the Hood*, by Alvina Ruprecht, 17–42. Ottawa: Carleton University Press.

Yanow, Dvora, and Peregrine Schwartz-Shea, eds. 2014. *Interpretation and Method: Empirical Research Methods and the Interpretive Turn*. 2nd ed. Armonk, NY: M. E. Sharp.

Zehfuss, Maja. 2002. *Constructivism in International Relations: The Politics of Reality*. Cambridge: Cambridge University Press.

6 A profession of faith, intersectional decoloniality, and beyond

Despite the profound discussions and struggles between multiple scholars, intellectuals, activists, politicians, and leaders, the problem of difference continues to confront the various kinds of boundaries and tendencies that emerge from the epistemic assumptions of each formation. How is it possible, then, to create a decolonial form of praxis while also accounting for epistemic levels of difference? Moreover, how can we create such a possibility while also committing to the struggles of multiple anti-colonial approaches, constructing a fruitful and reflexive criterion to stop deconstruction momentarily? How is it possible to build a way of knowing, being, and enacting that is devout to multiple struggles, voices, and projects at the same time? This multiplicity demands the de-universalization of anti-colonial discourses in order to listen to multiple struggles simultaneously, but how is it possible to avoid their epistemic invalidation? How much do they need to de-universalize and deconstruct? How is it possible to avoid the homogenization that takes place when anti-colonial and colonial discourses become equally classified within "domination"?

In order to answer these questions, I analyze the work of Silvia Rivera Cusicanqui. Similar to Fausto Reinaga, Rivera claims that some of her notions emerge from collectively shared ideas (Rivera 2018, 17), but I focus on how she synthesizes and constructs an approach; a method that can help us to think about the contradictions of colonialisms (Rivera 2010a, 69). Throughout her political and academic life, Rivera has written several books and articles, which, as the editors of her book *Sociología de la Imagen* assert, unapologetically and explicitly combine knowledge production and political action (Rivera 2015, 7). Much of her work is connected to Indianista concerns against racism and ethnic injustices (Rivera 2010c, 179). Moreover, her perspective was strongly influenced by the Andean context of Katarismo and Indianismo (Rivera 2015, 287). She was guided by the work of Reinaga and his focus on issues of colonial racism as well (Rivera 2010c, 13–14). Despite this intellectual background and her connection with other forms of Indianismo, Rivera introduces anarchist insights, ecological concerns, and feminist theories into Indianista discussions and into her construction of praxis (Rivera 2015, 289). She also takes into account the work of Michel Foucault, but she asserts that his focus on racism limits his investigations of colonialism and his analysis of alternatives (27). In some of her later books, Rivera has engaged the work of other decolonial authors such as Walter Mignolo and Catherine Walsh, critiquing their perspectives and seeking possibilities to move beyond some of the limitations that they sustain (Rivera 2018, 27). From her work as the coordinator of the Workshop of Oral Andean History (THOA for its initials in Spanish), as well as from her engagement with other scholars, Rivera thus constructs an innovative approach, which includes tensions and dilemmas in order to study multiple problems of colonialism and forms of struggle at the same time. Within this intellectual context, Rivera synthesizes an innovative way of knowing, being, and enacting decoloniality, which offers a possible answer to some of the questions of the problem of difference. According to Rivera, much of this decolonial praxis results from listening to indigenous oral histories in Bolivia. She carefully listens to indigenous insights, finding convergences of voices, which help her to construct another way to think about politics and act in the world (Rivera 2015, 18).

Cosmology and epistemological equivalence

Similar to Reinaga, Rivera begins to construct her epistemic notions from cosmological ideas of Pacha and equality in difference (Rivera 2018, 57). Reinaga stated that the existence of the Cosmos was the first foundation that enabled and guided the rest of his approach (Reinaga 2014, 6:403). From this notion of Pachamama, the author constructed a definition of cosmic coexistence, which presupposed a specific form of cosmological equality (6:227). Despite the equality of all the entities of the Cosmos, Reinaga assumed the possibility of accessing the essence of things "out there;" he essentialized the Cosmos, creating a foundational bedrock and universalizing a particular way of knowing, being, and enacting. To the contrary, Rivera avoids this epistemic tendency. The author asserts that the "co-participation" of an interpreter in relationships, as well as in a "dialogue with other subjects," enables her to construct a possibility of knowing (Rivera 2015, 25, translation by author). Here, the author applies the notion of equality in difference to the epistemological dimension of her own approach. Knowledge appears as the result of a relationship among equal subjects. The knower is hereby regarded as another equal member of the Cosmos; she does not have a "greater right" to define it or a more "human" capacity to know it. The author thus includes a possibility of *epistemological* equality in difference or "equivalence.". Unlike the work of Reinaga and much of Indianismo, this "Indio epistemology" renounces the essentializing possibility of accessing the very characteristics of objects or entities out there (Rivera 2018, 90, translation by author). Rivera gives up the unequal epistemological connection between a knowing subject and a knowable and controllable object. Instead, all the entities of the Cosmos hereby become equal subjects (Rivera 2018, 90). Due to this de-essentialization of the Cosmos, Rivera moves the possibility of knowing away from the essence of entities and towards experiences of *relationships*. Here, a knowing subject does not reach the very essence of another object; instead, she only experiences a *relationship* established momentarily by a complex and sometimes polysemic focus on the commonality and difference that can reconstruct that connection. Rivera thus prioritizes a relational understanding of Andean Cosmology and of epistemic equality in difference.

Due to this definition of co-participation and relationality, Rivera renounces the notions of objectivity, correspondence, and epistemological authority that emerge from the capacity of accessing the very essence of objects. Since she moves beyond the theory of "truth correspondence" between language and the real world (George and Campbell 1990, 272), Rivera applies the cosmological notion of equality in difference to the possibility of knowing, which now tends to equalize every experience of relationships in the Cosmos. Here, neither "inheritance" nor "co-substantiation" authorize any single knower or form of knowledge above "others." Instead, Rivera regards the Cosmos as composed by epistemologically equal subjects, who can experience relationships in different, but also equally valid ways. The author thus validates multiple and even contradictory experiences of relationships. According to Rivera, this notion of multiplicity, polyvalence, and polysemy emerges from Andean ideas of diversity, which include equal relationships of symbolic and productive exchange (Rivera 2018, 46).

To discuss this possibility of knowing further, Rivera uses the notion of "senti-pensar" (Rivera 2015, 228). To senti-pensar entails a rejection against the universality of philosophies of "reason" or the generalization of complete foundations that are designed to universalize a single kind of knowledge, knower, and project. Senti-pensar is a possibility of thinking based on complex feelings and to feel based on complex thoughts. It is a possibility of using multifaceted, polysemic, and even contradictory experiences of relationships in order to know; it is a possibility to think "con las entrañas" and with the Cosmos from multiple memories (Rivera 2018, 121).

Of course this possibility of expressing and reconstructing experiences of relationships does not entail some kind of correspondence between knowledge and relationships themselves. That is, senti-pensar is not a direct epistemological bridge between the meanings expressed by some and "objective" relationships. Instead, the sources of senti-pensar are the momentary, context-dependent, and inexplicably complex feelings and thoughts that are used by an interpreter to reconstruct experiences of relationships meaningfully. The complexity of "feelings" and "thoughts" thus mediates these experiences of relationships, turning Rivera's approach into an analysis of interpretations (Rivera 2015, 183). Similar to Foucault, Rivera thus avoids constructing yet another pre-definition of her own relationship with meanings, which would then create an overarching boundary and characteristic of "real" relationships. Foucault achieves this goal by avoiding the definition of "proximity" while Rivera renounces a complete pre-definition of senti-pensar, allowing for meanings to remain unstable and untamed.

Consistent with the cosmology of equality in difference, senti-pensar is, then, just another *relationship* that enables the possibility of reconstructing experiences of relationships; it is an epistemological relationship constructed from a possibility of equal *co-participation*. This epistemic notion of equality in difference has important implications for the ways in which Rivera defines *meaning*. Her field of inquiry includes a possibility of mapping meaningful "convergences" or "discursive atmospheres," which emerge from the synthetization of texts, voices, and images (Rivera 2015, 23–24). Rivera's sociology of images is "… a spirit, a tendency, a vital attitude that centralizes its impulse in grasping/narrating the experience of a situated and self-conscious sense of social existence" (25). The sociology of images thus seeks to know through a form of "… narration, a syntax between images and text that tells the story of what was *lived*" (22). Meanings are thus interpreted from texts, voices, and images, which are understood as reconstructions of experiences of relationships.

Throughout much of her work, Rivera highlights the importance of oral histories, which unveil the complexity and popular experiences that are often obfuscated or silenced by the formality of writing (Rivera 2018, 16). For example, the author analyzes how radio stations revived the history of Tupak Katari in Aymara while critiquing the dictatorship of 1971–1978 (128). Here, the importance of orality leis in its emphasis of the dynamic aspect of identity and relationality. Rivera states that writing tends to be more rigid than orality, but the two are related and often interact in dynamic ways as well (131). The author also highlights how memories re-actualize the past to think politically in the present, creating different forms of agency and collective desire (132). According to her, memories are constantly re-codified into victories or into careful warnings about what needs to be done and how we need to proceed; they are an exegesis and an invention/creation that often emerges in clandestine meetings, oral myths, legends, rituals, ceremonies (138). Hence, Rivera understands the past as *memories*, which are meanings that reconstruct experiences of relationships from the here/now of a present. Memories are not regarded as the actual experiences of past relationships themselves. Instead, they hereby become current *reconstructions* of past experiences of relationships. As a result, the author does not view memories as the "authentic" and "factual" past of "humanity" (Rivera 2015, 183). Instead, memories are a re-actualization of the past under the light of the present (Rivera 2018, 138).

From these meanings, Rivera synthetizes "convergences" (Rivera 2015, 24). She connects reconstructions of relationships and synthetizes them into weaved narrations. These "discursive atmospheres" allow for the interpretation of a lived and empirical realm called "taypi," which is a dynamic and multi-layered map of relationships. The meaning-related patterns interpreted by Rivera in her sociology of images thus entail a possibility of weaving multiple narrations into dynamic maps of experienced relationships. Unlike the plurinationalist understanding of identity, however, Rivera does not aim to settle yet another "real" map of identities; she does not objectivize or generalize a particular set of identities. Instead, Rivera invites us to think about the fluid practices that are anchored in daily exchanges and interactions, weaving complex and changing constructions of meanings (126). This understanding of practices, meanings, convergences, and taypi avoids the "masculine understanding of identity," which fixes rigid maps of bounded and mono-logical identities for a territory, stereotyping and settling notions of minorities that are based on characteristics of the body and particular symbols (126).

Epistemological equivalence and its de-authorizing effect

The epistemic connections between cosmological equality in difference, co-participation, senti-pensar, meanings, convergences, and taypi form the enabling or constructive side of Rivera's epistemic approach, which creates a way of knowing relational multiplicity. Despite this epistemic possibility, the consistency between the cosmology of equality in difference and the epistemological idea of co-participation includes a de-authorizing effect and deconstructing side, which deliberately prevents Rivera from creating yet another universalizing platform of validity, authority, and legitimacy.

The de-authorizing effect of this epistemic approach first emerges in the cosmological understanding of equality in difference. At this level of analysis, the perspective synthetized by Rivera avoids further defining and fixing an ontological characteristic or essence of co-participation; she renounces the ontological elevation, enactment, and specification of a particular kind of relationality, which would then act as an overarching criterion of judgement to determine what relationalities are more "real and equal." Hence, the author discusses co-participation, senti-pensar, convergences, and meanings, but she analyzes this epistemic realm while allowing for *multiple, polysemic, untamed*, and *dynamic* possibilities of relationships. To achieve this goal, Rivera does not epistemically elevate a universalized essence for any of these ideas; she does not fix the "real" characteristics of the Cosmos, avoiding the possibility of establishing a meta-consistency that would pre-determine what kinds of relationships could be regarded as more "real." Unlike colonial and anti-colonial discourses, Rivera does not elevate a particular definition of "reality," knowledge, relationship, equality, power, and struggle. She does not validate, at this level of analysis, a particular kind of knowledge, which would then determine the "real" relationship of "humanity," establishing notions of equality and determining the power axis that ought to be resisted. Similar to Foucault's notion of a deficit in the definition of the unit of discourse (i.e., the statement), Rivera uses an epistemically undetermined or at least un-enacted notion of senti-pensar, which then leads to the multiple and dynamic forms of relationships that emerge as weaved narratives. Hence, the cosmology of equality in difference is hereby held open towards the understanding of multiple ways of knowing, creating the possibility of encompassing a diversity of "realities," relationships, equalities, and power axes.

The problem that emerges at this level of analysis is that the cosmological notion of equality in difference renounces the possibility of classifying ways of knowing. At this cosmological level, all relationships, including "colonial" relationships, are regarded as equally valid in their multiplicity. At this level, there is no bedrock to judge relationships. As other authors have affirmed, even the essentializing understandings of epistemics that lead to universalized bedrocks and othering effects can be understood within relational perspectives (Mignolo and Walsh 2018). Hence, how is it possible to classify or judge relationships if they are all equally different and valid? How is it possible to separate and resist the "colonial" tendencies of particular relationships?

This cosmological tendency to deconstruct judgement and action can also be analyzed in the discussion of the epistemology that emerges in this level of Rivera's work. At this level of analysis, Rivera sustains her own position as an equal co-interpreter, co-participant, or subject, who also experiences relationships. Here, the author does not only avoid ontological classifications of relationships but also follows the implications of this equality in difference towards the de-authorization of herself as a knowing subject. The patterns of meanings that she interprets to make up convergences emerge from her momentary senti-pensar, which is a possibility of synthesizing narrations from the reconstruction of experiences of meaning-related relationships. The momentary meanings that she produces appear, however, to be equally valid. Within this cosmological level of analysis, the epistemological understanding of senti-pensar does not grant to Rivera any authority above other voices. In the case of Reinaga, the "Indio" became the knower of the "Cosmos" and the main agent that guided or ruled the rest of "humanity." Instead, Rivera's possibility of accessing knowledge does not entail an epistemological form of self-authorization. In other words, epistemology itself turns into another equal relationship. As a result, Rivera undermines her possibility of defining the "real" characteristics of a knower and she gives up the classification and hierarchicalization of other ways of being. This understanding of epistemological equality enables Rivera to understand the differences of multiple voices, but it also prevents her from being able to have the authority that is presupposed when actions demand the transformation of others. If all voices are equally different and equally authorized, how can someone demand that other voices transform their oppressive tendencies?

Finally, the cosmological notion of equality in difference undermines the possibility of constructing a single and rectilinear understanding of temporality. Since this cosmology avoids single ontological foundations of what is "real" and single authorizations of who knows "reality," the approach cannot provide a bedrock to organize the history of the past, topography of the present, and destiny of the future. Here, linear or dialectical understandings of temporality become problematized, opening the possibility of studying multiple narrations of time and history. Despite this possibility, how does Rivera think of decolonial action against oppressions? How does she enact possibilities to move beyond "oppressive" relationships, voices, and projects of civilization?

Due to this form of cosmological equality in difference or equivalence, Rivera's approach is a critique of objectivity emerging from "fragmented" visions of society, which precariously begin to construct a more encompassing way of knowing (Rivera 2015, 91). Here, each relationship, voice, and project appears as an equal moment of co-participation, senti-pensar, meanings, and convergences. Despite using an enabling possibility of knowing, then, Rivera's cosmological equality leads towards the de-elevation of any single way of knowing, any single knower, and any single project. In a way, then, the problem of difference leads towards the de-objectification and de-universalization of the sociology of images itself, which, in turn, undermines the possibility of demanding change from anything or anyone. Accordingly, Rivera asserts that multiplicity always sustains an element of uncertainty and incommensurability (Rivera 2018, 48). Moreover, this de-elevating tendency is consistent with Andean cosmological notions of Pacha, which entails a space called *Khä Pacha*. According to Rivera, this place includes a void, deficit, or abyss, which can lead to the de-authorization, invalidation, deconstruction, and disintegration of "human action," but can also represent a different kind of starting point.

> This is the world of what does not yet exist, of what is unknown, which emerges as a force in permanent displacement, which confronts a permanent disjunction: everything can become ruins and all human actions can become catastrophe, or else, it can redeem the world of what exists and turn into an act of liberation and accomplishment. The disjunction present in the abysmal nature of Khä Pacha is thus an ever-present danger, which is perceived in the social world as a risk of dissolution and stagnation, but can also create the possibility of renovation and realization of more complete human potential.
>
> Rivera 2015, 212

Due to her understanding of equality in difference, critique of objectivity, and idea of Khä Pacha, Rivera shows that this relational view of Cosmology does not provide a pre-determined path of decolonial praxis by itself. In other words, the focus on relationships, together with the de-essentialization of epistemics in the separation between language and the essence of objects "out there" enables a much broader understanding of difference, but this form of de-elevation does not offer the possibility of decolonial praxis. As other authors have pointed out, "absolute relationality of all identities – the fact that something is only in relationship to something else – is an obstacle for the project that pretends to allow the subaltern to speak for her/himself" (Viaña, Claros, and Sarzuri-Lima 2010, 32–33, translation by author). How is it possible, then, to invalidate the "colonial" and oppressive aspects of some relationships if all ways of knowing are equally valid? How is it possible to de-authorize the colonial tendencies of certain voices if all ways of being are equally authorized? How is it possible to delegitimize the homogenizing tendencies of colonial projects if all ways of enacting are equally legitimate?

Profession of faith

Unlike much of Revolutionary Indianismo, the later work of Reinaga, and the project of plurinationalism, Rivera's approach sustains the epistemic tension that emerges between the notion of equality in difference and political action. Instead of generalizing the deconstructive tendency that emerges from the idea of Khä Pacha, however, Rivera still creates a form of decolonial *classification* and *praxis,* which allows for multiple equalities, voices, and projects to be momentarily sustained. Contrasting the post-structuralist tendency to generalize domination and to homogenize all universalizing discourses, the author sustains the importance of the enabling side of meaning, reminding us that senti-pensar is also a way of reconstructing relationships and sites of solidarity. From this reminder emerges a possibility of thinking about what needs to be epistemically prioritized, which also determines what needs to be deconstructed and how much.

To achieve this goal, Rivera makes a "… profession of faith, which is based on the idea that decolonization can only be realized within practice. This would be, however, a reflexive and communicative practice founded in the desire of recuperating a memory and our own corporality" (Rivera 2015, 28). That is, the cosmological understanding of equality in difference and the epistemological notion of senti-pensar do not include an endogenously consistent form of validation, authorization, and legitimation. To construct such a classifying boundary, Rivera makes a "profession of faith;" she makes a decision to settle a momentary ontological, epistemological, and decolonial platform of equality, which can enable a possibility to demand change from "colonial" relations. This explains why Rivera asserts that her field of knowledge ultimately relies on the political "energy of desire" (302); it emerges from the desire of transformation and resistance against suffered colonialisms. This notion of classification is not some kind of philosophically universalized bedrock; it is an epistemic platform that appears equally valid within the relational cosmology of equality in difference, but Rivera still *decides* to elevate it over the universalizing tendencies that emerge from "colonial" ways of knowing, being, and enacting.

Rivera thus creates a possibility of decoloniality by acknowledging or having "faith" in the "fact of colonialism" (28). Similar to the fact of inheritance, the fact of reason, the fact of desire, and the fact of the Cosmos, this "fact" acts as an epistemic condition of possibility from which Rivera can create a classification of relationships, voices, and projects. Here, Rivera constructs a possibility of acknowledging the non-arbitrariness of the voices that denounce the existence of colonialisms. In order to achieve this goal, Rivera uses an ontological strategy that is similar to the post-structuralist notion of the archive and its presupposition of sharedness. Rivera deploys the idea of "convergences," which connects the different meanings that are interpreted in different moments of co-participation and senti-pensar. In this sense, the meanings that reconstruct relationships appear to include an ontological element that enables their connection and synthetization; it allows for the interpretation of weaved narratives and "discursive atmospheres." In turn, this link presupposes a non-arbitrary form of sharedness; it includes a status of validity for the statements, pictures, texts, and significations that the author connects. Since Rivera views the convergences that she finds as more than arbitrary or purely subjective synthetizations, she regards the connection between meanings as existing beyond her own, individual, and arbitrary moments of interpretation.

As this discussion begins to unveil, Rivera uses the profession of faith to settle and elevate a meta-relationship, boundary, and equality at the epistemic level. Then, the author can classify "coloniality" and demand change. This possibility entails two interrelated epistemic tendencies of classification, which begin to show how decolonial praxis surges within this approach. The first aspect of this platform of classification and bedrock is that the notion of sharedness demands the equalization of ways of knowing, being, and enacting. Since the problem of difference is settled yet again, Rivera defines another form of equality, which is granted to the different discourses that make up the "atmospheres" of a particular taypi. This equalization of interpreted ways of knowing, being, and enacting then judges the universalizing tendency of discourses that contradict this form of equality; it denounces the epistemic over-expansion of ways of knowing, being, and enacting that organize, discipline, or kill "others." In other words, the notion of non-arbitrary "convergences" allows the author to focus on the continuities, connections, and sharedness that can be established between meanings throughout space and time. This entails an the ontological condition of possibility that allows her to weave together the narratives of struggle, agency, and enactment in Bolivia. Then, the notion of a continuity and a sharedness among meanings emphasizes the non-arbitrary status of some ways of knowing, being, and enacting. From this idea emerges a form of equality that can be granted to the reconstructions of relationships. Insofar as discourses violate this settled definition of epistemic equality, they now become classified as "colonial." That is, the presupposition of a social sharedness of meanings hereby becomes elevated as the kind of relationship and equality that judges whatever contradicts it; it is a meta-relationship that judges other relationships.

In order to achieve this goal, Rivera also needs to re-authorize herself above the cosmological equality in difference among subjects and she has to appear capable of making the judgement that emerges from the "equality" of sharedness. Since she makes a profession of faith, she can in fact authorize herself to know, be, and enact this "equality;" she can locate herself above the cosmological equality of relationships, judging discourses and demanding transformation from the tendencies that violate "equality." This epistemological strategy of authorization is similar to the post-structuralist possibility of moving above foundationalisms, but Rivera adds a second epistemic clarification, which puts a stop to deconstruction. Unlike much of post-structuralism, Rivera explicitly prioritizes the continuity and sharedness of meanings that have been hidden under the totalizing and universalizing tendencies of "colonial" discourses; she explicitly commits her epistemic validation, authorization, and legitimation to the prioritization of the meanings that *confront* colonial universality, *fracturing* their domination and demanding transformation. Similar to some post-structuralist scholars who have in fact moved beyond the generalization of domination and deconstruction (e.g., George and Campbell 1990; Doty 1997; Edkins and Zehfuss 2014; Weber 2016), Rivera re-emphasizes the sharedness and equal validity of localized ways of knowing, being, and enacting while also claiming a possibility of desubjugation. In this sense, the author calls for the possibility of acknowledging "colonialism" as a fact, an "ethos" or a "structure" that reproduces itself daily in the oppression of the voices that confront it (Rivera 2018, 25).

In a way, then, the "reality" of multiple decolonial voices emerges from the sharedness that is presupposed in the connections of different meanings denouncing colonialisms. Additionally, Rivera constructs her epistemological bridge with this "reality" through the notion of co-participation, which connects her own possibility of interpretation with the non-arbitrariness of meanings through the same sharedness that is presupposed in converges. Similar to post-structuralism, then, Rivera presupposes sharedness and "proximity," but she prioritizes the non-arbitrariness of othered ways of knowing, being, and enacting in order to stop deconstruction, respecting localized struggles, voices, and projects insofar as they are not confronted from below by other continuous and shared voices. The relevance of this epistemic strategy, which I illustrate below, lies in the possibility of constructing criteria to avoid the homogenization of all foundationalist discourses, momentarily respecting the relationalities, equalities, agencies, and projects that emerge once colonial universalities are fractured.

Unlike the work of other decolonial and post-colonial authors (e.g., Said 1978; Mignolo 2000; Estermann 2006; Mignolo and Walsh 2018), however, Rivera explicitly avoids the temptation to re-objectify, re-structuralize, or sediment her epistemic profession of faith. Despite the classifying force of the boundary that emerges from the settlement of an epistemic notion of meta-equality of relationships, the author sustains the reflexivity of the cosmological abyss that constantly undermines all strong foundations. Unlike many universalizing epistemic platforms, the author acknowledges her moment of elevation, validation, authorization, and legitimation as an incomplete profession of faith. In this sense, Rivera does not define *how* convergences entail sharedness; she avoids pre-determining and fixing the characteristics of the shared connections between meanings, which could create settled ideas of intersubjectivity, structure, lifeworlds, or archives. Rather, the notion of a non-arbitrary connection among meanings has to remain indeterminate to allow for multiple reconstructions of relationships, voices, and projects. Instead of determining a settled characteristic of meanings, Rivera creates a more open and dynamic form of classification. This boundary invalidates the over-expansion of universalized discourses, voices, and projects, but it also sustains the possibility of localized multiplicity in a much more dynamic manner.

Additionally, Rivera explicitly creates a basis of knowledge from a "profession of faith." Despite her moment of self-validation, self-authorization, and self-legitimation, then, Rivera acknowledges her ontological, epistemological, and political moment of epistemic elevation as a decision, a leap of faith, and a desire, which is not understood as the "real" characteristics that correspond to the Cosmos itself. Her classification does not emerge from the very "reality" of the Cosmos, "reason," "desire," "inheritance," or "heritage;" it is a profession of faith. This explains why it is so important to think about cosmology, moving beyond exclusive foci on ontology, epistemology, and temporality. At the level of cosmology, Rivera sustains a tension that prevents the pre-definition, elevation, and/or universalization of yet another strong foundation. The author thus teaches us to stop before generalizing any single tendency within the problem of difference, avoiding the definitive sedimentation of any single construction of knowledge, equality, power, struggle, or relationality. The approach even cautions us against the generalization of deficit, domination, abyss, deconstruction, or Khä Pacha. Instead, Rivera makes a reflexive profession of faith, which changes the characteristics of epistemics by sustaining the tension of the problem of difference at the level of cosmology, precariously fixing an epistemic platform at the level of ontology, epistemology, and temporality. The author creates a reflexive locus of enunciation at the level of praxis.

The profession of faith in the equal sharedness of ways of knowing, being, and enacting, together with the emphasis of confrontation, constructs a possibility of creating an "ethical compass" (Rivera 2018, 80), but Rivera achieves this goal without assuming that normativity emerges directly from a universal foundation of "reality." In a sense, the cosmological notion of equality in difference does not provide a consistent way of prioritizing the profession of faith over colonialisms. The voices related to wounds of colonialisms are not more "real" than the discourses that claim to know them. This epistemic precarity could lead to a pragmatic understanding of the profession of faith, but Rivera also emphasizes the normative importance of this decision. In epistemic terms, the idea of the Khä Pacha could construct the profession of faith as an equally arbitrary decisions among diverse bedrocks of classification, but Rivera's normative concern for marginalized and agentic confrontations puts much more weight on her profession of faith than on other epistemic possibilities. That is, her normative concern for the different experiences of suffering caused by the universalizing tendencies of colonialisms elevates her profession of faith over the colonial faith on "reason" or "desire."

Precarious boundaries and decolonial praxis

Once the sociology of images introduces the profession of faith, difference can be constrained and classification can emerge, but the approach has to retain its precarious validation and the interpreter has to sustain her/his reflexivity.

To construct this kind of decolonial action, Rivera validates difference while also invalidating the hierarchicalization of differences. In order to begin analyzing how Rivera creates this possibility of decoloniality, I deploy the notion of intersectionality that is discussed by a number of feminist scholars (e.g., Crenshaw 1991; Cho, Crenshaw, and McCall 2013; Collins 2015; Collins and Bilge 2016; Méndez 2018). Rivera has important differences with some notions of intersectionality, but the concept fruitfully describes part of the praxis that surges from her work.

Rivera begins the construction of her decolonial praxis from the non-arbitrary status of memories and meanings of confrontation. This epistemic elevation of the equality of relationships, voices, and projects above "coloniality" allows for Rivera to focus on the *fracturing* that happens when meanings denounce the hierarchical organization of "others." The annexation of "others" as "inferior" results from the universalization of epistemically elevated ways of knowing, being, and enacting. As a result, Rivera prioritizes moments, voices, and projects of confrontation, which fracture the hierarchicalizing and homogenizing tendencies of universalized discourses; she constructs a clear commitment to those who resist and/or suffer "colonialism." Once confrontations are acknowledged, Rivera allows for the coexistence of equally valid ways of knowing, being, and enacting. The author constructs a more dynamic and complex realm where coexistence emerges in the fruitful dialogue that sustains differences (Rivera 2018, 84). In this sense, a bottom up form of heterogeneity confronts the homogenizing tendency of universalized discourses and it radicalizes itself (22).

This kind of boundary leads to two interconnected forms of political praxis. On one side, the emphasis of an othered relationship, voice, and project creates a first form of *resistance* against its hierarchical organization. In each confrontation of a hierarchy and the forms of violence that emerge from it, Rivera traces a validated struggle, authorized voice, and legitimated project, which denounces and contradicts the ways in which the universalized discourse seeks to organize it, assimilate it, or kill it. That is, the equal sharedness of an othered way of knowing, being, and enacting epistemically elevates the moment at which this formation confronts the universalizing tendencies of dominant discourses, demanding an epistemic transformation and limitation of the over-extended discourse. For example, Rivera uses the meaning-related convergences between memories of "indigenous" experiences to analyze the years of the Nationalist Revolution in Bolivia. Based on these voices, she unveils how "progressive" policies promoted by unions and then by the government entailed civilizing models that continued oligarchic hierarchies against indigenous ways of being and knowing (Rivera 2015, 105). These confrontations not only denounced the hierarchy and violence suffered by "indigenous" peoples in Bolivia, but also aimed to construct another kind of relationship (54).

On the other side, the epistemic prioritization of confrontations simultaneously validates other relationships, authorizes other voices, and legitimizes other projects; it listens to other "others." That is, despite the epistemic prioritization of a particular experience of ethnic equality above the coloniality of a Marxist project of civilization, Rivera also listens to other confrontations, avoiding "single axis thinking" (Cho, Crenshaw, and McCall 2013, 787). Each confrontation can thus enable a particular form of equality, identity, and project, but the broader epistemic prioritization of fracturing moments allows for other ways of knowing, being, and enacting to limit each other's validity, authority, and legitimacy. Accordingly, each struggle, voice, and project appears epistemically valued insofar as it does not claim to define, articulate, annex, colonize, discipline, or kill other ways of knowing, being, and enacting. Here, the othered can denounce the privilege of coloniality, but they also have to avoid becoming "colonial" themselves. Hence, Rivera not only avoids blindly deploying the "master's tools" in epistemic terms (i.e., renouncing strong foundations and bedrocks), but also in the way in which her own realm of coexistence enables heterogeneity and differences; she creates a possibility of classification and decoloniality that is respectful of differences in a much more encompassing sense than colonial or anti-colonial discourses. The sociology of images thus equally values a multiplicity of relationships, voices, and projects of equality; it creates an intersectional realm of tensions and coexistence by "disarticulating" heterogenous experiences (Rivera 2015, 220). For example, Rivera analyzes how Indianista unions, parties, and movements often silenced "women," while their economic activities inside and outside the household actually enabled "men" to participate in politics. The encounter between ethnicity and feminism thus leads to the inclusion of a much more complex study of colonial hierarchies and the confrontations hidden underneath them (179). This form of praxis resists the articulation and annexation of other "others;" it avoids the assimilation of struggles into logics that emerge from universalized forms of knowledge (Rivera 2018, 21).

Similar to other forms of pollical praxis and ideas of transformation, the epistemic faith that settles a notion of equality and elevates confrontations comes at a cost, which demands the transformation of the ways of knowing, being, and enacting that are integrated into this realm. In other words, Rivera enables multiplicity, but her field of knowledge and praxis comes at the cost of de-universalization; it takes away the universalizing tendencies of ontological, epistemological, and temporal assumptions by using its own epistemic profession of faith. Insofar as a discourse retains its epistemic tendency of universalization, moreover, Rivera's field of knowledge classifies it as "colonial." The possibility of resistance and disarticulation that prioritizes multiple struggles, voices, and projects, thus hierarchicalizes the universality of the discourses that annex, discipline, or erase "others." In order to enable a decolonial form of praxis, then, Rivera's field of knowledge includes a constraint against the respect of all differences.

The sociology of images begins by creating a field of inquiry that is designed to study a multiplicity of discourses. In order to achieve this goal, the approach analyzes the ontological, epistemological, and temporal source of universalization that is included in colonial discourses. Then, once it epistemically emphasizes the confrontations that emerge from "other" ways of knowing, being, and acting, the field transforms colonial discourses and reorganizes them into its own map. The sociology of images encompasses each set of convergences by using its own epistemic profession of faith, which deconstructs each endogenous tendency of universality, accommodating each discourse as equal parcels of a horizontal and yet multi-layered map. Hence, the sociology of images constructs its own bounded platform of validation, authorization, and legitimation from the idea of a "Ch'ixi" realm (Rivera 2015, 302). According to Rivera, this space of confrontations, tensions, and frictions emerges from Aymara religious notions, which construct a view based on complementary dualisms. Rivera explains this notion of equality through the idea of "Pacha." The Aymara notion of Pacha, includes a "… multiplicity of sacred spaces and entities, imbedded in the Aymara logic of complementarity, supplementation, and dialectical opposition" (208). In a sense, then, the Aymara notion of Pacha works as a *metaphorical* principle, which re-organizes life into a logic of equality that is based on the idea *complementarity*. This idea explicitly acknowledges the epistemic cost that is required from colonialities to become equalized within heterogeneity.

> Pacha is, at the same time, an abstract concept of *metaphorical and interpretative* nature, and a practical tool to walk the here/now of daily life. The syntax of Aymara culture is thus a form of *semiotic movement* that creates a method of *translation* and *integration* of present and future entities, even entities such as foreign cultures. Thus, Jesus Christ, development, democracy, history, and other figures are continuously integrated into the dynamic structures of Aymara cosmology, and they thus become parcels of a multipolar and broader form, which reverses the unitary and totalizing character of those words and, while doing so, erases their capitalized letters. (Rivera 2015, 207, italics by author)

The condition of possibility to charge this epistemic price of semiotic transformation, equalization, and de-universalization emerges from the profession of faith. Rivera's decision to prioritize subaltern confrontations allows the author to settle a particular boundary of equality, placing her own voice above "colonial" tendencies and henceforth demanding transformation. This is the epistemic moment that enables her to oppose the homogenizing, totalizing, and violent tendencies of universalized "colonialisms" (Rivera 2018, 36). This is how Rivera creates a possibility to resist the colonial siege of diversity (44). To some, Rivera's strategy of elevation, validation, authorization, legitimation, and classification might appear to be a contradiction because she aims towards the possibility of respecting differences, while also disrespecting some differences (i.e., colonial universalization). In other words, Rivera sustains an inconsistency between heterogeneity and her own demand of epistemic transformation, but that is precisely why the possibility of classification is a profession of faith, which is not assumed as a universalized or philosophically perfect foundation of "reality." Here, the level of cosmology moves the possibility of decoloniality beyond the Western demand of philosophical singularity and "perfection," which often universalizes single consistencies. That is, the possibility of classifying "coloniality" while also demanding a transformation does not emerge from the purity and oneness of the cosmological notion of equality in difference; it does not surge from a perfect correspondence of truth and reality. At the level of cosmology, the notion of equality in difference does not validate, authorize, and legitimatize any single way of knowing, being, and enacting above "others." Since she locates herself within this equality in difference, Rivera's approach, voice, and project cannot demand a transformation of "colonial" tendencies from this cosmological platform alone. Instead, she utilizes a reflexive profession of faith, which splits and decouples her discursive dimensions, sustaining a tension and creating a precarious kind of decoloniality at the same time. Cosmology thus retains a more consistent logic of equality in difference, while the levels of ontology, epistemology, and temporality become momentarily settled to construct a boundary of praxis.

Multiple memories, paths of transformation, and agents

Due to the epistemic elevation of multiple ways of knowing, being, and enacting, which leads to the prioritization of moments of confrontations, Rivera's approach complicates temporality and enactment. Throughout much of her work, Rivera demonstrates that convergences and continuities of marginalized *memories* often confront universalized organizations of linear history. As a result, several kinds of memories of multiple pasts and futures can thus be equally validated in the Ch'ixi realm (Rivera 2015, 73). Despite the possibility of including a multiplicity of memories and ideas of history, the Ch'ixi reconstruction of temporality classifies these meanings to demand the transformation of colonial projects. In consistency with the notion of intersectional decoloniality described above, the Ch'ixi realm validates memories of confrontation, which fracture universalized ideas of historical singularity, opening parallel ways to narrate other sets of convergences. Memories of struggles, resistance, and other ways of knowing, being, and enacting draw different histories, highlighting the ways in which universalized ideas can silence some of these experiences. The Ch'ixi realm thus uses its own construction of equality among multiple temporalities to judge and invalidate the epistemic tendency towards domination that is attached to universalizing narrations of linear history such as the ideas of "development," "evolution," "modernization," "revolution," etc. (88).

In order to achieve this goal, the re-validated past of confrontations is hereby understood as *memories* that narrate suffering of colonialities or moments of resistance against these hierarchies, but they can also contain other imaginaries of more balanced relationships of equality. In this sense, the present is epistemically emphasized, but in its "palimpsest" characteristics emerge threads from the most remote pasts; memories of the past that are re-actualized in front of us (Rivera 2018, 84). Hence, memories are presently re-actualized meanings that provide the possibility of different histories and multiple futures. Pasts are viewed as present actualizations (i.e., they are a present-pasts) used to imagine different futures in the now (i.e., they are past-futures to walk in the here/now) (Rivera 2015, 19). This notion of temporality refers to the following Aymara aphorism: "Quipnayra uñtasis sarnaqapxañani" (Looking back and forward – to the past-future – we can walk in the present-future). The interplay between memory and the possibility of projecting political action forward is thus understood as something active in the present (Rivera 2010a, 55).

The notion of the past as present memories thus creates an interplay that re-activates remembered moments in the present to imagine decolonial futures (Rivera 2010a, 55). However, Rivera also warns us that the future can be a constant danger, where differences confront each other endlessly and can lead to defeat or degradation (Rivera 2018, 91). This is a risk in the possibility of thinking multiple futures, but also in the coexistence of multiple pasts. Rivera shows how colonial, oligarchic, liberal, and Marxist pasts still coexist in the present of the Andes, deconstructing possibilities of unity in pacification and transformation (78). Accordingly, the future can be a danger that emerges from the colonial violence of singularity or the paralyzing tendency of pure multiplicity. This warning emphasizes again the context-dependent nature of a realm that emphasizes localized confrontations to create its moral compass.

This idea also complicates the understanding of bodies, which Rivera views as crisscrossed by the different ways of knowing, being, and enacting that coexist in particular contexts. Here, the body appears grey (i.e., Chi'xi), which is not a pure form of hybridity or a new construction of oneness, unity, singularity, and consistency. Instead, it is a grey made of multiple dots that are pure discourses of whiteness, blackness, etc. (Rivera 2018, 79). In this sense, the body is crossed by the purities of different discourses and their consistencies, creating a complex and inconsistent grey. Rivera thus avoids the possibility of understanding the body as yet another foundational source of unity, from which we can judge and hierarchicalize all other ways of being. Instead, the body becomes another taypi; another multi-layered map of relationships in tension and confrontation. In this manner, Rivera invites us to think about the complexity and inconsistencies of the body, creating a possibility to coexist in the radicality of difference (152). To the contrary, the universalizing tendencies of colonialities violently suppress the tensions of the body, preventing people from simply being.

The complex understanding of temporality thus creates a tendency towards differences and heterogeneity, which unsettles singularities. However, how can Rivera renounce the generalization of a consistent tendency towards a perfect multiplicity or the danger of generalizing deconstruction? Rivera achieves this goal by sustaining the circular temporality that surges from the possibility of momentarily drawing multi-layered maps (i.e., a taypi). She also re-applies the epistemic notion of Khä Pacha to her own approach to avoid universalizing and generalizing any perfect tendency, but I further discuss this cosmological stance in the conclusion. The Ch'ixi approach entails a notion of intersectional equality that emerges from the idea of sharedness to judge and classify different histories in particular contexts of confrontation. This notion might seem to create a linear form of narration, which could be ordered towards a universalized form of "intersectionality," but the Ch'ixi approach has at least two important differences with this kind of linear temporality. First, the Ch'ixi approach depends on moments of confrontation to settle momentary maps of relationships, struggle, and projects. That is, "intersectionality" and multiplicity cannot pre-define the taypi *a priori*. The "real" experience of class, gender, sexuality, ability, ethnicity, race, etc. cannot be determined and universalized because confrontation is the primary focus of the profession of faith. The approach emphasizes these moments and it continuously searches for parallel struggles, previously hidden voices, and hitherto erased projects. This construction of intersectional decoloniality is thus context-dependent and it demands a constant return to the possibility of listening for moments and voices of confrontation; it creates a demand for a circular process of returning to a blank canvas, which can only momentarily stop if continuous and/or shared voices do not confront a taypi from below.

Second, the Ch'ixi realm creates a dynamic definition of agency. In the multi-layered map of tensions and confrontations called taypi, the interpreted convergences of discursive expressions not only create a dynamic form of classification for ways of knowing, but also acquire an active role in the understanding of the boundaries of each "voice" and way of being. Since the characteristics of each relationship of equality and commonality depend on the meanings interpreted in the dynamic realm of the taypi, the definition of who participates in those relationships, who has the characteristics of each commonality, and who knows those forms of equality confronting hierarchies are also empirically dependent upon convergences. Accordingly, Rivera avoids authorizing a single "antenna," reasoning "man," or vanguard "proletariat." The convergence of discursive expressions remains as the source of contextual mapping, which momentarily validates a specific multiplicity of relationships to play against dominant discourses. Context-dependent multiplicities of equalities and commonalities thus emerge as concurrently validated possibilities of decoloniality. Then, the characteristics that are locally validated within each definition of a relationship (i.e., a way of knowing that includes a notion of equality) lead towards the definition of a particular agent that is most closely connected to those characteristics. The equal validation of a particular ontology leads to the epistemological authorization of a localized agent, which is connected to that way of knowing. Unlike universalized discourses, however, these agents are only authorized within the confines of the equality that emerges from the notion of sharedness; they are authorized within the limits that other "others" set against their universalization or colonization. In other words, the approach enables the possibility of understanding a multiplicity of agencies, which emerge from confrontations and multiple equalities. Accordingly, the Ch'ixi realm has to respect the cosmic mandate to learn and to listen (Rivera 2015, 270). This mandate to listen requires a constant return to the here/now, from which the interpreter can create new maps and paths; it demands a circular temporality.

Enacting an intersectional decoloniality in Bolivia: Ethnicity, gender, and ecology

Through these lenses, Rivera examines an Andean context of practices, which confronts particular expressions of colonialism and propose multiple alternatives; she enacts a distinct taypi, teaching us how it might be possible to apply some of the discussions that she has fruitfully synthetized and/or created. In much of her work, Rivera analyzes documents, paintings, letters, oral histories, and narrations in order to study a history of relationships that is based on ethnicity.

At first, Rivera analyzes how the pre-independence colonial era of Bolivia is reconstructed as a system of juridical separations between "indigenous" peoples and "Spaniards." This system was confronted because "indigenous" peoples viewed themselves as equal people who had to have the same kinds of rights and duties (Rivera and Morón 1993, 39, translation by author). In order to unveil this fracture, Rivera uses the letters written by Waman Puma to King Felipe III in 1613–1615. She asserts that Waman Puma reconstructed this colonial system as exploitative because Kings and the nobility were able to eat thanks to the work and the crops of "indigenous" peoples. Moreover, Rivera points out that these hierarchies often acted as the conditions of possibility for violent policies or actions suffered by "indigenous" peoples in the Americas (Rivera 2010c, 37, translation by author). By contrast, Waman Puma's letters turned colonial hierarchies upside down and he constructed Spaniards as inferior "gold-eating" beings (Rivera 2015, 183).

Rivera reconstructs the opposition against the hierarchicalization of "indigenous" peoples from narrations and memories related to experiences of resistance, which confronted colonialism through a search of separation and autonomy. On one side, resistance often included notions of pre-colonial relationships, which were more respectful of ethnic differences (Rivera and Morón 1993, 36). According to these memories, a multiplicity of ethnicities coexisted as equally respected economic and political units called ayllus. These relationships were not completely peaceful or perfect, but they entailed a higher degree of respect for differences than was allowed by the colonialism of the time. On the other side, memories reconstructed experiences of rebellions, which sought to revive pre-conquest relationships. The Inka movement of the 1500s thus appeared as an experience seeking to build an autonomous state. Another reconstructed memory of rebellion was related to the wars of the 1780s (41). The Tupaq Amaru and Tupaj Katari movements were thus viewed as reconstructed memories of resistance against forms of discrimination and segregation.

Despite these experiences of opposition and resistance, other reconstructions show the continuation of these ethnic and racial hierarchicalizations under different forms of colonial systems. The emergence of the independent Republic of Bolivia in 1825 is thus another form of segregation against "indigenous" peoples. Throughout this period, a limited form of liberalism was introduced as the official delineation of citizenship, which pretended to include the basic equality of all "human beings" (Rivera and Morón 1993, 34). Despite this idea of "universal" equality, the Bolivian Republic of the 1800s delineated an exclusionary notion of citizenship, which still negated the "humanity" of "indigenous" peoples. For example, Rivera uses the ethnographic paintings by Melchor María Mercado to analyze how he reconstructed the hierarchical system that he witnessed throughout his travels in Bolivia. Some memories also unveiled how, in the 1870s, the government of Bolivia legally forbid the ayllu. As a result, many communities lost their lands and means of survival (Rivera 2010c, 142). In the 1800s, the movement headed by Santos Marka Tula, Feliciano Inka Marasa, Faustino Llanki, Mateo Alfaro, and many others sought to use older laws in order to protect or regain access to lands (208). This movement, which later became known as the Alcaldes Mayores Particulares, aimed to create a notion of citizenship that could equally protect all individuals while also granting autonomy and self-government to "indigenous" communities.

After the Chaco War ended in 1935, Bolivia saw the re-consolidation of an oligarchic sector of society, but it also saw the emergence of unions and syndicates (Rivera 2015, 100). The memories gathered by Rivera showed how both of these forms of organization still included the same confrontation expressed by other memories of previous times. On one side, the oligarchic government still sought to continue a form of citizenship based on juridical segregation. On the other side, the more "progressive" movement of unionization transformed and co-opted "indigenous" forms of struggles under a different hierarchy. Rivera analyzes how indigenous notions confronted these hierarchies, for example, from memories about the path of the Warisata schools (101). These schools were either closed down by the Government or assimilated into more "progressive" forms of policies, which still marginalized indigenous notions of ayllu pedagogy (101). These "progressive" notions actually played along with governmental policies. Together, they sought to transform the "Indio" into a "clean agricultural worker" (102). These policies diagnosed "indigenous" practices as "unhealthy" or "anti-hygienic," seeking to transform ways of life and constructing everything "indigenous" as inferior or as "uncivilized" (103). Companies from the United States sold packages of soap, detergent, and "hygiene;" the United States government offered scholarships for Bolivian doctors, and the Bureau of the American Indian created a school curriculum based on the promotion of the "American way of life" (104).

Many of these unions became the platform of the 1952 Nationalist Revolution, which transformed the governmental notion of citizenship and sought to include "indigenous" peoples in a different manner. Here, the confrontation of hierarchies was experienced in relation to the governmental formation of a universalized idea of class, which created a notion of citizenship based on industrialized production, capitalist consumption, and "modernity" (Rivera 2015, 105). This idea of citizenship was embedded into the notion of "mestizaje," which sought to universalize a single Bolivian identity. Within this notion of citizenship, "indigenous" peoples were viewed as "peasants," who had to follow a process of modernization of agricultural practices. Much of this process was included in the reform of the education system, which took place in 1955. This reform imposed Spanish as the official language of Bolivia and sought to expand the reach of previous policies of "hygiene" (105). The construction of "indigenous" peoples as "non-modern" or "backwards" was also related to the land reform promoted by the government and its continuous negation of communitarian forms of ownership (Rivera 2010c, 173).

Rivera analyzes the confrontation of these hierarchicalizations from memories of histories that the Revolution sought to erase. According to the author, the 1952 Revolution created a reading of Bolivian history that sought to homogenize relationships, erasing the "indigenous" confrontations and struggles discussed above (Rivera 2015, 127). The Commission of History of Bolivian People, which was created by decree in 1954, thus sought to invalidate the oligarchic reading of history (107). Instead of a history of civilization based on conservative segregation, the Revolution reconstructed a history based on the idea of a series of class conflicts, which slowly and progressively led towards the formation of a more encompassing notion of universalized citizenship (107). Within this plot, the Revolution constructed "indigenous" peoples as a homogenous and oppressed class, which was liberated by the governmental decrees of mine nationalization and land reform (Rivera 2015, 110). The government of the Revolution and the leadership of Víctor Paz Estenssoro thus appeared to be the agents responsible for the liberation of Bolivian society from the chains of the old oligarchy (124). All other struggles for cultural, religious, and political forms of autonomy were thus erased. Rivera called this discursive erasure of other struggles and agencies miserabilism (151).

Despite the Revolutionary promotion of a universalized annexation or articulation of "indigenous" struggles through Marxist ideas, the memories collected by Rivera showed an opposition and confrontation against this hierarchicalization. In addition to other sources of memories related to experiences of the Revolution, Rivera analyzes the Indianista and Katarista reconstructions of confrontations. Rivera thus describes Indianismo and Reinaga's intellectual production in order to show how they emphasized the racial and ethnic hierarchy experienced by "indigenous" peoples through colonial and Bolivian history (Rivera and Morón 1993, 49). Notwithstanding Indianista struggles and confrontations against these continuing hierarchies, the fall of the Revolution in 1964 led to the rise of dictatorships, which eventually consolidated neoliberalism in Bolivia. According to Rivera, the dictatorships and the emergence of neoliberalism were experienced by conservative sectors of Bolivia as a reaction against the political mobilization that had emerged during the Revolution (90). This rise of neoliberalism entailed the re-imposition of notions of citizenship that were similar to the previous and more oligarchic ideas of the nineteenth century (90).

Neoliberalism was thus experienced by "indigenous" voices as yet another form of domestication and civilization now based on rules of consumption, which promoted European ways of life and aesthetics. They also imposed a European notion of labor, which devalued agricultural and non-urban forms of work (Rivera and Morón 1993, 93). Education continued to impose a single and officially recognized language (92). Moreover, whenever social or "indigenous" movements sought to resist these hierarchies, institutionalized ideas of "democracy" often led to repressive policies against political mobilization (95). Neoliberalism was also reconstructed as an experience of hierarchicalization because it did not recognize the ayllu as a communitarian form of political organization (Rivera 2015, 174). Within this context, Rivera discusses more contemporary reconstructions of confrontations. For example, she analyzes the symbolic production that continued through festivals and ancestral rituals, which were strongly revived within the water and gas wars of 2000 and 2003 respectively (171).

These voices and memories thus reconstructed diachronically organized experiences of confrontation against a particular kind of hierarchy and coloniality in Bolivia. They fractured the ways in which other discursive reconstructions of relationships pretended to grant universal equality while also ignoring confrontations (Rivera 2015, 143). These experiences revealed the long-lasting contradictions between colonial elites and "indigenous" and subaltern masses in Bolivia (145). Here, citizenship appears to be a continuous form of colonialism, which organizes each categorization of "non-citizens" as "others" who remain legally excluded or have to negate themselves in order to become equals within the boundaries of an official relationship (Rivera 2010c, 173). Pre-independence colonialism, oligarchic liberalism, nationalist Marxism, and neoliberalism thus created notions of equality bounded by ideas of citizenship, which reproduced colonial orders and hierarchies. These oppressive forms of colonialism undid the possibility of coexistence with "others" (Rivera and Morón 1993, 44, translation by author).

Throughout her historical account of ethnic confrontations in Bolivia, Rivera validates the ethnographic memories, voices, documents, paintings, films, and documentaries that continuously unveil these hierarchies and exogenously confront colonial boundaries of segregation, homogenization, coercion, and oppression. She validates a way of knowing and a set of voices that reconstruct a different relationship of equality. Despite this validation of "indigenous" memories and voices, she also avoids the universalization of their reconstructions of equality. In other words, Rivera validates the confrontation that emerges from a way of knowing, being, and enacting, but she also avoids viewing them as superior notions that can solve all other struggles, voices, and projects; she does not marginalize other "others."

> The plural meanings of history are re-created through the counterpoints between voices of men and women, workers and peasants, employees and manual workers, which, far from integrating themselves into a linear vision of history, stay as loose threads of an unfinished fabric, which will be weaved by the spectator.
>
> Rivera 2015, 78

Gendered confrontations

Thanks to the intersectional possibility of de-universalizing the masculine experience of an ethnic axis of power, Rivera is able to study other relationships simultaneously. Her focus on the convergences of expressions of confrontation and fracture between reconstructions of relationships thus leads to the analysis of another set of hierarchicalizations, also hidden beneath ideas of universalized equality. This focus enables Rivera to reconstruct a parallel history by following the diachronically organized gender-based confrontations that are traced throughout memories, documents, paintings, etc. According to Rivera, colonialism undid whatever form of previous respect might have existed for "women" and it introduced a widespread form of violation, rape, and violence (Rivera 2010c, 191).

These gender-based hierarchies were analyzed as confrontations found in a variety of sources, which showed a set of memories contradicting and thus deconstructing another coloniality. For example, Rivera asserts that the ayllu entailed a gender relationship that respected differences and also granted certain levels of equality between "women" and "men" (Rivera 2010c, 182). This relationship of "complementarity" between "women" and "men" allowed for the former to co-govern and to control the very boundaries of the community (183). From their own difference, "women" controlled the conditions of political power and inter-ethnic relations. As Rivera asserts, this relationship did not entail a perfect form of "egalitarianism;" instead, it sought to respect differences and grant equality at the same time. Here, "women" often formed intra-communitarian alliances, which controlled the realm of endogamy and the boundaries of the ayllu. This form of control balanced their power with "men" and enabled "women" to participate in the politics of the Inka state (185). "Women" thus had their own voice in politics, actively participated in the productive and economic structure of the state, organized domestic cycles, were the main weavers, and were often in charge of rituals (206). This religious role was important because it enabled "women" to have a key function in the symbolic production of the Inka state. (Rivera 2010c, 188). The Moon and the Sun ("feminine" and "masculine," respectively) thus represented two parallel lines of descendancy, creating humanity in a balance of power (188).

According to Rivera's empirical work, these notions were hidden under the patriarchal hierarchies that were diachronically attached to oligarchic, liberal, and Marxist discourses of colonial order. For example, Rivera analyzes how gender-related memories reconstructed oppositions against the Marxist discourse of "equality," which was institutionalized in 1952. In these confrontations, Rivera finds that, beneath the universalized notion of class-based equality promoted by the Nationalist Revolution, there was a hierarchicalization and erasure of "women." Throughout the Revolution, "women" appeared as "widows" of martyrs and soldiers or they were completely deleted from history (Rivera 2015, 158). The reorganization of history designed by the Revolution put class as the main system of oppressions, which became resolved by the government of Estenssoro. The role of "women" in these contradictions, and in the final resolution of history, was viewed as "companions," "widows," "sisters," or "wives" (162). As such, "women" were regarded as inactive, weak, and idle "victims" of previous systems of economic exploitation (42). Despite the official erasure of their agency, some of the memories taken into account by Rivera unveiled hidden confrontations, which remembered the anarchist feminist movements of the 1930s in Bolivia (Rivera 2015, 149). Additionally, Rivera shows how groups of "women" resisted beneath the discourse of the Revolution in festivals and markets, as well as in popular forms of organization and ancestral rituals (170).

Similar to the analysis of the patriarchal biases found in the class-based relationship that was promoted within the Revolution, Rivera examines Bolivian liberalisms. According to the author, the oligarchic and earlier forms of liberalism created notions of citizenship that were rhetorically universal, but only granted rights to male, mestizo, and Christian individuals. These "human rights" were thus not granted to "women," who could not own property and were only protected against domestic violence if the period of hospitalization lasted more than 30 days (Rivera 2010c, 204). The re-emergence of these notions of citizenship within the neoliberalism that began to surge in the 1960s transformed some of these legal forms of segregations, but it also continued these hierarchies. "Women" were still regarded as less "human" and thus erased from the realm of policies. In the national census of Bolivia, for example, the number of "women" was systematically underestimated, which created a mentality of "minority" and also decreased "women's" relevance in relation to the design of policies (212). Moreover, the "masculine" construction of "indigeneity" in Bolivia excluded "indigenous" "women" from this political dimension. The reform of the education system then proceeded to ignore their gendered experience and the demands that could have emerged from their positionality (214). These memories and voices thus showed a logic of hierarchicalization parallel to that of masculine ethnicity. The domestic exploitation of women in the household, which often included an extended amount of unpaid work, also showed the gender-based hierarchy even within similar ethnic categories. This form of hierarchy was often based on ideas of "natural" divisions of labor, but these memories and voices showed the confrontation lying beneath "natural" hierarchies (216).

These gender-based confrontations thus lead Rivera to analyze at least two separate struggles, but this fracture does not translate into the complete invalidation or deconstruction of other experiences of confrontation. Instead, Rivera emphasizes how multiple forms of struggles for different kinds of equality remain hidden beneath universalized discourses of Western and masculine equality. Her work thus separates confrontations and possibilities of equality hidden and articulated beneath the universalized forms of relationships that are imposed by the coloniality of some discourses. As a result, Rivera shows that even a universalized idea of ethnic equality can invalidate the reconstruction of other "others." The author considers gender confrontations as equally important because they can otherwise become ignored underneath male-based experiences of ethnic relationships (Rivera 2010c, 218). The encounter between Indianismo and feminism thus leads to the inclusion of a much more complex study of colonial hierarchies and the confrontations hidden underneath them (179).

Ecological confrontations

Notwithstanding the already complex map of parallel struggles and relationships charted by Rivera's analysis of convergences between memories, voices, and other sources, the examination of confrontations also leads the author to investigate the anthropocentric hierarchies between "nature" and "humanity" that are created by colonial discourses. To achieve this goal, Rivera discusses how a number of paintings, letters, and narrations confronted the colonial hierarchy established in the 1500s with "nature." These memories recalled Waman Puma portraying conquistadores as "others," who "ate gold" and whose insatiable appetite for material wealth was beyond "humanity" (Rivera 2015, 262). Similarly, Melchor María Mercado critiqued the hierarchies that emerged in post-independence Bolivia through paintings portraying notions of progress. In these paintings, Mercado described the dominant position of Christian men, who appeared above "Indios," "women," and "nature" (85).

Rivera also unveils this type of anthropocentric hierarchy through other memories and voices. Documents and voices related to the beginning of the neoliberal era in the 1960s, for example, showed the promotion of "development" based on the over-exploitation of raw material (Rivera 2015, 212). These notions were promoted by the World Bank and the United States Agency for International Development, which encouraged Bolivia to "modernize" through the usage of fertilizers in agriculture, liberalization of the financial market, development of the mining industry, construction of roads, etc. According to Rivera, notions of "progress" and "modernization" continued even after Juan Evo Morales Ayma became the president of Bolivia between 2006 and 2019 (219).

Thanks to the memories that Rivera analyzes in documents and different types of sources, these hierarchies of dominance over "nature" become confronted and fractured. For example, the author discusses how indigenous notions of ecological equality entailed a different definition of labor, which reconstructed the idea of exploitation as an unjust hierarchy not only among "humans," but also between "humanity" and "nature" (Rivera 2015, 180). The notion of a more balanced relationship with "nature" was attached to strategies of resistance against current policies of "development" (235). Rivera analyzes how "indigenous" peoples classified some of Morales' policies as violations of the rights of Pachamama and as the expansion of "human" dominance. Mining, road construction, deforestation, contamination, and the expansion of coca plantations were all understood to be the consequences of hierarchies related to industrialization, progress, and development (Rivera 2018, 170).

According to Rivera, this kind of ecological confrontation against anthropocentrism and exploitation can also be found in the letter of Waman Puma in the 1610s. Puma showed how the pre-colonial "Indio" of the mountains learned, from the Amazonian "Indio," to listen to "nature" (Rivera 2015, 270). This inter-ethnic relationship between communities not only illustrated the Inka's capacity to learn from other peoples, but it also showed their concern to establish more balanced relationships with "nature." The "Indio" of the Amazon tried to become the jaguar; they tried to view "nature" and "humanity" from the perspective of the animal world. This aim to reach an ecological perspective was not only regarded as a "cosmic mandate" to listen to "nature," but it was also a more general command to listen to all others in order to learn different relationships of equality and coexistence (270). "A mandate truncated by the colonial conquest and abandoned by many of the descendants of its creators, but no less valid because of that" (271). This "cosmic mandate" to listen to "others" and learn about new possibilities of equality thus included inter-human experiences and it also expanded to include "nature." (Rivera 2015, 178).

Conclusion

The decolonial praxis that Rivera's approach constructs requires constant attention for previously ignored confrontations, which emerge from the agency of silenced or violently hidden ways of knowing, being, and enacting. This demands continuously returning to a blank canvas and taypi in order to show momentary maps of overlapped struggles, voices, and projects that simultaneously decolonize the universalities of dominant discourses. Despite her focus on particular experiences of ethnicity, gender, and ecology, Rivera enables an approach and praxis that searches for other "others." The author momentarily settles her map of tensions and struggles, while also being aware of potential marginalizations that require a more open dialogue and a bottom-up mandate to listen. Accordingly, the way of enactment that emerges from the sociology of images is dynamic, circular, democratic, and reflexive, allowing us to think about decolonial praxis in different contexts. That is, the possibility of specification that emerges from Rivera's profession of faith does not close yet another epistemic circle of self-validation, self-authorization, and self-enactment, which could lead to the generalization of a particular struggle, voice, and project. Instead, the sociology of images sustains the dynamic movement that surges from the precarious validation of confrontations, weaving together multiple histories while considering other narratives.

This circular temporality and dynamic praxis has important implications. First, Rivera constructs an epistemically precarious boundary that undoes "otherness" more in general than the other loci of enunciation interpreted in previous chapters. The epistemic elevation of confrontations comes at the cost of de-universalization, which requires the limitation of the relationships that have overextended their reach to hierarchicalize "others," interiorizing externality or annihilating it. Once ways of knowing, being, and enacting abandon their privileged, dominating, and universalizing tendencies at the moments of confrontation and fracture, however, they become equal parcels whose capitalized letters have been erased. The "other" of the Ch'ixi realm (i. e., colonial ways of knowing, being, and enacting) thus becomes accepted as long as it renounces its dominating and universalizing privilege (Rivera 2018, 134). In this way, the Ch'ixi decolonial praxis deconstructs the binaries and colonial disjunctions that prevents us from being ourselves, whatever that may be (31). As Rivera asserts, we can find in the cacophony of contradictions and tensions a subjective intensity that renounces the ego, allowing us to encounter our own ignorance (134).

Second, Rivera moves beyond the romanticization of a particular "other," which would otherwise be able to impose his own way of knowing, being, and enacting upon everything else (Rivera 2018, 81)

Third, the approach avoids some of the issues that emerge when an anti-colonial discourse requires perfect epistemic foundations to legitimize political action. Since the approach epistemically elevates each way of knowing, being, and enacting at their moment of confrontation against universalisms and domination, it does not require them to represent, be, and enact a perfect kind of ontological "reality." That is, the ways of knowing, being, and enacting that are epistemically re-valued do not need to claim correspondence with a "pure" pre-colonial past, "ancestral" identity, "real" human nature, or "objective" structure. Instead, the profession of faith in the sharedness of convergences epistemically re-values the multiple "impurities" that confront universalisms and domination. Hence, the sociology of images validates, authorizes, and legitimizes those who are often caught in between; it listens to "hybrid" or "impure" differences, without the need to recuperate, for example, the "real" form of "indigeneity" (Rivera 2018, 124). Rivera illustrates this possibility throughout her analysis of the case of "Cholo" identities in Bolivia, which are often regarded as neither "Indio" nor "modern" (144). Instead, the "Cholo" represents yet another alterity that calls for the decolonization of mestizaje. Here, Rivera utilizes the decolonizing potential of an identity while also avoiding the essentialization, folklorization, and ornamentalization of Bolivian identities (147).

Fourth, Rivera renounces homogenizing definitions of "equality;" instead, she highlights an "equivalence" among differences (Rivera 2018, 148). This entails a contentious realm of tensions and fractures, which validates the differences negated by colonialism, freeing the possibility of creating a much more egalitarian dialogue among diverse ways of knowing (Rivera 2010a, 71). This understanding of equivalence among differences separates Rivera's work from the plurinational project of Morales and Álvaro García Linera because she avoids the articulating and assimilating tendency that emerges when one assumes to have access to the "real" identities that encompass everything in a particular territory.

Fifth, Rivera provides a mechanism to define what needs to be deconstructed and what can be momentarily respected. Unlike the tendency found in the work of some post-structuralist authors, Rivera achieves this goal by elevating shared and/or continuous confrontations, which emerge from the ways of knowing, being, and enacting that denounce a wound of colonialism and create a different loci of agency. In this sense, the author explicitly and unapologetically constructs a commitment to the causes of multiple "others." Since she deploys a fact of colonialism through her profession of faith, Rivera does not understand all universalizing discourses as equally oppressive; she highlights the wounds of colonialism to listen to their confrontation first. Here, Rivera momentarily elevates diverse subalterns through a reflexive and precarious epistemic strategy. Since she elevates these voices and their moments of confrontation, she stops the tendency towards the generalization of deconstruction, enabling a possibility of walking in a particular here/now; she allows for multiple worlds to coexist in a dynamic taypi. Hence, her approach first prioritizes the confrontation of dominant discourses by allowing for the subaltern to speak. Then, the universalizing tendency of particular subaltern projects becomes confronted by other "others," but this does not lead to the complete deconstruction that emerges from understanding everything as equally dominant. The approach also avoids philosophically generalizing deconstruction towards the endless promotion of a multiplicity that fragments everything and paralyzes action in the totalization of fear against othering. Instead, she deconstructs the universalizing tendency of a struggle, voice, and project when shared and/or continuous confrontations emerge, localizing a map or taypi within the limits that context-dependent confrontations set. Rivera stops deconstruction by listening to the convergences and continuities of meanings that confront over-expanded discourses in a particular context.

Thinking in a philosophically logical manner, the idea of confrontations could lead to a possibility of undoing labels altogether. Since it unveils the possibility of confronting whatever imposition demands the price of identity and undermines difference, the sociology of images could demand the logical deconstruction of all boundaries. In this sense, Lucy Taylor states that decoloniality should not lead to the parceling of bodies into ever smaller categories (Taylor 2012, 395). Instead, decoloniality should lead to the possibility of "being" without these limiting labels. As María José Méndez points out, however, the utilization of intersectionality and identities is a necessary, yet limited, step towards resisting domination, fracturing universalisms, and enabling difference (Méndez 2018, 17). According to the author, intersections are places of resistance and solidarity (16). They are moments of suffering and agency, denouncement and action, struggle and equality. In order to avoid the tendency towards homogenizing all discourses, which could generalize domination and demand endless deconstruction, the sociology of images thus needs to set a way to *use* labels against the civilizing projects that seek to erase them. Hence, the approach plays with labels and momentary boundaries to deploy the agentic possibility of solidarity that emerges from them. This is how Rivera puts a stop to the tendency to universalize a particular logic and philosophy, allowing for politics to listen to specific ways of knowing, being, and enacting against universalized and dominant discourses. Similar to Judith Butler, then, Rivera plays with power while also being aware of its risks.

> The mobilization of identity categories for the purposes of politicization always remain threatened by the prospect of identity becoming an instrument of the power one opposes. That is no reason not to use, and be used, by identity. There is no political position purified of power, and perhaps that impurity is what produces agency as the potential interruption and reversal of regulatory regimes.
>
> Butler 1990, xxviii

Sixth, Rivera's work explicitly includes ecological ways of knowing, being, and enacting. This confrontation of anthropocentric universalizations includes particularly interesting ramifications. At the most obvious and urgent level of analysis, the acknowledgement of nature as an equal alterity in the Cosmos leads to a possibility of re-connecting with "Pacha" and healing the planet (Rivera 2018, 150). In this sense, Rivera asserts that we should re-think markets to avoid accumulation while also allowing for exchange (45). Here, we could create a public sphere of exchange based on diversity, articulating networks of ecologies and signification. This is often the case in Andean cosmologies that regard exchange as a sacred relationship with deities and the Cosmos (49). This spiritual connection establishes a form of reciprocity and solidarity, where people live in a more balanced tension with other entities. That is, the relationship between different beings of the Cosmos does not entail a perfect "harmony" that is intelligible and thus definable by a particular knower. Instead, exchange entails a respectful tension that acknowledges its equivalence and solidarity. On the other side, the possibility of engaging with these moments of confrontation also emphasizes the importance of respecting difference even when they include radical incommensurabilities. As Méndez states, listening to indigenous cosmologies and the ways in which some of them construct ideas of equality with nature might be quite difficult, if not impossible, within ontologies that depart from ideas of individual reason (Méndez 2018, 18). In this sense, moments of confrontation might include epistemic levels of differences that are unintelligible to others, but still demand "equivalence" and de-universalization; they might entail an "ethics of incommensurability" (18).

Overall, then, the Ch'ixi project of the sociology of images aims to avoid the homogenizing and marginalizing tendencies of universalized discourses by enabling a dynamic, circular, and diversifying praxis; it seeks a possibility of promoting "rights of difference and of nature" (Rivera 2018, 18); a possibility of coexistence in the respect of differences (Rivera 2010a, 71). Hence, the praxical and unveiling power of this approach goes beyond the context of Bolivia not by universalizing a single and linear project of homogenization, but by enabling a way of thinking, being, and enacting the context-dependent heterogeneity of particular localities, which can only emerge from the wounds of colonialism of each loci of enunciation. In other words, the sociology of images teaches us to listen for confrontations that undo context-dependent manifestations of privilege and domination. Moreover, this project is not yet another form of liberalism. To the contrary, Rivera rejects homogenizing ideas of reason, anthropocentric individualism, citizenship, and development; she creates a praxis of heterogenization, which also requires redistributions, reparations, and other forms of equality that surge from the confrontations of universalisms, privilege, and hierarchies. This is a possibility of understanding difference, while also demanding the decolonization of the "structures" that have shaped our coexistence historically (Rivera 1990, 117).

To achieve this goal, the Ch'ixi approach does not talk about the "globe" or "globalization;" rather, it encourages us to think, be, and enact "planetarity" (Rivera 2018, 57). Due to the importance of relationships with "nature" and the capitalist destruction of the more-than-human, Rivera aims to think about the "planet," but she achieves this goal with bottom-up heterogeneity and difference in mind. She challenges the idea of "oneness" while also remembering that this is a single, irreplaceable, and finite planet (57). Hence, the author constructs the taypi as a zone of contact, where irreducible differences dialogue in a relationship of epistemic equivalence, contradicting each other and limiting the colonial tendencies of universalization that emerge when they internalize exteriority. Here, multiplicity, heterogeneity, difference, and diversity do not mean relativism; rather, they entail de-universalization, equalities, and confrontations. Furthermore, a "Ch'ixi world" would entail irreducible differences enacting each other into a broader patchwork of polysemy. This kind of space would not even allow for settled or fixed maps of heterogeneity because it would have to sustain the mandate to listen for new confrontations and tensions, which keeps the egalitarian friction against oneness alive (Rivera 2018, 84). In this sense, "planetarity" depends on the micro-politics of confrontations, which create "communities of difference" and acknowledge the possibility of multiple "self-poiesis" (84).

Here, the possibility of relationality becomes a basis from which we can construct multiple communities of equality, struggle, agency, identity, temporality, and projection. That is, each moment of confrontation becomes a moment of creation, from which a solidarity emerges in parallel to other forms of relationships and solidarity. Accordingly, Rivera understands relationalities within the idea of a multi-layered and juxtaposed set of communities that emerge from experiences of struggle and equality; they are moments that create binding effects of action and solidarity such as the struggle against the privatization of water in El Alto, Bolivia (Rivera 2018, 140). As the author points out, community is not hereby understood within the Western notion of nation and territory. This idea would re-solidify a singular way of knowing, being, and enacting within a bounded and territorial foundation. Instead, Rivera understands communities of difference as overlapping each other, crossing different boundaries, and trespassing all kinds of disciplining borders. Here, relationality becomes a cosmology that moves beyond foundationalist essentialization and objectification. In this sense, Rivera aims to avoid using "community" as another "magical word" that limits yet again the possibility of struggle, agency, and projection (114). This deterritorialization of relationships is highlighted by the increasing role of the virtual space that the Internet has created for communities of difference and loci of enunciation (120). Hence, this understanding of relationality allows us to establish agentic links of ally-ship beyond our geographic contexts of practice and action, enjoying other victories and accompanying other struggles (155).

Despite the logic of the decolonial praxis that emerges from the elevation of this way of knowing, being, and enacting, Rivera reminds us that her approach rises from the profession of faith in the fact of colonialism. That is, the abysmal threat of Khä Pacha still lurks under the certainty of praxis, denouncing the epistemic arrogance of assuming any possibility of accessing "reality" itself. In this sense, the entire edifice remains under the scrutiny of a reflexive cosmology, which constantly evaluates the normative implications of each profession of faith, subjecting all epistemic perspectives to constant dialogues and conversations. Here, Rivera avoids the unquestionable elevation of a particular epistemic edifice above everything else. Instead, the author sustains the tension that emerges when we try to seek equality without the price of identity, and difference without inaction or indifference. In this sense, Rivera's approach of decoloniality entails a circular temporality not only in its constant return to the map of confrontations, but also in all of its epistemic dimensions, which only settle a way of knowing, being, and enacting precariously and through a profession of faith. Thus, the Cosmos stays as a tension that cannot be universally settled, while ontology, epistemology, and temporality become momentarily and precariously fixed in a bounded way of knowing, being, and enacting. Rivera creates a "condition" for a Ch'ixi understanding and a moral compass, but she also questions the generalization of any single logic because she acknowledges epistemic equivalence (Rivera 2018, 80).

References

Ashley, Richard, and R. B. J. Walker. 1990. "Speaking the Language of Exile: Dissent Thought in International Studies." *International Studies Quarterly* 34 (3): 259–268.

Butler, Judith. 1990. *Gender Trouble: Feminism and the Subversion of Identity*. New York: Routledge.

Cho, Sumi, Kimberlé W. Crenshaw, and Leslie McCall. 2013. "Toward a Field of Intersectionality Studies, Applications, and Praxis." *Signs* 38 (4): 785–810.

Collins, Patricia Hill. 2015. "Intersectionality's Definitional Dilemmas." *Annual Review of Sociology* 41 (1): 1–20.

Collins, Patricia Hill, and Sirma Bilge. 2016. *Intersectionality*. Cambridge: Polity Press.

Crenshaw, Kimberlé W. 1991. "Mapping the Margins: Intersectionality, Identity Politics, and Violence Against Women of Color." *Stanford Law Review* 43 (6): 1241–1299.

Doty, Roxanne Lynn. 1997. "Aporia: A Critical Exploration of the Agent-Structure Problematique in International Relations Theory." *European Journal of International Relations* 3 (3): 365–392.

Edkins, Jenny, and Maja Zehfuss. 2014. *Global Politics: A New Introduction*. New York: Routledge.

Estermann, Josef. 2006. *Filosofía Andina: Sabiduría Indígena Para Un Mundo Nuevo*. 2nd ed. La Paz: Instituto Superior Ecuménico Andino de Teología.

George, Jim, and David Campbell. 1990. "Patterns of Dissent and the Celebration of Difference: Critical Social Theory and International Relations." *International Studies Quarterly* 34 (3): 269–293.

Inayatullah, Naeem, and David L. Blaney. 2004. *International Relations and the Problem of Difference*. New York: Routledge.

Méndez, María José. 2018. "'The River Told Me': Rethinking Intersectionality from the World of Berta Cáceres." *Capitalism Nature Socialism* 29 (1): 7–24.

Mignolo, Walter. 2000. *Local Histories/Global Designs: Coloniality, Subaltern Knowledges, and Border Thinking*. Princeton Studies in Culture/Power/History. Princeton, NJ: Princeton University Press.

Mignolo, Walter. 2011. "Epistemic Disobedience and the Decolonial Option: A Manifesto." *Transmodernity* 1 (2): 159–181.

Mignolo, Walter, and Catherine E. Walsh. 2018. *On Decoloniality: Concepts, Analytics, and Praxis*. Durham, NC: Duke University Press.

Reinaga, Fausto. 2014. *Fausto Reinaga: Obras Completas*. 10 vols. La Paz: Vicepresidencia del Estado Plurinacional.

Rivera Cusicanqui, Silvia. 1990. "Liberal Democracy and Ayllu Democracy in Bolivia: The Case of Northern Potosí." *The Journal of Development Studies* 26 (4): 97–121.

Rivera Cusicanqui, Silvia. 1999. "Sendas y Senderos de La Ciencia Social Andina." *Dispositio, Crítica Cultural En Latinoamérica: Paradigmas Globales y Enunciaciones Locales* 24 (51): 149–169.

Rivera Cusicanqui, Silvia. 2004. "La Noción de 'Derecho' o Las Paradojas de La Modernidad Postcolonial: Indígenas y Mujeres En Bolivia." *Aportes Andinos, Aportes Sobre La Diversidad, Diferencia e Identidad* 11: 1–15.

Rivera Cusicanqui, Silvia. 2010a. *Ch'ixinakax utxiwa: Una Reflexión sobre Prácticas y Discursos Decolonizadores*. Buenos Aires: Tinta Limón.

Rivera Cusicanqui, Silvia. 2010b. *Oprimidos Pero No Vencidos. Luchas Del Campesinado Aymara y Quechua, 1900–1980*. La Paz: La Mirada Salvaje.

Rivera Cusicanqui, Silvia. 2010c. *Violencias (Re) Encubiertas En Bolivia*. La Paz: La Mirada Salvaje.

Rivera Cusicanqui, Silvia. 2015. *Sociología de la Imagen. Miradas Ch'ixi Desde La Historia Andina*. Buenos Aires: Tinta Limón.

Rivera Cusicanqui, Silvia. 2018. *El Mundo Ch'ixi Es Posible: Ensayos Desde Un Presente En Crisis*. Buenos Aires: Tinta Limón.

Rivera Cusicanqui, Silvia, and Raúl Barrios Morón. 1993. *Violencias Encubiertas En Bolivia: Cultura y Política*. La Paz: Talleres Gráficos Hisbol.

Said, Edward W. 1978. *Orientalism*. New York: Vintage Books.

Shapiro, Michael J. 2004. *Methods and Nations. Cultural Governance and the Indigenous Subject*. New York: Routledge.

Taylor, Lucy. 2012. "Decolonizing International Relations: Perspectives from Latin America." *International Studies Review* 14 (3): 386–400.

Todorov, Tzvetan. 1982. *The Conquest of America: The Question of the Other*. Norman: University of Oklahoma Press.

Viaña, Jorge, Luis Claros, and Marcelo Sarzuri-Lima. 2010. "La Condición Colonial y Los Laberintos de La Descolonización." *Revista Integra Educativa* 3 (1): 13–36.

Weber, Cynthia. 2016. *Queer International Relations: Sovereignty, Sexuality and the Will to Knowledge*. Oxford: Oxford University Press.

7 The problem of difference and IR

Throughout previous chapters, I highlight how various ways of knowing, being, and enacting confront each other's boundaries, continuously re-posing a problem of difference: How is it possible to define "colonialism" and to create a decolonial praxis while also encompassing difference even at the level of epistemic politics? The importance of exploring this question lies in the possibility of knowing, being, and enacting multiple struggles, voices, and projects simultaneously. Additionally, this query carries us towards a decolonial examination of what needs to change and how much: What transformation does this kind of decoloniality demand in order to create possibilities of co-being, co-knowing, and co-enacting? Finally, the discussion aims to enable possibilities of praxis while also avoiding the othering tendencies of universalized bedrocks that draw single temporal goals of civilization and linear histories of homogenization.

As several authors have pointed out, the problem of difference has created important questions for International Relations (Ashley 1981; George and Campbell 1990; Milliken 1999; A. Tickner 2003; Inayatullah and Blaney 2004; Tickner and Blaney 2013; Blaney and Tickner 2017; Trownsell et al. 2019). In this chapter, I engage this discussion more explicitly, highlighting the contributions that emerge for the discipline from this genealogical discussion of the problem of difference and from my interpretation of Silvia Rivera Cusicanqui's work.

According to a number of authors, International Relations entered an "existential crisis" in the 1980s, and the field has not been able to close its methodological, theoretical, and political fractures since (Lapid 1989; Milliken 1999; Lynch 2014; Yanow and Schwartz-Shea 2014; Gofas, Hamati-Ataya, and Onuf 2018). Throughout much of this debate, epistemic politics unfolded towards the possibility of undermining positivist hegemony, questioning the existing boundaries of the discipline and diversifying the field (Yanow and Schwartz-Shea 2014; Kurki and Wight 2013). This philosophy of science uses an assumption of truth correspondence to validate and prove particular ways of knowing, authorize specific knowers, and legitimize certain approaches. Positivism elevates theories, intellectuals, and projects that claim to access an external and thus objective reality "out there" (Yanow and Schwartz-Shea 2014, 27).

The notion of truth correspondence entails at least three analytically separable dimensions. First, truth correspondence often connects *ontological* foundations of "reality" to "human" characteristics and commonalities. This aspect of correspondence entails the foundational consistency of a discourse. In this sense, Sylvia Wynter states that discourses often create isomorphic connections between "man" and the "human," which make a particular perspective appear more "objective" or "real," allowing us to experience them as truth (Wynter 1995, 29). Second, truth correspondence includes *epistemological and methodological* notions, which construct different kinds of connections between a knower and "reality." In the case of positivism, this bridge is established by regarding a methodologically purged form of language as a more direct representation of the world "out there." Then, whoever is deemed as a possessor of this kind of language becomes an authorized knower. Finally, truth correspondence entails constructions of *temporality*, which deploy ontological foundations as bedrocks that organize specificities of history within hierarchically echeloned narratives. The relationship between these dimensions of truth correspondence often constitute closed circles of intra-discursive self-validation, self-authorization, and self-legitimation. That is, discourses include epistemic conditions of reality, but they also create ways to assimilate historical specificities, "proving" their elevated notions of reality, agency, and temporality.

Despite much positivist resistance (e.g., Keohane 1988; Walt 1991; Mearsheimer 1994; King, Keohane, and Verba 1994; Gerring 2012) and "cartesian anxiety" (Campbell 2013, 229), interpretive discussions of methodology and theory have slowly undermined the disciplinary hegemony of this philosophy of science in International Relations (e.g., Enloe 1980; Ashley 1981; Onuf 1989; George and Campbell 1990; Ashley and Walker 1990; J. A. Tickner 1992; Grovogui 1996; Milliken 1999; Schwartz-Shea and Yanow 2012; Lynch 2014). Most saliently since the 1980s, interpretive intellectuals have chipped away the epistemic altar of positivists theories such as realism, liberalism, and Marxism. They have fruitfully critiqued notions of truth correspondence, carving out spaces in International Relations for and with feminist, post-structuralist, post-modernist, and social constructivist perspectives (Milliken 1999, 225). Others also highlight the important role of post-colonial, neo-Marxist, green, and queer theories (Dalby 2013; Lynch 2014; Weber 2016; Yanow and Schwartz-Shea 2014). Previously marginalized ways of knowing, being, and enacting have thus disputed the dominant boundaries of the discipline. The problem of difference at epistemic levels has questioned the certainties and walls of International Relations in spite of the continuation of colonial legacies (Inayatullah and Blaney 2004). In a sense, then, the "existential crisis" of International Relations is both the cause and the result of the confrontations that continue to emerge from different approaches and methodologies; it is a possibility of pluralization and diversification (Schwartz-Shea and Yanow 2012; Smith 2013).

As a number of authors point out, however, the generalization of difference, together with the renouncement of all epistemic bases, can impede the possibility of assertion and action. For example, Pierre Bourdieu criticizes "postmodernism" as a form of relativism that appears to unfold from Foucault's work.[1] Jürgen Habermas also mentions that the poststructuralism of Derrida and Foucault "... seems to be absorbed in a critique of reason radicalized through Nietzsche" (Habermas 1992, 5). Both authors find a tendency towards the construction of a self-destructing way of knowing in the implications that unfold from undoing foundations and truth correspondence. Wynter also affirms:

> It is only, therefore, because the individual subject is able to forget the fact of his/her being a represented subject, that he/she can "live with some repose, safety and consequence"; since were this individual subject to get out of the prison walls of his/her faith, even for an instant, his/her "self-consciousness would be destroyed at once."
>
> Wynter 1995, 33

Others also critique the epistemic notions that undermine all boundaries because they tend to abandon the struggle of those who are othered by dominant discourses (Estermann 2006; Viaña, Claros, and Sarzuri-Lima 2010; Alcoreza 2014). As I show in Chapter Five, the generalization of the philosophical implications that unfold from deconstructing foundations can also elevate anti-foundationalism above discourses, leading towards a process of deconstruction that categorizes all universalizing discourses as equally "dominant."

Epistemic, methodological, and theoretical discussions of International Relations thus seem to move between the othering effects of boundaries and the abyss of renouncing all bedrocks. The possibility of questioning positivists notions of truth correspondence has led to the diversification of discussions and the emergence of other theories, but the generalization of the logical implications that surge from respecting difference at the level of epistemics creates a threat against the enabling possibility of action in International Relations. This debate between positivisms, interpretivisms, and the potential implications of these methodological discussion has been the main divide in the study of international and global politics since the 1980s (Smith 2013, 5), and it continues to sustain a current struggle for "IR's soul" (Gofas, Hamati-Ataya, and Onuf 2018, 6).

Instead of finding a foundationalist, philosophically settled, logical, complete, and elevated solution to this crisis, I propose a way to sustain this tension between the deleterious effects of boundaries and their enabling side. Instead of constructing yet another self-assured epistemic foundation, I suggest a way to stay in the dilemma that emerges between using a possibility of judgement and the opportunity to abandon strong foundations; between sustaining International Relations and undoing its boundaries. Hence, I follow the teachings of Rivera and Indianismo to discuss the possibility of constructing International Relations as a permanently questioned and dynamic locus of interpretation, discussion, and praxis.

IR boundaries: The benefits of an existential crisis

The advantages of the fractures that have questioned the boundaries of International Relations can be examined by highlighting the othering effects of the approaches that benefited from a more closed, positivist, and bounded discipline. As I analyze in Chapter One, the genealogical focus on Bolivia unveils the effects and tendencies that emerge from the boundaries of liberalism and structuralist understandings of Marxism.[2]

In the case of liberalism, the construction of ontological realities and epistemic foundations changes throughout the history of Bolivia and international politics. Similar to John Locke, Simón Bolivar connects his definition of "reason" to a God-given human nature, which can be observed in the "civilized" peoples of the world. Reason thus appears as a representation of the essence and reality of "humanity," which then establishes the form of commonality that acts as a bedrock of equality, justice, and judgment. Then, those who have these characteristics are understood to be the authorized knowers that are epistemologically connected to reality itself. Truth correspondence is thus used to validate a liberal way of knowing and to authorize a liberal way of being. Finally, these epistemic connections legitimize a project, which organizes the past, analyzes the present, and draws the future. Ontology creates the basis of judgement to organize history while epistemology authorizes a particular agent to enact its specificities. This edifice leads to a hierarchically organized narration of epochs and places that are differentiated by their proximity to reality and their consistency with equality. Then, the observation of epistemically pre-selected aspects of history appears to be the proof that re-validates, re-authorizes, and re-legitimizes liberal ways of knowing, being, and enacting. This is how liberalism creates a closed circle of certainty, which endogenously reinforces the boundaries of the discourse.

These boundaries of validation, authorization, and legitimation create the othering tendency of liberalism, which marginalizes whatever is not consistent with the reality, agent, and history of the approach. Hence, liberalism excludes other forms of struggles such as indigenous notions of ethnic equality, silences other voices such as the political participation of those who are not "active citizens," and delegitimizes other notions of history such as Indianista ideas of transformation. These tendencies not only emerge in Lockean notions of human essence, but also in Kantian ideas of "reason" and Habermassian definitions of communicative action. In these constructions, the ontological status of "reality" and its validating effect emerge from different epistemic sources, but the discourses construct othering boundaries that surge from definitions of reason. The idea that "reason" corresponds to human nature, natural law, or the universal presuppositions of communicative action thus creates epistemic boundaries that exclude "others." For example, liberalism utilizes these boundaries to constitute notions of validated law, authorized citizens, and legitimized progress. By deploying this boundary, liberalism protects everything that is epistemically elevated against everything that is epistemically marginalized. Moreover, the observation and study of "others" entails the already classified proof of "reality." That is, whatever empirical observation does not fit the epistemically validated notion of equality, authorized idea of agency, and legitimized drawing of history becomes regarded as specificities of the hierarchically organized echelons of "others." They are the threat against "justice," "citizens," and "progress."

Throughout the history of Bolivia, this othering tendency has created different conditions of possibility for the violent and oppressive marginalization of everything that is regarded as "natural," "indigenous," "deviant," and/or "feminine." These boundaries of marginalization, othering, and violence are also concerning for International Relations due to the continuous saliency of liberal approaches in the discipline. For example, many textbooks of International Relations continue to prioritize liberal lenses above the diversity of approaches that now dispute spaces in the study of international and global politics (e.g., Dougherty and Pfaltzgraff 2001; Lamy et al. 2013; Goldstein and Pevehouse 2013; Mingst and Snyder 2014). The predominant presence of liberalism in peace studies also shows the need to question the epistemic sources of a certainty that often marginalizes and silences "others" in important circles of policy and international law (e.g., Chan 1997; Oneal, Russett, and Berbaum 2003; Paris 2004; Russett 2013).

According to Naeem Inayatullah and David Blaney, the positivist construction of an instrumental kind of "rationality" in liberalism has also reinforced similar colonial legacies and othering tendencies in the study of International Political Economy (Inayatullah and Blaney 2004). That is, other forms of liberalism also sustain assumptions of truth correspondence that continue to silence other ways of knowing, being, and enacting. According to the authors, "the liberal approach of international political economy, used by authors such as Robert Keohane, Robert Gilpin, and Stephen Krasner, creates othering hierarchies that sustain homogenizing and westernizing tendencies" (62). Based on positivist understandings of science, these scholars study how "rationality" leads to equilibria that improve over time. To achieve this possibility, the international system needs the kind of hegemony that provides an opportunity for collective goods (61). At first, this kind of "condition" entails hegemony, which seems culturally neutral and only emerging from the endowment of resources, but the two countries that have historically achieved this position are the United Kingdom and the United States (71). As a result, the "scientific" promotion of equilibrium includes a cultural bias that reinforces tendencies towards "Western" homogenization. The continuation of the "conditions" becomes the theoretical goal of a research that prioritizes the status of those who already promote and have these characteristics. In other words, these "conditions" become a renewed bedrock of judgement, which can be proved yet again through another assumption of truth correspondence. Additionally, the epistemic organization and isolation of causes and effects leads towards an idea of amelioration, which hides important aspects of colonialism and empire. The approach shows how equilibria lead to peace, but this epistemic isolation of a bedrock and its effects erases the previous costs of the establishment of these very conditions: Who paid for this "peace" or for this possibility of "collective goods"? What are the costs of the violence that erects hegemony and peace? More generally, what is the price of "reason"?

The analysis of multiple forms of liberalism shows that this tradition might include a possibility of change, discussion, expansion, and inclusion (Walzer 1990). That is, the history of liberalism might entail transformations that reshape different boundaries, creating more inclusive possibilities as time goes by. Despite this "progressive" argument, the study of Bolivia illustrates the violence of each elevated and sedimented boundary. Within liberal constructions of truth correspondence, each othering tendency only changes through struggles that are often governmentally and institutionally resisted in violent ways. The intra-discursive certainty and arrogance granted by different assumptions of truth correspondence construct impermeable boundaries that can only be expanded or deconstructed through exogenous and epistemically excluded confrontations. Liberalism thus omits the possibility of democratic relationships with whatever and whoever does not fit its context-dependent yet universalized boundaries. Furthermore, each kind of liberalism epistemically forfeits the possibility of questioning itself, renouncing opportunities of reflexivity and self-problematization.

Unfortunately, some of the approaches that confront the inequalities and injustices created by liberalisms often fall in the same epistemic trap of truth correspondence, creating other sets of boundaries and effects. For example, the case of Bolivia shows how structuralist notions of Marxism can begin from a different idea of "humanity," which emphasizes the undeniability of desire or interest. Within the Nationalist Revolution of 1952, intellectuals used notions of labor, which linked "humanity" to a necessity of relating to nature in order to survive. This connection locates "interest" as another representation of the essence of "humanity;" it creates a form of correspondence between a reality and a "human" characteristic. From this notion, Marxism creates a basis of judgement, justice, and equality. Moreover, those who labor and already relate to nature know this class-based equality; they are the "vanguard" and true agents of the Revolution. Then, this notion of equality becomes the bedrock that agents can deploy to re-organize history, analyze the present, and draw the future. Finally, the ontology of the approach pre-determines what needs to be observed in order to prove the theory and to specify its historical narration. As the Revolutionary emphasis on "science" and sociological "objectivity" illustrates, this positivist idea of observation emerges from the assumption of a direct connection between words such as exploitation, capitalism, feudalism, class, etc. and the "real" structures of societies throughout history.

To the contrary, all other notions of equality, justice, struggle, agency, and history became marginalized as "false," "traditional," "conservative," "reactionary," "backward," "Indio," or "feminine." This tendency can be found in the work of scholars who study international politics while also prioritizing class-based approaches that organize others as "mistaken," "traditional," "conservative," or "obstacles" (e.g., Petras 1989; Balibar and Immanuel 1991; Petras and Veltmeyer 2001, 2005; De La Barra and Dello Buono 2009). A number of scholars have tried to expand Marxist understandings of class and equality in order to study gender-based struggles or race-based injustices (e.g., Gimenez 2001; Belkhir 2001). Despite their efforts, much of the work by these authors continues to regard class equality as an overarching logic that assimilates other struggles. Thus, they often assume that class is the most important form of injustice, whose solution will trickle down into the amelioration of other forms of inequalities. In this way, they still hierarchicalize diverse forms of equality, sustaining forms of single-axis thinking. Class is hereby still regarded as the most real or objective structure of society.

As these cases of liberalism and Marxism illustrate, the notions of truth correspondence that ontologically, epistemologically, methodologically, and temporally elevate these theories marginalize "others" that do not quite fit the impermeable boundaries of the approaches. In turn, this elevation creates conditions of possibility for violence against everything and everyone that is "false," "untrue," "traditional," "irrational," etc. Additionally, methodologies of observation and investigation hereby appear to be possibilities to foreclose circles of self-validation, self-authorization, and self-legitimation. According to other authors, liberalism and Marxism were two of the three dominant approaches of International Relations during the 1970s (Lapid 1989; Kurki and Wight 2013). The boundaries of the discipline thus included the philosophical assumptions, theoretical constructions, historical narrations, and othering tendencies of these two approaches. Of course, the world that each perspective sought to construct was different, but positivist ideas of truth correspondence were commonly used to support the "findings" and specifications that were consistently organized within each approach. Thus, positivism is often regarded as the main commonality that bounded the discipline of International Relations before the so-called "third debate" of the 1980s (Lapid 1989; Milliken 1999; Kurki and Wight 2013; Yanow and Schwartz-Shea 2014; Lynch 2014; Gofas, Hamati-Ataya, and Onuf 2018). In addition to the dominance of this philosophy of science, then, the theoretical boundaries of liberalism and structuralist Marxism specified the characteristics that marginalized other forms of equality, agency, and history. This explains why several authors highlight the role of theories in the diversification of the discipline (Cox 1981; Cox and Sinclair 1996; Milliken 1999; Dalby 2013; Smith 2013; Yanow and Schwartz-Shea 2014; Lynch 2014; Weber 2016).

Thus, positivism played a methodological role in the erection of boundaries that also favored the theoretical construction of particular "others." Here, I am not stating that all the forms of truth correspondence that are included in my genealogical study are "positivist." In fact, the various definitions of epistemologies illustrate how discourses construct different kinds of bridges between knowers and realities. In the case of positivism, this connection of correspondence between language and an ontologically independent world is established through a notion of human experience, which appears to be a direct bridge between methodologically purged words and the objects that are "observed" or "sensed" (George and Campbell 1990; Habermas 1992; Milliken 1999; Schwartz-Shea and Yanow 2012; Yanow and Schwartz-Shea 2014). As others point out, positivism does not necessarily, or always, lead to notions of irreflexive certainty (Hamati-Ataya 2018, 23). Moreover, evidence can sometimes undermine the hegemony of some theories and their epistemic assumptions. For example, some authors highlight the relevance of the fall of the USSR, which undermined the dominance of Marxist, liberal, and realist approaches in International Relations, also enabling the pluralization of the discipline (Wendt 1999; Klotz and Lynch 2007; Kurki and Wight 2013). Despite these disproving, critical, and reflective possibilities, positivist notions of truth correspondence are often used to prove epistemically elevated realities, voices, and narrations. Hence, liberal peace studies, neoliberalism, and some forms of Marxism continue to use positivist assumptions to prove the boundaries and narrations of their approaches. These liberalisms and Marxisms assume truth correspondence, and they "observe" the reality that is epistemically validated, proving ways of knowing that are already elevated, and elevating assumptions that are already proven. In this sense, knowledge production and praxis often become parts of siloed dialogues that only take place within the boundaries of each discursive atmosphere. To the contrary, the confrontation that emerges from the ways of knowing, being, and enacting of "others" forces these disciplinary boundaries to open towards more democratic dialogues. In this sense, the fissures created by the existential crisis of International Relations undermine the exclusionary tendencies of at least two dominant approaches. Despite this advantage, the possibility of diversifying the discipline brings along its own set of questions and problems.

IR Boundaries: The problems of an existential crisis

In order to move beyond the colonial boundaries of approaches such as liberalism and structuralist Marxism, Indianista, amáutico, and plurinationalist intellectuals create their own possibilities of listening to those who have been othered. These authors fruitfully denounce the boundaries and effects of dominant discourses of civilization. The work of Fausto Reinaga, Ayar Quispe, Ramiro Reynaga, Álvaro García Linera, Juan Evo Morales Ayma, Esteban Alejo Ticona, and many others thus illustrates the importance of listening to "others" who confront the irreflexive biases of governmental projects and approaches, also creating innovative sites of agency and solidarity. Despite these contributions, the universalizing tendencies of anti-colonial notions create assimilationist, homogenizing, and violent tendencies against other "others." Moreover, this epistemically hierarchicalizing tendency forces everyone to select only one of the approaches as the "true" path of transformation and justice against "colonialism." In turn, this requirement creates an epistemic problem: How can intellectuals, practitioners, and activists choose among these equally universalizing discourses? The epistemic tendency of universalized singularity and the requirement of selection not only affect potential allies such as myself. More importantly, this tendency troubles those who are directly involved in the positionalities that each one of these anti-colonial discourses seeks to authorize. For example, revolutionary Indianismo, Indianismo Amáutico, and plurinationality claim to know, be, and enact the "Indio" in different ways. How do people who identify as such select from the exclusionary anti-colonialisms that emerge from each one of these universalizing epistemic platforms? Does the demand of singularity forfeit forms of ally-ship even among close experiences of colonialism? These questions highlight the problems that emerge from using the "master's tools" (Lorde 2018). As María José Méndez asserts, "so long as we do not unsettle our inherited colonial frameworks of assessing truth, we will continue to erase ways of being and knowing that might hold a promise for a more just future" (Méndez 2018, 22).

In order to solve this epistemic tendency of boundary construction and universalization, some intellectuals move towards the other side of the tension and they renounce the epistemic foundations that elevate particular ways of knowing, being, and enacting above "others." Hence, some of the intellectuals concerned with indigenous issues in Bolivia and the Andes have deployed post-structuralist notions (e.g., Estermann 2006; Viaña, Claros, and Sarzuri-Lima 2010; Alcoreza 2014). Other intellectuals use the insights of this approach to discuss the problem of difference in theories of International Relations (e.g., Ashley 1981; Der Derian 1987; Der Derian and Shapiro 1989; Ashley and Walker 1990; George and Campbell 1990; Milliken 1999; Walker 2010; Weber 2016). This perspective creates a way of knowing, being, and enacting that encompasses epistemic multiplicity. As several authors point out, however, some Foucauldian understandings of post-structuralism avoid committing to the calls and demands that emerge from "others" (Rivera 2015; Estermann 2006; Viaña, Claros, and Sarzuri-Lima 2010; Alcoreza 2014).

In Chapter Six, I analyze this tendency by focusing on the way in which Michel Foucault separates his field of inquiry from foundations, elevating a way of knowing above epistemic bedrocks, authorizing himself to deconstruct all universalizing discourses, and dismantling extra-discursive classifications of "oppression," "colonialism," etc. As a result, the author can deconstruct the arrogance that emerges from ontological, epistemological, and temporal assumptions, opening the possibility of studying multiple forms of knowledge, identity, and temporality at the same time. Moreover, this opening towards the study of multiple ontologies moves beyond the singularity of reality that often leads to the elevation of a particular definition of "human" commonality, equality, justice, and power. This deconstruction of foundations allows for a much more complex study of multiple power relations, which are examined discursively and within meaning.

Notwithstanding the advantages of this kind of multiplicity, Foucault also creates a tendency towards ignoring the differences between colonial and anti-colonial ways of knowing, being, and enacting. The introduction of power into a realm of pure discursivity renounces the possibility of utilizing power, equality, reality, and "human" characteristics as bedrocks of judgement against "coloniality." Instead, the generalized renunciation of extra-discursive foundations and bedrocks only creates a possibility of classification against universalization. Thus, any possibility of validating, authorizing, or legitimizing a boundary beyond philosophically ever-shrinking localities becomes "colonial," "dominant," "disciplining," etc. This tendency either leads towards the equal deconstruction of all struggles, assuming that domination is inevitable, or it creates another epistemic problem: How do post-structuralist approaches select what needs to be deconstructed in order to move beyond dominations? In other words, the approach either assumes that universalization is the main problem that should be resisted, due to its epistemic foundationalism and its tendency to internalize exteriority, or it accepts some processes of universalization to some extent. If the approach selects the latter path, how do we select what universalizing tendency and how much of it is acceptable? Any utilization of a criterion would lead towards yet another extra-discursive or elevated bedrock.

Consequently, since it tends to categorically homogenize all universalizing ways of knowing, being, and enacting, this kind of Foucauldian post-structuralism creates a lack of commitment with anti-colonial voices; it equally invalidates all universalizing discourses or avoids telling us how much deconstruction is necessary. Here, Revolutionary Indianismo, Indianismo Amáutico, plurinationalism, liberalism, and Marxism appear equally dominant and colonial. Thus, the problem of abandoning bedrocks is that we end up without any bedrocks to classify discourses, which is the condition of possibility for praxis. So, which one of these ways of knowing, being, and enacting should be deconstructed in order to desubjugate "others"? How can interpreters and activists prioritize the deconstruction of one or the other? What is more "dominant" and urgently oppressive? Or is desubjugation a pointless exercise that always ends up producing more complex forms of domination? Does this mean that deconstruction is a never-ending process? Or is there a possibility to put a momentary stop to deconstruction while also creating a moment that is less dominating? How can we determine how much deconstruction is necessary for this possibility? That is, how much does a way of knowing, being, and enacting have to change in order to abandon its dominant form? The generalization of anti-foundationalism does not answer these questions, and it tends to lead towards its own form of epistemic violence in the re-silencing and re-invalidation of "others." In a way, the approach becomes blinded against the inequalities suffered by "others" because it seeks to avoid the epistemic prioritization of any single definition of power and inequality. No particular notion of power appears extra-discursive. Power cannot be used as a possibility to determine how colonialism and anti-colonialism are different. Hence, anti-foundationalism abandons "others" in order to avoid creating other "others."

To steer clear of this kind of violence and generalization, approaches that aim to avoid the othering effects of boundaries while also sustaining the possibility of praxis need to examine how it might be possible to undo foundations while also prioritizing diverse "others." Only through this prioritization and judgement can an approach re-orient deconstruction and praxis against "dominations;" only in this manner can praxis commit to the "others" that are disproportionally disadvantaged. That is, the possibility of avoiding an epistemically aimless or never-ending tendency of deconstruction surges from a definition of a form of judgement, which presupposes a notion of power and inequality to guide praxis towards a commitment to "others." This commitment might entail a definition of power, privilege, or domination that might move beyond the previously discussed notions of class, citizenship, ethnicity, identity, etc., but the stance still requires some kind of classification of "coloniality;" it demands an idea of inequality in order to determine, explicitly or implicitly, who is "dominant" and who is an "other." This commitment towards "others" does not need to prioritize a single struggle, voice, and project above all other "others." A more encompassing form of praxis could move beyond single-axis thinking. However, this type of praxis still requires the determination of what is "domination." In other words, the prioritization of "others" demands an epistemic criterion and boundary, which needs to determine what equality is more valid. In order to sustain an encompassing form of classification that can take multiple struggles into account, one could say that domination is universalization in general, but then again, how is Indianismo different to liberalism? One could also affirm that domination is a classed, racialized, gendered, or sexualized form of power, but then again, what about other kinds of domination? What about other "others"? As I discuss in Chapter Six, this tendency to generalize particular forms of domination above other struggles also emerges whenever notions of institutionalization elevate discourses as the real "structures" of a society, disregarding other forms of resistance and the dynamic aspects of meaning. In this sense, notions of truth correspondence could continue to silence other "others."

As the previous, no doubt frustrating, paragraphs illustrate, the tension between the effects of boundaries and the renunciation of foundations can be uncomfortably circular, constantly returning to old or paralyzing assumptions for answers. Then, the limitations and issues that emerge from these answers summon the problem of difference yet again. In this sense, the problem of difference can be understood as a tension and a dilemma, which prevents the emergence of "perfect" solutions because epistemic answers either create or ignore "others."

A proposal for IR: Stay in the tension

Scholars of feminism, post-structuralism, post-colonialism, decoloniality, queer theory, green theory, constructivism, neo-Marxism, critical theory, interpretivism, and other approaches or methodologies have answered this problem in different ways (e.g., Said 1978; Todorov 1982; Butler 1990; George and Campbell 1990; Crenshaw 1991; Milliken 1999; Inayatullah and Blaney 2004; Shapiro 2004; Hoy 2005; Wolfe 2010; Cho, Crenshaw, and McCall 2013; Ari 2014; Rivera 2015; Weber 2016; Escobar 2017; Mignolo and Walsh 2018). A number of authors have fruitfully analyzed relational cosmologies to think about this dilemma as well (A. Tickner 2003; Tickner and Blaney 2013; Blaney and Tickner 2017; Mignolo and Walsh 2018; Querejazu 2018; Trownsell et al. 2019). My contribution concentrates on the work of Rivera and the discussion of Andean anti-colonial voices to discuss relationality and decoloniality.

Much of this work begins by renouncing the essentialist epistemic assumption of truth correspondence. Instead of starting from notions that connect meanings to ontologically independent realities, relational ideas can stay at the level of the meaningful constructions that emerge from moments of signification themselves. Here, meanings do not appear to spring from the very essence of distinct objects "out there;" instead, they construct worlds through the constitution of commonalities and differences, which simultaneously relate and separate identities. For example, Rivera creates a way of knowing from cosmological relationships of co-participation, which entail the possibility of constructing commonalities and differences among equal subjects. Then, this cosmological notion of relationality can be consistently sustained throughout the epistemic level of interpretation. The notion of ontological reality is thus transformed into a cosmology of indeterminate and equally experienced relationships. All notions of commonality and difference hereby appear as equivalent constructions of equality, power relations, struggles, and justice. Then, epistemology also becomes yet another indeterminate set of relationships. Thus, senti-pensar is not another pre-determined, elevated, and carefully defined bridge between a particular interpreter (i.e., a way of being) and an ontological reality "out there;" it is not another settled way of accessing some kind of independent and objective essence. Rather, senti-pensar entails the indeterminately complex possibility of co-participation that multiple kinds of interpreters enjoy in various relationships.

Within this multiplicity, relationality allows for diverse kinds of epistemic notions to coexist in equivalence. Since co-participation entails a form of equivalence among the experiences of the subjects that enter relationships, the multiple constructions of commonalities and differences that each of them expresses appear equally valid. Each notion of ontology thus becomes an equally valid characterization of relationships and each definition of epistemology is regarded as an equivalent construction of participation in relationships. Within this cosmological dimension, none of the definitions of epistemic relationships can be classified as an elevated way of knowing and a consistently authorizing way of being. At this level, interpreters are not enabled to elevate their own notion of equality and power relation; they cannot create some kind of classification between "colonialism" and "others." Consequently, the epistemological equality among multiple subjects undermines the authority that interpreters need to demand some kind of transformation from whatever they classify as "colonial," "oppressive," "dominant," etc.

This cosmology of relationality thus renounces foundations, bedrocks, essentialisms, truth correspondence, objectivity, and the possibility of accessing ontologically independent objects out there; it rejects the essentialist cosmologies of Western knowledge production. Here, different ways of knowing, being, and enacting appear as relationships that emerge from the experiences of subjects that equally co-participate in the cosmos. Similar to some of the epistemic ideas that surged in the so-called "linguistic turn," with authors such as Ludwig Wittgenstein (1958; 1969), as well as notions of interpretivism (Milliken 1999; Schwartz-Shea and Yanow 2012; Lynch 2014), post-structuralism (Foucault 1970; 1972; Der Derian and Shapiro 1989; George and Campbell 1990; Ashley and Walker 1990), and many others, this understanding of relationality entails a critique of epistemic elevation, objectivity, and universalization. Also, in accordance with some of these authors, Rivera is acutely aware of the dangers that emerge when the implications of anti-foundationalism are generalized towards an ever-deconstructing tendency that totalizes domination and homogenizes discourses. Hence, Rivera states that Andean cosmologies include a notion of Khä Pacha, which is the abyss that continuously threatens all human action. Due to this awareness, I interpret Rivera's approach as beginning from a cosmology that sustains the very tension of the problem of difference. On one side, the utilization of relationality allows us to abandon the essentialism that creates colonizing boundaries from the universalization of particular bedrocks and the interiorization of "others." On the other side, the cosmological notion of relationality alone does not provide a possibility of action and praxis, potentially ignoring the sufferings and constructions that "others" voice in the silencing edges of a domination that cannot be defined. In this cosmological realm, relationality is the problem of difference; it is the tension between multiplicity and praxis.

A proposal for IR: The profession of faith

Notwithstanding the circular and even paralyzing tendencies of the problem of difference, Rivera makes a profession of faith in the "fact of colonialism" (Rivera 2015, 28). This step entails a momentary and precarious split between the paradoxical logic of the relational cosmology and a possibility of walking in a particular here/now. Cosmology thus becomes a dimension of knowledge that always lurks underneath all possibilities of knowledge production and praxis, but its precarious separation also allows for reflexive and only momentary boundaries. In this manner, Rivera sustains the tension and dilemma of the problem of difference, constantly questioning all othering tendencies and all bedrocks, but she also enables a perilous and yet necessary form of judgment. The author thus acknowledges the cosmological arbitrariness of boundaries that are nothing but equivalent relationships. At the same time, however, she also recognizes the necessity of listening to particular experiences of relationality in order to demand transformations, authorize agents, and enact projects. Accordingly, the profession of faith appears to be a leap that sustains and yet freezes the indeterminate complexity and equivalence of pure relationality.

Rivera's sociology of images thus teaches us how to walk in the tension of the problem of difference, keeping the dilemma while also constructing possibilities of praxis. Moreover, the cosmological equivalence of each profession of faith demands a deep analysis of the boundaries of praxis that each stance constructs. For Rivera, the benefits of her approach emerge from her unapologetic and dynamic commitment to multiple "others."

Reflexive boundaries of intersectional decoloniality

Due to her personal experience, extensive empirical research, and profound theoretical knowledge, Rivera constructs her praxis and classification by deploying an epistemic notion of continuity and sharedness, which momentarily elevates the meanings that denounce particular forms of domination. Here, the fact that she finds and interprets meaningful "convergences" from multiple kinds of expressions such as texts, oral histories, paintings, etc. is regarded as a source of social sharedness, which elevates these meanings beyond the individual subjectivity of the interpreter. In other words, the idea that multiple anti-colonial ways of knowing, being, and enacting are socially shared locates these experiences above the universalizing tendencies of the discourses that construct them as "others." However, unlike some interpretivist and constructivist ideas of intersubjectivity (e.g., Cox and Sinclair 1996; Epstein 2008; Fierke 2013; Kratochwil and Ruggie 1986; Schwartz-Shea and Yanow 2012; Yanow and Schwartz-Shea 2014), this notion of socially shared meanings is not another disguised form of foundational reality; it is not "social reality" itself. Instead, this social status is a cosmologically arbitrary profession of faith; it is an epistemic assumption that emerges from the convergences that the interpreter finds among meanings, but this idea has to constantly sustain its reflexivity in order to avoid structuralizing interpretations, generalizing implications, and silencing other "others". This strategy is similar to the work of some post-structuralist authors who avoid the tendency to generalize domination, focusing on the enabling side of discourse and finding ways to stop philosophically endless processes of deconstruction (Wittgenstein 1958, 1969; George and Campbell 1990; Butler 1990; Campbell 2013).

Through this epistemic strategy, Rivera reflexively elevates a boundary that is based on the respect of differences that respect other differences; she creates a realm of heterogeneity and difference. Here, the assumption that convergences entail a degree of historical continuity and social sharedness becomes the commonality and precarious reality of discourses. Then, the notion establishes a form of equality among discourses and it builds an idea of power struggle. This boundary creates a separation among two different types of ways of knowing, being, and enacting. On one side, she finds ways of knowing, being, and enacting that, while being socially shared, universalize themselves above others who also enjoy this epistemic status. On the other side, those who have continuity and sharedness, but also suffer the othering effects of overly expanded discourses become the primary focus of the sociology of images, which follows these meanings to confront and fracture the universality of domination. Since the author first traces the prominent convergences of indigenous struggles in the Andes, the epistemic status of this way of knowing, being, and enacting confronts the ethnic and racial inequalities that are created by civilizing discourses such as liberalism and Marxism. Here, the construction of indigenous struggles creates a form of ethnic equality, indigenous agency, and anti-colonial transformation, which confronts the inequality of racism, Western rule, and modernity. The fact of colonialism thus emphasizes the social status of indigenous struggles, which elevates this way of knowing, being, and enacting above a form of universalization, coloniality, and epistemic privilege.

This politically fruitful yet cosmologically arbitrary epistemic status prioritizes this particular struggle, but it also avoids its universalization and it provides a way of stopping the generalization of deconstruction. The sharedness and continuity of indigenous struggles equalizes this construction against the privilege of colonial racism, but this idea avoids the demand to destroy everything that is "occidental;" it stops praxis before it demands complete assimilation. As I interpret it, Rivera's work emphasizes the meanings that can be analyzed as patterns of synthetized narrations. The interpreter weaves the fabric of plots from "convergences" that connect the cacophony of texts, paintings, voices, oral histories, legends, documents, documentaries, etc. These connections are the consistencies that are regarded as continuities or different forms of sharedness; they are the "convergence" that acts as the condition of possibility to construct "discursive atmospheres." Since indigenous struggles in Bolivia include this type of convergence throughout coetaneous and historical expressions, their epistemic status demands the transformation of the racist discourses that have continuously marginalized them. In a sense, this kind of praxis classifies and internalizes its own "others," which can only become equally accepted insofar as they pay the price of epistemic de-universalization. In other words, this is not a relativist approach; rather, it demands the decolonial deconstruction of the domination that othering practices entail. Despite this demand of transformation, Rivera's notion of praxis does not call for the complete destruction of everything related to "modern" ways of knowing, being, and enacting. As long as "modern" ways of knowing, being, and enacting lose their "dominating" characteristics, respect the confrontation of their privilege, renounce their interiorization of externality, and localize their notions, they can coexist as discourses that are equal due to their own sharedness. Deconstruction can stop at the moment of fracture and confrontation; at the point of internalization of exteriority.

Additionally, the prioritization of socially shared confrontations avoids the elevation of a particular struggle and the generalization of philosophically endless processes of deconstruction in another way: It stops these tendencies by demanding a possibility of listening to other socially shared and/or historically continuous meanings of confrontation. Hence, Rivera follows feminist understandings of equality, agency, and history, which have been continuously othered by colonial discourses and Indianista projects, to unveil another call for de-universalization and coexistence. Here, the continuity and socially shared aspect of another set of meanings calls for the epistemic equivalence of another "other." On one side, this possibility limits and fractures not only colonial discourses such as liberalism, but also the epistemic privilege of masculine understandings of Indianismo, enabling a realm where two anti-colonial confrontations have to be regarded as equivalent. On the other side, this confrontation of Indianismo does not lead to a demand of endless deconstruction. Instead, the sharedness of a feminist equality, agency, and project demands the deconstruction of universalizations until they enable the epistemic space necessary for yet another equivalent construction. Then, Rivera sustains the call to listen to others that are also regarded as socially shared ways of knowing, being, and enacting. This epistemic boundary of judgement leads the author to investigate an ecological experience of equality, agency, and history. Rivera thus narrates yet another set of meanings that confront the anthropocentric, human, and modernizing construction of colonialism. Of course, these ethnic, gendered, and ecological experiences are not isolated relationalities. Instead, the separated logic of each notion of relationality, equality, agency, and history can be best interpreted in their intersections, which modify the logic of other relationships. In this sense, notions of equality, agency, and transformation often become modified by the call that emerges from other ways of knowing, being, and enacting, which confront their universalization and heterogenize the taypi. Gendered experiences of ethnicity, racialized experiences of gender, gendered experiences of ecology, and so on thus confront each other, fracturing universalizations and creating a more complex diagnosis of epistemically equivalent struggles and propositions. Insofar as these meanings are socially shared and/or historically continuous, the interpreter has to include them in the map of struggles and alternatives that emerges as a guide for context-dependent praxis.

This boundary entails two possibilities of sustaining a more dynamic and reflexive kind of interpretation. On one side, the profession of faith is understood to be as a cosmologically arbitrary, or at least equivalent, moment of boundary construction. This understanding creates a different kind of boundary, which can be questioned from within the approach itself, without waiting for violently resisted voices that exogenously confront the boundaries of particular discourses. On the other side, the boundary contains a dynamic call to listen to multiple confrontations against universalizations. The boundary of decolonial praxis that Rivera constructs thus entails the dynamic prioritization of socially shared and/or historically continuous struggles, agencies, and histories. This boundary not only creates a context-dependent possibility of drawing maps, but also constantly demands the need to listen to other "others," which might have been previously ignored by a particular interpreter. Hence, Rivera emphasizes ethnic, gender, and ecological relationships, but other socially shared experiences of, for example, sexualized, aged, or ableist confrontations might complicate a particular taypi even further, localizing decolonial praxis from the bottom up.

Other approaches of decoloniality

This kind of epistemic strategy is in part similar to the work of other decolonial authors who consider multiplicity while also creating a condition of possibility for praxis. For example, Walter Mignolo states that decoloniality begins from an act of love that longs for the possibility of surpassing coloniality (Mignolo 2000, 272). This moment of decision is not a universal abstract; rather, it is a project that emerges from locality. Here, the notion of love creates a condition of possibility that focuses on the experiences of "colonial wounds" (37). In this sense, Mignolo seeks to construct a new kind of epistemology (273), which prioritizes multiple "others."

Despite these similarities, Rivera creates the fact of colonialism as an explicit "profession of faith," which does not re-claim truth correspondence. Her presupposition of sharedness in the idea of convergences is not the reality or structure of society itself. Instead, this criterion of epistemic elevation can be regarded as a cosmologically equivalent boundary, which she reflexively deploys to avoid the paralyzing and even Western-centric tendencies of generalized deconstruction. In this sense, Rivera does not solve the problem of difference; instead, she sustains it at the level of cosmology while also momentarily deploying a boundary that is not foundationally warranted; she changes the rules of the struggle to determine standards of knowledge production.

This fruitful way of understanding relational cosmologies and epistemics separates the work of Rivera from the decolonial approach of Mignolo. Despite his resistance to Western epistemics and universalization, Mignolo deploys a notion of geo-politics that territorializes the discourses that he is analyzing. This epistemic connection of correspondence between meanings and a spatial-temporal territoriality re-structuralizes particular forms of colonialism and decoloniality above other "others." Throughout his work, Mignolo narrates differences that are based on geo-political distributions of knowledges (Mignolo 2000, 115). This form of interpretation helps him to deconstruct particular colonialities that are "dominant" in specific contexts. Thenceforth, Mignolo unveils different loci of agency, but the territorial metaphor still creates a generalizing tendency of singularity in his understanding of difference. Much of his work regards each place and historical context as related to a particular construction of "coloniality." For example, Mignolo and Catherine Walsh assert that being from the "Third World" entails being "touched by" geo-politics that "matter" (Mignolo and Walsh 2018, 5). Here, geo-historical locations retain a causal and super-structural component, which ontologically exteriorizes the coloniality that Mignolo interprets. This strategy allows him to study the "pillars" of coloniality in particular geo-historical locations, prioritizing particular struggles, committing to specific "others," and enacting a strong form of praxis. However, the approach also sustains a hierarchical organization of struggles and ways of knowing, which prioritizes race and the organization of labor as the overarching logic of the domination that "operates" or exercises control over other experiences such as gender, sexuality, etc. (23). In this sense, Mignolo and Walsh create an assimilationist tendency, which organizes multiple ways of knowing, being, and enacting under a particular logic of domination, regarding this "structure" as more dominant in a particular geo-historical context than other experiences. In this sense, Mignolo and Walsh's notion of coloniality still sustains a structural tendency, which might emerge from the Marxist legacy of dependency theory and from the work of Anibal Quijano (Quijano and Wallerstein 1992; Quijano 2000, 2007).

This objectifying and structuralizing tendency can be found most clearly in Mignolo's separation between coloniality and modernity. These two sides of domination are conceived as constitutive, but their analytical separation creates a tendency to view them as ontologically distinct realms that determine each other; they are the two sides of the story (Mignolo 2018, 113). This ontological separation creates an assumption that objectifies a particular reading of society. On one side, Mignolo locates the "rhetoric of modernity," and on the other side he analyzes the "logic of coloniality" (139). Since the structure of coloniality appears as ontologically separated from meaning, language, or "rhetoric," this decoupling instance allows for Mignolo to elevate a more objective set of characteristics that decoloniality needs to oppose, but this epistemic elevation of his own interpretation also generalizes a particular experience of coloniality above other "others." Hence, Mignolo classifies "rhetoric" as domination, but "coloniality" becomes exploitation (146). This singularizing tendency assimilates multiple forms of coloniality and decoloniality under an overarching umbrella, which prevents us from listening to the ways in which multiple voices confront each other in their diagnoses of coloniality and alternatives of decoloniality. This tendency silences the heterogeneity of struggles, agencies, and temporalities that coexist in each particular context. In this sense, Mignolo still sustains the assimilationist tendencies of single-axis thinking.

Conclusion: The advantages of Rivera's approach

Unlike this epistemic tendency towards assimilation, the work of Rivera emphasizes the multiplicity that surges from contradictions, tensions, and fractures. In my interpretation of her work, this possibility within each multi-layered map allows us to understand contradicting logics of domination and different alternatives simultaneously. Rivera's boundary thus sustains two differences with Mignolo's definition of decoloniality. On one side, her possibility of committing to particular "others" emerges from a cosmologically equivalent profession of faith, which needs to sustain its reflexivity and self-problematization while also drawing a context-dependent map. On the other side, the map that Rivera draws encompasses the confrontations that emerge between multiple "others," understanding the ways in which different relationships cross and modify each other from diverse logics. This is the possibility that allows Rivera to understand gendered experiences of ethnicity, which do not unfold from masculine readings of race and exploitation. In fact, they modify masculine understandings of ethnicity, allowing Rivera to move beyond ideas of territorialization that include truth correspondence.

This difference between Rivera's work and Mignolo's approach not only allows for a more reflexive, dynamic, and complex understanding of heterogeneity, but also includes the possibility of respecting differences at the level of incommensurability. The work of Mignolo still emphasizes the need for a structuralized and overarching coherence or logic, which aims to explain and organize multiple experiences of oppression and diverse projects of transformation. Instead, Rivera uses incommensurability at a cosmological level that avoids claiming to know the real characteristic of all relationships or the overarching relationship that connects all relationships. Due to the equality among co-participant subjects, multiple forms of realities, agents, and projects coexist in a cosmology that chaotically avoids the singularity of civilizing order. At the level of cosmology, Rivera does not predetermine the logic of all relationships, sustaining a void or abyss of incommensurability. This cosmology thus helps us to live more comfortably with the humility of an epistemic uncertainty. Of course, the author makes her profession of faith and settles a praxis, but she still retains this uncertainty as an ever-present form of self-problematization. This is a powerful source of epistemic reflexivity, which can only be precariously settled in a localized manner.

Once the author makes her profession of faith, the boundary that emerges from this precarious moment of settlement emphasizes the sharedness or continuity of particular struggles. Despite this boundary, the notion of sharedness and confrontation does not require a complete cosmological understanding of the "other" that is calling for transformation. That is, the status of sharedness or historical continuity that we can assume from the convergences of a confrontation of a universality is epistemically enough to require us to listen to "others." Hence, interpreters do not need to understand "others" in complete or familiar ways; they do not need to assimilate "other" voices within a specific form of "coloniality" in order to allow them to confront epistemic privilege. Accordingly, Rivera allows for an element of incommensurability between the confronting "others" that are mapped in a specific taypi, enabling a form of heterogeneity that is much more radical than the project emerging from single logics of coloniality and modernity. As Méndez illustrates, this element of incommensurability is extremely important in listening beyond the colonial legacies of truth and singularity that kill (Méndez 2018, 18).

As a result of this cosmological element of incommensurability and the dynamic boundary of decoloniality, Rivera also avoids linear constructions of time. As I discuss in Chapter One, universalized constructions of ontologies and epistemologies can be related to designs of linear temporalities. To the contrary, Rivera begins by avoiding foundationalist assumptions of correspondence, and she only settles a reflective boundary. This possibility sustains the tension of the problem of difference at the level of cosmology, constantly requiring that interpreters problematize their criteria of classification and praxis. Hence, the author avoids the arrogance of truth correspondence, creating an epistemic need to return to the analysis of our assumptions and bedrocks; she builds a humbler opportunity of walking in a specific context.

In addition to this epistemic circularity of reflexivity, the boundaries of judgement that emerge as the logic of the moral compass create a circular demand to return to the drawing canvas every time that a map has been settled through interpretation. Hence, I see a second kind of temporal circularity in the work of Rivera. Due to the status of socially shared or historically continuous confrontations, the interpreter has to remain open to other ways of knowing, being, and enacting that might confront yet again the universalizing tendencies of particular struggles, agents, and projects. In other words, interpreters and agents can settle context-dependent maps, which can guide action in these localities, but they also need to continue listening for other "others."

These differences and implications show why it is important to understand relationality as epistemically detached from structural, territorial, geographical, or historical worlds "out there." This is how Rivera sustains relationality in a much more reflexive, dynamic, circular, bottom-up, and complex manner. Moreover, Rivera's work enables the possibility of moving the notion of a locus of enunciation away from geo-historical locations and towards relational positionalities. That is, the possibility of analyzing different loci of enunciation entails an examination of the epistemic assumptions and boundaries of each construction. Then, the selection and elevation of a particular locus of interpretation and praxis becomes possible thanks to a reflexive and momentary profession of faith.

Notes

1 Pierre Bourdieu mentions in "Pascalian Meditations," for example, that post-modern philosophers are "… inclined to see assertion as an injunction of order, to see the logic as a thought police, to see the claim to scientificity as a mere truth effect designed to secure obedience or as a disguised aspiration to hegemony inspired by the will to power …" (1997, 29) Then, in later pages, he links this form of post-modern negation of assertions together with the radical critique against universalisms found, for example, in Foucault's work (107).

2 Of course, a more complete discussion of the discipline should include an analysis of the epistemic boundaries created by realist approaches, but the scope of my case and genealogy leads me to leave this discussion for another time. Additionally, many authors have successfully shown the limitations of realism and its epistemic assumptions (e.g., Ashley 1981; J. A. Tickner 1988).

References

Alcoreza, RaúlPrada. 2014. "Epistemología Pluralista." In *Pluralismo Epistemológico*, edited by Amílcar B. Zambrana, 13–55. Cochabamba: FUNPROEIB Andes. https://es.scribd.com/doc/296610165/Pluralismo-Epistemologico.

Ari, Waskar. 2014. *Earth Politics. Religion, Decolonization, and Bolivia's Indigenous Intellectuals*. Durham, NC: Duke University Press.

Ashley, Richard. 1981. "Political Realism and Human Interests." *International Studies Quarterly* 25 (4): 204–236.

Ashley, Richard, and R. B. J. Walker. 1990. "Speaking the Language of Exile: Dissent Thought in International Studies." *International Studies Quarterly* 34 (3): 259–268.

Balibar, Étienne, and Immanuel Wallerstein. 1991. *Race, Nation, Class Ambiguous Identities*. London: Verso.

Belkhir, Jean Ait. 2001. "Marxism Without Apologies: Integrating Race, Gender, Class: A Working Class Approach." *Race, Gender & Class Journal* 8 (2): 142–171.

Blaney, David L., and Arlene B. Tickner. 2017. "Worlding, Ontological Politics and the Possibility of a Decolonial IR." *Millennium: Journal of International Studies* 45 (3): 293–311.

Bourdieu, Pierre. 1997. *Pascalian Meditations*. Stanford, CA: Stanford University Press.

Butler, Judith. 1990. *Gender Trouble: Feminism and the Subversion of Identity*. New York: Routledge.

Campbell, David. 2013. "Post-Structuralism." In *International Relations Theories: Discipline and Diversity*, edited by Tim Dunne, Milja Kurki, and Steve Smith, 223–247. Oxford: Oxford University Press.

Chan, Steve. 1997. "In Search of Democratic Peace: Problems and Promise." *Mershon International Studies Review* 41 (1): 59–91.

Cho, Sumi, Kimberlé W. Crenshaw, and Leslie McCall. 2013. "Toward a Field of Intersectionality Studies, Applications, and Praxis." *Signs* 38 (4): 785–810.

Cox, Robert W. 1981. "Social Forces, States and World Orders: Beyond International Relations Theory." *Millennium: Journal of International Studies* 10 (2): 126–155. doi:10.1177/03058298810100020501.

Cox, Robert W., and Timothy J. Sinclair. 1996. *Approaches to World Order*. Cambridge: Cambridge University Press.

Crenshaw, Kimberlé W. 1991. "Mapping the Margins: Intersectionality, Identity Politics, and Violence Against Women of Color." *Stanford Law Review* 43 (6): 1241–1299.

Dalby, Simon. 2013. "What Happens If We Don't Take Nature for Granted?" In *Global Politics: A New Introduction*, edited by Jenny Edkins and Maja Zehfuss, 39–61. New York: Routledge.

De La Barra, Ximena, and Richard A. Dello Buono. 2009. *Latin America After the Neoliberal Debacle: Another Region Is Possible.* London: Rowman & Littlefield.

Der Derian, James. 1987. "Mediating Estrangement: A Theory for Diplomacy." *Review of International Studies* 13 (2): 91–110.

Der Derian, James, and Michael J. Shapiro, eds. 1989. *International/Intertextual Relations: Postmodern Readings of World Politics.* New York: Lexington Books.

Dougherty, James E., and Robert L. Pfaltzgraff. 2001. *Contending Theories of International Relations: A Comprehensive Survey.* 5th ed. New York: Longman.

Enloe, Cynthia. 1980. "Women: The Reserve Army of Army Labor." *Review of Radical Political Economics* 12 (2): 42–54.

Epstein, Charlotte. 2008. *The Power of Words in International Relations: Birth of an Anti-Whaling Discourse.* Cambridge, MA: MIT Press.

Escobar, Arturo. 2017. *Designs for the Pluriverse: Radical Interdependence, Autonomy, and the Making of Worlds.* Durham, NC: Duke University Press.

Estermann, Josef. 2006. *Filosofía Andina: Sabiduría Indígena Para Un Mundo Nuevo.* 2nd ed. La Paz: Instituto Superior Ecuménico Andino de Teología.

Fierke, Karin Marie. 2013. "Constructivism." In *International Relations Theories: Discipline and Diversity*, edited by Tim Dunne, Milja Kurki, and Steve Smith, 187–205. Oxford: Oxford University Press.

Foucault, Michel. 1970. *The Order of Things: An Archaeology of Human Sciences.* New York: Vintage Books.

Foucault, Michel. 1972. *The Archaeology of Knowledge, and The Discourse on Language.* New York: Vintage Books.

George, Jim, and David Campbell. 1990. "Patterns of Dissent and the Celebration of Difference: Critical Social Theory and International Relations." *International Studies Quarterly* 34 (3): 269–293.

Gerring, John. 2012. *Social Science Methodology: A Unified Framework.* Cambridge: Cambridge University Press.

Gimenez, Martha E. 2001. "Marxism, and Class, Gender, and Race: Rethinking the Trilogy." *Jean Ait Belkhir, Race, Gender & Class Journal* 8 (2): 23–33.

Gofas, Andreas, Inanna Hamati-Ataya, and Nicholas Onuf, eds. 2018. *The SAGE Handbook of the History, Philosophy and Sociology of International Relations.* Los Angeles: SAGE.

Goldstein, Joshua S., and Jon C. Pevehouse. 2013. *International Relations.* 6th ed. Boston, MA: Pearson.

Grovogui, Siba N'Zatioula. 1996. *Sovereigns, Quasi Sovereigns, and Africans.* Minneapolis: University of Minnesota Press.

Habermas, Jürgen. 1992. *Postmetaphysical Thinking: Philosophical Essays.* Boston, MA: Beacon Press.

Hamati-Ataya, Inanna. 2018. "Crafting the Reflexive Gaze: Knowledge of Knowledge in Social Worlds of International Relations." In *The Sage Handbook of the History, Philosophy and Sociology of International Relations*, by Andreas Gofas, Inanna Hamati-Ataya, and Nicholas Onuf, 13–31. Los Angeles: SAGE.

Hoy, David Couzens. 2005. *Critical Resistance: From Poststructuralism to Post-Critique.* Cambridge, MA: MIT Press.

Inayatullah, Naeem, and David L. Blaney. 2004. *International Relations and the Problem of Difference.* New York: Routledge.

Keohane, Robert O. 1988. "International Institutions: Two Approaches." *International Studies Quarterly* 32 (4): 379–396.

King, Gary, Robert O. Keohane, and Sidney Verba. 1994. *Designing Social Enquiry: Scientific Inference in Qualitative Research.* Princeton, NJ: Princeton University Press.

Klotz, Audie, and Cecelia Lynch. 2007. *Strategies for Research in Constructivist International Relations.* New York: M. E. Sharpe.

Kratochwil, Friedrich, and John Gerard Ruggie. 1986. "International Organization: A State of the Art on an Art of the State." *International Organization* 40 (4): 753–775.

Kurki, Milja, and Colin Wight. 2013. "International Relations and Social Science." In *International Relations Theories: Discipline and Diversity*, edited by Tim Dunne, Milja Kurki, and Steve Smith, 14–36. Oxford: Oxford University Press.

Lamy, Steven L., John Baylis, Steve Smith, and Patricia Owens. 2013. *Introduction to Global Politics.* 2nd ed.Oxford: Oxford University Press.

Lapid, Yosef. 1989. "The Third Debate: On the Prospects of International Theory in a Post-Positivist Era." *International Studies Quarterly* 33 (3): 235–254.

Lorde, Audre. 2018. *The Master's Tools Will Never Dismantle the Master's House.* London: Penguin.

Lynch, Cecelia. 2014. *Interpreting International Politics.* New York: Routledge.

Mearsheimer, John J. 1994. "The False Promise of International Institutions." *International Security* 19 (3): 5–49.

Méndez, María José. 2018. "'The River Told Me': Rethinking Intersectionality from the World of Berta Cáceres." *Capitalism Nature Socialism* 29 (1): 7–24.

Mignolo, Walter. 2000. *Local Histories/Global Designs: Coloniality, Subaltern Knowledges, and Border Thinking*. Princeton Studies in Culture/Power/History. Princeton, NJ: Princeton University Press.

Mignolo, Walter. 2018. "The Decolonial Option." In *On Decoloniality: Concepts, Analytics, Praxis*, by Walter Mignolo and Catherine E. Walsh, 105–279. Durham, NC: Duke University Press.

Mignolo, Walter, and Catherine E. Walsh. 2018. *On Decoloniality: Concepts, Analytics, and Praxis.* Durham, NC: Duke University Press.

Milliken, Jennifer. 1999. "The Study of Discourse in International Relations: A Critique of Research and Methods." *European Journal of International Relations* 5 (2): 225–254.

Mingst, Karen A., and Jack L. Snyder. 2014. *Essential Readings in World Politics.* 5th ed. New York; London: W. W. Norton & Company.

Oneal, John R., Bruce Russett, and Michael Berbaum. 2003. "Causes of Peace: Democracy, Interdependence, and International Organizations, 1885–1992." *International Studies Quarterly* 47 (3): 371–393.

Onuf, Nicholas. 1989. *World of Our Making: Rules and Rule in Social Theory and International Relations.* London: Routledge.

Paris, Roland. 2004. *At War's End: Building Peace After Civil Conflict*. Cambridge: Cambridge University Press.

Petras, James. 1989. "State Terror and Social Movements in Latin America." *Journal of Politics, Culture and Society* 3 (2): 179–212.

Petras, James, and Henry Veltmeyer. 2001. "Are Latin American Peasant Movements Still a Force for Change? Some New Paradigms Revisited." *The Journal of Peasant Studies* 28 (2): 83–118.

Petras, James, and Henry Veltmeyer. 2005. *Social Movements and State Power: Argentina, Brazil, Bolivia, Ecuador*. London: Pluto Press.

Querejazu, Amaya. 2018. "Encountering the Pluriverse: Looking for Alternatives in Other Worlds." *Revista Brasileira de Política Internacional* 59 (2). doi:10.1590/0034-7329201600207.

Quijano, Aníbal. 2000. "Coloniality of Power, Eurocentrism, and Latin America." Translated by Michael Ennis. *Nepantla: Views from South* 1 (3): 533–580.

Quijano, Aníbal. 2007. "Coloniality and Modernity/Rationality." *Cultural Studies* 21 (2–3): 168–178. doi:10.1080/09502380601164353.

Quijano, Aníbal, and Immanuel Wallerstein. 1992. "Americanity as a Concept, or the Americas in the Modern World-System." *International Journal of Social Sciences* 134: 583–591.

Rivera Cusicanqui, Silvia. 2015. *Sociología de la Imagen. Miradas Ch'ixi Desde La Historia Andina*. Buenos Aires: Tinta Limón.

Russett, Bruce. 2013. "Liberalism." In *International Relations Theories: Discipline and Diversity*, edited by Tim Dunne, Milja Kurki, and Steve Smith, 94–114. Oxford: Oxford University Press.

Said, Edward W. 1978. *Orientalism*. New York: Vintage Books.

Schwartz-Shea, Peregrine, and Dvora Yanow. 2012. *Interpretive Research Design: Concepts and Processes*. New York: Routledge.

Shapiro, Michael J. 2004. *Methods and Nations. Cultural Governance and the Indigenous Subject*. New York: Routledge.

Smith, Steve. 2013. "Introduction: Diversity and Disciplinarity in International Relations Theory." In *International Relations Theories: Discipline and Diversity*, edited by Tim Dunne, Milja Kurki, and Steve Smith, 1–12. Oxford: Oxford University Press.

Tickner, Arlene. 2003. "Seeing IR Differently: Notes from the Third World." *Millennium: Journal of International Studies* 32 (2): 295–324.

Tickner, Arlene B., and David L. Blaney. 2013. *Thinking International Relations Differently*. New York: Routledge.

Tickner, J. Ann. 1988. "Hans Morgenthau's Principles of Political Realism: A Feminist Reformulation." *Millennium: Journal of International Studies* 17 (3): 429–440.

Tickner, J. Ann. 1992. *Gender in International Relations: Feminist Perspectives on Achieving Global Security*. New York: Columbia University Press.

Todorov, Tzvetan. 1982. *The Conquest of America: The Question of the Other*. Norman: University of Oklahoma Press.

Trownsell, Tamara, Amaya Querejazu Escobari, Giorgio Shani, Navnita Chadha Behera, Jarrad Reddekop, and Arlene B. Tickner. 2019. "Recrafting International Relations through Relationality." *E-International Relations* (blog). January 8, 2019. https://www.e-ir.info/2019/01/08/recrafting-international-relations-through-relationality.

Viaña, Jorge, Luis Claros, and Marcelo Sarzuri-Lima. 2010. "La Condición Colonial y Los Laberintos de La Descolonización." *Revista Integra Educativa* 3 (1): 13–36.

Walker, R. B. J. 2010. *After the Globe, Before the World*. New York: Routledge.

Walt, Stephen M. 1991. "The Renaissance of Security Studies." *International Studies Quarterly* 35 (2): 211–239.

Walzer, Michael. 1990. "The Communitarian Critique of Liberalism." *Political Theory* 18 (1): 6–23.

Weber, Cynthia. 2016. *Queer International Relations: Sovereignty, Sexuality and the Will to Knowledge*. Oxford: Oxford University Press.

Wendt, Alexander. 1999. *Social Theory of International Politics*. Cambridge; New York: Cambridge University Press.

Wittgenstein, Ludwig. 1958. *Philosophical Investigations*. New York: Macmillan.

Wittgenstein, Ludwig. 1969. *On Certainty*. Edited by G. E. M. Anscombe and G. H. von Wright. Translated by Denis Paul and G. E. M. Anscombe. Oxford: Blackwell Publishing.

Wolfe, Cary. 2010. *is Posthumanism?* Minneapolis: University of Minnesota Press.

Wynter, Sylvia. 1995. "The Pope Must Have Been Drunk, The King of Castile a Madman: Culture as Actuality, and the Caribbean Rethinking Modernity." In *Reordering of Culture: Latin America, the Caribbean and Canada in the Hood*, by Alvina Ruprecht, 17–42. Ottawa: Carleton University Press.

Yanow, Dvora, and Peregrine Schwartz-Shea, eds. 2014. *Interpretation and Method: Empirical Research Methods and the Interpretive Turn*. 2nd ed. Armonk, NY: M. E. Sharp.

Concluding thoughts

Throughout the book, my main goal is to analyze the problem of difference in order to re-imagine International Relations in more decolonial, intersectional, reflexive, and also plural ways. The genealogical dispute of the problem of difference among colonial, anti-colonial, post-structuralist, and intersectionally decolonial intellectuals provides a fruitful opportunity for International Relations to learn a way of constructing a reflexive locus of interpretation and praxis, but this genealogy has broader implications for the plurality of the field as well. On one side, then, some of the implications of this book unfold more directly from within the characteristics of intersectional decoloniality and the discussions of Andean intellectuals such as Silvia Rivera Cusicanqui and Fausto Reinaga. The possibility of sustaining the problem of difference at a cosmological level, the epistemic reflexivity that unfolds from this tension, the dynamic boundary of the approach, the ability to draw multi-layered maps of contextualized heterogeneity, the intersectional commitment to listen to multiple "others," the opportunity to create a self-problematized moral compass, and some of the other aspects discussed in the previous chapter are benefits that can help International Relations in a decolonial manner. On the other side, the implications of Rivera's work, together with some of the ramifications of my genealogical analysis, draw a way of thinking about the plurality of International Relations and the relationship between different approaches more in general.

First, the approach shows that boundaries often entail epistemic moments of decision, desire, or faith, which are cosmologically and relationally equivalent. In my interpretation of Rivera's work, cosmological assumptions alone do not always pre-determine politics and types of praxis. Instead, the author begins from a relational understanding of cosmology to highlight her "desire for change" and the "fact of colonialism," prioritizing a boundary that is cosmologically equivalent. Here, her explicitly normative, decolonial, bottom-up, circular, and transformational boundary emphasizes the importance of a decision and/or a "profession of faith." This notion of an explicit split between cosmology and epistemic boundaries not only creates a reflexive possibility of praxis, but also locates other boundaries and approaches as cosmologically equivalent constructions. This idea can help in the pluralization of the relationship among multiple approaches of International Relations and beyond, understanding the epistemic equivalence of different perspectives that are studying, critiquing, being, and enacting politics. Here, each approach appears to be another "profession of faith" and/or epistemic decision that is cosmologically equivalent. As a result, relationality undermines the altar that each set of epistemic assumptions erects for itself, weakening the elevation that each discourse claims above "others." Accordingly, relationality decreases the seldom disputed importance of epistemics. Then, the notion of equivalence emphasizes the relevance of assessing approaches in relation to the ways in which they create othering effects and possibilities of praxis. Since the problem of difference continues to lurk underneath the equivalence of multiple approaches, the othering tendencies of each boundary continue to be the main concern of analysis and dispute among equivalent perspectives. In other words, the problem of difference and its tension between praxis and multiplicity continue to sustain a struggle that questions the tendencies of each perspective. Hence, the cosmological equivalence among approaches demands an explicit understanding of the othering tendencies or the lack of commitment of particular approaches, creating a more transparent possibility of dialogue that moves beyond the veil of *a priori* epistemic elevations. This cosmology asks how equivalently different epistemic professions of faith create diverse boundaries. Here, the problem of difference is a cosmological realm that enables and questions equivalently different discourses. Rivera's notion of cosmological relationality and the problem of difference thus encourage other approaches to explicitly state their othering tendencies or stances. This possibility constructs a much more democratic space of dialogue among cosmologically equivalent boundaries and discourses. This cosmology of relationality thus allows us to critique each other beyond the artificial walls of siloed paradigms. Furthermore, the perspective abandons the primordiality of self-assured epistemics in the production of knowledge, concentrating debates on the praxis and othering effects of each discourse.

Second, cosmological equivalence creates a deeper possibility of ally-ship among approaches that construct different boundaries. For example, the cosmological equivalence of each particular approach of decoloniality constructs a possibility of dialogue and ally-ship that does not require the same kind of epistemic platform, boundary, and praxis. This type of discussion could fruitfully connect many of the approaches that are concerned with the problem of difference and the oppression of "others" while also avoiding a requirement of assimilation or homogenization. Feminist (Crenshaw 1991; Cho, Crenshaw, and McCall 2013; McCall 2005; Sjoberg 2006; Tickner and Sjoberg 2013; Collins 2015; Méndez 2018), post-structural (George and Campbell 1990; Doty 1997; Milliken 1999; Zehfuss 2002; Campbell 2013; Edkins and Zehfuss 2014), post-colonial (Doty 1996; Grovogui 1996; Inayatullah and Blaney 2004; Shapiro 2004; Agathangelou and Ling 2009; Agathangelou 2013), decolonial (Rivera and Morón 1993; Rivera 2010b, 2015, 2018; Mignolo 2000; A. Tickner 2003; Escobar 2010; Viaña, Claros, and Sarzuri-Lima 2010; Taylor 2012; Tickner and Blaney 2013; Ticona 2013; Alcoreza 2014; Richards 2014), queer (Butler 1990; Agathangelou 2013; Weber 2016), green

(Wolfe 2010; Cudworth and Hobden 2013; Eckersley 2013), and constructivist scholars (Onuf 1989; Lynch 2009, 2014), together with many others who trespass the boundaries of these theories in complex ways, could thus acknowledge their cosmological equivalence and their epistemic differences at the same time, learning from each other and creating possibilities of solidarity to practice politics in spite of some of their divergences.

To me, the notion of cosmological equivalence and the idea of professions of faith create a condition of possibility for a dialogue that respects difference even at the level of epistemic politics, while also demanding some kind of reflexive praxis and commitment. This notion can help us to move beyond the overly disciplined, bounded, and departmentalized communities that often prevent people from walking together against colonialisms. Moreover, the possibility of starting from ideas of equivalence undermines the altars that we might create for ourselves, often ignoring the complexity of struggles that other "others" denounce or act against. How often do students, intellectuals, leaders, activists, and so on feel close to the ideas and actions of others who also marginalize them? How often do scholars and intellectuals push each other away due to their own certainties, arrogance, and institutionalized positions of power? How is this epistemic, institutional, and intellectual competition a form of resistance against injustices?

To the contrary, the notion of equivalence creates a realm where concerned ways of knowing, being, and enacting can dialogue and confront each other in a much more cosmologically democratic manner. Here, we can ask each other how diverse approaches settle their own boundaries. What similarities do these approaches share in their ways of knowing, being, and enacting? What differences do they create once they take their own epistemic steps towards praxis? How do these approaches confront each other's epistemic privilege? This last question highlights the possibility of creating particular ways of knowing, being, and enacting, while also having to listen for "other" others who might confront our own privilege at the point at which we begin to assimilate them. In this cosmology, ally-ship becomes a democratic possibility of confrontation, solidarity, and action at the same time; it is a process of learning, teaching, coordinating, and acting simultaneously.

Of course the consistent implications of these discussions return in a circular manner towards the possibility of questioning my own interpretations, boundaries, decisions, and privilege. This requirement of self-problematization can emerge not only from the discussions that I hope to have in the near future with other scholars, colleagues, friends, students, activists, intellectuals, allies, etc., but also from the potential effects or ramifications of the interpretation that I propose throughout this book.

My positionality as an "interpreter:" Methodological and ethical issues

Hoping to contribute to the discussions of the problem of difference in International Relations and beyond, I explicitly enter the genealogical debate that I study. Unlike other authors, who investigate Andean voices to "return" knowledge (Estermann 2006, 10), however, I seek to listen and learn in order to debate the boundaries of a discipline that can be a more open, and yet committed, locus of enunciation. This goal leads me to learn from intellectuals that have moved far beyond some of the most prominent approaches of the discipline (e.g., Quispe 1988; Rivera and Morón 1993; Ticona 2000; Reinaga 2014; Linera 2014; Rivera 1999, 2010a, 2010b, 2015, 2018). Then, I take these insights into account in order to discuss the problem of difference and to re-imagine International Relations. By analyzing anti-colonial voices such as Indianismo and the critical work of decolonial authors such as Rivera, I thus seek to enter the debate of the problem of difference from a particular locus of interpretation, aiming towards particular boundaries, explicitly intervening from a situated concern, and avoiding the pretense of "translating" their work. I aim to re-imagine International Relations and the problem of difference to know, be, and enact intersectional decoloniality, while also thinking about a more pluralistic possibility of dialogue and debate.

In this sense, my own intervention in the discussion moves away from interpreting Indianista discourses or describing the work of intellectuals such as Rivera and Fausto Reinaga to tell "them" what they are "really" saying. This is not the work that emerges from a "historical duty of returning" (Estermann 2006, 10). Clearly, many of us living in the "West" have forms of privilege that need to be undone, but telling "others" what to do only exacerbates the colonial problem. To me, this kind of "duty" still assumes that "others" do not have agency, re-constructing a colonial throne for intellectual "white saviors." Instead, I aim to turn an analysis and praxis upon my own struggle, agency, and enactment. My work extends to realms such as the classroom, my daily life, university committees, and politics more in general, but much of what I learn and do is related to International Relations as well. Throughout this book, I thus participate explicitly in the debate to define the problem of difference from a particular locus of enunciation and mainly towards the effects of a specific set of boundaries. Hence, my work does not aim to expropriate and return that which intellectuals already know. Instead, I aim to accept their call to imagine a different kind of "planetarity" and decolonial praxis (Rivera 2018, 57). This invitation localizes our struggles and positionalities, while also confronting the oppressions that affects us and the privileges that we sustain.

Of course this goal still includes an ethical and methodological dilemma in the interpretation and synthetization of the meanings that are practiced and created by other intellectuals. On one side, I aim to avoid the "symbolic extractivism" that emerges when other scholars are not fully acknowledged as equal interlocutors of a pedagogical process of discussion and learning (Rivera 2018, 25). As it is inevitable in any process of interpretation and research, however, I encounter tension between listening to the meanings practiced by others and recognizing the symbolic violence of any process of synthetization. Hence, I acknowledge the contributions of many intellectuals in the genealogical struggle that I narrate to discuss the problem of difference, but I am also aware of the polysemic characteristic of meanings and the differences that might emerge between my interpretations and the "real" intentions of the authors themselves.

Similar to the problem of difference between foundations and othering effects, however, this tension is only paralyzing if positivist notions of truth correspondence and objectivity continue to be the elevated criteria that are deployed to judge knowledge production. Clearly, evidence plays an important role in my process of interpretation, which is why I sought to cite the documents, books, articles, interviews, pamphlets, speeches, and works of the different intellectuals that helped me in this process, but I do not claim to have accessed the real "essence" of their "intentions" or ideas. Instead, I construct "concept-metaphors" (Rivera 2018, 17), which aim to deepen discussions of the problem of difference and decoloniality in, for, and beyond International Relations. Concept-metaphors are thus synthesized interpretations that recognize the polysemic characteristic of meanings while also aiding in the goal of imagining other ways of thinking (Rivera 2018, 147). In a sense, then, I make a methodological and reflexive profession of faith in order to avoid renouncing my commitment of interpretation, struggle, and praxis; I assume the convergences of meanings that I interpret as including an element of sharedness and historical continuity, which moves my interpretations beyond my own subjectivity and/or arbitrariness.

Once this methodological assumption precariously validates my process of interpretation, I create a boundary that classifies four loci of enunciation: colonialism, anti-colonialism, post-structuralism, and intersectional decoloniality. Here, I narrate a genealogy of struggles and confrontations between different loci of enunciation, which are themselves understood as sets of relational differences and commonalities momentarily practiced and thus dynamically changing in different "discursive atmospheres" (Rivera 2015, 24). Each set of commonalities and differences creates consistent boundaries that momentarily fix particular definitions of relationships with "others." That is, each locus of enunciation includes particular meanings of difference and commonality that entail cosmological, ontological, epistemological, and temporal notions. In turn, the struggle between these dynamic loci of enunciation makes up the epistemic politics that I follow and interpret in a genealogy centered in the Andes, but also implicating intellectual practices from many other spaces and realms. As this genealogical process of interpretation moved forward, however, the question of the problem of difference came back yet again to seek the possibility of decoloniality itself. It questioned my own capacity to separate any particular kind of "other" or to classify any kind of difference; it created a circular tendency, where all possibilities of constructing classifications became unwarranted or invalidated. Due to the theoretical tendencies of these struggling loci of enunciation towards either othering boundaries or a lack of commitment, the problem of difference and its dilemma consumed the very genealogy that I had designed to analyze this issue. The discourses that I analyzed and my own methodological decisions could not escape the tension of the problem of difference. Despite this tendency, Rivera provides a different kind of stop to the problem of difference and she allows us to settle boundaries of classification momentarily and reflexively; she teaches us that making a profession of faith between cosmologically equivalent positions is necessary in order to avoid ignoring the differences of "others."

Therefore, I decided to follow the notion of a profession of faith, refusing to renounce my commitment towards "others," which include my own experience in terms of latinidad in the United States and in other ways that I am not ready to share here. As a result, I re-deployed the notion of sharedness and historical continuity in order to separate anti-colonial notions from colonial discourses, elevating the demands of "others" above the colonial privilege that seeks to dominate and oppress them. Here, the profession of faith helps me to establish a reflexive and explicitly decolonial criteria to separate the four loci of enunciation that I narrate in this genealogical dispute of the problem of difference. From this interpretive basis, I was then able to analyze the implications of this genealogy for International Relations. Admittedly, this form of classification emerged from a repetitive and circular process of back and forth between all the chapters of the book. The genealogical plot that you read here is thus the final product of a synthetization and interpretation that framed all my work only at the end of a learning process. At this point, then, I leave a momentarily and precariously settled map of struggles and questions, hoping to contribute towards a possibility of knowing, being, and enacting decoloniality, but also encouraging a more democratic and plural locus of interpretation for International Relations and international politics more in general.

References

Agathangelou, Anna M. 2013. "Neoliberal Geopolitical Order and Value: Queerness as a Speculative Economy and Anti-Blackness as Terror." *International Feminist Journal of Politics* 15 (4): 453–476.

Agathangelou, Anna M., and L. H. M. Ling. 2009. *Transforming World Politics: From Empire to Multiple Worlds*. New York: Routledge.

Alcoreza, Raúl Prada. 2014. "Epistemología Pluralista." In *Pluralismo Epistemológico*, edited by Amílcar B. Zambrana, 13–55. Cochabamba: FUNPROEIB Andes. https://es.scribd.com/doc/296610165/Pluralismo-Epistemologico.

Ashley, Richard, and R. B. J. Walker. 1990. "Speaking the Language of Exile: Dissent Thought in International Studies." *International Studies Quarterly* 34 (3): 259–268.

Butler, Judith. 1990. *Gender Trouble: Feminism and the Subversion of Identity*. New York: Routledge.

Campbell, David. 2013. "Post-Structuralism." In *International Relations Theories: Discipline and Diversity*, edited by Tim Dunne, Milja Kurki, and Steve Smith, 223–247. Oxford: Oxford University Press.

Cho, Sumi, Kimberlé W. Crenshaw, and Leslie McCall. 2013. "Toward a Field of Intersectionality Studies, Applications, and Praxis." *Signs* 38 (4): 785–810.

Collins, Patricia Hill. 2015. "Intersectionality's Definitional Dilemmas." *Annual Review of Sociology* 41 (1): 1–20.

Crenshaw, Kimberlé W. 1991. "Mapping the Margins: Intersectionality, Identity Politics, and Violence Against Women of Color." *Stanford Law Review* 43 (6): 1241–1299.

Cudworth, Erika, and Stephen Hobden. 2013. "Of Parts and Wholes: International Relations Beyond the Human." *Millennium: Journal of International Studies* 41 (3): 430–450.

Doty, Roxanne Lynn. 1996. *Imperial Encounters: The Politics of Representation in North-South Relations.* Minneapolis: University of Minnesota Press.

Doty, Roxanne Lynn. 1997. "Aporia: A Critical Exploration of the Agent-Structure Problematique in International Relations Theory." *European Journal of International Relations* 3 (3): 365–392.

Eckersley, Robyn. 2013. "Green Theory." In *International Relations Theories: Discipline and Diversity*, edited by Tim Dunne, Milja Kurki, and Steve Smith. Oxford: Oxford University Press.

Edkins, Jenny, and Maja Zehfuss. 2014. *Global Politics: A New Introduction.* New York: Routledge.

Escobar, Arturo. 2010. "Latin America at a Crossroads: Alternative Modernizations, Post-Liberalism, or Post-Development?" *Cultural Studies* 24 (1): 1–65. doi:10.1080/09502380903424208.

Estermann, Josef. 2006. *Filosofía Andina: Sabiduría Indígena Para Un Mundo Nuevo.* 2nd ed. La Paz: Instituto Superior Ecuménico Andino de Teología.

George, Jim, and David Campbell. 1990. "Patterns of Dissent and the Celebration of Difference: Critical Social Theory and International Relations." *International Studies Quarterly* 34 (3): 269–293.

Grovogui, Siba N'Zatioula. 1996. *Sovereigns, Quasi Sovereigns, and Africans.* Minneapolis: University of Minnesota Press.

Inayatullah, Naeem, and David L. Blaney. 2004. *International Relations and the Problem of Difference.* New York: Routledge.

Linera, Álvaro García. 2014. *Identidad Boliviana. Nación, Mestizaje y Plurinacionalidad.* La Paz: Vicepresidencia del Estado. Presidencia de la Asamblea Legislativa Plurinacional.

Lynch, Cecelia. 2009. "A Neo-Weberian Approach to Religion in International Politics." *International Theory* 1 (3): 381–408.

Lynch, Cecelia. 2014. *Interpreting International Politics.* New York: Routledge.

McCall, Leslie. 2005. "The Complexity of Intersectionality." *Signs* 30 (3): 1771–1800.

Méndez, María José. 2018. "'The River Told Me': Rethinking Intersectionality from the World of Berta Cáceres." *Capitalism Nature Socialism* 29 (1): 7–24.

Mignolo, Walter. 2000. *Local Histories/Global Designs: Coloniality, Subaltern Knowledges, and Border Thinking*. Princeton Studies in Culture/Power/History. Princeton, NJ: Princeton University Press.

Mignolo, Walter. 2011. "Epistemic Disobedience and the Decolonial Option: A Manifesto." *Transmodernity* 1 (2): 159–181.

Milliken, Jennifer. 1999. "The Study of Discourse in International Relations: A Critique of Research and Methods." *European Journal of International Relations* 5 (2): 225–254.

Onuf, Nicholas. 1989. *World of Our Making: Rules and Rule in Social Theory and International Relations.* London: Routledge.

Quispe, Felipe. 1988. *Tupak Katari Vive y Vuelve… Carajo*. La Paz: Ediciones Pachakuti.

Reinaga, Fausto. 2014. *Fausto Reinaga: Obras Completas*. 10 vols. La Paz: Vicepresidencia del Estado Plurinacional.

Richards, Patricia. 2014. "Decolonizing Globalization Studies." *The Global South* 8 (2): 139–154.

Rivera Cusicanqui, Silvia. 1999. "Sendas y Senderos de La Ciencia Social Andina." *Dispositio, Crítica Cultural En Latinoamérica: Paradigmas Globales y Enunciaciones Locales* 24 (51): 149–169.

Rivera Cusicanqui, Silvia. 2004. "La Noción de 'Derecho' o Las Paradojas de La Modernidad Postcolonial: Indígenas y Mujeres En Bolivia." *Aportes Andinos, Aportes Sobre La Diversidad, Diferencia e Identidad* 11: 1–15.

Rivera Cusicanqui, Silvia. 2010a. *Oprimidos Pero No Vencidos. Luchas Del Campesinado Aymara y Quechua, 1900–1980*. La Paz: La Mirada Salvaje.

Rivera Cusicanqui, Silvia. 2010b. *Violencias (Re) Encubiertas En Bolivia*. La Paz: La Mirada Salvaje.

Rivera Cusicanqui, Silvia. 2015. *Sociología de la Imagen. Miradas Ch'ixi Desde La Historia Andina*. Buenos Aires: Tinta Limón.

Rivera Cusicanqui, Silvia. 2018. *El Mundo Ch'ixi Es Posible: Ensayos Desde Un Presente En Crisis*. Buenos Aires: Tinta Limón.

Rivera Cusicanqui, Silvia, and Raúl Barrios Morón. 1993. *Violencias Encubiertas En Bolivia: Cultura y Política*. La Paz: Talleres Gráficos Hisbol.

Shapiro, Michael J. 2004. *Methods and Nations. Cultural Governance and the Indigenous Subject*. New York: Routledge.

Sjoberg, Laura. 2006. *Gender, Justice and Wars in Iraq*. New York: Lexington Books.

Taylor, Lucy. 2012. "Decolonizing International Relations: Perspectives from Latin America." *International Studies Review* 14 (3): 386–400.

Tickner, Arlene. 2003. "Seeing IR Differently: Notes from the Third World." *Millennium: Journal of International Studies* 32 (2): 295–324.

Tickner, Arlene B., and David L. Blaney. 2013. *Thinking International Relations Differently*. New York: Routledge.

Tickner, J. Ann, and Laura Sjoberg. 2013. "Feminism." In *International Relations Theories: Discipline and Diversity*, edited by Tim Dunne, Milja Kurki, and Steve Smith, 185–202. Oxford: Oxford University Press.

Ticona, Esteban Alejo. 2000. *Organización y Liderazgo Aymara, La Experiencia Indígena En La Política Boliviana, 1979–1996*. Cochabamba: AGRUCO, Agroecología Universidad Cochabamba, Universidad de la Cordillera.

Ticona, Esteban Alejo. 2013. *El Indianismo de Fausto Reinaga: Orígenes, Desarrollo y Experiencia En Qullasuyu-Bolivia*. Ecuador: Universidad Andina Simón Bolívar.

Todorov, Tzvetan. 1982. *The Conquest of America: The Question of the Other*. Norman: University of Oklahoma Press.

Viaña, Jorge, Luis Claros, and Marcelo Sarzuri-Lima. 2010. "La Condición Colonial y Los Laberintos de La Descolonización." *Revista Integra Educativa* 3 (1): 13–36.

Weber, Cynthia. 2016. *Queer International Relations: Sovereignty, Sexuality and the Will to Knowledge*. Oxford: Oxford University Press.

Wolfe, Cary. 2010. *is Posthumanism?* Minneapolis: University of Minnesota Press.

Zehfuss, Maja. 2002. *Constructivism in International Relations: The Politics of Reality*. Cambridge: Cambridge University Press.

Index

Printed in Great Britain
by Amazon

40239126R10143